HENRIETTA MARIA

HENRIETTA MARIA

Charles I's
Indomitable Queen

ALISON PLOWDEN

SUTTON PUBLISHING

First published in the United Kingdom in 2001 by
Sutton Publishing Limited · Phoenix Mill
Thrupp · Stroud · Gloucestershire · GL5 2BU

British Library Cataloguing in Publication Data
A catalogue record for this book is available from the British Library

ISBN 0-7509-1882-9

Typeset in 10/12½pt New Baskerville.
Typesetting and origination by
Sutton Publishing Limited.
Printed and bound in England by
J.H. Haynes & Co. Ltd, Sparkford.

Contents

List of Illustrations

Principal Characters

Henry Rich, Viscount Kensington and Earl of Holland, 'the wooing ambassador'
James Hay, Earl of Carlisle
Mamie St Georges, Lady of Honour to Henrietta
Inigo Jones, Surveyor of the King's Works
Daniel du Plessis, Bishop of Mende, Grand Almoner to Henrietta
Father Philip, confessor to Henrietta
Maréchal de Bassompierre, French special envoy
Theodore Mayerne, royal physician
Madame Peronne, royal midwife
Thomas Wentworth, Earl of Strafford, Lord Deputy in Ireland
Geoffrey Hudson, the queen's dwarf
Richard Weston, Earl of Portland, Lord Treasurer
Father Cyprien de Gamache, Capuchin friar
William Laud, Archbishop of Canterbury
William Prynne, Puritan lawyer and pamphleteer
Gregorio Panzani, unofficial papal envoy
George Con, papal agent
John Hampden, MP, bringer of the great ship-money case
Walter Montagu, Catholic convert and friend of Henrietta
Henry Jermyn, later Earl of St Albans, Master of the Horse and friend of
    Henrietta
John Pym, MP, leader of the opposition
Carlo Rossetti, papal agent
George, Lord Goring, one of the 'Army Plotters' and royalist commander
William Cavendish, Earl of Newcastle, royalist commander in the north
Edward Nicholas, Secretary of State
Madame de Motteville, French lady in waiting and friend of Henrietta
James Butler, Earl of Ormonde, Viceroy in Ireland
James Graham, Marquis of Montrose, royalist commander in Scotland
Edward Hyde, later Earl of Clarendon, royalist councillor

At the French Court

Armand du Plessis, Cardinal Richelieu
Cardinal Mazarin, French chief minister

Miscellaneous

Sir Thomas Fairfax, parliamentary commander in the north
Oliver Cromwell, parliamentary commander
Robert Devereux, Earl of Essex, parliamentary commander
Giovanni Rinuccini, papal envoy to Ireland

Chronology

1600
19 November   Birth of Charles I

1609
25 November   Birth of Henriette Marie de Bourbon

1610
14 May   Assassination of Henri IV
17 October   Coronation of Louis XIII

1615
25 November   Marriage of Louis XIII and Anne of Austria

1623   Visit to Spain by Charles, Prince of Wales, and the Duke of
                Buckingham

1625
27 March   Death of James I and accession of Charles I
11 May   Proxy marriage of Charles and Henrietta celebrated in Paris
12 June   Henrietta arrives at Dover
18 June   Opening of Charles I's first parliament
12 August   Dissolution of parliament

1626
2 February   Coronation of Charles I
6 February   Opening of Charles I's second parliament
15 June   Dissolution of parliament
21 July   Dismissal of Henrietta's French household

1627   War with France
May–November   Expedition to the Île de Rhé

1628
17 March   Opening of Charles I's third parliament
7 June   The king accepts the Petition of Right
23 August   Assassination of the Duke of Buckingham
September–
  October   Expedition to La Rochelle

1629
10 March   Dissolution of parliament. Beginning of the Personal Rule of
                Charles I

14 April	Treaty of peace between England and France
13 May	Premature birth and death of Henrietta's first child

1630

29 May	Birth of Charles, Prince of Wales, later King Charles II
5 November	Treaty of peace between England and Spain

1631

4 November	Birth of Princess Mary, later Princess of Orange

1632

November	Publication of *Histrio Mastix*, William Prynne's attack on the theatre
	Death of Frederick, Elector Palatine
	Death in prison of Sir John Eliot

1633

18 June	Coronation of Charles I in Scotland
19 September	William Laud created Archbishop of Canterbury
14 October	Birth of James, Duke of York, later King James II

1634

October	Issue of ship-money writs to coastal districts
15 December	Arrival in England of Gregorio Panzani, unofficial papal agent

1635

August	Second ship-money writ extended to inland counties
28 December	Birth of Princess Elizabeth

1636

17 July	Arrival in England of George Con, papal agent
10 December	Dedication of the queen's chapel at Somerset House

1637

17 March	Birth of Princess Anne
23 July	English prayer book imposed on Scotland, resulting in riot in St Giles Cathedral

1638

February	National Covenant circulated in Edinburgh
June	Judgement given for the king in the ship-money case
16 September	Birth of Louis XIV
18 October	Arrival in England of Marie de Medici

1639

29 January	Birth and death of Princess Catherine
April/June	The first Bishops War
May	Henrietta attempts to raise money from the English Catholics to help the king
August	Carlo Rossetti replaces George Con as papal agent
22 September	Thomas Wentworth returns from Ireland

1640

13 April	Opening of the Short Parliament

5 May	Dissolution of the Short Parliament
8 July	Birth of Henry, Duke of Gloucester
August–October	The second Bishops War
3 November	Opening of the Long Parliament
11 November	Arrest of Thomas Wentworth, Earl of Strafford
15 December	Death of Princess Anne

1641

3 March	Arrest of Archbishop Laud
March	The Army Plot
22 March	Opening of Strafford's trial
2 May	Marriage of Princess Mary and Prince William of Orange
8 May	Attainder of the Earl of Strafford
12 May	Execution of Strafford
26 June	Carlo Rossetti leaves England
10 August	Charles I visits Scotland
18 August	Marie de Medici leaves England
October	Rebellion breaks out in Ireland
24 November	Charles I returns to London
November	Parliament presents the king with the Grand Remonstrance

1642

4 January	The king attempts to arrest the Five Members
10 January	Flight of the royal family to Hampton Court
23 February	The queen and Princess Mary sail for Holland
July	Death of Marie de Medici
22 August	The Royal Standard is raised at Nottingham
23 October	Battle of Edgehill

1643

13 February	The queen lands at Bridlington
14 May	Death of Louis XIII and accession of Louis XIV
23 May	The queen is impeached by parliament
13 July	The king and queen are reunited at Oxford
20 September	First battle of Newbury
8 December	Death of John Pym

1644

19 January	Scottish army invades England in support of parliament
16 June	Birth of Princess Henrietta Anne at Exeter
2 July	Battle of Marston Moor
14 July	The queen sails from Falmouth

1645

10 January	Execution of Archbishop Laud
14 June	Battle of Naseby; the King's Cabinet, containing secret correspondence with Henrietta, is captured by parliament
10 September	Prince Rupert surrenders Bristol

1646

17 April	The Prince of Wales arrives in Jersey
5 May	The king gives himself up to the Scots at Newark
June	The Prince of Wales arrives in Paris
August	Princess Henrietta Anne and her governess escape to France

1647

30 January	The Scots hand the king over to parliament
June	The army seizes control of the king
11 November	The king escapes from Hampton Court and makes for the Isle of Wight

1648

20 April	The Duke of York escapes to Holland
8 July	The Scottish 'Engagers' invade England in support of the king
17–19 August	The Scots defeated at Preston
30 November	The king is removed to Hurst Castle by the army
6 December	Pride's Purge of the House of Commons
23 December	The king is taken to Windsor

1649

January	Trial and execution of Charles I
5 February	The Prince of Wales is proclaimed king at Edinburgh
15 August	Oliver Cromwell arrives in Dublin
September/ October	Cromwell storms Drogheda and Wexford

1650

16 June	Charles II lands in Scotland
3 September	Cromwell defeats the Scots at Dunbar
8 September	Death of Princess Elizabeth at Carisbrooke Castle

1651

1 January	Charles II crowned King of Scotland at Scone
3 September	Battle of Worcester
13 October	Charles II escapes to France

1652

Wars of the Fronde break out again in France. There is fighting in Paris, and the English royal family have to leave for St Germain

1653

March	The Duke of Gloucester arrives in Holland
June	Gloucester goes to Paris

1654

July	Charles II is required to leave France
November	Henrietta attempts to convert the Duke of Gloucester and Charles sends the Marquis of Ormonde to remove him

1655

November	Treaty of Westminster signed between France and the English Commonwealth

1656
February   Mary, Princess of Orange, visits her mother in Paris

1658
3 September   Death of Oliver Cromwell

1659
May   Resignation of Richard Cromwell. End of the Protectorate. The Rump Parliament is recalled

1660
February   General Monck enters London and orders the reinstatement of MPs excluded in Pride's Purge
March   The Long Parliament dissolves itself
25 May   Charles II lands at Dover
3 September   Secret marriage of the Duke of York and Anne Hyde
13 September   Death of the Duke of Gloucester
1 November   The queen and Princess Henrietta Anne arrive in England
24 December   Death of the Princess of Orange

1661
January   The queen and Princess Henrietta Anne return to France
30 March   Marriage of Princess Henrietta Anne and Philippe d'Orléans

1662
11 May   Marriage of Charles II and Catherine of Braganza
28 July   Henrietta returns to England

1665
March   Anglo-Dutch war breaks out
June   Henrietta leaves England for the last time

1666
January   France enters war on the side of the Dutch

1667
July   Peace of Breda ends the Dutch war

1669
January   Secret negotiations for a treaty between the Kings of England and France
9 September   Death of Henrietta Maria

Note on Dates

There were two calendars in use during the seventeenth century. Continental Europe used the Gregorian or New Style system of dating, while England still clung to the Julian or Old Style calendar and was thus ten days behind the rest of Europe. In this book I have used New Style for continental events, Old Style for those in England, indicating where they overlap, but it should be noted that the Venetian ambassadors in London continued to date their dispatches according to the New Style.

CHAPTER ONE

Madam of France

Sir, if your Intentions proceed this way . . . you will find a Lady of as
much loveliness and sweetness to deserve your Affection as any
Creature under Heaven can do.

Henry Rich to Prince Charles

On the morning of Tuesday 18 February 1623 two young men wearing
false beards and calling themselves John and Thomas Smith left New Hall
in Essex en route for Dover. They first attracted attention at Gravesend
where, having no small change, they over-tipped the ferryman so
extravagantly that he suspected they were up to no good and hurried off
to alert the local justices.

The mysterious travellers passed unhindered through Rochester but at
Canterbury the mayor arrived to arrest them as they were changing
horses, alleging a warrant from the Council, so that the taller of the two
Smiths was obliged to pull off his beard and reveal himself as George
Villiers, newly created Marquis of Buckingham, the king's favourite man
and chief minister. He was going covertly, he explained, and with such
slight company, in order to take 'a secret view of the forwardness of his
majesty's fleet', then in preparation on the Narrow Seas. He did not
reveal that his companion was the 22-year-old Charles, Prince of Wales, or
that their ultimate destination was not Dover but Madrid, where they
planned to conduct a personal courtship of the Spanish infanta and, they
hoped, bring her back with them to England as the prince's bride.

These optimistic knights errant, or the 'Knights of Adventure' as they
were presently dubbed, were joined at Dover by Francis Cottington, the
prince's secretary, and his confidential bedchamber servant Endymion
Porter, who was taken along for 'his natural skill in the Spanish tongue'.
After a stormy six-hour crossing to Boulogne, during which both knights
were unromantically seasick, the party set off for Paris which they
reached on the evening of the second day and found lodgings at an inn
in the rue St Jacques.

Next morning Buckingham and the prince took the precaution of
buying themselves large periwigs 'for the better veiling of their visages'
before starting out to see the sights. These, of course, included the
French court and they were able to get a good look at the king and the

1

queen-mother at dinner without being challenged. Emboldened by this, and having 'a great tickling' to add to the history of their adventures, they persuaded the queen's chamberlain, as a courtesy to a pair of curious foreign tourists, to admit them with a crowd of other spectators to watch the queen, the princess Henrietta Maria and a bevy of other 'fair dancing ladies' rehearsing for a masque which was to be performed before the king.

Early the following day they left for Bayonne on the Spanish frontier, but the Prince of Wales had in fact been recognised in the street by a sharp-eyed young woman who had once sold linen in London and an embarrassed English ambassador was forced to send a letter posting after him warning him that his presence in the country was known. Lord Herbert urged his royal highness to make all the haste he could out of France and take care not to do anything which might annoy the authorities on the way.[1]

In retrospect Charles's contemporaries naturally fastened on the occasion of his first glimpse of his future wife as being the most significant moment of his 1623 adventures. Charles himself, however, was apparently concerned only with gazing upon the young Queen of France, who happened to be a sister of the Infanta Maria for whose sake the whole crazy enterprise had been undertaken. There is nothing to suggest that he so much as noticed the thirteen-year-old Henrietta.

The princess, sixth child and third daughter of Henri IV and his second wife Marie de Medici, had not as yet attracted much notice in the outside world. No official rejoicings or salvos of cannon had greeted her arrival on 25 November 1609, although all the usual formalities were observed. Her father, the princes of the blood and principal ministers of state were present to witness the birth and the king took the newborn infant from the midwife and, holding her up, recognised her as his own before passing her over to the care of Madame de Montglat, official *gouvernante* of the royal children. He did not seem at all disappointed that the baby was another girl. On the contrary, he is supposed to have been especially fond of his name child, who was thought to be very like him. But then Henri IV was known to love all children, which was just as well since he had sired fourteen of them – six legitimate offspring and eight acknowledged bastards, progeny of a string of mistresses. The latest addition to this extended family appeared both healthy and lively. When her eldest brother, the eight-year-old Dauphin, was admitted to see her in the first hours of her life and took her hand, he exclaimed with delight when she clasped his fingers, saying, 'Laugh, laugh, *ma soeur*! Laugh, little child!'[2]

Henrietta's first public appearance was at her mother's long-deferred coronation. Throughout the ten years of her marriage the unfortunate

Marie de Medici had been forced to suffer the humiliation of sharing her husband with one predatory mistress after another – the Marquise de Verneuil even hinted at the existence of a pre-contract between herself and the king – but had never yet been granted the courtesy of a crowning. Whether influenced by his reluctance to spend the money or by the persistent prophecies, disseminated by de Verneuil, that his wife's coronation would be quickly followed by his own death, Henri had so far always managed to resist her importunities. But now, in the winter of 1609/10, he was preparing to go to war with the Hapsburg rulers of Austria over a disputed succession to the Rhineland duchy of Cleves and Marie had seen her opportunity, insisting that for the safety of the realm her position as queen (and consequently, of course, the legitimacy of her children) must be established beyond doubt before he left for the front. Reluctantly, therefore, he had given in and the date of the ceremony was fixed for 13 May. All six royal children were present at St Denis to see their stout blonde mother, resplendent in cloth of gold, enjoy her moment of triumph, the two youngest, Gaston, Duc d'Anjou, and six-month-old Henrietta being carried in their nurses' arms.

Next morning the king, who was noticed to be very melancholy 'upon some presages and tokens of his death', sent for little Gaston and Henrietta to be brought to him to divert his thoughts.[3] His children, he had once told the Duc de Sully, were the prettiest in the world and his happiest hours were spent playing with them. That afternoon he drove out from the Louvre to visit Sully, who was ill in bed. As his coach turned into the rue de la Ferronerie it was held up in the traffic and a tall red-haired man, who had been stalking it unnoticed through the narrow congested streets, hoisted himself up on to one of the wheels and stabbed the king three times, the second blow fatally severing the aorta.[4]

Henri le Grand of Bourbon and Navarre, the pragmatic Huguenot warrior, best remembered for his much-quoted declaration that '*Paris vaut bien une messe*' and his seemingly insatiable sex drive, had always been suspected by right wing Catholics of aligning himself with heretics and by Protestants of selling out to the Catholics. Nevertheless, he had been a strong and successful ruler who had gone a long way towards restoring French prestige and prosperity after the disastrous religious civil wars of the previous century, and news of his death spread panic through the court and city. No one yet knew whether this was the beginning of a *coup* planned by Spain, by the Huguenots, by the queen – perhaps the prelude to another Bartholomew's Day massacre. Sully rose hastily from his sickbed and ordered the Swiss Guard to be mobilised, and that night the royal children were huddled together for safety in one room of the grim old fortress palace of the Louvre. But as the hours passed and it became clear that <u>the assassin, a Catholic fanatic called François Ravaillac, had acted alone</u>, albeit with Spanish encouragement, panic began to subside. The following day the young Dauphin was presented to the Parlement as <u>Louis XIII and Marie de Medici claimed the regency</u>.

Henrietta's next public appearance, still in her nurse's arms, was at her father's funeral where the aspergillum was put into her hand and, with the rest of her brothers and sisters, she sprinkled holy water on the coffin. In October she was present at her brother's coronation, carried this time by the Princesse de Condé, but as soon as the various ceremonies were over she and the other children were removed from Paris, where already rumblings of dissatisfaction over the queen-mother's conduct of the regency could be heard.[5]

Most of Henrietta's earliest years were spent in the pleasantly rural setting of <u>St Germain-en-Laye</u>, some two hours' journey by coach from the capital. There had been a castle on the site for centuries, but the building Henrietta knew – a brick and stone chateau in the Renaissance style – was only about fifty years old and Henri IV had added a still newer and smaller summer residence on the wooded hill overlooking the Seine. This somewhat flimsy, hurriedly built construction (the court had prophesied that the first frosts would bring it tumbling down) was chiefly famous for its gardens, reached by two broad flights of steps leading down from a gallery or terrace.

One admiring visitor wrote:

Under these steps a grotto had been most artfully contrived, in the middle of which a fountain had been made of sea shells and coral. A griffon spouted out water and nightingales, by a contrivance worked by the water, sang most charmingly. All sorts of shells were to be seen, and coral mingled with lovely coloured stone. . . . The floor was made of coloured pebbles which were so set that they formed innumerable little pipes through which the water was forced up to the vaulted roof from which it fell again like heavy rain, so that one could neither stand above nor below without being wetted. The walls were full of recesses in which all sorts of figures stood, in metal, in marble, in shellwork, nearly all of whom spouted out water. Many of the figures moved, such as smiths striking on an anvil, birds who sung and flapped their wings, lizards and frogs and serpents poised on the rocks, spouting water with many curious movements. . . . In the middle of the grotto there was a figure of Neptune with his trident, who came out of a pool riding in a chariot. We could see him emerge on the surface, turn right round and disappear anew under

4

the water. On the left hand of the steps another grotto had been constructed in which a water-organ had been placed. Against the walls yellow roses made of shells were seen against a black background. In short there were so many lovely things that one could not notice them all in a brief visit.[6]

The grottos and fountains were not the only delights of the new chateau at St Germain. On the level ground beside the river were laid out shaded walks, trellised roses and alleys of fruit trees imported by Henri from his native south, plus a colourful display of flower beds, still something of a novelty in an age of rigidly formal garden design. All the same, it was surely the spouting wonders in the grottos, contrived by the Italian genius Tomaso Francini, which fascinated the children. St Germain was used as a nursery for all the king's numerous family, and not only the children of France but the sons and daughters of Gabrielle d'Estrées and the son and daughter of Catherine de Verneuil were brought up together in the old chateau in one large, unwieldy household ruled over by Madame de Montglat.

By the time Henrietta had begun to toddle the *troupeau*, as it was known, was beginning to disperse. Louis now had his own establishment and round of kingly duties, although he insisted on being allowed to return to St Germain from time to time to see his brothers and sisters. The second boy, apparently never named and known only by his title of Duc d'Orléans, had always been sickly and died in November 1611 at the age of four-and-a-half. The other two princesses, Elisabeth and Christine, were growing up – there was a gap of almost seven years between Elisabeth and Henrietta – so it was natural that her principal companion and playmate should have been her next brother Gaston, who had inherited the Orléans title. Dressed alike in white satin, brother and sister shared their public christening. They had both been baptised at birth, but it was the custom of the French royal family to complete the ceremony of admission into the church when the children were old enough to know what was happening and were able to recite the Pater Noster and Ave. So, on 15 June 1614, the remaining acts and ceremonies of the sacrament of baptism, which involved anointing with oil and salt, were administered by the Cardinal de Bonzi, and Gaston and Henrietta Maria were officially named before an admiring audience at the Louvre.

Marie de Medici, who was very particular about such matters, had attended the christening but her children seldom saw her at St Germain. When the two-year-old Henrietta went down with a feverish illness, the queen regent sent a servant to make enquiries, demanded to be kept informed and arranged for a doctor to be on call. She ordered Madame de

Montglat to ensure that her little daughter received every care but does not appear to have visited the invalid herself. So, for little Henrietta it was Madame de Montglat who represented nursery security and authority, and her first surviving letter was addressed to Mamangat, as the children called her. 'I pray you excuse me if you saw my little sulky fit which held me this morning. I cannot be right all of a sudden; but I will do all I can to content you; meantime, I beg you will no longer be angry with me, who am and will be all my life, Mamangat, Your affectionate friend, Henrietta.'[7]

Another familiar, perhaps less formidable member of the household was Mamangat's daughter, Mamie St Georges, who held the position of sub-governess and may well have dictated that stilted little note of apology. Gaston and Henrietta are said to have shared a learned tutor, the orientalist François Savary de Breves, at one time ambassador to the Ottoman court, but it seems likely that this was more of a courtesy title than an actual teaching post, for the children's academic education remained a pretty sketchy affair. Years later Henrietta was to regret that she had never been taught any English history.

She learnt to dance at an early age, mastering the steps of the corranto, galliard and bourrée, the branle and saraband. She is said to have had a good singing voice and amateur theatricals were a favourite pastime at St Germain. She was taught to ride and thoroughly drilled in all the arcane mysteries of court etiquette and protocol, learning who could claim the honour of handing the king his shirt at the morning levée or the napkin at mealtimes; whose rank entitled them to a fauteuil, or chair with arms, and who must be content with a mere stool.

Lessons were frequently interrupted by attendance at public functions and in September 1614 Henrietta was present with the rest of the family for the celebrations marking Louis' thirteenth birthday, when he was considered to have come of age. She was also present at the betrothals of the princess Elisabeth to the Infante Don Philip of Spain and of King Louis to the Spanish Infanta Anna, when Paris was *en fête* for three days, with pageants and processions jostling one another in the streets and squares, the nobility parading on horseback in all their finery, fountains spouting wine and the city ablaze with illuminations. In the summer of 1615 the whole court took to the road, travelling south to Bordeaux, where the two brides were to be exchanged, and Henrietta was there to watch as her thirteen-year-old sister departed in floods of tears to begin a new life among strangers.[8]

The Spanish marriages had been engineered by Marie de Medici in order to buy peace with France's powerful neighbour and long-standing rival for continental dominance. By the early years of the seventeenth century the all-pervasive Hapsburg family ruled over Spain and Austria and a handful of central European statelets. The kingdom of Naples was

[margin note: "ANNE OF AUSTRIA"]

theirs, as was the Duchy of Milan and the southern provinces of the Low Countries. Henri IV had always striven to contain Hapsburg expansionism and resist the threat of Hapsburg encirclement. His widow, understandably enough, opted for appeasement. Henri had, after all, been a vigorous and experienced war leader. His son was a neurotic immature adolescent. France, still divided by bitter sectarian conflict and plagued by a quarrelsome and assertive nobility, was in no position to go looking for trouble abroad. The queen wanted a quiet life and was prepared to pay whatever price was necessary to get it.

The court made its way back to Paris by leisurely stages and the queen-mother and her two younger daughters were greeted by the loyal bourgeois militia drawn up in the rue d'Orléans. They went on to inspect the sumptuous new palace which the queen was having built in the Luxembourg park and Marie was pleased to see how well the work had been progressing during her absence.[9]

The return from Bordeaux marked the high point of the queen-mother's career but popular resentment over her extravagance and mismanagement, together with the greed and overweening presumption of the Concini, her low-born Italian cronies, was slowly reaching boiling point. In April 1617 that point was reached and Concini, or the Maréchal d'Ancre as he had become, was shot dead by a member of the royal bodyguard while 'resisting arrest' and his corpse subsequently torn to pieces by the Paris mob. His wife, who had been Marie de Medici's foster-sister, was also seized, tried on a charge of witchcraft and sentenced to death, while the queen mother was bundled off in disgrace and under guard to house arrest at Blois. Fifteen-year-old Louis now declared himself to be a king indeed, although, in fact, real power swiftly passed into the hands of his own not very distinguished crony Charles d'Albert de Luynes, soon to be created Duc de Luynes.

The queen's request that her youngest daughter should be allowed to accompany her into exile had been refused and the princess Henrietta remained at court. In February 1619 she was present at the wedding of her next sister, Christine, to the Duke of Savoy's heir, Victor Amadeus, Prince of Piedmont, who would, it was hoped, not only help to counter Hapsburg influence in northern Italy but also prove a useful ally in case the queen-mother decided to join with the princes of the blood in taking up arms against the king.[10]

Shortly after the wedding the queen mother succeeded in escaping from the castle at Blois and made for Angoulême, refusing to communicate with Louis 'any otherwise than by lamentable complaints'. Eventually a meeting was arranged and a family reunion took place in September, the king being accompanied by Henrietta as well as by

Christine and her husband, who were on their way to Turin. Marie burst into tears on seeing her son, exclaiming 'how you have grown!' But she would not return to Paris, and as a loose cannon at large in the provinces she continued to represent a threat to the security of the crown.

It is said that Henrietta dared not take her mother's side in the quarrel 'to the displeasure of her brother', in case she damaged her own marriage prospects.[11] The youngest of Henri le Grand's children was ten years old now and during that summer her future had been coming under serious consideration; so much so that by the end of the year arrangements to marry her to her cousin Louis de Bourbon, Comte de Soissons, had reached an advanced stage – the king apparently hoping that such an alliance would buy the loyalty of at least one member of the restive Condé branch of the royal family. Unfortunately, in June 1620 the sixteen-year-old Comte spoiled his chances by slipping away from court, together with the Ducs de Longueville and Vendôme, in order to join the queen mother at her headquarters in Anjou. But Louis was standing no more nonsense from his mother. He led a businesslike army against her to suppress the nascent rebellion and by September Marie was back in the family fold, having been obliged to surrender unconditionally.

Although de Soissons continued to hover hopefully in the background, Henrietta's affairs had temporarily come to a standstill, and it was left to the Duc de Luynes to make the next move by putting out some cautious feelers at the English court. The idea of an English alliance was not a new one. Marie de Medici had always wanted all her daughters to be queens, and plans to marry the princess Christine to King James's elder son, the handsome, athletic Henry, Prince of Wales, had been discussed at government level before that young man's untimely death in 1612, while Henri IV is reputed to have thought of marrying Henrietta in England when she was still in her cradle. Some time in the autumn of 1620, therefore, de Luynes, who had once been the king's falconer, sent an obscure individual named du Buisson across the Channel, ostensibly to buy horses for the Prince de Condé but carrying secret instructions to try to find out how the English would react to the idea of a French marriage for their prince.

De Luynes had not seen fit to warn the resident ambassador at the court of St James about the true nature of his henchman's mission, and M. Le Comte Leveneur de Tillières was appalled when he discovered that a person without breeding or wit was being trusted anywhere near so sensitive a matter. Du Buisson, who apparently blurted out his proposition in words 'more explicit than the state of the affair permitted', was rebuffed politely enough. King James regretted that he was unable to accept the King of France's flattering offer, as he was already engaged with Spain on his son's behalf. However, when he next saw de Tillières, James could not resist expressing his surprise and disappointment, both at the choice of envoy and the manner in which this unseasonable suggestion had been made. Much mortified, the ambassador hastened to disown du Buisson as an ignorant upstart with no official status, adding loftily that it had never been the custom to go looking for husbands for the daughters of France.

Undeterred by this débâcle, de Luynes now prepared to dispatch his brother Honoré, the Maréchal de Cadenet, to London at the head of a suitably imposing special embassy. De Cadenet, accompanied by a large retinue of high-class gentlemen, landed at Dover on New Year's Day 1621, and during a three-day visit was lavishly entertained to receptions, banquets and hunting parties. He was granted an audience with the king, but had no more success than the despised du Buisson in presenting the case for an Anglo-French marriage alliance. The de Luynes brothers had their own reasons for wanting to keep England and Spain apart but, at least according to the scornful de Tillières, they knew nothing of foreign affairs and would, in any case, have stood no chance of persuading James, for whom good relations with Spain were particularly important just then.[12]

The war which had overshadowed the last two decades of the Elizabethan century was long over now, although far from forgotten by those generations of Englishmen for whom their old enemy would always be equated with Antichrist. The king did his best to ignore these inconvenient prejudices. Nervous and pacific by nature, he liked to see himself in the role of international arbiter standing aloof from the bigoted sectarianism of others, and had sought to emphasise his neutral status by marrying his daughter, another Elizabeth, to the Elector Frederick of the Rhineland Palatinate, titular leader of the German Protestant princes. Unfortunately, this union, personally successful and popular among his own subjects, was to be responsible for pushing the would-be British Solomon further into the arms of his Catholic allies. In 1619 the Lutheran nobility of the kingdom of Bohemia rose in revolt against their Hapsburg overlords and the impressionable Frederick had accepted their offer of the crown, with consequences which were to prove catastrophic for all concerned. The Austrian Hapsburgs experienced no difficulty whatever in dealing with the rebellious Czechs, driving Frederick not only out of Prague but from his Rhineland territories as well, and turning him, his English wife and numerous progeny into stateless, penniless refugees. Thus, by 1621 the King of England found himself in honour bound and under considerable public pressure to go to the aid of his daughter and son-in-law; Elizabeth had always been a favourite with the people and it also had to be remembered that, unless and until her brother married and started a family, she and her children were next in line for the English throne.

9

Something clearly had to be done and, military intervention on any meaningful scale being neither practicable or affordable, James was obliged to turn to the Spanish Hapsburgs in the not very realistic hope that the concluding of a dynastic alliance with the Stuarts would be a sufficient inducement for them to coerce their Austrian cousins into at least restoring Frederick to the Palatinate. Negotiations for a marriage between the Prince of Wales and the Infanta Doña Maria had already been in progress for more than five years, and in 1621 showed every sign of continuing for another five. The principal sticking point was, of course, religion, the Spaniards demanding, among other things, that the infanta should be guaranteed full and free exercise of her faith surrounded by a Catholic household of her own choosing; that any children of the marriage should be baptised and brought up as Catholics until they reached years of discretion; that all persecution of the English Catholics should cease forthwith and all the laws penalising them be repealed by the English parliament.[13] The king knew very well that the English parliament would do no such thing, but towards the end of 1622 he gave his private assurance that he would no longer enforce those laws, and on the strength of that assurance the Spanish government at last agreed to apply to Rome for a dispensation to allow the marriage to take place.[14]

It was at this point that Prince Charles, who had now, for reasons which remain obscure, succeeded in convincing himself that he was madly in love, came to the conclusion that his only chance of cutting through the impenetrable thickets of Spanish obfuscation and procrastination would be to go to claim his bride in person. It was the one grand romantic gesture of his life and predictably it ended in a total fiasco. Buckingham quarrelled with the Spanish king's chief minister; Charles's attempt to see the infanta alone only exposed him to embarrassment and he was warned privately by the queen – she who had been Elisabeth of France – that his suit was hopeless; while Doña Maria herself, a solemn, ultra-devout young woman, made no secret of her revulsion at the prospect of marriage to a heretic. This apart, it quite soon became clear that, marriage or no marriage, Spain had not the slightest intention of ever making any attempt to restore the Palatinate. By October the two luckless swains were back in England humiliated and furious, and the old king, delighted to have his 'sweet boys and dear venturous knights' safely home again, announced that 'he liked not to marry his son with a portion of his daughter's tears'.

Although negotiations were not finally broken off until the spring, it was obvious that the Spanish match was a dead letter, to the immense and freely expressed relief of the nation. Charles and Buckingham (who had been created a duke during his absence) were now planning to recover the Palatinate by force of arms and the talk was all of war with Spain. Parliament, which met in February 1624, voted £300,000, some of which was to go towards the cost of an Elizabethan-style naval expedition, but Buckingham and the prince wanted an all-out war by land and sea. The duke, though, was aware that unilateral action was not a realistic option – to have any chance of success a continental campaign would need powerful continental support, and that could only come from France, where fourteen-year-old Henrietta Maria was still unspoken for.

It was now the turn of the English to put out feelers and even before he left Spain the Duke of Buckingham had sent an emissary, in the habit of a Franciscan friar, to Paris. This rather mysterious individual, who possessed useful contacts at the French court, was able to get an interview with the queen-mother, telling her that if she was willing to consent to a marriage between her daughter and the Prince of Wales, he would 'take care so to arrange matters as to carry it into execution'. Since the sudden death of de Luynes at the end of 1622 Marie de Medici had regained a good deal of her former influence, and she gave her visitor a purse full of money and enough encouragement to send him over to London with an optimistic report for his master. De Tillières, who was once more being sidelined, commented sourly that Buckingham apparently preferred to deal with an ignorant busybody of a friar and an ambitious match-making mama than with the properly accredited ambassador.[15]

The French, who had been following the progress of events in Madrid with interest, were understandably suspicious in case they were being used in an attempt to extract better terms from Spain; but in January 1624 King Louis sent James a present of twelve falcons, twelve huntsmen in livery and twelve horses with trappings to match as 'a complimentary overture for the purpose of improving their relations', and the Venetian ambassador in Paris heard that they would like the prince 'to show some courtesies to Madame such as he lavished on the Infanta'.[16]

In February the first explicit approach was made with the dispatch of that experienced charmer Henry Rich, Viscount Kensington, in the capacity of semi-official Cupid. Arriving at the Louvre on a Sunday, his lordship made for the apartments of his old friends the Duc and Duchesse de Chevreuse and found them getting dressed for a masque which was to be performed that evening. 'I had not been there above an hour,' he wrote in his first report to Buckingham, 'but the Queen and Madam [Henrietta] came thither, where they staid a great while. And it was observed, that Madam hath seldom put on a more chearful Countenance than that Night. There were some that told me I might guess at the Cause of it. My Lord, I protest to God, she is a lovely, sweet young Creature. Her Growth is not great yet, but her Shape is perfect;

and they all swear that her Sister, the Princess of Piedmont (who is now grown a tall and goodly Lady) was not taller than she is at her Age.'[17]

Kensington had half expected to encounter some hostility from the young Queen of France but, on the contrary, he told the prince 'she asks of you with all the expressions that are possible of joy, for your safe return out of Spain; and told me, that she durst say you were weary with being there and so should she, though she be a Spaniard.' She seemed to be all in favour of the new marriage, saying she was sorry that Charles had only seen her sister-in-law at a distance and in a dark room when he had paid that fleeting clandestine visit to Paris, and Kensington thought she would prove a useful ally. 'She made me show her your Picture, the which she let the Ladies see, with infinite Commendations of your Person.'[18]

It would not be proper to show Henrietta herself the miniature of Charles which the 'wooing ambassador' was wearing on a ribbon round his neck, nor, of course, could she ask him, but she was bursting with curiosity to see it and 'at the last . . . desired the Gentlewoman of the House where I am lodged, that had been her Servant, to borrow of me the picture, in all the secrecy that may be, and to bring it unto her. . . . As soon as she saw the party that brought it, she retired into her Cabinet, calling only her in; where she opened the Picture in such haste as showed a true Picture of her passion, blushing in the instant at her own guiltiness. She kept it an hour in her hands, and when she returned it, she gave it many praises of your Person.' Kensington was most anxious that Madam's little secret should be kept, telling Charles that he would rather die a thousand times than it should be published, 'since I am by this Young Lady trusted, that is for Beauty and Goodness an Angel'.[19]

Although the Spanish ambassador was going round saying that the Prince of Wales could not have two wives, and the Comte de Soissons ostentatiously cut him dead, Kensington's mission continued to prosper. Writing on 24 February, he assured the prince that the queen-mother was eager for the match, having more than once expressed her 'great favour and good will' towards it, while as for Madam: 'Sir, if your Intentions proceed this way . . . you will find a Lady of as much loveliness and sweetness to deserve your Affection as any Creature under Heaven can do.' Kensington was obviously a trifle concerned about Henrietta's smallness, but 'her Growth is very little short of her Age; and her Wisdom infinitely beyond it. I heard her discourse with her Mother, and the Ladies about her with extraordinary discretion and quickness. She dances (the which I am a witness of) as well as ever I saw any Creature. They say she sings most sweetly, I am sure she looks so.'[20]

The ambassador was by this time on excellent terms with all the royal ladies and had been able to have several long chats with Henrietta, during one of which they talked about ladies riding on horseback, which she said was rare in France, but frequent in England, and then 'expressed her Delight in that Exercise'.[21]

Kensington now felt confident enough to ask the queen-mother's permission to speak more freely to the princess on his master's behalf. When she wanted to know what he intended to say, he explained that he wished to present the prince's service 'not by way of Compliment any longer, but out of Passion and Affection' which Henrietta's outward and inward beauties had kindled in him; how His Highness was resolved to contribute the uttermost he could to the alliance in question, and would think it the greatest happiness in the world if its success were to give him the opportunity of expressing his devotion in a better and more effectual manner. All this he spoke 'with some little other such like amorous language'. Reassured, Marie de Medici smiled knowingly and said, '*Allez, allez. Il n'y a point de danger en tout cela. Je me fie en vous. Je me fie en vous.*' 'Neither did I abuse her trust,' Kensington told Buckingham, 'for I varied not much from it in delivering it to Madam, save that I amplified it to her a little more, who drank it down with joy, and with a low Courtesie acknowledged it to the Prince, adding that she was extremely obliged to His Highness and would think herself happy in the occasion that should be presented of meriting the place she had in his good grace.' Kensington then turned to 'the old Ladies that attended', telling them that since the queen had given her approval, they could now talk openly about the affair and let them know that his master had their princess's picture in his cabinet and often 'fed his eyes' on it, since he could not yet have the happiness of beholding her in person. All which, 'and other such-like speeches', the princess, standing by, took in 'without letting any one fall to the ground'.[22]

Matters had now reached the point where serious negotiating could begin, and by the end of May Kensington had been reinforced by James Hay, Earl of Carlisle, an experienced diplomat, who arrived bearing the official proposal of marriage. The two envoys got down to business with the French commissioners, de Vieuville and Ville-aux-Clercs, but it quickly became apparent that Lord Kensington had been right when he had warned James and Buckingham that, in his opinion, the military alliance and the marriage should be treated as separate issues. 'For I doubt whether it may not be thought a little dishonourable for this King to give his Sister conditionally, that if he will make War upon the King of Spain his brother, we will make the Alliance with him.'[23] The Venetian ambassador put it rather more succinctly when he remarked that 'they cannot sell the princess as the price of tumult'.

This came as a serious disappointment to Buckingham and Prince Charles, but while Louis was anxious to keep England and Spain apart and prevent any further extension of Hapsburg dominance over the German states, he had no particular desire to see the Calvinist Frederick restored to the Palatinate. It was true that control of the Rhine valley would make it easy for Spain to bring troops up from northern Italy to the Low Countries, but Louis did not want a war with his brother-in-law; in any case, if France could hold the Valtelline, the Swiss valley which commanded the Alpine route between Hapsburg Milan and Hapsburg Tyrol, she could cut Austro-Spanish lines of communication just as effectively and much less expensively. So although the English ambassadors continued to press for a definite commitment from the French to enter into a league 'not only defensive but offensive for the Palatinate', they could get nothing in writing. 'It is true that they do offer unto us this King's word for their assistance, and that their Ambassador shall give his Majesty the like assurance' wrote Carlisle to Charles in October; 'but what assurance can be given to the verbal promise of this people, who are so apt to retract or give new interpretations to their former words . . . Your Highness, out of your excellent wisdom, will easily discern.'[24]

Meanwhile, the details of the marriage contract were being hammered out and it was not long before the question of toleration for the English Catholics came up again, but it seemed at first as if this time it might not prove too serious an obstacle. De Tillières had been recalled, as being 'too much of a Jesuit', and his replacement, the smooth-talking Marquis d'Effiat, was indicating that the French would be content with 'reasonable advantages for religion'; while in Paris de Vieuville gave the Earl of Carlisle to understand that their requirements would be satisfied by a letter from James promising not to persecute his Catholic subjects.

Unfortunately, it appeared that de Vieuville had been speaking without authority. By the beginning of August he had lost his place as Louis' chief minister and the king was disclaiming all knowledge of any undertakings he might have given to the English envoys. Worse still, the new chief minister, Cardinal Richelieu, lost no time in demanding that a clause expressly guaranteeing freedom of worship for the English Catholics should be included in the marriage contract. This evidence of French bad faith provoked a furious reaction in London and Prince Charles told Carlisle 'if you find they persist in this new way that they have begun in making an article for our Roman Catholic subjects, dally no more with them but break off the treaty of marriage, keeping the friendship in as far terms as you can'. To Lord Kensington the prince wrote in even blunter terms. 'The Monsieurs have played you so scurvy a trick that if it were not for the respect I have for the person of Madam, I would not care a fart for their friendship.' Neither the prince nor his father had ever shown as much enthusiasm for the French marriage as they had for the Spanish. Even now James was still hankering after a Spanish alliance and he drafted an angry dispatch to his ambassadors, accusing Louis of trying to find excuses for breaking the treaty and ordering them to end the negotiations altogether if he continued to be unreasonable.[25]

Negotiations might indeed have been broken off in a fog of petulance and mutual distrust had not the Duke of Buckingham and the diplomats on both sides of the Channel intervened to smooth ruffled Stuart feelings. It was explained to Louis and Richelieu that it would be politically impossible for James to make any formal promises regarding the English Catholics. After the collapse of the Spanish marriage project he had been obliged to promise a suspicious parliament that he would never agree to any relaxation of the recusancy laws as a condition of any future marriage contract, and could not now publicly go back on his word.

Richelieu, a practical man of affairs as well as a cardinal, could see the difficulty but he had to have something more than an off-the-record undertaking. For one thing, his own position was not yet entirely secure, and he could not afford to alienate the Dévots, as the right-wing French Catholic faction was known. Then there was the question of national prestige. The French could not be seen to agree to part with their princess on lesser terms than the Spanish had been prepared to part with theirs. Papal permission for Henrietta's marriage to a notorious heretic had also to be obtained and, according to information coming out of Rome, Urban VIII would refuse to grant a dispensation unless the treaty contained some definite provisions for the relief of the English Catholic community.

In the end, of course, a compromise had to be reached and on 13 September Marc Antonio Morosini, the Venetian ambassador in Paris, reported that the religious question holding up the English match had been settled. 'The king and Prince of Wales promise in a separate written document, which the Secretary of State will also sign, that the Catholics of the kingdom shall enjoy the same privileges and exemptions at the instance of the Most Christian [King of France] as were conceded to the Catholic [King of Spain] in the negotiations with him. They shall be allowed to live in the profession of their faith, without molestation, and shall not be persecuted or compelled in any matter of conscience.'[26]

Morosini was being optimistic in believing the religious question settled, for the status of the 'separate written document' – the Escrit Particulier or Escrit Secret as it came to be known – continued to be a matter of contention well into October. The English were still trying to persuade the French to accept a simple letter signed by the king alone, but, wrote Carlisle on the 18th, 'we did sing a song to the deaf, for they would not endure to hear of it'.[27] After much argument the English had to give way and agree to 'the formality of an Escript', which would form part of the treaty but remain separate from the main articles and not be made public.

During all these months, while ambassadors and politicians squabbled endlessly over details, the young girl whose future was being decided was growing increasingly restive. Henrietta was fifteen now and it seemed as if life was passing her by. 'Madame already styles herself bride of the Prince of England and future queen of the two kingdoms,' wrote Morosini from Paris on 16 November. 'She is impatient of all delay and constantly importunes her mother and brother to bring it to a conclusion.'[28]

But things were now at last beginning to move. Although the papal dispensation had not yet arrived, Richelieu, hearing that the influential Spaniard Count Gondomar was planning to return to England and alarmed that James might even at this late stage be persuaded to call the marriage off, decided to go ahead anyway and on the evening of 23 November (N.S.) the treaty was signed on the French side. 'They lighted bonfires for the marriage,' reported Morosini two days later, 'fired all the guns of the Arsenal, and yesterday gave a ball in the Louvre.' The treaty still contained no mention of the Palatinate, but Carlisle and Lord Kensington – or Earl of Holland as he now was – had had an audience with Louis and been given a solemn promise that the French would pay the mercenary captain Ernest Mansfeld for six months and allow an English expeditionary force under his command to cross French territory on its way to the relief of the Rhineland.

A French delegation headed by the Secretary of State Ville-aux-Clercs now prepared to cross the Channel, taking the treaty and the Escrit Particulier with them for ratification. King James and his son were at Newmarket and the signing ceremony took place at Cambridge on 12 December. The church bells were rung and the Venetian ambassador in London, Zuane Pesaro, informed the Doge that by the king's orders the city was illuminated with bonfires. 'The Tower fired many guns', continued Pesaro, 'and I also for the dignity of your Serenity and to celebrate the alliance of the two crowns, lighted several bonfires and glutted the people here with an abundance of beer and wine.'[29]

The Londoners had no objection to the beer and wine, but there was little or no support for the French marriage in the country at large. Sir Simonds D'Ewes, the parliamentary journalist, believed that 'the English generally so detested the Spanish match as they were glad of any other which freed them from fear of that', although he added that 'wiser men feared much danger would ensue to the gospel and true religion by this marriage'.[30] This was a moderate view. Zuane Pesaro, writing in October, had observed that 'the marriage . . . pleases few and is opposed by infinite passions. . . . The Catholics do not favour it', he went on, 'partly because they desire no other union than the Spanish, partly because they think that the French ambassador is not acting entirely for their advantage.' 'Good'

Englishmen, thought Pesaro, *were* pleased, 'but the English in general and the Puritans abhor this alliance . . . the Puritans desire no marriage, except with the reformed religion, because that is their interest.'[31]

The Puritans would have abhorred the French alliance still more had they known what exactly the king and the Prince of Wales had set their names to at Cambridge that December. The marriage contract itself followed much the same lines as had previously been agreed with the Spaniards. Henrietta was to be given every facility to practise her religion, with properly ornamented chapels provided in all her residences where the Word of God might be preached, the sacraments administered, the mass and all divine offices freely celebrated according to the Roman rite. She was to have an ecclesiastical establishment of twenty-eight priests headed by a bishop who would be allowed to go about in public wearing their religious habits where appropriate, and her 'family' or household was to consist entirely of French Catholics chosen by the King of France. Any children of the marriage were to be brought up by their mother until they were twelve years old, and if she became a widow she was to be free to return to France if she so wished, taking all her goods and jewels with her. The king and the prince had also signed the so-called Escrit Particulier, the 'separate written document' or secret clause, in which James undertook to grant his Catholic subjects even greater liberty of conscience than they would have enjoyed by the terms of the Spanish treaty. They were, in short, to be free to practise their religion without fear of molestation in their persons or property; always provided, of course, that they behaved with discretion and continued to render that obedience which good and true subjects owed to their king.[32]

Charles now sent his fiancée a formally worded 'love letter' together with his portrait and a gift of jewellery; before the end of the year, King James had given orders that the recusancy laws were to be suspended and those Catholics currently imprisoned for religious reasons released. All proceedings against Catholics in the church courts were to be dropped and any fines imposed since the amnesty of 1623 returned to them. Preparations were begun for a fleet to fetch the bride and it was hoped she would be in England and the marriage consummated by the end of January.

The bridegroom certainly hoped so. Not, it must be said, for romantic reasons but because both he and Buckingham were anxious to be able to present parliament with a *fait accompli*. The Puritan tendency in the Commons might grudgingly be prepared to concede that a Popish queen and her personal servants must be allowed their mass, but they might well turn awkward over some of the articles in the treaty. There would certainly be trouble if once they got wind of the secret article, and trouble with parliament was the last thing Charles and Buckingham could afford at a time when they were desperate for money to fund Mansfeld's expedition. In the event, the Crown was forced to borrow against its parliamentary expectations and Mansfeld set sail from Dover at the end of January 1625. He was, however, hopelessly handicapped by orders from James not to set foot on any territory belonging to Spain and by the fact that the French had now gone back on their promise to allow him to land at Calais. His troops, a wretched rabble of 'raw and poor rascals' scraped up from the dregs of the population, untrained, ill-fed, barely clothed and in some cases armed only with cudgels, had consequently to be diverted to Holland where, in the dead of winter with nothing prepared for them, desertion, disease and starvation did their usual work – 'all day long we go about to seek victuals and bury our dead' complained one of the officers – and the survivors quickly disintegrated into marauding bands of looters and murderers.

Mansfeld's failure was a bitter disappointment to the Elector Palatine and his wife, a humiliation for the all too obviously toothless British lion, and had done nothing to improve Anglo-French relations. These deteriorated still further in February when the papal dispensation finally arrived, but came accompanied with French demands for further concessions. 'This unworthy people . . .', wrote Lord Carlisle, 'are grown so indiscreetly and unreasonably presumptuous as to impose a new treaty upon us.' It appeared that they were using the People's 'borrowed name' to try to extort 'no less than a direct and public toleration not by connivance, promise or escrit secret, but by a public notification to all the Roman Catholics of all his Majesty's kingdoms whatsoever'.[33] The Venetians also heard that as well as the children being brought up by their mother until their thirteenth year, the Pope was now asking for a guarantee that they would be brought up as Roman Catholics; but the English, who had reason to believe that the dispensation had, in fact, been issued unconditionally, were furious. 'A round sharp negative' to these new extravagant demands made by 'inconstant and perfidious monsters' with no sense of honour or gratitude was Lord Carlisle's advice and King James, who fully shared his ambassador's opinion of the Monsieurs, needed no persuading. 'They say his Majesty constantly repeats that he will not alter the things agreed upon in the smallest degree,' reported Zuane Pesaro on 14 March. According to Pesaro the French thought they could get anything they wanted – 'feeling sure that they held the fish securely hooked in Buckingham, who could only maintain his fortunes by the help of France' – and in Paris they were angrily blaming the present impasse on the inflexibility of the English ambassadors.[34] For a few days it looked as if the alliance might yet be shipwrecked and d'Effiat in London had once more to use all his tact to calm the waters. In a final burst of horse-trading, from which Buckingham held himself conspicuously aloof, James agreed to a few minor modifications but stood firm on the substance of the treaty and Richelieu, apparently satisfied that he had now wrung every last drop of advantage from the situation, gave Carlisle a written promise that the marriage would definitely take place within thirty days.

It had already been agreed that Buckingham would represent Charles at the proxy wedding and escort the new Princess of Wales back to England. Some £40,000 had been set aside for his expenses and he had begun to send some of his baggage down to Dover when the king developed a fever and soon his condition was giving cause for serious concern. At fifty-eight James Stuart was a sick old wreck of a man who constantly slobbered, belched and scratched himself, and suffered from a variety of distressing ailments from indigestion and gout to colic and diarrhoea. However, this illness seems to have taken everyone by surprise. On 24 March the embassy in Paris was warned that the Duke of Buckingham would not be able to leave his majesty 'in such a condition as he now is', and three days later came the news that the king was dead.

1625

The first act of the new king was to confirm all the members of his father's Privy Council in their offices and, contrary to some people's expectations, it appeared that the old king's death would cause no more than a temporary hiccup in the wedding preparations. Also contrary to some people's expectations, it was plain that the Duke of Buckingham's position as favourite would not be affected by the change of sovereign. The duke, to do him justice, was genuinely distressed by the loss of his 'dear dad and gossip', but he had been comforted by the new king who told him that, though he had lost one master, he had gained another who would cherish him no less, and this was being made obvious by 'the most transparent evidence'. The two men were to be seen constantly in each other's company and an Italian resident in London reported that the duke had not only been confirmed in all his offices, 'which are numerous and of the highest importance', but had also been made a Gentleman of the Bedchamber and presented with a golden key as a symbol of his privileged right to come and go anywhere in the royal residences as and when he wished. 'In fine,' concluded Amerigo Salvetti 'nothing is done without him.'[35]

One thing, though, would have to be done without him, and that was the proxy wedding due to be celebrated in Paris within a month. Buckingham would have to be present at King James's funeral which could not be arranged for another six weeks, and it was therefore agreed that the Duc de Chevreuse, who was distantly related to King Charles through his Guise great-grandmother, should instead represent the bridegroom. This change of plan inevitably involved more delay while the details were discussed between London and Paris, and it was not until nearly the end of April before Sir George Goring was able to leave for France carrying the necessary documentation.

By this time the last of the difficulties with Rome had been removed and the Pope had written to Henrietta, who was also his god-daughter, urging her to become the Esther of the oppressed English Catholics, the Clothilde 'who subdued to Christ her victorious husband', the Aldiberga whose marriage to the Kentish King Ethelbert had brought Christianity to England, and reminding her that the eyes of the whole spiritual world would be turned upon her. The Holy Father had always harboured the gravest misgivings about the wisdom of the marriage and told the princess that, had it not been for the hope afforded by her character that she, as queen of a heretical country, would be the guardian angel and protectress of her co-religionists, he would not have granted the dispensation.[36] According to some, he had only done so in order to avoid the scandal of the marriage going ahead without it.

By the beginning of May the way was finally clear for the betrothal ceremony, which took place in the king's audience chamber at the Louvre on Thursday the 8th, and three days later, on Sunday, 11 May (N.S.) – it was May Day in England – Henrietta Maria de Bourbon was married to Charles Stuart on a specially erected stage at the door of the cathedral of Notre Dame. It was late in the afternoon before the bridal procession appeared at a window of the nearby archbishop's palace and began to make its way along a gallery or walkway raised on pillars swathed in violet satin leading to the west door of the church. The diminutive bride wore a gown of cloth of gold and silver encrusted with diamonds and gold fleur de lys, and a train so heavy that the three ladies carrying it had to co-opt a spare gentleman-in-waiting to walk underneath and take some of the weight on his head. She was supported by her two brothers and preceded by the princes of the blood, the marshals, dukes and peers of France, 'their clothes strewn with diamonds and wearing robes of inestimable value'. Everyone present, in fact, was positively incandescent with gold and silver, crimson and purple, diamonds and other precious stones. Louis, it was said, looked like 'the glorious sun outshining the other stars'.

The proxy bridegroom, in a suit of black velvet slashed with cloth of gold, took his place beside the bride and the Cardinal de la Rochefoucauld performed the short wedding ceremony, after which George Goring hurried away on the first stage of his journey to inform the King of England that he was at last a married man. The new Queen of England, together with her relations and the rest of the company, then moved on into the body of the cathedral for the nuptial mass, only the

English and Dutch ambassadors as good Protestants and the Duc de
Chevreuse as King Charles's representative remaining outside. The mass
was followed by a banquet and the celebrations continued for several
days, with firework displays, illuminations, salvos of cannon and a lavish
entertainment at the Luxembourg Palace provided by a triumphant
queen-mother.[37]

It had been supposed that Henrietta would now set out at once for the
coast and there was some talk of Charles crossing the Channel to meet her
at Boulogne. Instead Henrietta lingered and it was Buckingham who
crossed the Channel, reaching Paris on 24 May. His arrival caused quite a
sensation. Described as 'the best made man in the world, with the finest
looks', he made his appearance at the French court 'with so much charm
and magnificence that he won the admiration of all the people. The ladies
of the court were filled with joy (and something more than joy); the court
gallants were openly envious; and all the husbands at court were consumed
with jealousy.'[38] The duke was taking the opportunity to display some of the
sumptuous wardrobe he had assembled in expectation of acting the part of
proxy bridegroom, including a suit of purple satin embroidered all over
with rich orient pearls said to be worth £20,000 and which he had
apparently intended to wear at the wedding, but he told the Venetian
ambassador that his only purpose now was to hasten the departure of the
bride, as King Charles was dying with impatience and love.[39] Charles was
certainly impatient, finding the delay 'too insupportable to bear'. His
ardour, though, was still driven more by financial necessity than any other
cause. Financial necessity was making the first parliament of the reign a
matter of urgency, and once it was in session the king would not be able to
leave London to greet his wife in proper style.

Buckingham spent a week as the guest of the Duc de Chevreuse and, in
the intervals between cutting a considerable dash on the Parisian social
scene, found time to follow up the other purpose of his visit, which was to
renew his efforts to persuade the French to join his proposed anti-
Hapsburg league. He was unsuccessful. Richelieu, preoccupied just then
with problems of internal security – the Huguenots of La Rochelle had
recently come out in revolt – remained resolute in his refusal to commit
his master to taking part in any doubtful foreign adventures in order to
oblige the English. This was a bitter disappointment to the duke, who
had built all his plans for the recovery of the Palatinate and the
discomfiture of Spain around a French alliance; the king's marriage,
which had taken so much diplomatic effort to arrange, would be of very
little use without the political and military partnership it had been
intended to supplement. Buckingham was used to getting what he
wanted and it has been suggested that angry frustration may well have

coloured his future attitude towards Henrietta who, with her tiresome baggage of priests and chapels, now looked like being a great deal more trouble than she was worth.[40]

The duke and the new queen had already clashed over Cardinal Barberini, the papal legate who was on a visit to Paris; he scolded her for going out to greet the cardinal when he came to call on her and Henrietta retorted that she considered this courtesy no more than was due to the Pope's representative. Some optimistic Englishmen, hearing that Madam of France had been presented with 'divers of our Common Prayer Books in French', had raised hopes of her possible conversion, but there was never any question of that. However inadequate her secular education, Henrietta's religious instruction, supervised by the nuns of the Carmelite convent in the Faubourg St Jacques, had been extremely thorough and her faith was an integral part of her life, strong and uncompromising.

She was now, at long last, almost ready to set out on her journey. Rumours were beginning to spread in England that the delay had been caused by papal machinations, that 'something more is to be performed for the Catholic cause before we shall see her'; but in fact it appears to have been due partly to Louis' indisposition – he had been suffering from a feverish cold – and partly to the complicated logistics involved in getting the whole of the royal family on the road at the same time, not to mention the two hundred or so members of the establishment which was going to England with Henrietta, plus her elaborate and extensive trousseau, several sets of chapel plate and furnishings, and a 'great bed' with red velvet curtains.

May had turned into June before everybody and their belongings had been marshalled, packed and loaded up and the Venetian ambassador was able to report that the Queen of England had left Paris in state, 'amid shouts of applause and a countless throng of people'. As befitted a daughter of France on her bridal journey, Henrietta was escorted as far as St Denis by the city archers, the militia, the craft guilds, the trumpeters and various other civic bodies all determined to give Madame a good send-off. Louis accompanied his sister as far as Compiègne, before turning aside for his beloved Fontainebleau, while the rest of the caravan jolted on towards Amiens, where the queen-mother succumbed to her son's cold and took to her bed, causing yet more delay. But in England they were running out of patience – 'the people and the members of parliament are complaining, laying the blame on France' – and Charles was sending increasingly peremptory messages 'urging the queen not to stay anywhere, but to come straight to him'. It was therefore agreed that she should go on to Boulogne without further ado and with only her brother Gaston of her immediate family to see her safely on board ship.

Henrietta said goodbye to her mother on 16 June, receiving a maternal blessing and a long letter of motherly advice and spiritual exhortation, which she was to keep always with her to be re-read at frequent intervals, so that her mother might seem ever to be near giving counsel and assistance. In this letter (actually written by Father Bérulle, a leading light in the French religious revival movement) the bride was reminded that without God she was nothing and that as He had blessed her by making her a Christian and a Catholic – the highest rank she could ever hold – so must she give thanks to Him while on earth, never forgetting that she had been called into the world for a great and glorious purpose. She was being sent now into a foreign country expressly to protect the Catholics there and must do her utmost to persuade the king her husband to relieve their sufferings. Nor should she forget all those unhappy Englishmen who, because of their heresy, were afflicted by God and must in her charity use her influence and her prayers to help them to see the error of their ways and return to the true faith. After God and religion her duty was to her husband and she must love and honour him, being always humble and patient to his will, while at the same time remembering to love his soul and salvation and pray daily for his conversion.[41]

This was inspirational stuff, but although she had promised her brother and the Pope to ensure that her children were brought up by Catholics and also to observe their intentions 'as well in what concerns me and mine, as in what may be useful and advantageous to religion and to the Catholics of Great Britain', there is little to suggest that the youthful Henrietta was fired by any very great enthusiasm for the role of crusader. Nor indeed does she appear to have felt any very great sorrow at parting from her mother. After all, she still had her much loved governess and mother substitute, Mamie St Georges, who had been with her since nursery days and was going to England with her as Lady of Honour. She was also still surrounded by the comfortingly familiar faces of her French household. Yet it is noticeable that in all the careful provisions made for her physical and spiritual welfare in the godless island, no one had thought it necessary to equip the new queen with even a few words of the language.

Two days after leaving Amiens the bridal party arrived at the coast and the Mayor of Dover, writing on 9 June (O.S.), informed Secretary of State Conway that 'a mariner reports that the queen reached Boulogne yesterday, about 5 o'clock p.m., in good health and very merry. This man saw her viewing the sea, and so near that it was bold to kiss her feet, so that her Majesty was over shoes, and then returned with great pleasure.'[42]

As well as her first sight of the sea, Henrietta was now having her first encounter with the English dignitaries who had crossed over to welcome her. These included a party of ladies, all relations of the Duke of Buckingham – his mother, his sister, the Countess of Denbigh, and his niece, the Marchioness of Hamilton. Also present was Sir Toby Mathew, son of an Anglican bishop but a recent convert to Catholicism, who had come along to act as interpreter and who wrote to tell Buckingham's wife that the queen was 'more grown' than he had expected. 'And whatsoever they say,' he went on, 'believe me, she sits already upon the very Skirts of Womanhood. Madam, upon my Faith, she is a most sweet lovely Creature, and hath a Countenance which opens a Window into her Heart, where a Man may see all Nobleness and Goodness; and I dare venture my Head that she will be extraordinarily beloved by our Nation, and deserve to be so.'

Mathew thought he could discern a little remnant of sadness 'which the fresh Wound of parting from the Queen Mother might have made', but which may just have been a sudden shyness among so many incomprehensible strangers – at any rate she was soon chattering away happily enough to Toby Mathew, who was later to become a close friend and who found her 'full of Wit' with a lovely manner of expressing it.

Certainly Henrietta does not appear to have been moping. She was fascinated by the sea and insisted on going out on the water of the harbour in a little boat with only Gaston for company. The courage required for this escapade quite astonished Toby Mathew. 'I dare give my Word for her, that she is not afraid of her own Shadow who could find it in her Heart to put herself, at the first sight, upon an Element of that Danger and Difficulty for mere Pastime. Unless it were', he added archly, 'that she might carry some Steel about her, and there is some Adamant at Dover, which already might begin to draw her that way.'[43]

The travellers were held up for several days at Boulogne by a summer storm blowing in the Channel and Buckingham, who had enlivened the journey from Paris by conducting a flirtation with Queen Anne, Louis' pretty but neglected young wife, seized the opportunity to make a quick dash back to Amiens, where Anne had remained with Marie de Medici, in order to pay a sentimental farewell. This naturally gave rise to a good deal of gossip which was equally naturally relayed to Louis, who promptly joined the ranks of jealous husbands, thus muddying still further the already muddy waters of Anglo-French relations.

By 22 June the weather had improved sufficiently for Henrietta to go on board the *Prince* and set sail with an escorting flotilla of twenty ships into the future for she was so woefully unprepared – although, to be fair, no one on that June day in Boulogne could reasonably have foreseen what was lying in wait for the new little Queen of England.

CHAPTER TWO

La Reine d'Angleterre

[The queen] is thoroughly French, both in her sentiments and habits. The marriage has not changed her one whit . . . and does not seem likely to do so by a long way.

The Venetian Ambassador's report, July 1626

'Mam's ill luck at sea' was later to become a by-word in the Stuart family and that first Channel crossing, which lasted for twelve hours, was quite choppy enough to be unpleasant. The fleet, firing off its guns in salute, finally entered Dover harbour some time after eight o'clock on the evening of Sunday 12 June by the English calendar, and Henrietta was carried straight up to the castle, where she was to spend the night. *1625*

Thomas Howard, the Earl Marshal, was there to receive her, but the French were shocked by the almost total lack of ceremonial. The king was not present – he and the court were waiting at Canterbury – and Dover Castle, 'un vieux bâtiment fait à l'antique', proved to be a dank and depressing medieval fortress quite devoid of modern comforts. The rooms which had been prepared for the queen were very poorly furnished, and the bed such as in France would not have been considered fit for a palace servant. Henrietta, tired out and suffering from the after-effects of seasickness, was probably too glad of a bed on dry land to worry unduly about its lack of grandeur; but her retinue, most of whom had to go out into the town to find their lodgings – it was raining, needless to say – were more than somewhat disenchanted, especially when they recalled the many glowing reports of English wealth and magnificence they had heard from the Lords Carlisle and Holland.[1]

Messengers were sent hurrying off to tell the king that his laggard bride had arrived at last, and at ten o'clock on the Monday morning he rode into the castle where Henrietta was still at breakfast. She immediately went downstairs to meet him, dropping on her knees and making a little speech proper to the occasion: '*Sire, je suis venue en ce pays de Votre Majesté pour être usée et commandée de vous.*' She would have kissed his hand, but he raised her to her feet, 'wrapt her up in his arms and kissed her with many kisses'. After a few minutes rather stilted conversation she noticed that he seemed to be looking down at her feet and, thinking that perhaps he was wondering if she was wearing high heels, she proceeded to display her shoes, saying: 'Sir, I stand upon mine own feet; I have no helps by art. Thus high I am and am neither higher nor lower.'[2]

The king and queen then retired into a private room for about an hour. At the time of his marriage Charles Stuart was twenty-four. A puny baby and ricketty child, famously slow to develop, he had grown into a healthy if somewhat undersized young man – he is thought to have been about five foot four inches tall. An addiction to vigorous physical exercise had strengthened his bandy legs, but he suffered from a painful stammer – 'a difficulty in his speech which prevents him talking easily', according to the Venetian ambassador – and although he was said to have improved significantly both in looks and self-confidence as a result of that unfortunate trip to Spain, his appearance at this time was unremarkable and his manner stiff and awkward. Henrietta, by contrast, was described as 'nimble and quick'. A vivacious brunette, her big black eyes were probably her best feature, for she was a skinny little thing, so small that her head reached only to her husband's shoulder.

We do not know what they made of each other at this first encounter, although Leveneur de Tillières, the former ambassador, who had returned to England as Henrietta's chamberlain, thought she was seriously disappointed, feeling she had been deceived as to both Charles's physical and mental attributes, and from that moment began to regret the vanity of her desire to be queen of a country which she had been led to believe was an earthly paradise. De Tillières himself considered that the king made a very poor impression, arriving quite casually dressed and with only a handful of companions.[3]

We do not know either what passed between the newly-weds in that first private hour, although, according to one account, she shed a few tears and he kissed them away, 'professing that he would do so, till she had done, and persuading her she was not fallen into the hands of strangers, as she apprehended tremblingly, but into the wise disposal of God, who would have her leave her kindred, and cleave to her spouse'. According to Charles himself, Henrietta also told him that, being young and inexperienced, among people whose ways were strange to her, she would very likely make mistakes, but if she did she hoped he would not leave it to a third person but tell her about them himself, so that she could avoid repeating them.[4]

When they reappeared, the queen presented all her servants, 'by name and quality in order', and the company then sat down to dinner. The king carved his wife a generous portion of venison and pheasant which she ate heartily, ignoring her confessor who was hovering behind her chair, whispering reproachfully that it was the eve of St John the Baptist and should be fasted.[5]

After dinner everyone got ready to leave for Canterbury and the king and queen had their first quarrel, caused by Mamie St Georges following the queen into her carriage and sitting down with her. The king, possibly unaware that in France the dame d'honneur always expected to stay close beside her mistress and who, in any case, had planned to give the Duke of Buckingham's mother and sister the honour of riding with his wife, promptly ordered her out again. This provoked a shrill torrent of protest from Henrietta, who seems to have panicked at the prospect of being parted from her friend – even the sympathetic de Tillières felt she made rather an exhibition of herself. Charles, unmoved by tears and prayers, stood firm until the French ambassadors intervened, pointing out that the queen was alone in a crowd of people whose language and religion were unfamiliar and that she naturally clung to the person in whom she had greatest confidence.[6] The king gave way reluctantly, but he did not forgive Madame St Georges, while Henrietta angrily resented the fact that he had deferred to the ambassadors' persuasions and not to her pleas. It was a foolish little episode and a bad omen.

At Barham Downs, just outside Canterbury, the local dignitaries and their wives were waiting to greet the royal party and escort them to Lord Wotton's house, where they were to spend the night. This would be Henrietta's wedding night and she retired early to a bed usually occupied by foreign diplomats in transit and which was grudgingly admitted to be slightly better than the one at Dover. Charles, who had no taste for the sort of ribaldry and high jinks which frequently accompanied a bride bedding, admitted only two of his gentlemen to help him undress and then, with his own hands, secured all the doors giving access to the bridal suite.[7] What followed seems only too likely to have more resembled a rape than the tactful initiation of an unawakened, under-developed adolescent girl; Charles, who was himself quite possibly still a virgin, would certainly have lacked either the experience or sensitivity necessary to make the occasion anything other than painful and traumatic. Next morning, having presumably proved his manhood to his own satisfaction, he was described as being 'jocund' and unusually talkative, but Henrietta appeared 'very melancholy'.

The king and queen now went on to Cobham near Gravesend, where they stayed for one night, before entering their barge for the last stage of the journey to London. On the way, Henrietta was treated to 'the beautiful and stately view' of fifty ships of the navy royal lying at anchor along both shores which saluted her with a volley of fifteen hundred great shot, while the Tower guns discharged such a peal that, it was confidently asserted, she could never before have heard the like. By the time they reached London Bridge their majesties had been joined by a flotilla of many hundreds of small craft, and 'infinite numbers' of spectators lined the river banks, hung out of windows and packed into wherries, barges and lighters on the water. One ship, 'whereupon stood above a hundred people, not being balanced nor well tied to the shore, and they standing all upon one side, was overturned and sunk, all that were upon her tumbling into the Thames'. Luckily, though, it seems there were no casualties, everyone being fished out by the spectators on the other boats. It was raining again, but the windows of the royal barge had been left open and the queen could be seen waving to the crowds, 'all the people shouting amain'.[8]

In spite of her Frenchness, her Catholicism and her outlandish name, the English had been quite pleasantly surprised by their first glimpses of their new queen, and the Welshman James Howell, who had seen her on the bowling green at Barham Downs, was enthusiastic, considering her in true beauty a great improvement on 'the long-woo'd Infanta', a faded blonde, big-lipped and heavy-eyed, a typical Hapsburg in fact. By contrast, this daughter of France, this youngest branch of Bourbon, was of a more lovely and lasting complexion, with 'Eyes that sparkle like Stars'.[9] Others, less complimentary, commented on her pallor, thinking she might be 'a little touched with the green sickness' or chlorosis (a form of anaemia affecting pubescent girls), and on her lack of height, although acknowledging that she was still young enough to grow taller. There was also some lingering optimism that she might still be young enough to be persuaded to change her religion, and a story was circulating that, on being asked if she could abide a Huguenot, she had replied smartly, 'Why not? Was not my father one?' There had been some hesitation over how Henri le Grand's daughter should be addressed – Henriette or Henrietta seeming altogether too fanciful for English taste – and she was prayed for, rather doubtfully, as Queen Henry, until the king settled the matter by announcing that she was to be known as Queen Mary, the name by which he called her himself.[10]

The king and queen had now reached Whitehall, the rambling palace village which sprawled along the river bank from Charing Cross to Westminster and which had changed very little since the days of the Tudors – the French thought the furniture had not changed since the days of Queen Elizabeth. True, an ambitious rebuilding programme was at the planning stage, but so far the only visible sign of innovation was the Palladian banqueting house, designed by Inigo Jones and faced with Portland stone, rising somewhat incongruously above the huddled Tudor brick and timber. In normal circumstances the court would not have been in town in mid-summer, always an unhealthy season, and plague was bad that year, with the bills of mortality rising steadily. But circumstances

were not normal in 1625. The much-postponed opening of parliament
could wait no longer and on Saturday 18 June the king went down to
Westminster to address the assembled Lords and Commons.

The members came crowding into the Upper Chamber, eager for their
first sight of the new monarch, still very much of an unknown quantity to
most people. The French minister Henri-Auguste Ville-aux-Clercs, who had
come to England the year before for the signing of the marriage treaty, had
written of the then Prince of Wales: 'He is either an extraordinary man or
his talents are very mean. If his reticence is affected in order not to give
jealousy to his father, it is a sign of consummate prudence. If it is natural
and unassumed the contrary inference may be drawn.'[11] One thing,
though, was already abundantly clear – the new monarch was very different
from his father. Gone were the casual, disorderly ways of the old court.
Dignity, respectful demeanour and regularity were now being insisted
upon. 'From which', observed Amerigo Salvetti within days of James's
death, 'everyone may readily conjecture how much weight His Majesty will
attach to deference and obedience.' His Majesty had made it known that
no one was to attempt to gain access to him unofficially by the backstairs or
by bribing the servants. In future all approaches must be made in public
and on set days. Nor would he allow members of the nobility or Privy
Councillors to enter the private apartments uninvited, 'as they have been
in the habit of doing during the last reign'. Instead, everyone 'is to take his
place in the ante-chambers according to his rank, as was the usage in the
time of Queen Elizabeth'.[12] The moral tone of the royal household had
also changed, as the 'fools and bawds, mimics and catamites' who had
surrounded the late king melted away, and courtiers who could not quite
bring themselves to abandon their previous debaucheries found it wiser to
practise them in corners, out of sight of the temperate, chaste and serious
Charles.[13]

The opening of parliament marked another departure from precedent.
King James had been accustomed to harangue his faithful Lords and
Commons with 'long rambling quaint orations'. His son, by contrast, was
brief and to the point, his speech resolving itself into a terse demand for
cash to pursue the war with Spain, the initiative for which, he insisted,
had come from the Commons. 'I pray you remember that this being my
first action and begun by your advice and entreaty, what a great
dishonour it were, both to you and me, if this action, so begun, should
fail for that assistance you are able to give me.'[14]

The Commons, however, seemed to remember that it had been Charles
and Buckingham who had led the war party in 1624, and while they had
no objection in principle to war with Spain they were demonstrably
reluctant to put up the money for it – especially bearing in mind how the

last year's subsidies had been squandered. In June 1625 the members were more concerned with debating what was to them the far more important issue of the state of religion, believing as they did that if it were undermined God would bless none of their undertakings. The Puritan faction had been unconvinced by the king's denial of rumours that he was not 'so true a keeper and maintainer of true religion as he professed'. They remained deeply suspicious that, in spite of all assurances to the contrary, concessions had been made to the Catholic community as part of his marriage treaty, and wanted to see a vigorous anti-Catholic campaign with strict enforcement of the penal laws.

The state of religion was a subject of peculiar delicacy for Charles just then. In spite of parliament's misgivings as to the soundness of his views, he was unquestionably a committed member of the Church of England, even if he favoured a branch which might loosely be described as High Anglicanism. His faith would always be a matter of great importance to him and was, like his wife's, strong and uncompromising. Nevertheless, in his anxiety to secure the French alliance, he had made promises he could not keep, allowing himself to become trapped in a situation from which there was no honourable exit and sowing the seeds of an ineradicable and eventually fatal distrust in the minds of a powerful body of English public opinion. Meanwhile his government found itself in the rather embarrassing position of trying to keep everybody happy as a predictably ill-tempered atmosphere developed at court.

On Friday 17 June, the day after her arrival in London, 'the queen was at her first mass in Whitehall, which was mumbled over to her majesty at eleven of the clock, what time she came out of her bedchamber in her petticoat, with a veil upon her head, supported by the Count de Tilliers, her lord chamberlain, and followed by six women'. On the following Sunday she went privately to high mass at Somerset House – or Denmark House as it was more generally known, having been made over to King James's wife, Anne of Denmark – where the Duc and Duchesse de Chevreuse were staying and where there was a temporary chapel. The fact that there was still no permanent place of worship ready for Henrietta's use was an early cause of complaint by the French. According to one of the regular newsletters sent by Dr Meddus, rector of St Gabriel, Fenchurch Street, to his friend the Reverend Joseph Mead of Cambridge, the priests were being very importunate to have the chapel finished at St James's but had received a sharp set-down from the king. 'His answer (some told me) was, that if the queen's closet, where they now say mass, were not large enough, let them have it in the great chamber; and if the great chamber was not wide enough, they might use the garden; and if the garden would not serve their turn, then was the park the fittest place.

So, seeing themselves slighted, they grow weary of England, and wish themselves at home again.'[15] This was a wish heartily reciprocated by the English, who grudged the expense involved in feeding and housing so many foreigners – and popish foreigners at that. The men, they complained, were arrogant and over-dressed, while not one of the women in the queen's train was worth looking at, with the possible exception of the Duchesse de Chevreuse, 'who, though she be fair, yet paints foully'.

The Venetian ambassador had already begun to notice ominous cracks opening up on the surface of the Anglo-French entente, but these were not allowed to interfere with the series of lavish entertainments held to celebrate the royal marriage. On Tuesday 21 June, at a ceremony in the *1625* Great Room at Whitehall, the articles of the treaty were read aloud in English and French in the presence of the king and queen, the Duc de Chevreuse, the French ambassadors and the whole court. The union was then announced to have been lawfully consummated and Henrietta, making her first official public appearance, was proclaimed queen. After this the king hosted a grand dinner party followed by dancing, and Zuane Pesaro commented that 'it was a fine sight to see the splendour of the liveries and the carriage of the French ambassadors at the palace, richly be-jewelled and dressed'. Next day it was the turn of the Duke of Buckingham, who feasted the visitors 'with such magnificence and prodigal plenty, both for curious cheer and banquet, that the like hath not been seen in these parts'. One especially choice dish had apparently arrived of its own accord: 'a sturgeon, full six feet long, that afternoon leaping into a sculler's boat, not far from the palace, was served in at supper.' But, in the opinion of one disgruntled Englishman, 'in all these shows and feastings there hath been such excessive bravery on all sides, as bred rather a surfeit than any delight in them that saw it'.[16]

The French continued to complain that they were not being treated with proper respect, and that the promises contained in the Escrit Secret were being broken. Back in May, on the day of his proxy wedding, Charles had instructed the Lord Keeper, John Williams, 'to forbear all manner of proceeding against His Majesties Catholic subjects', but his majesty's Catholic subjects were forbidden to attend the queen's mass and, as Zuane Pesaro pointed out, as long as the penal laws remained on the statute book, 'certain ministers will always have the power to enforce them'. Amerigo Salvetti, writing to the Duke of Tuscany early in July, also remarked on French dissatisfaction when they realised that the English Catholics were not enjoying all the liberties they had been led to believe would now be granted, and went on to describe the astonishing state of ignorance and misapprehension prevailing among 'those who had charge of the negotiations in France. . . . They apparently believed, or induced others to believe, that the English are a sort of Spanish Catholics, different from the French, and they have acted without looking closely into the subject or understanding it.'[17]

Another cause of dissension was the appointment of several non-Catholic Englishmen as officers in the queen's household. This was certainly in breach of the spirit, if not the letter of the marriage contract and the French ambassadors were disputing it, but Salvetti did not think they would be successful. He believed the household would eventually be mixed with a good many English and contain fewer French, 'with regard to whom the prevalent wish is to send them to their homes'. But although there was plenty of squabbling and name-calling between the Londoners and the numerous hangers-on attached to the queen's entourage, the real animosity was reserved for Henrietta's priests. As well as her Grand Almoner, the Bishop of Mende, a close relative of Cardinal Richelieu, and the venerable Father Bérulle, they included twenty-four Oratorians, an order founded by Bérulle, and it was the sight of these individuals going about in their clerical habits, mumbling their daily masses and apparently having unrestricted access to the queen's private apartments which did most to raise the hackles of all good Protestants.

The Londoners were also beginning to revise their first cautiously favourable impression of Henrietta herself. So far they had seen very little of her. 'She does not show herself much to the English ladies and gentlemen of her court,' wrote Salvetti, 'probably because she cannot converse with them except through the unpleasant intervention of an interpreter.' Certainly the language barrier was causing problems, but on at least one occasion that summer Henrietta had not needed an interpreter to make her wishes plain and an Englishman who had joined the throng at the palace hoping to catch sight of her remarked that the queen 'howsoever little of stature, is of spirit and vigour, and seems of a more than ordinary resolution. With one frown, divers of us being at Whitehall to see her being at dinner, and the room somewhat overheated with the fire and company, she drove us all out of the chamber. I suppose none but a queen could have cast such a scowl.'[18]

As June turned into July the plague was killing several thousand a week and the infection had begun to spread westward from the city. It was no longer possible to keep parliament sitting and by the time the king ordered an adjournment, most of the members were already leaving for the country. The court, too, was on the move, out to the comparative safety of Hampton Court, but Charles had not forgotten the episode of Mamie St Georges and the coach at Dover and, according to de Tillières, insisted on making the journey in a small carriage in which there was room only for himself and Henrietta and a couple of English ladies. The queen, says de Tillières, was annoyed and could not help showing her resentment.

It was by now painfully obvious that all was not well between husband and wife and, with his usual sublime self-importance, the Duke of Buckingham decided to take on the role of marriage guidance counsellor, warning Henrietta that the king would no longer put up with her coldness towards him. Apparently believing that it would be easy to bully her, Buckingham went on to threaten that if she did not mend her ways she would become the unhappiest woman in the world, adding that he knew she disliked him, but this did not worry him as he was assured of his master's good will. Again according to de Tillières, Henrietta was shaken by this unexpected attack, but answered coolly that she was not aware of having given her husband any cause for complaint and she did not believe he would ever wish to make her unhappy. As for the duke, she had never looked unkindly on him and was quite prepared to live on civil terms with him if he would do the same with her. Next day he was back again, this time to demand that the queen should agree to accept his wife, sister and niece as ladies of the bedchamber. Henrietta replied that she was perfectly satisfied with the ladies she had brought from France but would be willing to refer the matter to the judgement of the French ambassadors. The duke was persuasive, the ambassadors disposed to be compliant, but the Bishop of Mende, horrified at the thought of exposing a vulnerable young princess to the evil influence of such Huguenot ladies, vetoed the idea as soon as he heard about it, thus incurring Buckingham's particular enmity.

Henrietta was no sooner installed at Hampton Court than cases of plague began to appear in the neighbourhood and the king, who had gone off to the royal manor of Oatlands for a few days' hunting, sent instructions that his wife was to move to Windsor. She had expected him to meet her there, but instead he returned to Hampton Court for no other reason, it seemed, than to ensure that it was Buckingham's niece, Mary Hamilton, and not Mamie St Georges who travelled with her. It was all the duke's doing, says de Tillières. As he escorted the queen to her carriage, he could see 'le Buckingham' standing talking loudly to the king, as if to demonstrate his authority. Unfortunately, even Windsor proved unsafe and, when a member of the king's own guard fell ill and died, yet another move had to be hastily organised. This time Henrietta went to Nonesuch, the fantastic prodigy house in the Surrey countryside built by Henry VIII back in the 1540s to impress the French. Charles was staying at nearby Woking, but he came over two or three times to see the queen and always with some trivial complaint about the conduct of her household manufactured by Buckingham or the Earl of Carlisle who, de

Tillières was convinced, were determined to make mischief. It was so sad, he sighed, that this promising young king, married to a beautiful, high-born princess, should allow himself to be manipulated by men like the duke, who cared only for their own interests.[19]

Parliament had been summoned to reconvene at Oxford on 1 August, but its second session was to be even shorter and less successful than the first. Fear of infection – plague stalked the court wherever it went – was making everyone jumpy. The members, too, were annoyed at being made to leave their homes at harvest time and almost at once king and Commons were at loggerheads again. The king was still asking for money – the two subsidies which had been voted at the end of June represented only a fraction of what was wanted – while the Commons had returned obstinately to the subject of religion. But this time Charles and Buckingham, desperate for the means to equip the fleet they were planning to send against Spain, were prepared to make concessions: all religious orders, except the priests attached to the queen's household, would be banished from the realm; the children of Catholic families currently being educated abroad would be recalled, and the Catholics generally required 'punctually to obey the special laws to which they are subjected'. It was even said that Buckingham had suggested some new anti-Catholic regulations. Unhappily, this was not enough to prevent certain members of the Commons from continuing to ask awkward questions. They wanted an account of how the supplies voted in 1624 had been spent. They wanted more details about the king's intentions – war with Spain had still not been declared and parliament had not yet even been told exactly who the fleet was going to attack – and they wanted to know how any future grants were to be spent and who was to administer them. More ominously, 'they spoke of the necessity for correcting abuses. . . . They condemned the authority of a single individual and said that matters should be done by council.'

There was no secret as to the identity of this 'single individual'. Buckingham had been growing increasingly unpopular during the past year, but any hint of danger to his favourite touched Charles on his most sensitive spot, as did any threat to his own sovereignty, and on 12 August he dissolved parliament, declaring that his condition would be too miserable if he could not command and be obeyed: 'he would employ one or many or nobody in his councils.' The Venetian ambassador put it rather more succinctly when he observed that the interests of the duke's safety had prevailed over the needs of the Crown and public affairs.[20]

After the débâcle at Oxford the king and queen, who had been staying at Woodstock, left for Hampshire. There could be no question as yet of returning anywhere near the plague-ridden capital and in any case the king, who was still determined somehow to get the fleet to sea before the autumn gales set in, wanted to be within reach of the Channel ports. He sent Henrietta to Titchfield, the Earl of Southampton's property near Netley, while he retreated to Beaulieu on the other side of Southampton Water, where he would be able to get some hunting in the New Forest.

Very much to everyone's relief the French ambassadors and their retinues had now gone home, and Father Bérulle had also been recalled, but the question of the queen's household had still not been settled and the ambassadors were not at all happy over the way she and her people were being treated. Buckingham had so far failed to get any of his female relations appointed to the bedchamber, although Pesaro reported that 'the ladies enter the queen's apartment, as they say, by permission' and, according to de Tillières, Henrietta was still being pestered by the duke, who told her that she was behaving more like a silly little girl than a queen. This may have been a veiled allusion to her continued aversion to the physical side of married life, which was causing her to have rather too many headaches when her husband came over to Titchfield and which led him to accuse her of denying him his conjugal rights. Other men, including Buckingham of course, had told him that if she was their wife they would not stand for it. Nor was this by any means his only cause for complaint, but if she was really unwell, he would have to wait until she felt better to tackle her about them. Henrietta retorted that there was no time like the present, but Charles does not seem to have taken up the challenge.[21]

There were some other unfortunate incidents at Titchfield. One Sunday morning Buckingham's sister, the Countess of Denbigh, had arranged for the local parson to come and preach a sermon for the benefit of the Protestant members of the household without first asking the queen's permission. The French chose to regard this as a deliberate provocation and Henrietta, together with a number of her ladies and other attendants and their pet dogs, reacted by walking to and fro through the hall where the service was being held, talking and laughing, making mock hunting cries and generally creating so much disturbance that the preacher was unable to continue. Accusation and counter-accusation followed and the minister concerned later claimed that some of the queen's servants had been taking pot-shots at him while he was sitting on a bench in his garden. De Tillières, called upon to investigate, dismissed this as nonsense. It was only a couple of lackeys shooting birds. One of their guns might have gone off by mistake, but they could not possibly have been aiming at the minister, who was on the other side of a hedge. In any case, if the marks on his garden bench had really been made by bullets, the man would certainly have been dead. On another occasion, when the king and queen were both at dinner, the rival Catholic and Protestant chaplains descended to pushing and shoving and trying to shout each other down in saying grace, so that the king 'in a great passion, instantly rose from the table, and, taking the queen by the hand, retired into the bedchamber'. It all sounds amazingly childish, but this sort of thing could generate some very unchildish rancour. The French were said to be 'full to the throat with disgust' and the feeling abroad was growing that instead of true friendship, nothing but discords and disputes between the two nations seemed to have resulted from the marriage so that they were in danger of losing the advantages which the world had hoped to gain from this alliance 'through vanity and lightness'.[22]

Cardinal Richelieu had previously been willing to show some flexibility over the composition of the queen's household, but now, disturbed by the reports of the returning ambassadors and needing to placate the French Dévots, he prepared to send Jean de Varinières, Marquis de Blainville, on a special mission to England with instructions to make strong representations on behalf of the embattled Catholics and insist that no Englishwomen or Protestants should be admitted to the queen's service. De Blainville had also been briefed by a worried Marie de Medici to enquire into her daughter's various marital problems and 'remove all shadows that pass between their Majesties'. But Buckingham had been warned by Thomas Lorkin, his agent in Paris, that de Blainville, 'a prying, penetrating and dangerous man', was no more than a spy coming to make mischief, so that when he arrived, towards the end of October, he got a chilly reception from the king, who told him that any measures taken against the Catholic community had been necessary for the good of the state and, in any case, were nothing like so severe as had been reported. As for his wife's household, Charles meant to be master of it and appoint anyone he saw fit. He had already settled with his kinsman, the Duc de Chevreuse, all that he felt able to concede and if there were those who hoped for more, they were deceiving themselves. The ambassador repeatedly begged him to remember and to keep the solemn promises he had made in the secret clauses of his marriage treaty, but in vain, and that very evening the king sent a message to Comte de Tillières ordering him to swear in three English Protestants as grooms of the queen's guard chamber. The Duke of Buckingham, who had just succeeded in getting the fleet off to Spain and was now preparing to leave on a diplomatic mission to the Hague, managed to snatch a few days to see de Blainville, but although he seemed a good deal friendlier than the king had been, the ambassador could not persuade him to promise anything.[23]

The queen's entourage was continuing to blame Buckingham for the distressing failure of the royal marriage. It was he, they maintained, who carried tales to the king about his wife's frivolous behaviour and encouraged him to find fault with those innocent little pleasures and pastimes it was only natural she should enjoy at her age – Henrietta was about to celebrate her sixteenth birthday. She, not understanding what she was doing wrong, put her husband's attitude down to unreasonable crossness and coldness and kept out of his way as much as she could. A state of affairs, wrote de Tillières, which suited the duke and his henchman the Earl of Carlisle very well; afraid of losing their power over the king, they missed no opportunity of poisoning his mind against the queen. This was especially easy for Buckingham, 'the king having no other sentiments than his and seeing only through his eyes'.[24]

Charles, increasingly irritated by the French in general and de Blainville in particular – 'the French ambassador does not cease to press the business for which he came to this court, without profit and with greater ill-feeling' – was, for his part, convinced that it was the 'monsieurs' surrounding his wife who were the source of all his marital problems. He and Henrietta had been living apart for most of the late summer and autumn. She had moved from Titchfield to the Earl of Pembroke's Wilton House, while he, after visiting the fleet at Plymouth, had settled at nearby Salisbury. It was November before the plague had abated sufficiently for it to be considered safe for them to return to Hampton Court together, and it was from there, on the 20th of the month, that the king wrote to his beloved Steenie (the pet name bestowed on Buckingham by King James) to say that he thought he would soon have cause enough 'to put away the monsieurs', either for attempting to steal his wife away, or for making plots with his subjects. He was still hunting after definite proof, 'yet seeing daily the maliciousness of the monsieurs, by making and fomenting discontentments in my wife, I could tarry no longer from advertising of you, that I mean to seek for no other grounds to cashier my monsieurs'.[25]

Having successfully negotiated a treaty with Denmark and the United Provinces, Buckingham was planning to travel on to France and Charles, clearly anticipating maternal thunderbolts, 'this being an action that may have a show of harshness', took the precaution of enclosing another letter to Steenie which could, if necessary, be shown to Marie de Medici. 'You know what patience I have had', he wrote, 'with the unkind usages of my wife, grounded upon a belief that it was not in her nature but made by ill instruments, and overcome by your persuasions to me, that my kind usages would be able to rectify those misunderstandings. . . . But I am sure you have erred in your opinion; for I find daily worse and worse effects of ill offices done between us, my kind usages having no power to mend anything. Now, necessity urges me to vent myself to you in this particular, for grief is eased being told to a friend; and because I have many obligations to my mother-in-law (knowing that these courses of my wife are so much against her knowledge, that they are contrary to her advice) I would do nothing concerning her daughter that may taste of any harshness, without advertising her of the reasons and necessity of the thing. . . . You must, therefore, advertise my mother-in-law, that I must remove all those instruments that are causes of unkindness between her daughter and me, few or none of the servants being free from this fault in one kind or other.'[26]

In spite of being resolute to do the business, 'and that shortly', Charles told Steenie he would 'put nothing of this in execution until I hear from you' and a few days later was reporting that: 'As for news, my wife begins to mend her manners; I know now how long it will continue, for they say it is by advice; but the best of all is, they, the monsieurs, desire to return home; I will not say this is certain, for you know nothing that they say can be so.'[27]

In the event, the monsieurs stayed where they were, for the present at least. It seems likely that Buckingham, still pursuing his dream of enticing France into a grand anti-Spanish, anti-Hapsburg league, had counselled more patience; but the duke was to be frustrated in his hopes of making another spectacular appearance at the French court. The French ambassador in Holland told him flatly that he would not be welcome until King Louis' legitimate demands, as expounded by the Sieur de Blainville, had been satisfied. There was also, of course, the little matter of the duke's amatory advances to Louis' wife, which that monarch had not forgotten or forgiven.

Buckingham was, therefore, obliged to return home, to be met with news of the humiliating failure of the great naval expedition against Spain. Inadequately financed with borrowed money (some of it borrowed from the queen's dowry), its commanders ranging from the mediocre to the useless, the men unpaid and unwilling, the fleet had never even looked like achieving any of its objectives; and the ill-found ships with their ragged, starving, mutinous crews which now came limping back to port demonstrated beyond all possibility of doubt that the Elizabethan glory days were a thing of the past.

Amazingly, neither Charles nor Buckingham seemed particularly cast down. The talk was all of getting another task force together and writs were issued for a new parliament. Meanwhile, the court prepared to celebrate Christmas, the queen even making a daring foray into town to do a little shopping at the Royal Exchange, 'going nimbly from shop to shop', until she was recognised and had to beat an embarrassed retreat under the disapproving eyes of the Londoners.

Although Henrietta's first six months in England had been a considerable disappointment and she had missed the greater luxury, warmth and gaiety of home, she does not appear to have been actively unhappy. Royal brides were not brought up to expect romantic happiness and if Charles, with his stammer, his chilly, undemonstrative ways and obsessive passion for order – dividing his days into rigid compartments devoted to prayer, exercise, business, eating and sleeping, must sometimes have seemed like a creature from another planet to his eager, mercurial little wife, at least he had no obvious vices and, unlike her father, kept no mistresses to plague her or challenge her position. It was true that the Duke of Buckingham was almost as formidable a competitor as a mistress but, supported and cushioned by her French household, Henrietta had so far contrived to keep herself amused without taking too much thought for the future.

This had been comparatively easy during a summer spent in the more relaxed atmosphere of the country as refugees from the plague. But summer was over now. The plague, which had killed some 60,000 of the king's subjects, was finally in retreat and in the New Year the court was back at Whitehall, getting ready for the much-delayed coronation. This had been set for Candlemas Day, 2 February, but was to be held without the customary recognition procession and shorn of much of 'the magnificence characteristic of the ceremonial; it being resolved, from motives of economy, to save [the] three hundred thousand crowns which it would have cost and to use the money for other important and needful purpose'.[28]

The king and queen should, of course, have been crowned together, but a ceremony taking place in a Protestant church, performed by Protestant clergy, presented the French government and the Catholic hierarchy with a peculiarly intractable problem. 'The queen's bishop' (that is, Mende) had at first 'pretended and stood to have the crowning of her', but this having been indignantly vetoed by the Archbishop of Canterbury, Mende had gone over to France to consult the authorities at the Sorbonne and bring back 'the resolution of the French court'.

'They entered upon many negotiations to secure some compromise,' reported Zuane Pesaro. It was suggested that the ceremony might take place outside the church, as did the marriage in France, 'and that a Catholic bishop or the Archbishop of Canterbury, not as an ecclesiastic but [as] a lay peer of the realm, should perform the coronation'. But since the English refused to allow the smallest departure from the practices of their church, it seemed that the queen's coronation would have to be postponed indefinitely or else abandoned altogether. 'This concerns France', Pesaro went on, 'more because her prerogatives will be less, and already men say she will be queen consort of the king, but not the crowned queen of England or of Great Britain.'[29]

In the event, Henrietta was not only not crowned but was not even present in the Abbey to see her husband crowned, although 'she was

[margin: 1626]

39

offered to have a place made fit for her'. Instead, she stood at the window of a house by the palace gate to watch the 'going and returning', but certain officious passers-by did not fail to remark that her ladies could be seen in the background 'frisking and dancing' in their usual unsuitable fashion.[30] While it is certainly unfair to lay all the blame on the sixteen-year-old queen, conditioned as she was to accept the church's ruling on such matters without question, the English people understandably took her rejection of the crown matrimonial as a calculated insult which they never forgave, and it was an error of judgement which would come back to haunt her in years to come.

Four days after the coronation Charles was due to ride in state to the opening of parliament and the Comte de Tillières made arrangements for the queen to view the procession to Westminster from one of the galleries in Whitehall; but the ever-helpful Duke of Buckingham had intervened, suggesting to the king that her majesty would be much better off seeing the show from the windows of his mother's apartments in another part of the palace complex. This involved going outside, across a garden wet and muddy underfoot. It was also raining and at the last moment Henrietta decided to decline the duke's kind invitation, pointing out that her coiffure would be quite spoilt. Charles appeared to acquiesce, although reluctantly, until – at least according to de Tillières – Buckingham told him that a king who let it be seen that his own wife would not obey him could hardly expect to be able to assert his authority over parliament. The French ambassador had now arrived on the scene and managed to persuade the queen to brave the weather, but this only made things worse. The king, believing that she had given way to de Blainville rather than to his wishes, sent Buckingham to order her to return to her own rooms. When she and the ambassador protested, it was represented as yet more defiance and Charles lost his temper, insisting that she return immediately – or he would put off his entry into parliament until another day. Henrietta, forced to traipse back through the damp garden, was justifiably irritated, complaining bitterly about being made to look ridiculous in front of everybody and at the duke acting as messenger.[31]

Cardinal Richelieu had recently been heard to remark in some exasperation, 'we made that alliance expecting to marry England to France rather than to marry individuals', and now this latest squabble between husband and wife looked like turning into an international incident. The already unpopular de Blainville found himself becoming a convenient scapegoat for royal tantrums and was blamed for having given the queen bad advice. He was told he would no longer be welcome at court and was barred from visiting the queen. When Henrietta heard about this from the ubiquitous Buckingham, she declared she would rather die than shut out her brother's representative, going on to say she was sorry that her husband, who had so many enemies, should add to them by offending France. The Venetian ambassador did what he could to smooth things over, but without success and de Blainville, having demanded and been refused a public audience of the king, retreated into the country in a great state of umbrage. Meanwhile the king and queen were not on speaking terms, Charles refusing to see his wife until she apologised. In the end she went to him and asked what she had done to displease him so excessively, to which he replied, after some hesitation: '*Est ce que vous m'avez assuré qu'il pleuvait quand je vous ai dit qu'il ne pleuvait pas.*' She thought this hardly seemed a very serious crime, but if he really believed it to be so, she would do the same and begged him to think no more about it.[32]

The quarrel was patched up. It was agreed that de Blainville might visit the queen privately to bring her letters from her family, and Zuane Pesaro reported that the king and queen had resumed sleeping together. But the physical side of the marriage remained unsatisfactory, and late one evening the Duke of Buckingham approached Mamie St Georges to warn her that the king was still complaining about his wife's coldness towards him. Mamie replied that she thought the queen lived very well with her husband and his majesty could not expect more from a strictly brought-up young princess. Buckingham agreed that she behaved amiably enough during the day, but at night it was different. She never meddled in such matters said Mamie primly and neither should anyone else. Nevertheless, according to de Tillières, Buckingham then told Charles that she had promised to speak to the queen, making it clear that if Henrietta now became more responsive in bed, he would have Madame de St Georges to thank for it. All which, thought de Tillières, was further evidence of the duke's malice and the weakness of the king – the former seeking to penetrate the secrets of the bedchamber and to persuade the latter that his wife's natural virtue and modesty was actually no more than an unnatural aversion to his lovemaking.[33] The English, of course, were equally convinced that Henrietta's priests were also prying into what went on behind the royal bedcurtains and that 'these bawdy knaves would, by way of confession, interrogate her how often in a night the king had kissed her', and that they had such influence over her that she obeyed them when they told her that today was the feast of such and such a saint and she must not let the king approach.[34]

On Shrove Tuesday, 21 February, Henrietta created quite a sensation by presenting a pastoral play which she and twelve of her ladies had been rehearsing since Christmas. The scenic effects, designed by Inigo Jones, and the costumes were much admired, as was the acting talent of the performers – her majesty in the leading part, needless to say, 'surpassing all the others'.

Amateur theatricals had been a favourite pastime of the late queen, Anne of Denmark, and Charles himself as a child of nine had appeared in one of his mother's productions, wearing a green satin tunic sewn with gold flowerets; but members of the royal family had hitherto contented themselves with walk-on parts, designed to display them and their finery to best advantage. Henrietta, in her element in the world of music and dance and romantic make-believe, was more ambitious, learning by heart and reciting several hundred lines of French verse with great aplomb. The king, worried in case her debut might be greeted with disapproval, had ensured that the audience was limited to a carefully selected few, but even so there were those who found the spectacle shocking, especially as some of the young ladies were disguised as men with beards! 'I have known the time when this would have seemed a strange sight', wrote one gentleman, 'to see a Queen act in a play, but *tempora mutantur et nos* [times change and so do we].'[35]

Henrietta's performance may also have seemed further evidence of her wilful refusal to make any attempt to adjust to her new surroundings, for she, who so often appeared sulky and stand-offish to her husband's people, was invariably merry and voluble among her own compatriots. The queen, remarked the percipient Venetians, 'is thoroughly French, both in her sentiments and habits. The marriage has not changed her one whit; it has not made her English and does not seem likely to do so by a long way.'[36]

While his wife continued to attract hostile criticism, the king, now wrestling with his new parliament, was about to discover that the rising tide of popular indignation against his best friend had begun to reach dangerous levels. Determined that this time religion should not be an issue, Charles had abandoned any pretence of toleration for his Catholic subjects. 'All the laws hostile to them are enforced without distinction of rank or quality,' reported Amerigo Salvetti, and the authorities had recently come to arrest a number of Catholics attending mass at the French ambassador's house, which resulted in a free fight and equally free exchange of insults between the pursuivants and the embassy servants.

But the religious question had been temporarily put on one side by the House of Commons, where smouldering resentment against the arrogance and incompetence of the Duke of Buckingham had now found a powerful voice. Sir John Eliot was a West Countryman who had seen with his own eyes the starving exhausted survivors of the ill-fated expedition to Spain dropping dead on the streets of Plymouth, and on 10 February he rose to deliver a veiled but devastating attack on the favourite. 'Is the reputation and glory of our nation of a small value?' he demanded. 'Are the numberless lives of our lost men not to be regarded? I know it cannot so harbour in an English thought. Our honour is ruined, our ships are sunk, our men perished; not by the sword, not by the enemy, not by chance, but, as the strongest predictions had discerned and made it apparent beforehand, by those we trust.'[37]

If the king was to pursue the war and have any hope of being able to restore his sister and brother-in-law to their Palatinate, he had to have money to prop up his Scandinavian allies and pay the English troops in Dutch service, but the parliamentary session was already reaching a familiar stalemate – the Commons stubbornly refusing to grant supplies until their grievances had been redressed, grievances 'all springing from one root'. Led by Eliot, the campaign against Buckingham gathered momentum throughout March and April and a list of the members' principal complaints was prepared, thinly disguised as questions which needed answering. Had not the duke, by the appointment of unworthy officers and general maladministration, caused the fleet to incur its recent disaster and, in any case, should he not, as Lord Admiral, have gone in person to command? Had not the crown revenues been seriously depleted by the lavish grants of land and money bestowed on him, his friends and relatives? Had not the commonwealth suffered from his sale of honours, offices and ecclesiastical dignities, and was it fitting that he should himself enjoy so many great offices of state? Added to this was the lingering suspicion that he favoured the Romish sect, for were not his mother and his father-in-law known to be recusants?[38]

The Commons were anxious to assure the king of their continuing loyalty and regard, but Charles, as always fiercely protective of his beloved Steenie, made it clear that he would tolerate no enquiry into the proceedings 'not of any ordinary servant, but of one that is most near unto me'. He delighted to honour the duke, who had always served him most faithfully and had never meddled or done anything concerning the public except by his special directions. 'I would not have the House to question my servants,' he repeated, 'much less one that is so near me.' A fortnight later the House was threatened by the Lord Keeper Coventry that unless money was forthcoming within the next three days, the king could not guarantee that the sitting would continue, and Charles added a warning of his own: 'Remember that Parliaments are altogether in my power for their calling, sitting and dissolution; therefore, as I find the fruits of them good or evil, they are to continue, or not to be.'[39]

Even this failed to impress the Commons, who now began defiantly to draw up a bill of impeachment against Buckingham and on Tuesday 9 May a deputation from the Lower House arrived in the Lords ready to present a catalogue of thirteen charges, 'the duke sitting there, outfacing his accusers, outbraving his accusations, to the high indignation of the Commons'. It was left to Sir John Eliot to make what amounted to the opening speech for the prosecution, in which he denounced Buckingham's vanity, his abuse of power and reckless squandering of the king's treasure on 'his superfluous feasts, his magnificent buildings, his riots, his excesses' – no wonder the government was short of money – and went on to compare him to Sejanus, the villainous favourite of the Emperor Tiberius. Charles retaliated by having Eliot and another member, Sir Dudley Digges, arrested and sent to the Tower, but such was the outcry in the Commons over this flagrant breach of privilege that both men had to be released again.

In spite of all this, and some other accusations relating to that crazy trip to Spain in 1623 now being levelled against him by the Earl of Bristol, no one seriously believed that Buckingham was in any immediate danger – not, at any rate, while the king continued to stand by him. As Amerigo Salvetti remarked, 'although the people cry "crucify him", they have in reality no power to do him any harm'. But, as once before, Charles was taking no chances where Steenie's safety was concerned and on 15 June, after one more fruitless attempt to blackmail the Commons into passing a subsidy bill, he abruptly dissolved his second parliament – so abruptly that when the Lords tried to make him see how dangerous this would be to the State and begged him to let them sit for a few more days, he is said to have retorted 'not for another minute'. 'What will become of us now, God knows,' lamented Joseph Mead in Cambridge, 'but so fatal and invincible a destruction in times of so great danger cannot but produce a woeful event, unless God be extraordinarily merciful to us.'[40]

Certainly the year 1626 was so far proving deeply unsatisfactory for the king, both at home and abroad. That spring France signed a treaty with Spain without reference to her English allies, thus not only seeming to confirm every Englishman's worst suspicions about French duplicity but also putting an end to any lingering hopes of being able to create a viable anti-Hapsburg league, and Anglo-French relations cooled to near freezing point. De Blainville had now received his recall, much to everyone's relief, and the latest English delegation in France returned home at the end of March, but not before they had endured an uncomfortable interview with the queen-mother, who complained angrily about the lack of consideration with which her daughter was being treated. Henrietta still had no settled establishment and was being denied the power to appoint even a single servant of her own choosing to her household – something which had been freely granted in her marriage treaty. She was becoming more and more dissatisfied with this sort of behaviour, added Marie de Medici, and she would have given her right hand not to have married her daughter in England. The ambassadors, Lord Holland and Dudley Carleton, pacified the indignant mama as best they could, assuring her that the queen's affairs would be better managed from now on and promising that she would, in future, have complete control over her household.[41]

Unfortunately French suspicions about English bad faith were also about to be confirmed, for Charles was now insisting that his wife should agree to accept the Marchioness of Hamilton, the Countess of Denbigh and the Countess of Carlisle – Buckingham's niece, sister and mistress respectively – as her ladies of the bedchamber. Henrietta protested that he had always said he wanted her to follow the example of his mother, who had never had more than two bedchamber ladies, but if she was to be forced to have three Englishwomen, she would much prefer the Duchess of Buckingham, whom she knew to be virtuous, to the Countess of Carlisle, whom she disliked. Charles replied brusquely that that was nonsense, she had no business to take dislikes to people and Henrietta gave in, but with a bad grace, saying 'she would never have confidence with those ladies'.[42]

Another outstanding bone of contention was the appointment of officers to administer her dower lands, which were now at last being assigned to her, and the Venetians reported that the queen had sent her husband a note with the names of those she wished to be appointed, 'but his Majesty, angry perhaps about the affair of the ladies, seems to have thrown it aside without reading it, saying that he meant to be master and dispose of her officers as he pleased'.[43]

The couple's next quarrel took place without witnesses and was described by the king himself. 'One night, when I was in bed, [my wife] put a paper into my hand, telling me it was a list of those that she desired to be of her revenue [i.e. administer her estates]. I took it, and said I would read it next morning; but withal told her that, by agreement in France, I had the naming of them. She said there were both French and English in the note. I replied, that those English I thought fit to serve her I would confirm; but for the French it was impossible for them to serve her in that nature. Then she said, all those in the paper had breviates [recommendations] from her mother and herself, and that she could admit no other. Then I said, it was neither in her mother's power nor hers to admit any without my leave; and that, if she stood upon that, whomsoever she recommended, should not come in. Then she bade me plainly take my lands to myself; for, if she had no power to put in whom she would in those places, she would have neither lands nor houses of me; but bade me give her what I thought fit in pension. I bade her then remember to whom she spoke; and told her she ought not to use me so. Then she fell into a passionate discourse, how miserable she was, in having no power to place servants, and that business succeeded the worse for her recommendation; which, when I offered to answer, she would not so much as hear me. Then she went on saying, she was not of that base quality to be used so ill. Then I made her both hear me, and end that discourse.'[44]

Henrietta had expected, naturally enough, to follow the normal custom of rewarding her own people, but it was not exactly tactful to have nominated the Bishop of Mende, who, with Mamie St Georges, headed the list of Charles's *bêtes noires*, to be Steward of her jointure property – a prestigious position which had, in any case, already been earmarked for the Earl of Holland. Andrea Rosso of the Venetian embassy heard that 'the quarrels between their Majesties do not cease, but even become more and more bitter. It seems', he went on, 'that the queen herself spoke to the king and told him that she desired no more for the regulation of her household than his mother Queen Anne enjoyed.' The king had replied that his mother was quite a different sort of woman and from then on the dispute had degenerated into an unedifying exchange of personalities, the queen retorting that there certainly was a great difference between a daughter of Denmark and one of France and of the House of Bourbon. A daughter of France was no great thing, said Charles sourly. Henrietta had brought nothing with her but her dowry, and being the youngest was of even less account.[45]

July was a miserable month all round. It was another drenching summer with the prospect of another bad harvest to come and the king, having once more demonstrated his inability to manage his parliaments, was again in dire financial straits. But his most immediate problem was the apparently irretrievable breakdown of his marriage. According to de Tillières, when the king did visit his wife he told her it was only for the sake of appearances and not out of any affection for her, and these days he scarcely spoke to her except to scold. On one occasion he took offence because she gave her companions permission to sit down in his presence, and another time, when she was unwell with a feverish cold and such bad toothache that she was rolling on the floor in agony, he only laughed and told her not to make such a fuss.[46] De Tillières was admittedly a prejudiced witness, but just the same it was obvious that some sort of crisis was approaching and it seemed that Charles had now found a convincing pretext for dismissing the French household, which he still maintained was not only the cause of all his marital difficulties, but was also forming a separate enclave at court and stirring up trouble among the Catholic community.

The English Catholics had so far derived very little benefit from the Catholic queen. On the contrary, Salvetti, writing in April, gave it as his opinion that their affairs 'never were in a worse state than at the present time with every appearance of decline rather than improvement', and in June he observed that no one was able to escape the rigorous application of the penal laws. No one, that is, but the queen and her servants. Ever since her arrival Henrietta's observance of her religious duties had been exemplary – or regrettable, according to point of view – and during Holy Week she and her ladies had gone into retreat at Somerset House, where a long gallery had been divided and fitted up with cells and an oratory, and 'there they sang the hours of the Virgin and lived together like nuns'. On Holy Thursday, reported Salvetti, the queen had walked all the way to St James's Palace, 'the distance of a mile', to visit the still unfinished chapel which had been begun for the Spanish Infanta.[47]

This excursion was repeated when, at the end of June, Henrietta again went into retreat at Somerset House for 'a special season of devotion', and this seems to have been the occasion of her controversial pilgrimage to the site of the gallows at Tyburn, where she stopped to pray for the souls of those Catholic saints and martyrs who had suffered there 'so openly that the people noticed it and were scandalised'. Since the Catholic martyrs were commonly regarded as traitors by the Protestant Londoners, this gesture by the queen was provocative to say the least and later had to be denied by the French.

Just exactly what did happen at Tyburn remains a little obscure and by the time the story reached the king it had very probably been embellished with such picturesque details as the queen having been forced to walk barefoot by her 'luciferian confessor', who rode along beside her in his coach.[48] At all events, it appears to have finally decided the king to 'cashier' the monsieurs, and before the end of July that experienced diplomat Dudley Carleton was dispatched to Paris with instructions to explain and justify their expulsion.

The French royal family, said Charles, were aware of the various 'unkindnesses and distastes' which had fallen out between his wife and himself and which, as everyone knew, he had hitherto borne with great patience, 'ever expecting and hoping an amendment; knowing her to be but young, and perceiving it to be the ill crafty counsels of her servants for advancing of their own ends, rather than her own inclination'. He traced the root of the trouble right back to the arrival at Dover and his refusal to allow Mamie St Georges to ride in the royal coach. According to Charles, this had caused Madame St Georges to take offence and set his wife 'in such a humour of distaste' against him that ever since that day she had behaved with so much coldness and disrespect towards him 'that it were too long to set down all'.

He did, however, set down quite a lot. When Henrietta had first come to Hampton Court, he had sent some of his councillors to see her with a request that the same order which had been kept in his mother's house should be observed in hers, but her only answer was to say 'that she hoped I would give her leave to order her house as she list herself'. When he later reproached her, quite calmly of course, for publicly flouting his authority, she had not only refused to acknowledge her fault but had spoken to him so rudely that he really could not bring himself to repeat her words. And he had other causes for complaint – such as, for example, the way she avoided being in his company and how, when he had anything he wanted to say to her, he had to use one of her servants as a go-between, or else he was sure to be rebuffed. Then there was her 'neglect of the English tongue and of the nation in general', and he went on to refer to their more recent disagreements. Thus, he concluded, 'having had so long patience with the disturbance of that which should be one of my greatest contentments, I can no longer suffer those that I know to be the cause and fomenter of these humours to be about my wife'. Charles did not think that Louis could fairly seek to make an issue over an action 'of so much necessity', especially bearing in mind that he had dismissed his own wife's Spanish attendants and with less reason.[49]

Needless to say, it did not occur to Charles that he might have shown Henrietta more understanding, or that her physical withdrawal might have been the result of his own clumsiness in claiming his 'rights'. Nor did he have the sensitivity to recognise that her obstinate attachment to her French household and language was the natural reaction of one thrust into an alien environment among uncongenial strangers. 'She dislikes many things', observed the Venetians, 'and preserves her inclination more for France and the French than for England and her husband.' To be fair to the king, who never found personal relationships easy and was doubly handicapped by his speech impediment and having to communicate in a language other than his own, the difficulties of establishing any sort of sympathetic rapport with the frightened, hostile child who was his wife must often have seemed insurmountable.

The abrupt departure of an ambassador extraordinary to the French court produced a flurry of speculation among the diplomatic corps. 'It is thought that the object of the embassy is to obtain the other half of the Queen's dowry,' wrote Amerigo Salvetti on 31 July (N.S.) and in view of the king's well-known financial problems this seemed reasonable, although the Venetians guessed that Carleton might also be going to ask for the French to be recalled. They did not believe Charles would quite have the nerve to expel them, but they were becoming so impossible that, if Louis did not help him out, 'he will be compelled to take some step'. The French themselves suspected that the king was about to take some step, a suspicion heightened when they discovered that the ports had been closed behind the ambassador, but de Tillières, determined to get his side of the story told, did contrive to slip through the net.[50]

In view of the uncertain international situation, no lengthy summer progress had been arranged that year and the last weekend of July found the court in London for the betrothal of Mary Villiers, the Duke of Buckingham's little daughter, to the Earl of Pembroke's heir. The king was also waiting to hear that Carleton had got safely across the Channel, and by Monday the 31st he was ready to act. At about three o'clock in the afternoon he appeared in the queen's apartments, telling her he had something to say to her in his own room. Henrietta, who still had toothache, answered crossly that he could just as well say it where he was, and he then ordered her to dismiss the two ladies who were with her. When they had gone, he locked the door and proceeded to inform her that for her own good and the good of the country he was sending all her people back to France immediately, at the same time promising 'that in the future she would be better served and with more decorum'.

Although the king must have expected some kind of protest, he can hardly have been prepared for the storm that now broke over his head. Henrietta burst into floods of tears and prayed him to relent in a manner 'which would have moved stones to pity' – but not Charles. She fell to her knees before him. She grovelled. If she could not have Mamie St Georges, then surely she might keep de Tillières' wife. She sobbed and screamed 'loud enough to split rocks' according to one account, and begged at least to say goodbye to her friends. When that, too, was refused, she rushed to the window and smashed the glass with her fists, clinging to the iron grating in a frantic attempt to reach the interested crowd which had gathered in the courtyard below. Charles, appalled by this shamefully public loss of control, dragged her away, her hair dishevelled, her dress torn, her hands cut and bleeding.[51]

Meanwhile the Secretary of State Edward Conway was breaking the news of their impending deportation to the senior members of the French household. Led by their bishop, they at first tried to stand their ground, Mende claiming diplomatic immunity and declaring that he could not leave unless his master the king of France commanded him. But he was told that 'the king his master had nothing to do here in England; and that, if he were unwilling to go, England would send force enough to convey him away hence'. The yeomen of the guard were then summoned to eject the lesser servants from the queen's lodgings and lock the doors after them, the women howling and lamenting 'as if they were going to execution' instead of down the road to Somerset House.[52]

Charles had planned to take his wife straight out to Nonesuch, apparently hoping that a change of scene would help to take her mind off the loss of her companions. He also seems to have hoped that the French would accept their dismissal and go quietly. Unfortunately it was not as simple as that. For one thing, Henrietta, having cried herself to a standstill, had now gone on strike, refusing to eat or drink or go to bed unless she was allowed to keep at least one of her ladies. The French, too, were being difficult. On the morning after the great scene, the king had gone in person to address them and, in a brief prepared statement, told them that it was not his intention to offend the French nation or his good brother the king, but he had decided to possess his wife which he found he was not able to do while she remained surrounded by those (and he could have named names) who had caused so many 'jars and discontentments'. He therefore trusted they would understand if he now sought his own ease and safety, adding that he pardoned them all their offences and would try to get them favourably received by their master. This was too much for Daniel du Plessis, Bishop of Mende, who wanted to make it plain that they were only abandoning their posts under protest and because of 'the violence shown us by your Majesty'. 'We have a clear conscience,' he went on, 'having always discharged our duties properly and we need no other testimony with our master than our own actions.' He did, however, ask Charles to show compassion to the lower servants, who would need help with their travelling expenses.[53]

Getting rid of the French turned out to be a costly business, more than £22,000 in jewellery and cash having to be somehow scraped together for gifts and back wages. There were also the unpaid bills – £800 from the apothecary, £1,500 for the bishop's 'unholy water', as the Reverend Mead put it, and another £4,000 'for necessaries of the queen'. Mende told the secretary at the Venetian embassy that all the French had been obliged to lend money to the queen 'who was in the greatest necessity, as for eight months she had not received a penny from the king'. According to one of Joseph Mead's correspondents, Henrietta was said to owe her friends nearly £20,000 but, cross-examined by the king, she confessed that this sum had been greatly exaggerated.[54]

The date set for the departure of the household was Monday 7 August and a convoy of thirty coaches and fifty carts arrived in the Strand after dinner ready to transport them to Rochester. But the French sat tight, saying they would not leave until they had orders from their king or, alternatively, until their debts were paid. When Charles heard that they 'contumaciously refused to go', he lost his temper and dashed off an angry note to Steenie: 'I command you send all the French away tomorrow out of the town. If you can by fair means (but stick not long disputing), otherwise force them away; driving them away like so many wild beasts, until you have shipped them; and so the devil go with them!' Next morning, therefore, the captain of the guard, accompanied by a businesslike force of his yeomen, together with heralds and trumpeters, arrived to proclaim his majesty's pleasure, 'which, if it were not speedily obeyed, the yeomen of the Guard were to put it in execution, by turning all the French out of Somerset House by head and shoulders. . . . Which news', observed Mr John Pory, writing to Joseph Mead on 11 August, 'so soon as the French heard, their courage came down and they yielded to be gone the next tide. . . . So on Tuesday night they lay at Gravesend; on Wednesday night at Rochester, yesternight at Canterbury; and tonight they are to lodge at Dover, from whence God send them a fair wind.'[55]

The rest of the king's subjects were equally relieved to see the back of the foreigners, especially, of course, the priests, who were widely believed to have been 'the most superstitious, turbulent and Jesuited' to be found in all France, and to have shamefully tyrannised the poor young queen. Besides this, it was rumoured that some of the French about her majesty had not only 'practised with the Pope on the one side and the English Papists on the other side, but have had intelligence also with the Spaniard'.

Recriminations pursued the travellers all the way to the coast when it was discovered that the queen's wardrobe stored at Somerset House had been comprehensively plundered, leaving her with 'but one gown and two smocks to her back' and when 'these Frenshe freebooters' were ordered to return her majesty some apparel, 'they sent her only one old satin gown keeping all the residue to themselves'. Mamie St Georges reacted furiously to accusations of theft, declaring that the queen herself had given some of her dresses away to her maids as keepsakes, and when their luggage was searched at Dover, she remarked bitterly that if they had been thieves it would not have done them much good, as everyone knew the English were too poor to be worth robbing.[56]

Some people hoped that, freed from the opposition of her priests, the queen might now begin to appreciate 'the sweetness of Liberty' but, in spite of official assurances that she was in good spirits, there were no immediate signs that Henrietta was becoming reconciled to her new circumstances – rather the contrary. The Comte de Tillières' wife feared she would cry herself to death, such was her despair. In a letter smuggled out to the comtesse, Henrietta declared herself to be '*tout à fait prisonnière*' – the king was even following her to the close-stool – and she addressed a series of tearstained appeals to her family in France. She was the most miserable creature in the world, she told her brother, and her only hope was that he would have pity on her. She begged Cardinal Richelieu, as being the person most able to assist her, for help in her affliction, and asked her mother to send some diplomatic representative over to England as soon as possible, otherwise her treatment would go from bad to worse.[57]

According to the Comtesse de Tillières, no Frenchman was permitted to come near the queen, on pain of death, but, in fact, the clearance had not been complete and about twenty members of the original household still remained. Henrietta had, after all, been allowed to keep two of her women servants, her old nurse and her dresser, Madame Ventelet. There were also half a dozen or so kitchen staff and twelve musicians. Two English priests, Fathers Potter and Godfrey, said to be of milder temper and 'far from the Jesuits' faction and humour', had been added to the strength, but were rejected by the French as having denied the Pope's supremacy. There was also one Frenchman, Father Viette, 'the silliest of them all' in John Pory's opinion, and Philip Preston, a Scottish Benedictine who became the queen's confessor.

Alvise Contarini, the new Venetian ambassador, who had arrived in London on the day after the exodus from Somerset House, reported that the queen was actually being waited on in great state and with more decorum and punctuality than before, but the queen was not appeased and wrote to her mother: 'Have pity on my misery . . . I have no hope but in God and you. Remember that I am your daughter, and the most afflicted person in the world; if you do not take pity on me I am beyond despair.'[58]

Henrietta was never averse to a little self-dramatisation, but there is no doubt that this time her shock and distress were genuine. She had now been in England for over a year, during which time her situation had grown steadily more uncomfortable. The terms of her marriage treaty had been ruthlessly disregarded and her friends torn from her. The English Catholics she had been supposed to help were no better off. She felt herself threatened by her husband's favourite, the most powerful figure in the land – it is said that on one occasion Buckingham had gone so far as to remind her that there had been queens in England who had lost their heads – and now she was surrounded by his female relations. Her husband was cold and unloving and, perhaps worst of all, she had not succeeded in becoming pregnant. She would be seventeen in three months' time and she was in black despair.

CHAPTER THREE

The Tenpenny Knife

The king has now so wholly made over all his affections to his wife,
that I dare say we are out of danger of any other favourites.
Thomas Carey to the Earl of Carlisle, 21 December 1628

By the middle of August the dust of the great palace upheaval was slowly beginning to settle. Buckingham's wife, mother and mother-in-law had been added to the queen's household and his father-in-law, the Earl of Rutland, became her Chamberlain. Other appointments included Sir George Goring as Vice Chamberlain and Lord Percy as Master of her Horse (the Countess of Carlisle had been born a Percy); the Earl of Holland was her Steward and George Carew, Earl of Totnes, her Receiver or Treasurer. Several of these individuals were either Catholics or had Catholic sympathies, but unfortunately from Henrietta's point of view – apart from the fact that they were all more or less closely connected with the Duke of Buckingham – they were all English. Young Lady Strange, recently married to the Earl of Derby's heir, had failed to get a place with the queen because, although a Protestant, she also happened to be French.

The Venetian ambassador reported that the extreme formality with which she was now waited on, 'so different to French custom and familiarity', had begun to weary her majesty 'who leads a very discontented life'. She was apparently undergoing a crash course in English, not being allowed to speak or write except in the presence of her English ladies and this had led to several 'angry discussions' between her and the king. Contarini had his first official audience out at Nonesuch, where he was received by the king and queen together, which was considered an unusual mark of honour, but the ambassador found Henrietta still very depressed and inclined to shed tears when in conversation with someone sympathetic to France. 'The queen continues in affliction as usual', he wrote a little later, 'more especially as she is watched by the argus eyes of those in whom she has little confidence.' It seemed that whenever the king was away on one of his everlasting hunting trips, Buckingham's niece, Mary Hamilton, slept in her room, so that she was surrounded day and night by the duke's relatives.[1]

1626

Meanwhile, Dudley Carleton had been having a frustrating time in France. It was 11 August before he saw the French king and Louis, who had already heard the other side of the story from de Tillières, gave him a frosty reception, saying that he considered his sister had been cruelly treated and that he was sending a special ambassador of his own over to England to conduct an enquiry into the matter. When he had received his envoy's report, he would decide what action to take. The French court was displaying great indignation over the expulsion of the household – the queen-mother in particular expressing herself deeply grieved over her daughter's troubles and remarking bitterly that 'the English habitually spoke fair and acted ill' – but all the same, the reaction was less violent than might have been expected. This was partly due to the fact that Richelieu, disturbed by rumours of a possible Anglo-Spanish rapprochement, saw no reason to make too big an issue out of Henrietta's problems, and partly to the French royal family's preoccupation with the dissension in its own ranks – a conspiracy involving Louis' younger brother, Gaston d'Orléans, and two of his bastard half-brothers, and aimed at overthrowing the cardinal's government, had recently come to light.

The choice of ambassador with the best chance of making sense of the deteriorating situation across the Channel had fallen on François, Seigneur de Bassompierre, Marquis d'Harouel and Maréchal de France, soldier, diplomat, courtier and one-time crony and comrade-in-arms of Henri IV. An amiable, experienced man of the world in his late forties, Bassompierre would, it was hoped, have better luck than the hapless de Blainville. To begin with, though, the omens were not favourable. The Comte de Tillières, that well-known expert on English affairs, who was also Bassompierre's brother-in-law, had been selected to accompany him, but King Charles made it clear that the Comte would not be welcome – his majesty was not risking the return of any of the queen's former allies – and Bassompierre was therefore obliged to travel alone. He landed at Dover on 27 September to be greeted with such a conspicuous absence of the usual courtesies that, as he presently remarked to Alvise Contarini, he almost doubted whether he was an ambassador or no. It was customary for an envoy on a special mission to be lodged and entertained at his hosts' expense, but Bassompierre had been obliged to find his own accommodation, renting a house in Leadenhall Street for which he was paying £50 a week.

Given the coldness of his welcome, he was surprised to receive, on the evening of his arrival in London, a private and informal visit from the great Duke of Buckingham himself offering 'all manner of assistance and friendship'; but, recorded the ambassador, 'he begged me not to tell that he had been to see me, because he had done it without the king's knowledge, which I did not believe'. On the following day Bassompierre had a ceremonial visit from the Venetian ambassador – the Venetians, always nervous of Hapsburg ambitions in northern Italy, took a close interest in the welfare of the French alliance – and that evening he went privately to see 'Bocquinguem' at York House, where he was much impressed by the richness of the decor. Bassompierre had no illusions about the sincerity of the duke's friendship but found him an amusing companion and, in any case, it was obviously sensible to keep on good terms with the all-powerful favourite.

An irritating complication now arose over the presence in the ambassadorial retinue of one of the controversial priests who had come to England with Henrietta, and a royal official appeared in Leadenhall Street on behalf of the king to command Bassompierre 'to send back to France Père Sancy of the Oratory'. 'This', declared the ambassador, 'I absolutely refused, saying that he was my confessor and that the king had nothing to do with my family; that if I was not agreeable to him, I would leave his kingdom and return to my master.'[2]

There, for the moment, the matter rested and on Sunday 1 October Bassompierre had his first audience at the palace, although he was warned to confine himself to a brief and purely formal exchange of compliments. It seemed that the queen was still so distressed by the loss of her servants that the king was afraid she might 'commit some extravagance' and burst into tears in front of everybody. Alvise Contarini thought the marshal's mild address was 'almost too humble, and more becoming a courtier than an ambassador' but even so Henrietta, who was clearly still in a highly emotional state, could be seen to be on the verge of tears as she left the audience chamber. The Frenchmen in Bassompierre's train were surprised by the plainness of her dress, which they attributed to 'discontent', but may equally well have been connected with the depredations of her departed servants or the fact that, at least according to the Venetians, the queen was so short of money that she had not the wherewithal to buy herself a ribbon.

Bassompierre had been promised a private interview with Charles when they would be able to talk business at their leisure, but as he was being escorted out to his coach, the Secretary of State Lord Conway came up to tell him that the king would not receive him again unless he first dismissed his chaplain and sent him back to France. The ambassador had had his doubts about the wisdom of bringing Father Sancy back to England (he had been foisted on him by the queen-mother), but felt that a disproportionate amount of fuss was being made over a man who, as far as he was aware, was not guilty of any offence and had neither been accused nor condemned. Speaking loudly enough to be heard by the bystanders, he said he thought the king ought to be satisfied with his undertaking to see that Father Sancy did not show himself at court or in the city and had no contact with anyone outside his own household. If this was not acceptable, then he, Bassompierre, would have to seek further instructions from the king his master who would not, he believed, allow him to grow old in England.[3]

After this no more was heard about sending Father Sancy home and four days later Bassompierre was finally granted his private audience but, the ambassador reported, he was treated 'with great rudeness and found the king very little disposed to oblige my master'. Charles had launched into a passionately self-justificatory tirade against the malicious, insolent and generally insufferable behaviour of Henrietta's French attendants. He would not allow anyone to interfere with the government of his realm, his subjects or his wife, 'from all of whom, without exception, he meant to have unconditional obedience'.

According to Bassompierre, 'the king grew at length so warm as to exclaim to the ambassador: "Why do you not execute your commission and declare war?"' Keeping his temper with difficulty, the ambassador replied that he was not a herald to declare war, but 'a Marshal of France to make it when declared'. At this point, the Duke of Buckingham suddenly appeared, thrusting himself between king and ambassador and announcing that he had come to keep the peace between them, a dramatic gesture which Bassompierre considered to be 'an instance of great boldness, not to say impudence'. However, the atmosphere now lightened somewhat and the interview ended with the king personally conducting the ambassador to the queen's apartments, having apparently 'conceded a great deal'.

But Bassompierre was too old a hand to be taken in by amateurs at the diplomatic poker game. In conference with Buckingham he made it clear that if Charles was not prepared to do business in a civilised fashion, he would have no choice but to return to France without more ado; having first, of course, made sure that all the other ambassadors at court knew exactly why he was being obliged to leave. If, on the other hand, the English government wanted to negotiate, he asked for a panel of commissioners to be appointed to hear what he had to say, so that the matter could be discussed 'without reserve' and a conclusion reached one way or the other. While waiting for the duke and the Council to digest his ultimatum, Bassompierre wrote gloomily to Richelieu that he thought Charles was so set against the re-establishment of any French officers round the queen that it would be a 'waste of time to think of persuading him to it'. As for himself, he was so disgusted by the way he had been treated that he only wanted to go home; for, as he told his brother-in-law, 'I languish here without hope of effecting anything'.[4]

Buckingham had, however, decided that the ambassador must be given some satisfaction and during the following week Bassompierre was able to have a number of wide-ranging informal discussions with such leading political figures as the Earls of Pembroke, Carlisle and Holland and the Lords Conway and Carleton. He was also now in daily contact with the queen which gave him a useful opportunity of observing the state of the royal marriage at first hand – on one occasion when he was with Henrietta, her husband came into the room and she promptly picked a quarrel with him. After this, wrote Bassompierre, 'the king took me into his chamber and talked to me for a long while, making many complaints of the queen his wife'.[5]

A fair-minded man, Bassompierre was beginning to see that Charles might have a legitimate grievance; that the French household had perhaps been guilty of forming '*une petite république particulière*' within his court and that Henrietta, young and inexperienced though she was, had been at best foolish, at worst deliberately perverse in her refusal to adapt to English ways. The ambassador was, in short, coming round to the Venetians' opinion that the queen would be happier if she fell in with her husband's wishes. With this in mind he was trying to establish better relations between Henrietta and Buckingham, and on 15 October brought the duke to the queen's apartments 'where he made his peace with her', something which, Bassompierre recorded in his journal, 'I brought about with infinite difficulties'. The king then came in 'and he also was reconciled with her and caressed her very much'. Unfortunately, on the very next day Bassompierre himself fell out with the queen, apparently under the impression that she was not being open with him.[6]

The ambassador had by this time formally presented his case for the reinstatement of some part at least of Henrietta's former entourage to the ten commissioners appointed to hear him, and on 27 October he was summoned to receive their answer. This began with a long-winded defence of the dismissal of the French attendants which, declared the commissioners, had violated neither the letter nor the spirit of the marriage treaty, the said persons having been sent back as offenders, who had by their ill conduct disturbed both the affairs of the kingdom and the domestic happiness of his majesty and the queen 'his dearly beloved consort'.

All the old familiar allegations were rehearsed again. The Bishop of Mende and his priests, aided and abetted by M. de Blainville, had intrigued to stir up dissension among his majesty's subjects, 'exciting fear and mistrust in the Protestants, encouraging the Roman Catholics, and even instigating the disaffected in Parliament against every thing connected with the service of the king'. The same priests had celebrated mass in illegal assemblies, used the queen's house as a rendezvous for

Jesuits and other undesirables and 'laboured to create in the gentle mind of the queen a repugnance to all that his majesty desired and ordered'. They had endeavoured to inspire her with a contempt for the English nation and encouraged her to neglect the language, 'as if she neither had, nor wished to have, any common interest amongst us'. Worst of all, they had abused their influence over her so far as to lead her to go in devotion to Tyburn, 'where it has been the custom to execute the most infamous malefactors', not one of whom had been executed on account of religion but for high treason. It was this act which, by implication, accused the king's glorious predecessors of tyranny in having put to death innocent persons which had provoked his majesty 'beyond the bounds of his patience' and driven him into taking action.

The commissioners then went on to deal with the non-fulfilment of the king's undertakings regarding the treatment of his Catholic subjects. This was broadly justified on the grounds of political expedience, but it was also contended that the article contained in the Escrit Secret which had promised freedom of worship to the English Catholics had been accepted by both sides 'simply as a matter of form, to satisfy the Roman Catholic party of France and the Pope'. The King of France might, however, rest assured that in all matters touching his sister's conscience the terms of the treaty would be strictly adhered to and that, for the sake of his dear consort, Charles would 'show all the indulgence to the Roman Catholics which the constitution and the security of the state will allow'.[7]

Bassompierre immediately asked to reply, addressing the company with 'great vehemence'. The only time when he appeared to feel himself on slightly shaky ground was over the much-discussed visit to Tyburn. He could not deny that this had taken place, but insisted it had happened merely by chance in the course of an evening stroll through Saint Gemmes [St James's] Park and the adjoining Hipparc [Hyde Park]. He did strenuously deny that the queen had gone in procession to offer public prayers, or that she had approached within fifty paces of the gallows and knelt there with a rosary in her hands. It was, though, surely natural to have thought a little of God in such a place, and if she and her companions had been moved to say a quiet prayer for all those who had died there, they had done the right thing. However wicked these men may have been, they had been condemned to death not to damnation and no one had ever been forbidden to pray for their souls. 'To conclude,' declared the ambassador, a touch defiantly, 'I deny formally that this action has been committed, and offer, at the same time, to prove that they would have done very well to commit.'[8]

Bassompierre's oration had lasted for more than an hour and he felt satisfied that he had never spoken so well in his life, but next morning, when he was due to meet the Council again, he had completely lost his voice – a misfortune which he attributed in part to the foggy London weather and in part to his exertions of the previous day. However, he seems to have recovered sufficiently to be able to take part in the final round of negotiations which were opened in conciliatory mode by Dudley Carleton, who spoke of the damage which might result from a rupture between their two countries and proposed that they should make every effort to come to an amicable agreement. 'We then went to work', says Bassompierre, 'and found no great trouble in it, for they were reasonable and I was moderate in my demands.'[9]

In fact, most of the details had already been settled in behind-the-scenes discussions between Bassompierre and Buckingham, who had overridden the Privy Council's reluctance to sanction the return of another pack of mischief-making Catholic clergy, and it was agreed that 'for her conscience' Henrietta should have twelve priests, providing none of them were Jesuits or Oratorians, with a bishop to act as their governor and the queen's Grand Almoner. The chapel at St James's Palace was to be finished and another would be built at Somerset House, now her official town residence. She was to have two ladies of the bedchamber, plus three bedchamber women, a seamstress and laundress 'of her own nation', and there would also be two physicians, an apothecary and a surgeon, a chamberlain, an equerry, a secretary, two gentlemen ushers and a handful of lesser servants, making a French establishment of about thirty individuals. It was further agreed that all the priests currently detained in English prisons should be released and the activities of the pursuivants curtailed.[10]

Bassompierre celebrated the occasion by giving the assembled councillors 'a magnificent entertainment', and then went to the queen 'to bring her the good news of our treaty'. On Sunday 29 October he had *1626* a private audience with the king, when Charles 'confirmed and ratified all that his commissioners had negotiated and concluded with me, which he showed me in writing'. Monday was Lord Mayor's Day and Bassompierre accompanied the queen in her coach to the City to see the pageant, which the ambassador considered 'to be the greatest that is made at the reception of any officer in the world'. While they waited in 'Schipsay' [Cheapside] for the procession to pass, he and Henrietta and Buckingham played a friendly game of cards and afterwards the duke took him to dine with the Lord Mayor, 'who that day gave a dinner to more than eight hundred persons'.[11]

Everything seemed to be going so smoothly that it came as a nasty shock when, two days later, the queen again quarrelled with her husband and turned on Bassompierre, accusing him of not having done nearly enough for her. The ambassador, who had been meticulous throughout in keeping her informed of his progress, was understandably annoyed. If that was how she felt, he would take his leave the very next day and go back to France without finishing the business. What was more, he would tell Louis and her mother that it was all her fault. On returning to Leadenhall Street he was met by Father Sancy, who began to ask him to make further representations to the Council on the queen's behalf, and Bassompierre realised that the chaplain had been going behind his back, encouraging Henrietta to make unreasonable demands. He saw now why the English had been so unwilling to have him back and Father Sancy, too, got the rough edge of his tongue. Next day, when Henrietta sent for him, he refused to obey the summons and his firmness had the desired effect, for the Earl of Carlisle presently came to beg him to visit an apologetic queen and friendly relations were re-established.[12]

On Sunday 5 November the Duke of Buckingham entertained the king and queen, the French ambassador and all the court 'with great feasting and show'. The feast, at which the food appeared as if by magic from above, was followed by a masque, culminating in a spectacular marine view 'representing the sea which divides England from France'. Above it could be seen Marie de Medici, sitting on a regal throne among the gods and beckoning to the King and Queen of Spain, the Elector Palatine and the Prince and Princess of Piedmont – all of them so true to life that Henrietta had no difficulty in recognising her mother and sisters – to come and join with her in putting an end to the discords of Christendom.[13]

The party, which Bassompierre thought the most magnificent affair he had ever attended, went on into the small hours and continued over the following day, the king, 'very jocund and merry, being entertained royally with plays and desports', staying on till suppertime. 'Whereupon', remarked the Reverend Joseph Mead, 'some people stick not to prate that his majesty is in very great favour with the duke's grace.'[14]

Although there were several matters still outstanding, such as final arrangements for paying over the second half of the queen's dowry, reinstating an amnesty for the English Catholics and an increasingly serious Anglo-French maritime dispute, Bassompierre was now anxious to go home, but it was another fortnight before he was able to extricate himself from a belated bearhug of English hospitality and set out for the coast.

The journey was to turn into something of a nightmare. The weather was frightful – 'a storm detained me fourteen days at Dover, which cost me 14,000 crowns', recorded the ambassador mournfully – and it was the second week of December before he was able to get across the Channel. But delay, expense, seasickness and the loss overboard of two carriages and 40,000 francs' worth of new clothes bought in London were not his only problems. The Duke of Buckingham had made a last-minute decision to accompany him on a peace mission to the French court and the harassed Bassompierre had to use all his powers of persuasion to prevent his impulsive friend from making a potentially catastrophic diplomatic gaffe, 'so far as giving him to understand that he would not be received'. The duke remained unconvinced, but did reluctantly agree to wait until he heard if his visit would be welcomed.

When he finally reached Paris just before Christmas, Bassompierre found, as he expected, that 'the coming of the Duke of Bourkinkam was not agreeable'. He also found that his own carefully constructed compromise settlement was not agreeable either. On the contrary, 'the Louvre resounded with angry voices raised against him'. They say, reported the Venetian ambassador, Giorgio Zorzi, that 'he has left the queen without support and with no good Frenchman at her side; that he yielded too much to the English and did not stand up for the French. In short, they criticise every article of the treaty and find fault with all.' This ingratitude shown to so skilful and prudent a public servant was widely blamed on the jealousy of Cardinal Richelieu, who, according to Zorzi, writing from the embassy in Paris, 'wants to rule this kingdom alone and cannot support the growing fortune of the Marshal Bassompierre'.[15] In fact, by this time relations between England and France had reached such a point of simmering hostility that probably no compromise, however carefully contrived, would have been acceptable. Apart from religion, an issue which continued to fester just below the surface – representatives of the English Catholics were complaining that Bassompierre had made very little effort on their behalf – the most immediate cause of dissension was 'the great maritime question', which Amerigo Salvetti thought must be remedied quickly, 'for otherwise the two nations will soon be on the road to a complete rupture'.[16]

Trouble at sea went back as far as the beginning of 1625, when the royal marriage negotiations were at a delicate stage and Buckingham, in his capacity as Lord Admiral, had authorised the loan of eight English ships to France, on the understanding that they would be used in the Mediterranean to enforce a blockade of Genoa, one of the Hapsburg client statelets. Instead, to the special fury of the Puritan party, they had gone no further than the Bay of Biscay, where they formed part of a French naval squadron which comprehensively defeated the Huguenots off La Rochelle, and the English government had been trying to get them back ever since. Of more urgent concern in 1626 was the seizure by the English of French merchant vessels sailing from Spanish ports and suspected of carrying contraband of war to the Spanish Netherlands. This had led to protracted and bad-tempered disputes over the law of prize and retaliation against English merchants trading in French ports.

Matters began to come to a head in the autumn, when the Earl of Denbigh, cruising off Ushant, captured three valuable French ships believed to be laden with Spanish cargo. This aroused acute resentment in France and in December the authorities at Bordeaux seized the entire English wine fleet, some two hundred vessels with 2,000 butts of Gascony wine on board, lying ready to sail in the mouth of the Garonne. It was a calculated and massive act of reprisal and caused panic in the city of London, where several thousand families depended on the wine trade for their livelihood. 'The populace here is practically frantic,' reported Alvise Contarini and, as the merchants clamoured for action, Contarini's sources were saying that if the king called parliament now, he would find the whole nation eager for war with France, 'all for the sake of avenging this affront'.[17]

Meanwhile, life at court went on much as usual. Amerigo Salvetti told the Duke of Tuscany that her majesty the queen, although no doubt feeling the difficulties of her position 'in this extremity of animosity between the two countries', was acting with perfect calmness and Henrietta seems to have been very little affected by the developing crisis. It is true that one of her French musicians, who had been teaching her to play the lute, was arrested about this time and sent to the Tower, but this seems to have had more to do with his improper advances to the Earl of Carlisle's daughter, another of his pupils, than with the political situation and the queen continued to be absorbed in rehearsals for a masque and ballet she was planning to present during the Christmas season. She was still suffering intermittently with toothache, so the performance, pronounced 'very pretty' by the Venetian ambassador, had to be postponed until the middle of January. It was a lavish affair – a thousand yards of satin and taffeta were said to have gone into the making of the costumes – and the king was seen to be taking a close interest in the details of the production, carefully 'placing the ladies' gentlewomen with his own hands' and leading the dancing which followed. For a monarch now facing the prospect of war with both great European powers at once, Charles, too, was behaving with perfect, almost unnatural calm.

His most immediate problem, of course, was money, or the lack of it. After the 1626 dissolution an attempt had been made to persuade the lieges 'lovingly, freely and voluntarily' to hand over the cash that would have been collected from them had parliament passed the relevant legislation. When this optimistic appeal fell, unsurprisingly, on stony ground, the government resorted to the old expedient of a forced loan, an always unpopular form of back-door taxation which, on this occasion, met with widespread resistance. However, as obstinate non-payers, or 'loan recusants', could be bound over to appear before the Privy Council and imprisoned for contempt, some £300,000 was eventually raised and ear-marked for the navy, now in a dangerously run-down condition, with ships lying unrigged and derelict, their crews unpaid and mutinous.

In March 1627 Captain John Pennington, commanding a squadron of fifteen men-of-war reluctantly financed by the London bankers, sailed from Falmouth with orders to patrol the coast of France and intercept and take all the French and Spanish shipping which came his way, while letters of marque were issued to anyone who fancied his chances as a privateer. A pinnace belonging to the Earl of Warwick brought a Portuguese prize worth £10,000 into the Scilly Isles and his lordship was presently rewarded by a visit from the queen, who went by water to Blackwall, where she dined on board his ship the *Neptune*. The party then travelled on by water to Greenwich, returning to town on horseback: 'The earl attending her majesty to Somerset House, forty or fifty riding before bareheaded, save her four priests with black caps.' Henrietta and her ladies were masked and all wearing little black beaver hats, 'but her majesty had a fair white feather in her hat'.[18]

A very satisfactory number of prizes were now arriving in the southern ports. 'Captain Pennington hath taken four great French ships, richly laden, valued at £100,000 at least and brought them into the West Country,' wrote one of Joseph Mead's correspondents on 27 April, and the Duke of Buckingham, resplendent in military costume with 'an immense collar and a magnificent plume of feathers in his hat', was already organising another ambitious foreign adventure. This time the expedition was intended to bring succour to the embattled Huguenots of La Rochelle which would, it was hoped, destabilise the French government and encourage Richelieu's enemies to turn on him. 'Through the malcontent princes and the Huguenots', wrote Alvise Contarini, 'the [English] government counts on kindling a conflagration, especially through the king's brother, whose character is notoriously disposed to receive such impressions.'[19] Buckingham also hoped that being seen going to the aid of French Protestants would re-establish his reputation and 'win him back the affection of the people'. He is said to have boasted that before the end of the summer he would be more honoured and beloved by the Commons than even the Earl of Essex – hero of the successful assault on Cadiz back in 1596 – had ever been.[20] This time the duke intended to command in person and on 14 May he entertained the king and queen to a sumptuous farewell supper party at York House, with an accompanying masque 'wherein first comes forth the duke, after him Envy, with divers open-mouthed dogs' heads, representing the people's barking; next came Fame; then Truth'.[21]

In fact it would be another six weeks before preparations were complete and early in June the king went down to Portsmouth to inspect the task force assembling there, going aboard every ship in the fleet, visiting the soldiers and 'seeing them exercised'. Enough money had been raised from the sale of prize goods to pay the troops, but they remained a pretty rough-and-ready lot and the officers grumbled about the poor quality of the new conscripts, predicting that they would be only too likely to mutiny, desert or get drunk at the first opportunity. Nevertheless, thanks largely to Buckingham's efforts this expedition did seem to be rather better planned and equipped than most, and as he and Charles dined in state together on board his flagship, the *Triumph*, they were both in confident high spirits.

For Henrietta, left behind in London, it was a lonely and depressing summer. According to the Venetian ambassador, she had offered to try to mediate a reconciliation with her brother, but the king had forbidden her to interfere. Contarini thought this was probably just as well, 'as she is very young and has no counsellor at hand'. Certainly she was feeling very cut off from her friends and family, complaining that she had not heard from her mother for months 'just as if they had entirely forgotten her in France'.[22]

Normal cross-Channel intercourse was now virtually at a standstill, anyone attempting to travel in either direction being regarded with deep suspicion, and even diplomatic couriers were liable to be arrested at the ports. But when news filtered through that Gaston's wife had died in childbirth and that Louis himself had been ill with fever, Henrietta got permission to send Henry Jermyn, one of the gentleman of her Privy Chamber, with messages of condolence and enquiry. To Marie de Medici she wrote that she would have no peace of mind until she knew her brother was definitely on the mend, adding that Charles shared her concern 'which he has commanded me to assure your majesty from him, and what a desire he has to see a perfect intelligence between your majesty and himself . . . and that you would be pleased to regard him as your good son. As for me, madam, it would be the greatest satisfaction that could ever happen to me.'[23]

Buckingham finally sailed on 27 June with a fleet of close on a hundred ships, carrying an army some six thousand strong, and set course for the Bay of Biscay and La Rochelle. The king, meanwhile, had returned to London. There was no question of any long progress being undertaken that year and Charles was confining himself to small 'hovering journeys' in the vicinity of the capital. He and Henrietta met briefly at Whitehall at the beginning of July before he left for Theobalds and Henrietta started for St Albans on her way to Wellingborough, a small market town on the banks of the river Nene in Northamptonshire with something of a reputation as a watering place – its chalybeate springs were thought particularly efficacious for ladies hoping to become pregnant.

Tradition says that the queen and her entourage camped in tents in a field round the so-called Red Well, where she conscientiously drank the iron-rich water and worried about her failure to conceive. She was also worried about money and had written to the Lord Treasurer Marlborough complaining that she had only received half the £2,000 she had been expecting for her private use 'at her coming from London'. She reminded him of his promises and her wants and asked for the payment of other sums due to her, without which 'she would not be able to pay her servants'.[24]

All the same, she seemed to be enjoying her little holiday and the king, replying to a query about his wife's plans, remarked rather irritably that he had no idea how long she meant to stay at the Wells, 'for I will expect no certainty in women's determination'. But he suggested she might come via Cambridge and Audley End to join him at Theobalds.[25]

After the storms and scenes of the previous year it looked as if the royal couple were at last beginning to learn to get along together in reasonable harmony. Alvise Contarini heard that the king had told his wife how much he regretted the necessity of having to make war on her country and that she had replied politely, expressing equal regret but saying frankly that she wished her husband all success, 'being more interested for him than for anyone else'.[26] This sounded promising and Charles, in a letter to Steenie dated 13 August, had added a postscript: 'I cannot omit to tell you, that my wife and I were never on better terms; she, upon this action of yours, shewing herself so loving to me, by her discretion on all occasions, that it makes us all wonder at and esteem her.'[27]

The news from France was not good. The expedition had succeeded in establishing a bridgehead on the strategic Île de Rhé, just offshore from La Rochelle, and had laid siege to the principal fortress at St Martin. But the hoped-for support from 'the malcontent princes' and Huguenot leaders showed no sign of materialising. Even the Rochellois were proving disappointingly lukewarm. Only a few hundred volunteers had come out to join their self-appointed deliverers and soon urgent appeals for reinforcements and supplies were reaching London. Charles, with Steenie's welfare at stake, flung himself wholeheartedly into the business of raising money and recruits, attending regular Council meetings and bullying the exchequer and the commissioners responsible for collecting loan payments; Henrietta, bored as well as lonely, was reduced to consulting a clairvoyant.

Eleanor Davys (or Davies), an eccentric lady with a considerable reputation for accurate prophecy, had been summoned to wait on the queen as she came from evening service on All Saints' Day, escorted by Lord Carlisle. According to the account later provided by the oracle herself, Henrietta's first question was 'when she should be with child?

I answered, "Oportet habere tempus".' This having been interpreted by Carlisle as 'soon, or in a short time', the queen went on to ask 'what success the Duke would have. . . . Answered again, as for his honor, of that he would not bring home much, but his person should return in safety with no little speed.' Lady Eleanor (she was the Earl of Castlehaven's daughter) then told the queen that 'for a time she should be happy. "But how long?" said she. I told her sixteen years, that was long enough.' At this point the king arrived and the consultation came to an abrupt end. Since she was said to have foretold her late husband's death three days before the event, Charles's displeasure was perhaps understandable and her ladyship was warned to leave off her predictions regarding his affairs; although, again according to her own account, this did not prevent her from telling people, when Henrietta did eventually become pregnant, that his first-born son 'should go to christening and burying in a day'.[28]

As far as Buckingham was concerned Eleanor Davys proved to have been only too accurate, and ten days after her encounter with the queen he was on his way home bringing very little honour with him. For all the king's valiant efforts the administrative machinery (and the money) needed to keep an expeditionary force adequately supplied in the field simply did not exist, and in September Colonel Edward Conway had written to his father, the Secretary of State: 'The army grows every day weaker; our victuals waste, our purses are empty, ammunition consumes, winter grows, our enemies increase . . . we hear nothing from England.'[29]

By October the situation was becoming desperate. An attempt to storm the vital St Martin fort had failed and the French were now landing in strength further down the coast. With sickness spreading among his troops and winter coming on fast, it was obvious that Buckingham could no longer postpone a retreat to the ships. He left it almost too late. The English rearguard was attacked by the advancing French as they were crossing a narrow causeway and bridge over the salt marshes on the northern side of the island and were cut to pieces in the resulting confusion: 'The passage being choked up, the enemy had the killing, taking and drowning of our men at the bridge at his pleasure.' Casualties from disease – principally dysentery, or 'the bloody flux' – as well as from enemy action had been heavy and fewer than three thousand survivors, nearly half of them sick or wounded, all of them hungry, ragged and dispirited, straggled ashore at Plymouth and Portsmouth in the second week of November.[30]

It needed no prophetess to predict the angry public reaction to this latest fiasco – 'the greatest and shamefullest overthrow the English have received since we lost Normandy' – nor was there any doubt as to who would be held to account for it in the public mind. But while the people cursed their favourite hate figure, the king was receiving him 'more familiarly and kindly than ever, if that is possible'. Alvise Contarini heard that 'the entire blame is laid on the delay of succour, for which they say the king himself apologised to the duke, while praising his courage and capacity'. Charles had sent his own coach down to Portsmouth for him, and one observer commented bitterly that 'those of the court run to meet him as if he were returned from some conquest'.[31]

Only the queen was absent from the welcoming committee, her majesty having taken to her bed with some minor indisposition, but Contarini thought it was probably because she did not know how to cope with this admittedly awkward social occasion. Louis had released all the English prisoners taken at Rhé and sent them over to his sister as an early Christmas present, but the forty-odd captured regimental and company colours were now on display in Notre Dame and the King of France was reported as having remarked that if he had known his brother of England longed so much for the Île de Rhé, he would have sold it to him for half the money it had cost him.[32]

In spite of everything it seemed that Charles and Buckingham were still hell-bent on continuing the war. Charles told the Venetian ambassador that while he had not the remotest idea of ever gaining 'a span of territory' from France, he considered himself responsible for the Rochellois and as long as Louis was determined to destroy their stronghold, he was no less resolved to support it, 'as otherwise my word and my promises would be void and that I will never allow'. Buckingham was even more hard-line in his attitude. 'The French have no wish for peace,' he declared. 'They have vowed to destroy La Rochelle and we to save it at any cost. So long as this punctilio exists, it is useless to think or speak of peace.'[33]

Charles was talking airily of sending an army of twenty thousand men to La Rochelle, 'in order to help all the Huguenots from that place', and appeared at the christening of Buckingham's infant son wearing a long soldier's coat covered with gold lace. He was now mortgaging Crown lands and had extracted a loan of £120,000 from the City of London on the security of his rents from landed property. The total sum raised amounted to £263,000, but this would be nothing like enough and it became obvious that, however reluctantly, the king was going to have to call another parliament. *the 3rd*

It met on 17 March and Charles, never one to waste any charm on this disobliging body, opened the proceedings by informing the members that they had been summoned for the sole purpose of providing him with the means of pursuing what most of them were now convinced was a ruinous foreign policy. He would use but few persuasions, he announced, for if the maintenance of 'the true Religion, Laws and Liberties of this State, and the just Defence of our true Friends and Allies' was not sufficient, then no eloquence of men or angels would prevail.[34]

Unfortunately the Commons' view of the laws and liberties of the state was beginning to differ widely from that of their sovereign lord and, ignoring all appeals not to waste time in 'tedious consultations', they were soon once more immersed in discussion of their numerous grievances. These were presently embodied in a document known as the Petition of Right, demanding an end to extra-parliamentary taxation, arbitrary arrest, the compulsory billeting of the military on private householders (something which was giving rise to much bitter complaint by the householders concerned) and the issuing of commissions of martial law. The Petition passed both Houses and was presented at the end of May. During the following week the king attempted to evade the issue and the temperature of the Commons rose to boiling point. As usual Buckingham was the focus of attack. 'The Duke of Bucks is the cause of all our miseries,' cried the lawyer Edward Coke. 'That man is the grievance of all grievances.' Then, on 7 June, Charles gave way, accepting what was, in effect, an attempt to place definite limitations on his prerogative.

'This sudden resolution on the part of the king to please his subjects was entirely unexpected', wrote Amerigo Salvetti, 'and has caused the greatest joy and contentment to the people in general who show their feelings by extraordinary demonstrations, and by the ringing of bells, and by fireworks in every part of the city.'[35] The House of Commons showed its feelings by passing a subsidy bill, but a gang of youths was reported to have pulled down and burnt the old scaffold on Tower Hill, saying that they would have a new one built for the Duke of Buckingham. A few days later things turned very nasty when a certain John Lambe, an astrologer and quack doctor who had been consulted by Buckingham and was known as 'the Duke's wizard', was set upon and hacked to death by a London mob. Joseph Mead heard that the 'barbarous rabble which mauled and mangled Dr Lambe, did it in reference to the duke his master, as they called him, whom, they said, had he been there, they would have handled worse, and would have minced his flesh, and have had every one a bit of him'.[36]

The city seethed with the wildest rumours – that the duke was a Spanish agent, that he was plotting to take over the country and drive out the king, that he had soldiers in every place waiting to cut the throats of all good Englishmen or make them slaves, and a placard was found nailed to a post in Coleman Street bearing the words: 'Who rules the kingdom? The king. Who rules the king? The duke. Who rules the duke? The devil.'[37] As well as rumours, tales of omens proliferated. The duke's portrait had fallen from the wall in the high commission chamber at Lambeth; he had had a violent nose-bleed; his father's ghost had been seen three times walking at Windsor Castle warning that unless he mended his ways he would be suffered but a short time to live. Eleanor Davys, though, was prophesying that his time was not till August.

The king never for a moment wavered in his support of his friend but, apart from giving orders that Dr Lambe's murderers be caught and punished and that the City Watch should be doubled, he and the queen appeared untroubled by the current outbreak of public hysteria. The royal physician, Theodore Mayerne, who saw them both in June, told the Earl of Carlisle that 'the king and queen are well and live together with a satisfaction which all their true subjects and honest people ought to wish'. Back in March there had been persistent but sadly unfounded reports that Henrietta was pregnant at last and she was planning to pay another visit to Wellingborough.

She was still very short of money. Early in the year the king had instructed the Lord Treasurer to make over to her 'so many lands within the survey of the Exchequer or Duchy of Lancaster as amount to the clear yearly value of £6,000'. This was to make up her jointure to £28,000 a year, which would be about equal to the income enjoyed by the late Queen Anne.[38] As usual, however, the government machine moved with agonising slowness and the queen continued to complain of having nothing to spend. In July the Venetian ambassador picked up what he described as 'an amusing story on this subject'. It seemed that one day the queen asked the king for £2 to give as alms to a poor young Frenchwoman. When the king insisted on knowing who this person was, the queen replied, 'I, Sire, am the penniless pauper'. 'This piqued the king greatly,' observed Contarini, but then, he went on, the French always were given to exaggeration.[39]

Towards the end of July the king went down to Portsmouth to inspect the latest expedition being gathered for the relief of La Rochelle, now closely besieged by a French government army, and Buckingham joined him there on 14 August. Henrietta, meanwhile, had left for Wellingborough where, according to Amerigo Salvetti, she was staying 'more on account of her taste for the country, and because the dances of the peasantry amuse her, than for her bodily benefit from the waters which are so diluted by the rain that at the present time they are of little service'.[40]

The queen was still at Wellingborough when she received a letter from Lord Carleton dated Saturday 23 August. 'I am to trouble your Grace with a most Lamentable Relation,' he wrote. 'This day betwixt nine and ten in the morning, the Duke of Buckingham then coming out of a Parlor, into a Hall, to goe to his coach and soe to the King (who was four miles off), having about him diverse Lords, Colonells, and Captains, and many of his owne Servants, was by one Felton (once a Lieutenant of this our Army) slaine at one blow with a dagger knife.' Hearing the disturbance, the duke's wife and sister-in-law had come out into a gallery overlooking the hall in time to see 'the blood of their deerest Lord gushing from him; ah poore Ladies,' sighed Carleton, 'such was their screechings, teares, and distractions, that I never in my Life heard the like before, and hope never to heare the like againe'.

The assassin, a morose man with a grievance, had bought a tenpenny knife at a cutler's shop on Tower Hill and, having made his way on foot to Portsmouth, had mingled with the jostling crowd in the hallway of the duke's lodgings, waiting an opportunity to strike his victim down. He made no attempt to escape in the ensuing confusion. On the contrary, he came forward, 'saying boldly, "I am the Man, heere I am".' Questioned by Carleton, he said he was a Protestant in religion, and 'partly discontented' for want of eighty pounds back pay due to him, as well as having been unfairly passed over for promotion. But he maintained that private revenge had not moved him to 'this resolution'. Rather he had come to believe that 'in committing the Act of killing the Duke, hee should doe his Country great good service'.[41]

The king was at morning prayers when the news was whispered in his ear, but with his usual rigid self-control Charles 'continued unmoved and without the least change in his countenance till prayers were ended'. He then gave orders that Buckingham's widow should be moved to a safe place and that the ports should be closed immediately in case his friend's murder was the start of a wider conspiracy. He also summoned the Privy Council to wait on him at Portsmouth. Only after this did he retreat into his own rooms, there to collapse on the bed and give way to a passion of grief for Steenie. He remained incommunicado for two days and when he reappeared sought relief in a burst of furious activity, so it was said that in fourteen days after the duke's death [the king] discharged more business than the duke had done in three months. Charles was determined that the fleet should sail just as he and Steenie had planned and it was noticed that he seemed 'as much affected to the duke's memory as he was to his person'.[42]

The queen had left Wellingborough as soon as Carleton's letter reached her and hurried south to the king, who went to meet her at Farnham on 2 September. Henrietta had little reason to mourn the man whose overwhelming and all-pervasive presence had cast such a long shadow over her first three years in England, but her instinctive, generous impulse was to try to share the sorrow of those who would feel his loss the most and she went in person to comfort the bereaved duchess – 'an act on her part which has greatly gratified the king,' noted Amerigo Salvetti approvingly.[43]

The fleet sailed on 7 September and Charles then turned his attention to ordering a state funeral for the duke, 'as ample and sumptuous' as could be performed – until it was tactfully pointed out that the money might be better spent on paying off his debts, which had been found to amount to over £60,000. More difficult to point out tactfully was the undoubted fact that any show of public pomp and ceremony would simply invite public disorder, for the news of the favourite's death had been greeted with such widespread and unconcealed delight that, as Contarini reported, 'it has been very difficult in many parts of the kingdom to prevent bonfires and other rejoicings'. The murderer, too, was rapidly becoming a popular hero. In London the citizens were openly drinking his health, and the large crowds which gathered to see him brought to the Tower 'with a general voice cried, "Lord comfort thee! The Lord be merciful unto thee! or such like words".'[44]

In the end, the duke's body was virtually smuggled into Westminster Abbey 'in as poor and confused a manner as hath been seen . . . there being not much above a hundred mourners'. It was thought that the coffin, 'borne upon six men's shoulders', was in fact empty, the corpse having been interred secretly the day before as a precaution against mob violence. 'And this', observed Joseph Mead, 'was the obscure catastrophe of that great man.'[45]

Charles did not even have the satisfaction of crowning Steenie's memory with a victory, for his final attempt to relieve the starving Rochellois, who were now reduced to chewing on boiled cowhide and old gloves, was another dismal failure. On 16 October the town surrendered in sight of the English fleet and, as if to emphasise the futility of the whole campaign, the defeated Huguenots were granted generous terms by Cardinal Richelieu. There was to be no more political independence and no more defiance of the king, but wherever French Protestants had enjoyed liberty of worship before, they were to enjoy it still, and Protestants and Catholics would be equally welcome in the service of their country.[46]

By the time the fleet returned to port in November, people were beginning to come to terms with the disappearance of 'that great man' who for more than a decade had dominated every aspect of public life, and one consequence of his disappearance was already plainly visible. Within a fortnight of the duke's death the Venetian ambassador had written to his opposite number in Paris that it was believed 'the queen would henceforward have great influence', and again, at the end of September, he wrote, 'every day she concentrates in herself the favour and love that was previously divided between her and the duke'.[47] Amerigo Salvetti thought that 'were she not so youthful . . . it would be an easy matter for her to make the King do whatever she pleased, so much is he attached to her', and throughout the autumn the fascinated courtiers watched the royal romance unfolding before them. The Earl of Carlisle, on a diplomatic mission abroad, was told that he would find 'their master and mistress at such a degree of kindness as he would imagine him a wooer again, and her gladder to receive his caresses than he to make them'.[48]

In fact, of course, Charles was transferring all his emotional dependence on Buckingham to the nearest available substitute, and Henrietta, naturally outgoing and affectionate, and at last finding herself loved and wanted, was responding eagerly. Her nineteenth birthday was celebrated by a tournament, the king on horseback and determined to 'grow gallant every day more and more'. In December Carlisle's correspondent was writing that 'the King has now so wholly made over all his affections to his wife, that I dare say we are out of the danger of any other favourites', and fresh reports had begun to circulate that the queen was 'breeding child'.[49]

This dramatic improvement in the state of the royal marriage was especially welcome news to Alvise Contarini, who had been trying all year to promote peace between England and France, and he wasted no time in approaching the queen to ask for her help in furthering his efforts. It was never easy to interest Henrietta in politics and she seems to have remained largely indifferent to the progress of the war. Now, however, she thanked Contarini warmly for his goodwill, promising to speak to the king without delay, and he later heard she had told Charles that 'although she did not pretend to interfere in state affairs, yet the reconciliation with her brother concerned her greatly and she besought him to excuse her if she dared to recommend to him the negotiation already begun by me. . . . I know', added the ambassador, a touch complacently, 'that her entreaties have made an impression in addition to my own.'[50]

The surrender of La Rochelle appeared to remove the last serious obstacle to the ending of a pointless and expensive conflict, leaving the settlement of the queen's household the only problem still to be resolved. The English were maintaining that the arrangements negotiated by Bassompierre, which had after all been disavowed by the French, no longer applied and it was certainly true that the domestic situation had changed radically since his visit. The queen's household was now established and it would be difficult, if not impossible, to dislodge those English lords and ladies now in her service. In any case, the king was making it perfectly clear that he had no intention of allowing the French to return. He was so determined about this, wrote Contarini to Zorzi in Paris, 'that he would let all the rest go to ruin first'. Charles said repeatedly that he valued his peaceful home life more than anything else and was unalterably convinced that it would be wrecked if he once let any Frenchmen back anywhere near his wife. Nor did Contarini believe that the queen was particularly anxious to have them, 'foreseeing disagreements which might impede her growing influence'. Besides this, she had become accustomed to her English companions and no one could deny that she was being waited on with 'the greatest possible state and had nothing to desire with regard to the faith'.

Contarini thought it would be wiser to leave the whole question of the household open for the time being. Much better, he urged, to get the peace treaty signed, and then a discreet ambassador could bring things forward by degrees according to circumstances. He suggested that Henrietta should write to her mother to this effect, but was obliged to add a postscript to a letter to Zorzi dated 3 November: 'At this moment the queen . . . sends me word very confidentially that she does not want to displease the king by interesting herself too far in this matter, and asking me to supply her place by attesting that she is perfectly satisfied with the service and the court in its present state. . . . This confirms my belief that nothing will be gained on this point, that the king remains firm and to speak of it prejudices the queen herself, and so she is unwilling to move backward from the post of authority to which she is advancing.'[51]

The argument rumbled on into the New Year, with the French trying to revive the Bassompierre treaty and Charles obstinately refusing to budge. He had vetoed Richelieu's suggestion that the matter should be referred to Marie de Medici, 'because the daughter always agrees with her mother' and he could foresee a revival of 'the former causes of dissatisfaction, the mere shadow of which', according to Contarini, 'gives His Majesty more concern than all other political considerations'.[52]

But while the Venetians continued patiently to pick at the Gordian knot of the queen's household, cross-Channel traffic was gradually resuming. In January thirty ships laden with wine and other merchandise from France arrived in the Thames after a gap of two years, and Contarini was of the opinion that the mutual interests of the two kingdoms were 'gently compelling them to reunite'. Confirmation of the queen's pregnancy was also helping to hasten the peace process, and there was something else. On 20 January 1629 the parliament, prorogued the previous June, met again at Westminster but any hopes that, without Buckingham, king and Commons might get on better together were soon disappointed, as king and Commons became once more locked in combat over those old familiar bones of contention, finance and religion.

This time the financial dispute centred on tonnage and poundage, the customs duties levied on all imported and exported goods and which were traditionally granted to the sovereign for life by his first parliament. Charles's first parliament, however, had granted them for one year only,

[margin note:] 1629

which he had taken as a deliberate insult and had gone on collecting them anyway. Now the government, bearing in mind that the king had accepted the Petition of Right which demanded an end to extra-parliamentary taxation, was anxious to get a bill legitimising tonnage and poundage passed as quickly as possible; but the more radical members of the Commons insisted on first raising the religious question and expressing their alarm over the growing influence at court of the Arminian or reactionary High Church party.

When they finally got round to debating tonnage and poundage, it emerged that one of the merchants whose goods had recently been seized for refusing to pay was a member of the House, so that the sensitive question of privilege became involved with the equally sensitive issue of illegal taxation. When the Commons threatened to prosecute the customs officials concerned, the king forbade them to meddle with those who had acted by his special command. Tempers began to rise and Contarini noted that 'these affronts generate very great rancour and there is great fear of a rupture'.

This was not long in coming. On 25 February Charles adjourned the session for a week and, just as the members reassembled on 2 March, adjourned it for another week. The result was a furious row. The doors of the chamber were locked and the Speaker held down forcibly in his chair as the debate continued and Sir John Eliot introduced a series of resolutions condemning as 'a capitall enemye to the King and Kingdome' anyone who attempted to bring in either Popery, Arminianism or any new doctrine contrary to the Established Church; or who counselled the taking of tonnage and poundage without Act of Parliament. Any merchant who paid tonnage and poundage without Act of Parliament was to be accounted 'a betrayer of the libertie of the Subject' as well as a capital enemy of the state. Only when these resolutions had been passed and after 'some confused noyse and stirre', did the House move its own adjournment on what one observer described as 'the most gloomy, sad and dismal day for England that happened in five hundred years last past'.[54]

On 10 March Charles went down to the House of Lords in full royal regalia and dissolved his third parliament. Alvise Contarini did not think it would reassemble in the king's lifetime, adding that his majesty had been seen to return from the Lords 'in high spirits, as if he had freed himself from the yoke'. Whether Charles had given any serious thought to the future of parliament at this stage seems at least open to doubt. What was not open to doubt was the fact that he could no longer hope to wage war without the active cooperation of parliament, 'as to bark without being able to bite brings a government into discredit'.[55]

Serious Anglo-French negotiations sponsored by the Venetians were now in progress, and on 14 April Articles of peace were signed by both kings. A *status quo ante bellum* agreement, the treaty carefully skated round the fundamental differences between the two countries. Nothing was said on either side about the welfare of the other's religious minority and, while the English agreed to put an end to any further privateering attacks on French shipping, the vexed question of their right to stop and search neutral vessels trading with Spain was left open. The provisions of the queen's marriage contract were to be confirmed and any alterations to her household made 'to the mutual satisfaction of both sides, in conformity with what shall be deemed most fitting for the queen's service' – a form of words surely vague enough to save everyone's face.[56]

An official announcement that Henrietta's first child was expected in the summer had been made on 15 March and duly celebrated with bonfires and church bells. There was the usual queue of applicants for posts in the royal nursery, although it was thought the queen would want them all to be Catholics, and Contarini observed that 'in this as in future matters of similar importance the assistance of some representative of the Crown of France is required'. The queen-mother had, of course, been informed and found herself in something of a quandary, for the Princess of Piedmont was also expecting her first baby and the anxious grandmother-to-be naturally wanted both her daughters to enjoy the services of Madame Peronne, the best *sage femme* in France. Henrietta, carrying the responsibility of producing future kings, had prior claim, but for a while it was hoped that Madame Peronne might be able to look after Christine and still travel to England in time for the queen's delivery in July.[57]

The court had moved out to Greenwich and Contarini visited Henrietta there on 8 May to congratulate her on the happy conclusion of the peace. The treaty was publicly proclaimed two days later in a ceremony attended by all the chief officers of state, although Charles, who had not forgiven Louis for humiliating him at Rhé and setting up his captured standards in Notre Dame, refused to order the usual celebratory bonfires, maintaining that this was a reconciliation rather than a peace and, anyway, he did not know what the French were doing to mark the occasion.[58]

On Monday the 11th Henrietta came up-river to Somerset House to have a solemn Te Deum sung and on her return had stood up with her usual impatience before the barge touched the shore, so that the sudden jolt as it bumped against the landing stage made her lose her balance and fall backwards. She was in considerable pain for the rest of the day and by Tuesday it was clear that she was going into labour. Nothing was ready and in the ensuing panic 'the poor town midwife of Greenwich' was summoned to the palace; but when she realised that her patient was the queen, the wretched woman fainted in terror and had to be carried out. Fortunately, though, Peter Chamberlen, a leading obstetrician who had pioneered the use of forceps, was able to arrive in time to take charge of the situation, which he appears to have done very skilfully. It was a breech presentation, the child being turned 'overthwart' in its mother's belly, and for several hours Henrietta was in great pain and considerable danger. But at last, at about two o'clock in the morning of Wednesday 13 May, the baby was born. It was a boy, some ten weeks premature, who lived just long enough to be hastily baptised by one of the king's chaplains.

The king had been present throughout the proceedings, urging the doctor at all costs to save the mother before the child. He could, he said, please God, have other children and would rather save the mould than the cast, which, thought Contarini, was evidence of the great love he bore his wife. Henrietta had, in fact, survived her ordeal remarkably well. She had fallen into a deep sleep as soon as she was delivered and by the time Theodore Mayerne saw her, was recovering fast and 'full of strength and courage'.

All the same, it was a severe disappointment to both families, especially since, as Contarini observed, 'the premature delivery of the first child is usually an obstacle to posterity'. Various explanations, apart from the obvious one, were being put forward. According to some the queen had been frightened by two dogs fighting in her gallery, one of which had snatched at her and pulled her by the gown. Others blamed 'the violence of her exercises' and fondness for walking – walking uphill was considered seriously dangerous for pregnant ladies.[59]

Henrietta herself seems to have taken the whole thing philosophically and when her more fortunate sister successfully gave birth to a daughter, she wrote a graceful little note of congratulations to the Prince of Piedmont, saying almost casually, 'as to my loss, I wish to forget it'. Such sad mishaps were, after all, only too frequent at all levels of society, and the queen had at least now proved her ability to conceive. She was young, still only nineteen, and naturally optimistic. Probably, though, what mattered most to her in the summer of 1629 was the comforting knowledge that she now unquestionably occupied first place in her husband's affections. Henrietta, who had once asked Eleanor Davys for how long she should be happy, was now beginning the happiest decade of her life, innocently unaware of the existence of the great storm already gathering just below the horizon which would sweep that happiness away for ever.

CHAPTER FOUR

The Happiest Princess

. . . not only had I every pleasure the heart could desire;
I had a husband who adored me.
Henrietta Maria to Madame de Motteville

The weeks passed and the love affair between the king and queen continued to blossom. Towards the end of July Charles left for Theobalds while Henrietta went down to Tunbridge Wells, intending to complete her convalescence by taking a course of the waters, but they missed each other so much that, as the diplomat Francis Cottington wrote to Thomas Wentworth on 7 August, 'she is suddenly come from thence, and by great journeys meets with the king this night at Oatlands, whither he also returns to pay her in the same coin'.[1]

The newly arrived special envoy from France, the Marquis de Chateauneuf, was much impressed by the royal couple's public displays of affection. The king kissed his wife repeatedly in the ambassador's presence, saying complacently, 'you do not see that in Turin', home of the Prince and Princess of Piedmont, or, in a lower voice, 'at Paris', referring to Louis' loveless marriage.[2]

Chateauneuf had instructions from Richelieu to try to interest Charles in reviving his war with Spain, but quickly came to believe that England was now so weak that it would be useless to raise the subject of further military operations. In fact, preliminary negotiations towards ending the Spanish war were already in progress, something the Frenchman chose to ignore, indicating that he really considered the matter beneath his notice. According to the Venetians, 'his usual way of speaking is that they [the English] are poor folk, who can do neither good nor harm'. Instead he concentrated his efforts on cultivating his friendship with the queen, whom he was seeing on a daily basis and through whom 'he can always know everything'. Giovanni Soranzo, who had recently taken over from Contarini at the Venetian embassy, was of the opinion that Henrietta, although 'a very young princess and therefore disinclined for business', could easily be guided by an adroit ambassador and shown how to insinuate herself and find things out. 'There is no doubt', Soranzo went on, 'but that she will always be ready to meddle in affairs for the sake of her reputation if for nothing else.'[3]

However, to the disappointment of all those eager to make use of her influence to build up a pro-French party at court, Henrietta remained resolutely disinclined to meddle in affairs and Chateauneuf was obliged to resort to some rather low-level intrigue, encouraging her dislike of Richard Weston, the tight-fisted Lord Treasurer, who was beginning to emerge as the king's principal adviser and who was known to be strongly in favour of peace with Spain. The ambassador also became involved in the rivalry between Lord Holland and the pro-Spanish Earl of Carlisle, with the only immediately discernible result of causing a quarrel between the queen and Lucy Carlisle.

When it came to the final settlement of the queen's household, Chateauneuf found himself up against the king's well-known obstinacy and what he described as the queen's timidity. He had, he told the king, been instructed to ask for a bishop as Grand Almoner, an adequate number of priests to serve the queen's chapel, a lady of the bedchamber, a doctor and as many other household officers as her majesty might require. Charles was ready to concede some additional priests. He would even concede a Grand Almoner, but on no account whatever would he allow another trouble-making French bishop into the country. He had not forgotten the Bishop of Mende, with his arrogant, intrusive ways and irritating habit of strolling in and out of the queen's apartments at will. They want to send you another governor, he told his wife.

The king was reluctant even to discuss the appointment of any other French attendants and Chateauneuf got no help from the queen, who said she already had all the ladies she wanted. Any more coming from France would find they had nothing to do, and besides she really could not afford the extra expense. As for a doctor, if one was sent, he would have to be prepared to serve under Theodore Mayerne.

Chateauneuf might deplore Henrietta's refusal to assert her undoubted rights under the terms of her marriage contract, but there was little he could do in the face of her obvious determination not to risk any interference with her new-found married bliss with a doting husband who could scarcely bear to have her out of his sight. Councillors complained that they never got a chance to speak to the king these days, for he always hurried straight to the queen the moment he returned from hunting. Indeed he often said, so Henrietta told Chateauneuf, that he wished they could always be together and that she could go with him to Council meetings. It would never do, of course. What would the English say if they saw a woman taking part in the government!

Wrangling over the household dragged on into the autumn but with the queen now supporting her husband – too many foreigners, especially too many priests, would be bound to cause an outcry from the Protestant clergy who were powerful in parliament – and insisting that she was perfectly happy and content, the happiest woman in the world in fact, it was difficult for the French to maintain their position. Chateauneuf did his best, but after a while the demand for a bishop was quietly dropped. Instead it was agreed that eight Capuchin friars should be attached to the queen's chapel and Charles rather grudgingly promised to allow the queen-mother to select one lady of the bedchamber, but since the choice of candidate was too important to be made in a hurry no date was set and the whole matter left deliberately vague.[4]

In November it was being confidently reported that the queen was pregnant again and in January public prayers rendering thanks to the Almighty were being offered in the London churches. This time there would be no dangerous walking exercise or jolting about in unsprung coaches, for Marie de Medici had sent her daughter the present of 'a beautiful chaise' for taking the air, together with much good advice and a little heart on a chain which Henrietta told her mother she always wore round her neck, believing it brought such good fortune that she was afraid to be without it. 'I hope God may grant me the favour to go to the end of my term,' she wrote, 'and as to what depends upon me, I shall take all possible care of myself.' Charles also wrote to his mother-in-law, assuring her that Henrietta was indeed being so careful that he had no need to use other authority than that of love. 'The only dispute that now exists between us', he went on, 'is that of conquering each other by affection.'[5]

Preparations for the happy event were now well in hand and on 11 February Susan Denbigh, the first lady of the bedchamber, was issued with a warrant for £2,000 'for extraordinary provision of linen for the queen's lying-in'. The services of Madame Peronne had also been retained once more and M. Garnier, husband of the queen's nurse, dispatched in plenty of time to fetch her. Garnier was accompanied by Geoffrey Hudson, the queen's dwarf, 'a marvellous sight and the most perfect imperfection of nature that ever was born'. Hudson, a butcher's son and the Tom Thumb of his day, had been 'presented' to the queen by the Duke of Buckingham when he was nine years old and no more than eighteen inches high, having been concealed in a pie at one of the duke's lavish parties. Henrietta seems to have regarded him as some sort of special pet, but why he was detailed for escort duty on this occasion is not explained, unless it was for his curiosity value – certainly he was showered with expensive presents in France.

On their way home, towards the end of March, these oddly assorted travellers fell into the hands of the notorious Dunkirk pirates and were carried off to Gravelines. The news caused consternation at court. The queen was in tears; a courier went hurrying to Brussels with an urgent request to the Infanta Isabella, ruler of the Netherlands, to secure their release, and the Spanish ambassador, in London for the peace talks, was asked to write letters in their favour. The captives were duly set free, but whether their baggage – Hudson is said to have had at least £2,000 in jewels and a wagon-load of rich goods – was also returned intact is not entirely clear. Although this accident seems of slight importance, wrote Giovanni Soranzo, 'it caused so much disturbance that one of the lords here, laughing at their weakness, remarked to me that they were more upset at court than if they had lost a fleet'. There were also those who felt it rather served the queen right for not being content with an honest English midwife.[6]

By this time the new leiger, or resident, French ambassador, the Marquis de Fontenay-Mareuil, had arrived in England, bringing with him the Capuchins for the queen's chapel. The Capuchin friars, a reformed branch of the Franciscans, had a reputation for charity, for tactfulness and for the simplicity and piety of their way of life, so it was unfortunate that their first few days in London should have been marked by an unedifying display of uncharitableness towards another Order. When their Superior, Father Leonard, discovered that he was not, as he had been led to expect, going to take over from the Oratorian Father Philip as the queen's spiritual director, he took serious umbrage. So much so, in fact, that he threatened, with something suspiciously like a flounce, to take himself and his brethren back to France and had to be reminded of his Christian duty to stay and spread the Word among the benighted islanders. However, ruffled feathers were soon smoothed. Henrietta's refusal to part with Father Philip, who had been with her since the great exodus of 1626, was blamed on the machinations of the Marquis de Chateauneuf, and the Capuchins were installed in the pleasant house and garden which the queen had acquired for them adjacent to Somerset House. On the Sunday after their arrival, the third Sunday in Lent, they celebrated mass and the Reverend Father Esmé of Beauvais preached an eloquent sermon, taking for his text the lesson of the deaf and dumb man which 'furnished him with occasion to say that if, since the dismissal of the French and the war with France, the preachers were dumb to the queen, the master of all preachers, the Holy Ghost, had spoken to her heart'.[7]

The Capuchins had travelled in the cassocks of secular priests, but they now asked for and were given permission to resume the distinctive rough brown habits of their Order – a garb 'so extraordinary and so strange in this kingdom' that it naturally raised the hackles of the Protestant Londoners. The Catholic community, on the other hand, had taken fresh heart from the coming of the Capuchins, which 'made them dream of a new liberty', and they began to flock in ever-increasing numbers both to the queen's and the foreign ambassadors' chapels, so that the Council was soon forced to placate the Puritan tendency by issuing an order forbidding the king's subjects to attend religious services at the embassy chapels.[8] This, in turn, led to scenes reminiscent of the early days of the marriage and Soranzo reported that 'the first acts of violence against the Catholics' took place on 14 March, when guards were posted not more than twenty paces from the gates of the French, Spanish and Venetian ambassadors' houses and all the English coming out after mass were immediately arrested. One Sunday in April the pursuivants, reinforced by some local people, fell on a group of worshippers as they left the French embassy chapel. Some of them managed to break away and retreat back into the embassy courtyard, whereupon 'the French came forth with their naked swords to guard them, but were soundly beaten, and not without bloodshed, into their gates by the people, that with their rude weapons rushed upon them'.[9]

Rather more genteel methods were employed at the queen's chapel, where two gentlemen ushers stood at the door warning visitors to turn back if they were English; those who persisted were not arrested until the next day. There was, though, one unfortunate incident when Marie Aubert, the heavily pregnant wife of Henrietta's principal surgeon, was seized outside Somerset House by an over-zealous official, who disregarded her protests that as a member of the queen's French household she was exempt from the Council's order and dragged her away so roughly that she later miscarried.

Chateauneuf and Henrietta were both furious and blamed the Lord Treasurer Richard Weston for these new severities, but neither of them got much satisfaction from the king. The ambassador was told that it was not a good idea to excite the queen's feelings just now and, in any case, Charles would not allow any interference in the affairs of his household. When Chateauneuf tried to take a high tone, threatening possible reprisals against the Huguenots and exclaiming dramatically that his majesty could not prevent him from concerning himself in what touched the honour and conscience of the queen, Charles merely made some remark about the observation of his laws and brought the interview to a close. As for Henrietta, she was apparently given to understand 'that it was against the convenants of her contract of marriage that her chaplains should be used by any but herself and her own servants', while John Rous, the incumbent of Santon Downham in Suffolk, heard that the king had told his wife: 'I permit you your religion with your Capuchins and others; I permit ambassadors and their retinue, but the rest [of] my subjects I will have them live in the religion that I profess and my father before me.' Henrietta was still extremely cross and sulked for several days, refusing to speak to any of the lords of the Council, especially the Treasurer, but Charles did not relent and at the end of April it was being noted that 'the queen's chapel is still so strictly guarded that no subjects of his majesty may enter'.[10]

Chateauneuf had left for home by this time, having achieved very little during his ten months in England. The highly contentious problem of a belligerent's right to stop and search neutral shipping at sea remained unresolved, as did the French government's claims for compensation for past interference with their commerce. The ambassador had also failed in his efforts to get the queen's jointure secured by Act of Parliament and had to be satisfied with 'the best landed of the lords of the Council' acting as guarantors. Filippo Burlomachi, the international merchant banker, would now, it was hoped, begin to arrange payment of the second half of her dowry, but it would be another two years before that was finally settled.[11]

Henrietta was in good health and expected to be confined towards the end of May. She had intended to lie in at Greenwich, but several cases of plague had recently been reported in the town and it was decided that St James's, with its surrounding parkland, would be a better choice. A luxurious new bed, furnished with a set of embroidered green satin hangings valued at £675, was installed in the birth chamber and a messenger arrived from Marie de Medici bearing a gift of some charming baby clothes. Less welcome had been the arrival, apparently engineered by the busybodying Chateauneuf, of a French physician to assist at the accouchement. The king, seeing this as an attempt to force his hand and make him accept the man, 'a thing he cannot tolerate', took immediate, furious offence and, to the acute embarrassment of ambassador Fontenay-Mareuil, the unfortunate Dr Poix was sent packing without even being allowed to kiss the queen's hand.[12] Henrietta, with Madame Peronne in attendance and Theodore Mayerne on call, had shown no interest in him and, as it turned out, was to need little in the way of medical intervention. She went into labour at about four o'clock in the morning of Saturday 29 May 1630 and shortly before noon 'was made the happy mother of a Prince of Wales'. He was the first heir apparent to be born on English soil for very nearly a century and later that same day his father went in state to St Paul's to give thanks.[13]

There was no question about the health of this infant. Giovanni Soranzo, who saw him in his cradle before he was a week old, observed that 'so far as one can judge from present indications he will be very strong and vigorous' and went on, 'the nurses told me that after his birth he had never clenched his fists, but had always kept his hands open. From this they augur that he will be a prince of great liberality in the future.'[14]

The birth of the heir had been followed by all the bell-ringing, bonfires and bad verse customary on such occasions, but not everybody in the kingdom was celebrating. All those Protestants who saw Henrietta's

Henrietta's father Henri IV of France, by Frans Pourbus the Younger. (The Royal Collection © 2000. Her Majesty the Queen)

Henrietta's mother Marie de Medici (1573–1642), wife of Henri IV of France; portrait by Alessandro Allori. (Kunsthistorisches Museum, Vienna, Austria/Bridgeman Art Library)

Prince Charles in 1623, by Daniel Mytens. (From the Collection at Parham Park, West Sussex, England)

The royal favourite George Villiers, 1st Duke of Buckingham. Attributed to William Larkin. (By courtesy of the National Portrait Gallery)

Henrietta Maria in 1632; this Van Dyck portrait was hung in the king's bedchamber at Whitehall. (The Royal Collection © 2000. Her Majesty the Queen)

Charles and Henrietta dining in public at Whitehall, by Gerard Houckgeest. (The Royal Collection © 2000. Her Majesty the Queen)

The Banqueting Hall, Whitehall. The queen's 'dancing barn', it was the scene of many royal masques and other functions. (© Crown copyright. NMR)

The king and queen and the court at Greenwich, by Adrian van Stalbent. (The Royal Collection © 2000. Her Majesty the Queen)

Charles and Henrietta departing for the chase. (The Royal Collection © 2000. Her Majesty the Queen)

The queen's chapel at St James's Palace, engraving by Johannes Kip. (Pepys Library, Magdalene College, Cambridge)

The Queen's House at Greenwich. The exterior was designed by Inigo Jones. (Photo: John Bethell, Bridgeman Art Library)

Sir Thomas Wentworth (afterwards Earl of Strafford) and John Pym at Greenwich in 1628, by George Cattermole. (Victoria & Albert Museum, London/ Bridgeman Art Library)

Theodore Mayerne, the Stuart family physician. (By courtesy of the National Portrait Gallery)

Geoffrey Hudson, the queen's dwarf, pictured by Daniel Mytens. (The Royal Collection © 2000. Her Majesty the Queen)

Charles and Henrietta with the Prince of Wales and Princess Mary, by Van Dyck. (The Royal Collection © 2000. Her Majesty the Queen)

religion as a threat harboured grave misgivings about the sort of influence she might be expected to exert over the prince's upbringing, and there were those who would have much preferred her to remain childless. Until now the king's heir had been his Protestant and very popular sister Elizabeth, herself the mother of a number of sturdy Protestant sons, and some people had not hesitated to say that they could see no cause for joy in the queen's pregnancy, 'God having better provided for us in the hopeful progeny of the Queen of Bohemia'. The contemporary historian Peter Heylyn could remember being at a town in Gloucestershire when news of the prince's birth arrived, and while most of the parish, especially the younger members, rejoiced in the usual manner, 'from the rest of the Houses, being of the Presbyterian or Puritan party, there came neither Man, nor Child, nor Wood, nor Victuals, their doors being shut close all the evening as in a time of general mourning and disconsolation'.[15]

In fact, it seemed as if no one need have worried. Henrietta had brought two of her Capuchins with her to St James's, but the king made it clear that they were to have nothing to do with his son's baptism. He would attend to it himself and 'would satisfy the Most Christian King, his brother, on that point'.[16] The ceremony duly took place on 27 June and was performed according to the Anglican rite by William Laud, Dean of the Chapel Royal, the four-week-old prince being named after his father. The King of France and the queen-mother had been invited to be godparents and had accepted – rather amazingly in view of the fact that the Protestant baptism was in direct contravention of the marriage treaty – although neither of them sent proxies and were represented by the Duke of Lennox and the Duchess of Richmond, both close connections of the Stuart family. The duchess indeed always considered herself an extra godmother in her own right and 'shewed a more than ordinary bounty', presenting her 'godson' with a diamond ring worth £5,000 and scattering lavish tips in the shape of gold plate and jewels on the midwife, the nurses, cradle-rockers and everyone else 'that had done her honor and service'.[17]

The king had previously announced that all the nurses, rockers and other officers belonging to the queen's nursery were to be Protestants, but now he rather spoilt the effect by appointing the Catholic Countess of Roxburgh as governess. A face-saving excuse had to be found – 'the pretext of indisposition' – and the post went instead to the reliably Protestant Mary Sackville, Countess of Dorset.

Henrietta had made a good recovery from her childbed and by early July was able to join the king on his summer journeyings. A month later they both returned to town for a brief visit to see their son at St James's. The big, dark-eyed baby was thriving in a most satisfactory manner but he was undoubtedly something of a surprise to his doll-like mama, and in September she was writing to Mamie St Georges from Hampton Court: 'If my son knew how to talk, I think he would send you his compliments; he is so fat and so tall, that he is taken for a year old, and he is only four months: his teeth are already beginning to come. I will send you his portrait as soon as he is a little fairer, for at present he is so dark that I am ashamed of him.' However, he did not get any fairer and his mother was obliged to admit: 'He is so ugly, that I am ashamed of him, but his size and fatness supply the want of beauty.'[18]

The prince may have got his inches from that long lad his paternal great-grandfather, Henry, Lord Darnley, but his startlingly Mediterranean appearance unquestionably came from his mother's family. Some people have traced it to the Medici dukes of Tuscany, seeing a strong likeness to the fifteenth-century Lorenzo the Magnificent. Others again believe the resemblance is to his illegitimate uncle the Duc de Vendôme, and certainly the adult Charles II would seem to have inherited his genes from the pragmatic and priapic Henri IV.

It was a hot dry summer with a new sort of fever going about which struck down several members of the household, but the baby was unaffected. He continued to thrive and his parents to marvel at his size and fatness. All that summer, too, negotiations had been continuing in London and Madrid and finally, on 5 November, a treaty was signed putting an end to the war with Spain, thus marking England's withdrawal from any further engagement in the field of continental conflict. It was also a tacit recognition by Charles of his powerlessness to help his sister and her husband, whose brief occupation of the Bohemian throne had precipitated the Thirty Years War of Catholic versus Protestant and the Hapsburg family versus the Rest which was currently ravaging central Europe. It was true that a paper attached to the Treaty of Madrid contained some vaguely worded promises that Spain would do her best for the restoration of the Palatinate to its rightful owners, but Vicenzo Gussoni, writing from the Hague, remarked that this only went to confirm the general opinion 'that in the end the English have allowed themselves to be deluded'.[19]

Apart from disapproving on principle, like a good Frenchwoman – she had warned Charles more than a year before that the Spaniards would only deceive him – Henrietta had taken little interest in the treaty which was published in London in December to a general lack of popular acclaim because, again according to the Venetians, 'the peace is disliked by everyone and all know that it is dishonourable and prejudicial'.[20] The queen was, however, 'deeply interested' in developments currently taking place inside the French royal family circle, where her mother, increasingly jealous of Richelieu's rise to power, had been hoping to oust him from his position as Louis' confidant and chief minister. A stormy confrontation, known as the Day of the Dupes, resulted in the frustration of her intended coup and early in 1631 Marie de Medici was banished from the court and placed under house arrest at Compiègne. As once before she managed to escape and this time fled over the border into the Spanish Netherlands.

Her principal ally in France was the Marquis de Chateauneuf, who now led the faction plotting the cardinal's downfall and sought to enlist Henrietta's support, using as his instruments her faithful dresser Madame Ventelet and François de Rochechouart, Chevalier de Jars, who had taken refuge in England back in 1626 after a previous conspiracy against Richelieu and had become a great favourite at court. A gambler and adventurer, he was an amusing companion who played tennis with the king, made himself agreeable to the queen and had recently been doing a little spying on the side for Chateauneuf, until the resident ambassador grew suspicious and resorted to employing a burglar in order to get his hands on the enterprising Chevalier's private correspondence. De Jars' friends, headed by the queen, demanded restitution, but Fontenay defended his action on the grounds that he was entitled to use any means he considered necessary to expose possibly disloyal practices on the part of one of his master's subjects and Charles refused to interfere.[21]

Henrietta, who had never got on with Fontenay, now attacked him on the subject of the queen-mother's wrongs, declaring 'with some passion' that the removal of Richelieu from about the king was a perfectly reasonable request which Louis could not decently refuse, and she continued to complain that his ill-treatment of their mother was all Cardinal Richelieu's fault – ideas which, as Soranzo remarked, had been planted by Chateauneuf's intimates 'because they believe that with the fall of the cardinal no one but he could inherit his influence'.[22]

Henrietta had another reason for being on bad terms with her brother just then. Her new Grand Almoner had come to England in April but although the Abbé Duperron was, as requested, only a simple priest, the queen at first refused to receive him, knowing that his arrival would be followed by renewed attempts to persuade her to send her old friend and confessor back to France – the Fathers of the Oratory now being considered hostile to Richelieu. The affair dragged on through the summer and complaints were made at diplomatic level, but Henrietta was determined not to be separated from Father Philip. In the end she told Fontenay openly 'that she did not wish to be dependent on anything but her own good pleasure in what touched her household, and the Most Christian would gratify her by not meddling with it, with some other resentful expressions, so sharp that they will certainly compel the king, her brother, to take note of them and not to interest himself so much in her behalf, should occasion arise, as he has done in the past. Here,' added Giovanni Soranzo, 'they by no means regret that he should be to some extent estranged.'[23]

Throughout her life Henrietta was governed principally by her emotions. Heedless of the great political issues of the day – until, that is, they began to affect her directly – it was people who mattered to her; but while always a fiercely loyal friend (Father Philip stayed in his post and remained with her until his death), the queen could also make an unforgiving enemy, as anyone who incurred her displeasure quickly discovered. One of these unfortunates was Richard Weston who, in his capacity as Lord Treasurer, was engaged in the perennial struggle to make royal ends meet and had first come into collision with the queen over his efforts to reduce expenditure in the household. There was a story going round that when the old Duchess de la Tremoille came over from France to see her daughter Lady Strange and went to pay her respects at court, Henrietta, who was then still lying-in, had had to keep her curtains drawn in order to conceal the shabbiness of her surroundings, 'as they make the most miserable economies even in the things that show most'.[24]

Finance ministers making spending cuts are seldom popular and it did not help matters that Weston was always ill at ease with Henrietta. 'He had not that application and submission and reverence for the Queen as might have been expected from his wisdom and breeding', remembered Lord Clarendon, 'and often crossed her pretences and desires with more rudeness than was natural to him.'[25]

Weston was not short of other enemies and Soranzo reported that while Chateauneuf was in London, he and several of the queen's friends – notably the Earl of Holland, who coveted the Treasurer's pre-eminent place on the Council – had schemed to bring about his fall. Henrietta herself had become involved and had been persuaded to speak out against him to the king, but 'this did no good and only served to impair her influence somewhat'.[26] Chateauneuf had always seen Weston as an obstacle in the way of his own plans for bringing down Cardinal Richelieu, knowing he would do nothing to risk annoying the French establishment, but in the summer of 1631 a possible new line of attack opened up. From her refuge in Brussels Marie de Medici was angling for an invitation to London, something which would have suited Chateauneuf's purposes very well. The two queens between them would surely be able to persuade the king to dismiss Richard Weston and promote Lord Holland, who would then be in a position to help him to create difficulties for Richelieu. So, at least, he and the anti-Weston faction at court appear to have reasoned. But Charles had every confidence in his Lord Treasurer and no intention of advancing the lightweight Holland; nor did he intend to put his precious domestic peace at risk by having his mother-in-law to stay, remaining impervious both to Spanish suggestions that he might see his way to relieving them of her presence and to his wife's tearful pleas on her behalf.

In September an English lord returning from overseas brought Henrietta 'not only salutations from her mother, but an expression of the resentment she said she felt at seeing herself practically abandoned by her daughter at a time of her greatest need'. Henrietta was much upset by this blatant attempt at emotional blackmail, but although the king, to pacify her, agreed to send someone on a courtesy visit to the queen-mother, he administered a majestic rocket to the 'English lord' and clapped him in gaol for a few days for having presumed to approach his wife on such a politically sensitive matter without prior permission.[27] Weston and Richelieu remained secure in their respective masters' esteem and it was now clear to the sharp-eyed Venetians that the Queen of England's influence over her husband was by no means as strong as some people had rashly begun to assume.

None of this had affected the personal harmony between king and queen, and although distressed by her family's troubles Henrietta had not allowed them to interfere with any of her usual activities. The beginning of the year had been largely taken up with rehearsals for the masque, scripted by Ben Jonson and with costumes and sets designed by Inigo Jones, which the queen would present to the court at Shrovetide. The vernal theme of this ambitious production was established in the opening scene showing a landscape of little hills planted with trees and flowers, with fountains spurting from the hollows and the appearance, in a luminous cloud, of Spring herself, dressed in green and white and garlanded with more flowers. This pastoral idyll was disrupted by Cupid, who had quarrelled with the gods and gone off to make trouble in Hades by upsetting all the accepted behaviour patterns in the underworld – so that the Furies were depicted playing ninepins and Tantalus eating the fruit that before had been forever out of his reach, while Sisyphus bowled his stone along a level green. The dwarf Geoffrey Hudson and six infernal spirits performed a grotesque dance; the lights dimmed, heralding a storm which gave way to renewed calm, and Henrietta, in a costume of fresh greens decorated with gold and silver, was revealed in her bower as Chloris, goddess of flowers, surrounded by nymphs played by the ladies of her household. The clouds parted, the goddesses Juno and Iris appeared with their attendant nymphs and a three-dimensional mountain rose from beneath the stage, topped by the figure of Fame, who spread her wings and flew up into the heavens. The chorus sang a hymn in praise of Chloris and the actors stepped down out of their make-believe world to take their earthly partners from among the audience for the closing dance.[28]

In May the Prince of Wales had attained the dignity of his first birthday. 'I wish you could see the gentleman', wrote his mother to Mamie St Georges, 'for he has no ordinary mien; he is so serious in all that he does, that I cannot help fancying him far wiser than myself.' Although Henrietta did now seem to be making genuine efforts to adapt herself to English ways, she remained thoroughly French in all her personal tastes and was trying to arrange for a Parisian dressmaker to come over and measure her for new petticoat waists, as the last one Mamie had sent her was so heavy and narrow that she had not been able to put it on. 'I have still my velvet one', she wrote, 'got two years ago, which is so short for me and so far worn that I am greatly in want of another.' She also asked her friend for 'a dozen pairs of sweet chamois gloves' and for details of any new games currently fashionable in France. 'I assure you, that if I do not write to you as often as I might', she went on, 'it is not because I have left off loving you, but because – I must confess it – I am very idle; also I am ashamed to avow that I think I am on the increase again.'[29]

1631

The queen was indeed pregnant again and her baby was born at St James's Palace in the early hours of 4 November. It was a girl this time and no dark cuckoo in the nest, but a typical Stuart with brown eyes and reddish hair. The baptism, performed by William Laud, took place later that same day, the excuse being that the child was delicate, having arrived three weeks prematurely, but the more cynically minded believed that the real reason for the hasty private ceremony had been 'to save charges and prevent other christening'. The new princess was named Mary, and her godmothers were the Countesses of Carlisle and Denbigh, and her godfather the Lord Keeper Thomas Coventry.[30]

Henrietta made her usual rapid recovery and was soon once more immersed in her favourite pastime of planning the New Year masques. Old Ben Jonson was not involved this time, having quarrelled violently with Inigo Jones, and his place had been taken by the minor court poet Aurelian Townshend. Jones, now firmly established in the queen's confidence, was therefore able to give full rein to his genius for creating stunning visual effects without too much competition from the spoken word, although *Albion's Triumph*, the king's masque performed on 8 January, was a relatively restrained affair, portraying his majesty as the Emperor Albanactus, the embodiment of a benevolent autocrat bringing the blessings of peace and prosperity to a grateful people against a succession of classical backgrounds, while Innocence, Religion, Affection to Country and Concord hovered in the clouds over his head.[31]

The queen's masque, which should have followed a week later, had to be postponed until mid-February as Henrietta was suffering from a painful <u>eye infection</u>, but *Tempe Restored* was generally held to have been well worth waiting for. 'The queen', reported the new Venetian ambassador Vicenzo Gussoni, 'celebrated the end of the carnival by a sumptuous masque, performed with wonderfully rich decorations before a numerous assembly in the great hall of the royal palace.'[32] Based on a French original and telling of the conquering of sensual passion, as represented by the enchantress Circe, by the higher influences of reason and intellect, the production, which included an anti-masque or comic interlude featuring wild Indians and barbarians, was notable for the first appearance on stage of professional female singers as well as for some of Inigo Jones's most spectacular scenic triumphs to date.

The queen herself appeared as Divine Beauty –

> When Divine Beauty, will vouchsafe to stoope,
> And move to Earth: 'tis fit the Heavenley Spheres,
> Should be her Musicke: And the Starrie Troope,
> Shine round about her, like the Crowne she weares.

The Heavenley Spheres, eight musicians in 'rich habites' sitting on a cloud, were lowered from above, followed by two more clouds bearing the Starrie Troope. Then came yet another, greater cloud with still more stars, and above all 'in a Chariot of goldsmithes workes richly adorned with precious Jemmes, sat divine Beauty, over whose head appear'd a brightnesse full of small starres'. As Henrietta, in pale blue satin embossed and embroidered with silver, alighted from her chariot, the clouds rose again in reverse order, linking heaven to earth 'as in a Chaine' – a sight which was 'for the difficulty of the Engining and number of the persons the greatest that hath been seene here in our time'. For with the appearance of 'such as came downe in the ayre, and the Choruses standing beneath' there were now some fifty elaborately costumed persons assembled on the stage.

When the masquers had performed their main dance, the queen went to sit with her husband and the scene changed again into a shady wood with a different-coloured sky, in the midst of which Jove was discovered sitting on an eagle's back, hovering in the air 'with a glory beyond him'. At the same time Cupid came flying out from another part of the heaven, turning and soaring like a bird, while a chorus of five and thirty musicians serenaded them from below. This dazzling display of aerobatics brought the masque proper to a close, but the whole company, actors and audience, now took to the floor for the revels which lasted into the small hours. It had all been a triumphant success, showing off 'the magnificence of the Court of England' in a most satisfactory manner and the king, noted Gussoni, proved the pleasure he took in it 'by gaily taking part in the dancing'.[33]

The king and queen now left on a short holiday, going by way of Theobalds and Royston to Cambridge, where the university entertained them with three comedies, and then on to Newmarket 'for the pleasures of the country and hunting', although Henrietta joined in her husband's sporting activities so enthusiastically that she rather overtired herself. They were back in town for Easter, at the beginning of April, and a few weeks later were off again, to Greenwich this time, for more 'country pleasures'. Henrietta liked the country, in good weather of course, and enjoyed the opportunity of playing at rustic pastimes. Very soon after her first arrival in England it had been noticed that she loved to walk in the meadows beside the Thames and watch the haymakers at work, and how she would sometimes seize a rake or fork and 'sportingly' join in.

A sentimental yearning for the simple delights of rural life was not at all uncommon among those who were never likely to have to make hay or milk cows for real, and during that spring Henrietta organised a party of ladies and gentlemen to go on a maying expedition. 'The queen was dressed à l'Anglaise, and no sooner was a bush spied, with its beautiful load of white and pearly blossoms, than she sprang out of her coach, gathered the first bunch, and placed it in her hat.'[34]

There were other, equally pleasurable matters to occupy her attention at Greenwich, where Inigo Jones, in his capacity as Surveyor, was superintending the completion of the Queen's House, begun for Anne of Denmark but left unfinished at her death. Henrietta was taking a close interest in the progress of the building and employed a French artist to supply designs for chimney pieces and other decorative details. There were also the exciting plans for her new chapel at Somerset House to be finalised. Long gone were the days when Lady Strange had remarked rather scornfully that the queen 'interferes with nothing and thinks only of how to kill time'.

The 1632 summer progress took the court westward, to Salisbury and Beaulieu, but the second week of September found her majesty at Somerset House, ready to lay the foundation stone of the chapel which was to occupy the site of the old tennis court. This, according to one of the Capuchin fathers, had been very tastefully fitted up for the occasion in the form of a church. 'Rich tapestry served for walls; the most costly stuffs for roof; the floor was strewed with flowers, which diffused an agreeable odour. At the further end', he went on, 'was seen an altar, garnished with magnificent ornaments . . . the costliness and

90

workmanship of which rendered them worthy of being compared with Solomon's Temple.'

The queen, accompanied by the French ambassador and a number of other Catholic gentlemen and ladies, knelt on a red velvet cushion as her Grand Almoner celebrated high mass and granted some indulgences, 'while harmonious music ravished the heart'. After this, her majesty was ceremoniously handed a velvet-trimmed trowel and taking some mortar from a silver-gilt basin she threw it three times on to the stone, which bore a large silver plaque with a commemorative Latin inscription. She then distributed gifts among the workmen lavish enough to make them give shouts of joy, 'repeating a thousand times, "Long live the Queen! Long live the Queen!"'

A large crowd of spectators had turned out to watch this unusual ceremony and, as reports of it spread through the city, interest in the Capuchins was stimulated. 'People talked of them in their houses; they said they were persons so strange, wearing dresses so extraordinary, leading so austere a life, that everyone conceived a desire to see them. Accordingly, persons of quality, people of all conditions, who had never been out of the kingdom, came to see them, as one goes to see Indians, Malays, Savages, and men from the extremities of the earth.' England, remarked Father Cyprien de Gamache, was such an abundant country and the English so used to soft living that they were particularly impressed by the spartan nature of the Capuchins' accommodation.

The fathers were now beginning to find their way about the streets and gradually became an accepted part of the London scene, so that they were able to make a start on the missionary work for which their Order had been founded. 'All things being quieter', wrote Cyprien de Gamache, 'we acted with more freedom, but nevertheless with great moderation, taking care that nothing should appear and occasion a noise. The English language had become more familiar to us, and easier; one converted person brought several others, who were either related to him, or friends of his. . . . At every mass', he went on, 'there was a great number of communicants. We carried the sacraments to the Catholics in prison, and to the sick in various places in and out of the city of London, so commonly that this happened almost every day, and in such number that in one forenoon a single Capuchin carried the sacraments sometimes to eight sick persons in quarters and places far distant from one another.'[35]

Things may have been quiet in England, but on the European mainland some stirring events were taking place that autumn. Henrietta's younger brother, the unstable Gaston d'Orléans, had finally summoned up the courage to come out in open rebellion against Louis and Richelieu and had been crushed. His principal ally, the great nobleman

Henri de Montmorency, was taken prisoner and executed in October, but Gaston escaped and by early November had joined his mother in Brussels. Further to the east, the King of Sweden, whose recent string of victories over the Hapsburg armies had been putting new heart into the Protestant cause, was defeated and killed at Lutzen near Leipzig, and almost simultaneously came news that the unlucky Frederick, Elector Palatine and ex-King of Bohemia had died of fever, leaving a grief-stricken widow and a young family. There was another death that November. Sir John Eliot, who had been in close confinement in the Tower ever since those stirring March days which marked the end of the king's last parliament, had sickened and died in his prison cell, conspicuously unlamented by his sovereign.

Charles, whose past failures to help his sister and brother-in-law had been a constant cause of reproach among Protestant activists, now wrote urging her to make her home in England – 'I entreat you to make as much haste as you conveniently can to come to me.' But Elizabeth regretfully declined the invitation. The Queen of Bohemia knew that she would now have to fight for the rights of her eldest son as once she had fought for Frederick's, and that meant she must stay at her post in the Hague, as near to the scene of action as possible.

Meanwhile, the other exiled queen was still hoping to be offered asylum by her daughter's husband. Mr John Pory, indefatigable writer of newsletters, had heard from a correspondent in Brussels that 'the French there, with the queen mother and monsieur, made account to have kept a brave Christmas here at London, and for that purpose had trussed up their trinkets half topmast high; but it seemeth they reckoned before their host that should have been, K[ing] C[harles]'.[36] King Charles, supported by a nervous Lord Treasurer, continued resolute in his determination not to let Marie de Medici into the country and had dispatched his trusted confidential servant Will Murray to Flanders to try, as tactfully as possible, to persuade her to give up the idea of coming to England.

Unusually for him, Charles had been rather unwell just recently with a fever and rash on his face and chest which the doctors diagnosed as a mild case of smallpox. He himself made light of his indisposition and refused to stay in bed, 'but all the day long he is up in a warm room with a fur gown on his back, and is merry, and eats and drinks heartily', while Henrietta, heedless of the risk of infection, kept him company, helping to amuse him 'with some game or other'.[37] He was fully recovered by the middle of December and ready for the Christmas festivities, one of the high spots that year being a pastoral play which the queen, with some of her ladies and all the maids of honour, had been rehearsing for months. *The Shepheard's Paradise*, a romance loosely based, it has been suggested,

BUCKINGHAM

on Charles's and Steenie's long ago escapade in Spain, was an inordinately long and indigestible piece of work, heavily laced with gobbets of neo-Platonic philosophy. Written by Walter Montagu, a leading member of the queen's circle, it was said to be intended as well for her majesty's recreation 'as for the exercise of her English', which was even now apparently still far from perfect.

This would be the first time since her appearance in *Artenice* back in February 1626 that Henrietta had taken a speaking role in court theatricals and she worked conscientiously on the eight hundred turgid verses of her part as Bellesa, the Princess of Navarre – the ladies were said to have been coached by a professional actor from the Globe Theatre. The performance, with sets and costumes by Inigo Jones, took place on 9 January in the Lower Court at Somerset House before an audience 1633 hand-picked for the occasion. John Pory heard that the Lord Chamberlain had directed that 'no chambermaid shall enter, unless she will sit cross-legged on the top of a bulk'. On the other hand, 'no great lady shall be kept out, though she have but mean apparel, and a worse face, and no inferior lady or woman shall be let in, but such as have extreme brave apparel and better faces'.[38] In fact, the most important qualification for all the spectators, whatever their degree, would seem to have been sheer staying-power, for *The Shepheard's Paradise*, astonishingly, lasted for more than seven hours!

Although actresses might be acceptable in sophisticated court circles, popular prejudice against women on the stage remained as strong as ever. A company of French players which included actresses had recently been hooted out of the theatre at Blackfriars, and about the end of November 1632 William Prynne, barrister of Lincoln's Inn and Puritan polemicist, published his notorious *Histrio Mastix* – a comprehensive and uncompromising denunciation of the evils of all stage plays, players and play-going. Since the king and queen were both well known to be enthusiastic theatre lovers, this was at best impolitic but Prynne was sailing dangerously near the wind when he went on to assert that the frequenting of stage plays by kings and emperors had in the past been 'the just occasions of their untimely deaths', citing, among others, the example of Emperor Nero, murdered as he came from the theatre.

Prynne also attacked dancing, another favourite royal diversion, as 'heathenish, carnall, worldly, sensuall and misbeseeming Christians', as well as certain church practices, such as organ playing between the lessons, which he considered verged on the theatrical. But it was an entry in his Index under Women which excited the most public interest. 'Women actors notorious whores,' it ran. St Paul had specifically prohibited women from speaking publicly in church; how dared then 'any Christian woman be so more than whorishly impudent as to act, to speak publicly on a stage (perchance in man's apparel and cut hair) in the presence of sundry men and women'. Prynne always denied that this insulting reference was aimed at the queen, but the fact that it occurred right at the end of a work appearing so close to the date of her pastoral, well known to be in preparation, was too much for the authorities, and it was generally thought that his words were likely 'to cost him his ears, or heavily punished and deeply fined'.[39]

This turned out to be a pretty accurate forecast. The unlucky Prynne was arrested and brought before the Star Chamber charged with having published a libellous book against his majesty and the state, and was condemned to stand in the pillory while his ears were cropped and his book burned in front of him. He was further sentenced to perpetual imprisonment, to be fined £5,000, expelled from his Inn and stripped of his university degree.[40]

Across the Channel Nemesis was catching up with some other transgressors. In February 1633 Cardinal Richelieu was at last in possession of enough evidence to enable him to deal with the enemies who had been pursuing him for so many years, and both Henrietta's old friends, the Marquis de Chateauneuf and the Chevalier de Jars, who had rather unwisely returned home, were arrested and imprisoned. In March, Richard Weston's son Jerome, on his way back from a diplomatic mission in France, intercepted a letter from the Earl of Holland illicitly on its way to Paris by royal courier and found it to contain another letter written by the queen. These letters proved harmless enough, being no more than pleas on behalf of de Jars, but the episode led to a furious row between the rival Weston and Holland factions and Holland challenged young Weston to a duel. He told his father, who told the king, who promptly put a stop to it. Charles would not allow anything so uncouth as duelling among his servants and was particularly annoyed when he discovered that the combatants were to have met in one of the palace gardens. Lord Holland was banished to his house at Kensington and ordered to consider himself under arrest; but the court at once took sides, the queen's friends accusing Jerome Weston of cowardice and flocking out to visit the earl in open defiance of the king and the Lord Treasurer, who had recently been created Earl of Portland.[41]

The Venetian ambassador thought Holland would surely be ruined, despite having 'the favour and protection of the queen', but Charles evidently found it impossible to resist Henrietta's coaxing, especially perhaps because she was pregnant again. Holland escaped with a serious reprimand and was soon back in his accustomed place, having been officially 'reconciled' with Jerome.[42] It was, though, an unmistakable snub to the ambitious and manipulative coterie which had begun to gather round the queen and another indication that, however much he loved her, the king was not prepared to give in to his wife over any really significant matter of government policy. His support for the Westons had been unqualified and Portland remained securely in power and favour.

At the beginning of May the king left for the north for his much-postponed Scottish coronation, leaving the queen at Greenwich. It would be their longest separation to date and Henrietta was described as 'a perfect mourning turtle'. All the same, she managed to find some diversions. Going up-river with a fleet of boats to visit the widowed Duchess of Buckingham, she challenged George Goring to a race 'over a long course of the Thames'. The royal barque won and Goring had to pay her majesty 500 crowns, much to the amusement of all the ladies and cavaliers who were following the contestants in the other boats and no doubt laying bets on their own account.[43]

The king did not linger in the land of his birth. He was crowned at Holyrood on 18 June with enough accompanying ritual to cause some of those present to experience 'great fear of inbringing of Popery' and a month later, after a brief tour of the Lowlands, he was on his way home, travelling so fast that he covered the distance from Berwick to London in only four days. 'By this haste', remarked Vicenzo Gussoni, 'he wished to take the queen by surprise, so as to make his return more welcome to her when she was not expecting him.'[44]

Charles was concerned about his wife's health. Soon after his return she had tripped up on level ground and fallen and her anxious husband ordered her to go to bed at once. Fortunately no harm was done, but a few weeks later she was suffering from a bad cold and severe pains down her right side, which the doctors attributed to 'a troublesome pregnancy', and she herself told Mamie St Georges that she was 'not a little incommoded' by her size.[45]

About the middle of September Henrietta retired to St James's Palace, always her preferred venue for lying-in, to await her confinement and the baby, another boy, arrived safely on Monday 14 October. Captain John Pennington heard that the new Duke of York was 'a goodly, lusty child, God be thanked', but soon a story had begun to spread that the infant was ailing and no wonder, seeing that the queen had insisted on engaging a Catholic nurse! 'To the astonishment and remark of many', wrote Gussoni, 'she had persuaded the king to agree to her choice of a lady who openly professes the Catholic faith. . . . There was much to say about the oath to be required of her [this was the Oath of Allegiance first required of Catholics in the aftermath of the Gunpowder Plot], but in the end the queen overcame everything and induced the king to agree to

1633

an ordinary oath of fealty, such as is taken by other Catholics who take part in the queen's service.'[46] The baby prince survived in spite of his nurse's dangerous religious proclivities, and was christened James (after his grandfather) by William Laud, newly elevated to the Archbishopric of Canterbury.

That Christmas the king had 'invited' the Inns of Court to present him with a masque to demonstrate the legal profession's repudiation of William Prynne and his odious prejudices. Despite the considerable expense involved, the benchers responded with enthusiasm. Inigo Jones as usual was responsible for the sets and costumes and the schoolmaster-turned-dramatist James Shirley was made an honorary member of Grays Inn and commissioned to provide a script. This was written in close collaboration with a committee of senior lawyers, who had seen an opportunity to convey a discreet warning to the monarch, whose absolutist tendencies were beginning to give some people serious cause for concern.

The Triumph of Peace was staged at Candlemas and was chiefly remembered for the spectacular torchlight procession or 'riding show' of masquers, most of them law students, parading through the streets from Holborn to Whitehall. This 'numerous stately and glittering cavalcade' attracted a large and appreciative crowd of Londoners, who seldom got the chance to see anything of the colour and brilliance of court entertainments. There was such a crush in the Banqueting Hall, where the performance was to take place, that the king and queen had some difficulty reaching their seats, but everyone, including the king and queen, greatly enjoyed the show, which consisted largely of a series of comic interludes where a variety of bawds, wanton wenches, gamesters and other undesirables were vanquished by Peace, Justice and Law. Indeed, the king enjoyed it so much that he ordered a repeat performance. Unfortunately, though, the underlying message that the royal prerogative could not exist without the law – 'we cannot flourish but together' – had been wasted on his majesty.[47]

A fortnight later Charles was appearing in his own Shrovetide masque, admission strictly for ticket-holders only. Written by Thomas Carew, a poet of some distinction, *Coelum Britannicum* dealt with the theme of unity – of the king with his people, of his three kingdoms and, finally, the pure and perfect matrimonial union of the king and his queen. The very gods of Olympus are so impressed by their example that they mean to reform heaven on the pattern of the Stuart court and Jove has the word Carlomaria engraved on his ceiling. The king, of course, remains the dominant partner in this union, but the queen is granted full recognition of her place at his side as his 'twin' and 'royal half'.

> This royal pair, for whom Fate will
> Make motion cease and time stand still,
> Since good is here so perfect as no worth
> Is left for after ages to bring forth.

Coelum Britannicum ended with Charles and his attendant lords presented as the heroes of a New Age of Great Britain – an age of unity made possible by Stuart rule, with Religion, Truth, Wisdom, Concord, Reputation and Government all hovering in the clouds above Windsor Castle.[48]

The Christmas and carnival seasons over, the king and queen left for their annual visit to Newmarket before returning to Greenwich to get ready for the summer progress, which this year was to take them further afield than usual, the queen having apparently expressed a wish to see something of the 'northern parts'. At the end of May the Prince of Wales, sometimes styled Prince of Great Britain, celebrated his fourth birthday, the occasion being marked by a bull- and bear-baiting. There was an amusing incident when the Dutch ambassador came to take leave of the queen and paid his respects to the dwarf Geoffrey Hudson, who happened to be present, under the impression that he was the little prince! Realising his mistake too late, the poor man tried to apologise, 'which only made her majesty and the others who were standing by, laugh the more'.[49]

It was mid-July before the king and queen set out for the north, going by way of Belvoir Castle as far as Welbeck, where they were lavishly entertained by William Cavendish, Earl of Newcastle, at a cost, so it is said, of some £15,000. Fortunately, his lordship was one of the richest men in the country. Their return journey took the royal party to Nottingham, Tutbury, with its unhappy associations with the king's grandmother, Mary, Queen of Scots, and to Holdenby, Christopher Hatton's prodigy house which Charles would later know again in very different circumstances.

With the benefit of hindsight, it is possible to think of that summer of 1634 as the high point of the king's personal rule, and Charles certainly had superficial cause for complacency. 'Never was there private family more at full peace and tranquillity than in this glorious kingdom,' wrote Sir John Goring to Secretary John Coke, 'for we hear not of the least disorder therein from one end thereof to the other.'[50] The king's own private family life, too, seemed idyllic. He was completely happy in his marriage and there were three healthy children growing up in the royal nursery, with every likelihood of more to follow – tiny and fragile-looking though she might be, Henrietta Maria was proving surprisingly successful in fulfilling the first duty of a queen consort. She herself in later years would often recall this period of her life, telling her friend and confidante Françoise de Motteville that she had been the happiest and most fortunate of queens, 'for not only had I every pleasure the heart could desire; I had a husband who adored me'.[51] If only Charles had been able to change places with, say, one of his recent hosts and live like any wealthy private gentleman, a role to which he would have been ideally suited, ruling his local neighbourhood, indulging his passion for field sports and his undoubted flair for collecting works of art, then this blissful state of affairs might very well have continued undisturbed. As it was, the demands of the outside world would keep breaking in on that charmed inner circle which the royal couple had created around themselves.

There was a new French ambassador at court that autumn. Henrietta had openly disliked his predecessor and Jean d'Angennes, Marquis de Poigny, had been warned that he might find her majesty distant towards him at first. However, de Poigny, 'a cavalier of mature age and of admirable and open nature', seems to have made a favourable initial impression. This was rather spoilt when he tried to demand the dismissal of Madame Ventelet, the queen's dresser, and now almost the only survivor of the 1626 purge, who was suspected by Cardinal Richelieu of having had a hand in Chateauneuf's intrigues. The queen, faithful as ever to her friends, refused even to consider such a thing and the ambassador was told that the king was unwilling to order his household for the satisfaction of others. Madame Ventelet stayed where she was and de Poigny began to be 'looked at askance'.[52]

Richelieu had been disappointed by Henrietta's own involvement with Chateauneuf and with the Chevalier de Jars, whom she was still trying to get released from prison. The Cardinal had, in fact, been disappointed by her generally unhelpful attitude towards her homeland ever since her marriage, something he blamed largely on her identification with her tiresome mother and younger brother; but Gaston had now returned to France and was apparently fully reconciled with Louis. The meeting between the brothers took place at St Germain on 21 October 'with extraordinary demonstrations of affection on both sides' and this would, it was hoped, make Henrietta feel more sympathetic towards the cardinal's government.

Richelieu was also hoping to interest Charles in a triple alliance with the States of Holland in an effort to contain the disagreeably increasing power of Spain and the Austrian Hapsburgs. Since the death of the King of Sweden, the fortunes of the Scandinavian and German Protestants had been in sharp decline and that August they had suffered a crushing defeat at the hands of an imperial Hapsburg army. The French were aware that, given Charles's financial circumstances, there was not much to be got out of England but, reported the Venetians, 'they would be content if they could deprive Spain of the power of receiving any advantage from her'.

De Poigny was finding Charles irritatingly hard to pin down: he was always either away hunting or else 'engaged in other recreations', but his majesty told the Dutch ambassador that he was resolved to live at peace with everyone and did not wish to be more partial to one side than the other. 'He did not want the House of Austria to advance to excessive power,' he went on, 'but neither was the increase and too evident aggrandisement of France a thing to desire. He would be glad to see a universal adjustment, and would much rather employ himself upon that than in fomenting a war which had been carried on too long in Christendom.'[53] The little friend of all the world omitted to mention that he was just then seriously considering signing a treaty with Spain with the object of curbing Dutch and French naval power, and Anzolo Correr, the new Venetian ambassador in London, noticed that a resentful attitude of mind towards France was common in the king and his ministers, 'due to their natural antipathy to the French'.

Although it was clear by this time that Henrietta exerted very little political influence over her husband – or at any rate was making very little positive effort to do so – she was believed to disapprove of his pro-Spanish leanings, and Richelieu still reckoned that she might yet prove useful in helping to promote his foreign policy. The Cardinal had more reason to be pleased with the fruits of the other purpose behind her marriage for, according to Father Cyprien, the English Catholics were now enjoying 'a sweet and agreeable peace'.

In fact, there is really nothing to indicate that this gratifying state of affairs was due to any conscious plan of action on the queen's part. Her personal influence and example were important, of course. Her chapels at St James's and Somerset House were always open, and the edicts forbidding the king's subjects to attend mass there no longer appeared to be enforced. Many of her friends were either Catholics themselves or Catholic sympathisers – several of them became converts – and could count on her protection, while there are a number of scattered instances of indulgence being shown to individual Catholics as a result of her intercession; but there is no evidence that she was motivated by anything beyond a simple readiness to help any stray co-religionist who happened to approach her. Charles himself, freed from the nagging voice of parliament, gave no sign of wanting to pursue an aggressive anti-Catholic policy. As long as the Catholic community in the country did nothing to draw attention to itself and offered no threat to his authority, he seemed content to leave it pretty much alone. Indeed, just as his own high Anglican sympathies had often caused his more fundamentalist subjects to harbour grave suspicions as to the purity of his Protestantism, so, as time went on, hopes began to rise in Catholic circles over the possibility of his conversion, and even, just conceivably, of an English reconciliation with Rome.

In the spring of 1633 the Earl of Angus, a devout Scottish Catholic, had sent his kinsman, Robert Douglas, over to Rome armed with letters of recommendation from the queen and her confessor. His instructions were to approach Francesco Barberini, Cardinal Secretary of State and official Protector of England and Scotland, with a request that the Pope should be asked to consider raising one of the king's subjects to the cardinalate – both as a gesture of goodwill and to encourage Charles to establish regular diplomatic relations with the Holy See. A suitable candidate for a Red Hat, it was suggested, might be George Con, another Scot and a member of Barberini's own household.

Barberini hesitated. The plan was a bold one and might easily backfire on the papacy and the English Catholics by rousing the fury of the Puritan faction. He consulted his colleague Cardinal del Bagno, who was held to be something of an expert on English affairs and after protracted discussions – the Vatican never did anything in a hurry – it was agreed that the best course would be to send an unofficial envoy privately to London to assess the situation on the spot. Such an envoy could try to settle the damaging internal disputes which were currently causing scandal among the English Catholics, who had been without any overall guiding authority for some years now. He could also talk to the queen and try to discover just how much influence she really did possess and how far she was prepared to go for the furtherance of the Catholic cause.[54]

Cardinal del Bagno was inclined to be sceptical. The fact that Henrietta had never been crowned must, it was felt, count against her. Also it appeared that she and her ladies spent most of their time in dancing and other frivolous pursuits.[55] Nevertheless, the queen was now, in her mid-twenties, a mature wife and mother with a husband whose devotion to her had become a matter of international admiration. Surely the time had come to start taking her more seriously, to show her some support and give her a chance to redeem those solemn undertakings she had given her family and the Holy Father at the time of her marriage.

CHAPTER FIVE

The Catholic Queen

The Catholics are no longer hated or persecuted with the old severity. The public services in the queen's chapel are most freely frequented by very great numbers, while those of the ambassadors are crowded.

The Venetian Ambassador's report, 29 May 1637

It was not until December 1634 that the papal envoy finally reached England. Gregorio Panzani, a secular priest of Chiesa Nuova (St Philip's Oratory), was met on arrival by the queen's confessor who arranged for him to see Henrietta without delay, her active support and protection being essential to the success of his mission.

Panzani presented his letters of credence and proceeded to assure her majesty of the 'extraordinary respect' which both the Pope and Cardinal Barberini felt for her, and their appreciation of the fact that so much ease had been procured for the English Catholics by her influence. He went on to request, in the cardinal's name, that she would continue to 'shew herself a parent to that neglected handful of people and use her interest to bring them to a good understanding among themselves who of late had been unhappily divided'. Henrietta replied with suitable civilities, promising that nothing should be wanting on her part to further assist her co-religionists, and Panzani then explained that the Holy Father expected King Charles's Catholic subjects to be 'exact and scrupulous' in their civil allegiance, hoping that his majesty would not press them beyond the limits of their duty in matters of religion. He also asked that the king should be told of his arrival.[1]

Panzani had no official diplomatic status – in fact his visit was supposed to be an official secret – but he took lodgings near St Martin's-in-the-Fields, on the fringe of the Whitehall palace complex, and was soon making contact with such well-placed Catholic sympathisers as Secretary of State Francis Windebank and Chancellor of the Exchequer Francis, Lord Cottington. He was impressed by the degree of compliance, 'not to say affection', shown by the court party towards the Roman see. Not only were English Catholics able to attend mass at the various embassy chapels, as well as at those at St James's Palace and Somerset House but, he reported, Catholic schoolmasters were allowed to teach in several parts of the city of London, and even the king's own preachers 'often took occasion to run into the praises of the moderate papists'. Altars and images were mentioned with respect and many, 'in common conversation', wished for a reunion with Rome. The king himself, it was whispered, had been heard to say that 'he would willingly have parted with one of his hands rather than such a schism should ever have happened.' All this, Panzani concluded, 'was attributed to the influence the court had upon the minds of the people, and originally to the queen's religion, and to the king's uxorious temper'.[2]

Nevertheless, it was several weeks before the queen succeeded in persuading her husband to grant Panzani an audience and they had to be brought together privately in a 'remote and unsuspected place'. Charles greeted the Italian graciously, taking off his hat as a mark of respect, while Panzani kissed his hand before proceeding to give his majesty an account of his business in England, 'with an ample assurance of the great affection his holiness had for him, and a grateful remembrance of the kind treatment the Catholics had met with under his majesty's mild and prudent reign'. Charles returned these compliments 'in a very obliging manner', and went on to say that, as to the Catholics, 'he was resolved none of their blood should be spilt during his reign', although he could not conceal the provocations offered to him by some of their party – a reference to a recent Jesuit pamphlet defending the right of subjects to depose a heretical sovereign. Panzani could only reply in general terms, repeating that he knew it was the Pope's desire that the Catholics should be punctual in obedience to his majesty and that it was expected, or rather hoped, that in return they should enjoy reasonable indulgence in the practice of their religion. On which somewhat indecisive note the interview came to an end.[3]

Before he left Rome, Panzani had been warned not to meddle in politics and not to discuss controversial matters with non-Catholics but, encouraged – and misled – by the apparent cordiality of his welcome, he had already begun to discuss with Windebank and Cottington such highly controversial matters as a possible modification of the Oath of Allegiance and the appointment of a new Vicar Apostolic, or bishop, with spiritual authority over the Catholic community, to replace Dr Richard Smith, Bishop of Chalcedon, who had been driven out of England four years previously. Windebank objected that the Protestant clergy would never tolerate such a thing, but Panzani, hearing a rumour that there had been complaints about the queen's Capuchins – that they were too numerous and too inquisitive about state affairs – and that the king was planning to get rid of some of them, thought he could see a way round this. Early in February 1635 he wrote to Cardinal Barberini suggesting that the new bishop should succeed the Abbé Duperron, the queen's present Almoner,

1635

102

and that the Capuchins be replaced by English priests, who could not be accused of 'tampering in favour of a foreign power'. By this means, he pointed out hopefully, the queen's chapel would be served and the bishop could exercise his jurisdiction and make his visitations at convenient times and still 'comply with all the queen expected of him in quality of almoner'. Panzani considered the appointing of a bishop to be a matter of some urgency, if only to curb the pretensions of the Jesuits, who were doing their best to take control of the English mission, 'daily making new conquests and incorporating youths of the best families into their society', while the secular clergy were in an abandoned state, 'living under a kind of anarchy without an immediate head'.[4]

But the authorities in Rome were not pleased by the way in which Panzani had been exceeding his instructions, and Barberini wrote back ordering him in no uncertain manner to stop disputing over the Oath of Allegiance, about which there could be no compromise. Nor was there to be any more loose talk about reunification. As far as the bishop was concerned, he was also being far too hasty. 'Time is required to become acquainted with the factions of a country' and Panzani was still a stranger to the missionary priests who were his main enquiry. His task was to see, hear and observe and only then to 'endeavour to silence all past animosities'. It was definitely not his business to start trying to interfere in the queen's family and risk offending her.[5]

It seems unlikely that Henrietta was aware of Panzani's interesting plans for rearranging her household, for the court was especially gay that winter season, 'not a day passing without dancing and comedies'. At the centre of this social whirl had been the marriage of thirteen-year-old Mary Villiers to Charles Herbert, the young son and heir of the Earl of Pembroke. The Pembrokes were trusted friends of the king and queen, who loved Wilton and made it one of their favourite holiday resorts, while Charles had virtually adopted the dead Buckingham's children, being particularly fond of young Mary. The Villiers–Herbert wedding was, therefore, a very grand affair which took place in the queen's closet at Whitehall in the presence of the king, and afterwards 'by his command a most sumptuous banquet was given to the flower of the nobility'.[6]

The queen was also busy with rehearsals for her annual Shrovetide masque. *The Temple of Love*, devised by William Davenant, dealt with the by now familiar theme of platonic love, which consisted only of 'Contemplation and Ideas of the Mind', and was free from all 'sensual Appetite' or anything so gross as 'carnal Fruition'. Henrietta appeared as the island queen Indamora, a variation of her customary role as the semi-divine embodiment of chaste love, who rescues some noble youths from the seductive toils of certain evil magicians, the enemies of platonic love and pure thought, and 'by the influence of her beauty' succeeds in re-establishing a Temple of Chaste Love on the island of Britain. *The Temple of Love* had its first performance on 10 February with fifteen of the queen's ladies, who now formed a highly trained and competent *corps de ballet*, and 'nine gentlemen of title' in the cast. Scenery, stage machinery and costumes were felt to be well up to standard, and the production contained one of Inigo Jones's spectaculars – a seascape in which Indamora and her attendant nymphs glided across a lagoon fringed with tropical vegetation in 'a maritime chariot made of spongy rock stuff mixed with shells, seaweeds, coral, and pearl'. Altogether it was, in the opinion of one spectator, an occasion 'truly worthy of so great a queen'.[7]

The party season over once more, Charles, who was nothing if not a creature of habit, prepared to leave for Newmarket and the queen went with him, albeit a little reluctantly, because, as the Venetian ambassador put it, 'of the inconveniences of that country'. Certainly the climate of East Anglia in February could be remarkably cheerless and Henrietta came down with a feverish cold which kept her in bed for several days. She had, however, fully recovered by mid-March, in time to accompany the king on a visit of inspection to some of the ships he was having repaired and refitted.

Charles had recently embarked on an ambitious programme of naval expansion, in order, so it was given out, 'to secure the coasts of Great Britain and Ireland, and to free them from pirates and others that commit hostilities and insolencies there'. But a strong navy, desirable though it might be, had to be paid for and in the autumn of 1634 writs demanding the payment of ship-money had been issued to all the maritime counties which were, by ancient custom, obligated to contribute to the support of those vessels maintained by the crown for home defence and the protection of trade. This sudden resurrection in time of peace of an antique levy not imposed since the days of Elizabeth 'greatly stirred and exasperated' the lieges, and the city of London, ordered to provide the wherewithal for seven ships, well armed and equipped, took legal advice which was unanimously of the opinion that 'money could not reasonably be obtained from the people without infraction of the laws, by any way but the ordinary one of parliament'. Strong pressure was, however, brought to bear on the Lord Mayor and in the end, after much debate and grumbling, the city fathers reluctantly paid up.[8]

The grumbling continued, Anzolo Correr reporting that, although 'the lesser folk, who have least power agree to pay fairly readily . . . others of a higher condition do not follow this course, and they try to evade it as much as they can'. Some gentlemen, in fact, had let it be known that they did not intend to pay anything. 'They say that every law and custom exonerates them from such contributions, which can only be raised by the authority of parliament.' But, added the ambassador, 'as only a few seem inclined to follow their example, they will have to use the ointment of patience for their ills'.[9] Resentment over what looked uncommonly like a form of illegal extra-parliamentary taxation was increased by a suspicion that the king was expropriating 'some parcels of this money' for his own private use. 'The whole city cries out about this and complains bitterly.'[10] Nevertheless, when, in August 1635, demands for ship-money were extended to cover the inland counties, reaction was less hostile than might have been expected. 'Perhaps', commented Anzolo Correr, 'habit makes it less sensible, or at least more supportable.'

Although ship-money has become the best remembered, it was by no means the only source of revenue currently being tapped by the government. These ranged from so-called 'fiscal feudalism', such as exacting fines from all freeholders worth more than £40 a year who had not applied to be knighted and fees from those who had, and a revival of the centuries-old Forest Courts with power to impose fines for the technical offence of trespass on former royal game preserves, to the reappearance of monopolies, thinly disguised as 'patents', granting favoured individuals sole rights to the manufacture and marketing of a variety of commodities from soap to beaver hats.

The architects of the ingeniously contrived foundation underpinning the king's house of cards were the Attorney-General William Noy, with his encyclopedic knowledge and skilful manipulation of the law, and the Earl of Portland, whose management of the Treasury had at least kept court corruption and waste and royal extravagance within reasonable bounds. But Noy had died in 1634, unlamented by the propertied classes, to be followed in March 1635 by Portland, and thereafter there would be no one on the Council with either the administrative ability or the authority to assure the crown's continuing financial independence.

Competition to succeed to the Lord Treasurer's prestigious and powerful place was naturally intense – the leading contenders being the abrasive Thomas Wentworth, Lord Deputy in Ireland, sponsored by Archbishop Laud, and Francis Cottington, who was the queen's favoured candidate. But the king was in no hurry to come to a decision. He appointed a committee, chaired by Laud, to run the Treasury on a temporary basis, and it was a full year before he finally 'satisfied the curiosity of the court and ended the agitation of the claimants' by unexpectedly giving the top job to William Juxon, Bishop of London. Juxon was an honest, good-natured man, unlikely to tread on anyone's toes and possessing the added advantage of having no family interests to advance, but, reported Anzolo Correr, the court would rather on the whole that the choice had fallen on someone with greater experience of the world. 'They do not think that one who has never had occasion to deal with anything but ecclesiastical affairs can have the capacity required for discharging such an office.' Juxon, too, was known to be a protégé of William Laud and his promotion seemed to indicate the archbishop's growing ascendancy.[11]

Abroad it was hoped that, freed from Portland's restrictive influence, the king might now be persuaded to call another parliament, which would give him the means to take a more active part in foreign adventures. In Paris Cardinal Richelieu, who was on the point of declaring war on the Austrian Hapsburgs, certainly hoped so. He had been planning since January to send a special envoy over to London to try to breathe new life into his efforts to secure an anti-Spanish alliance and also, if possible, to put an end to Henrietta's long-standing hostility towards him; by a fortunate coincidence this individual was to arrive within days of Portland's death. Described as being 'a perfect courtier of ladies', the Marquis de Senneterre wasted no time in making himself agreeable to the queen and was soon reporting that her majesty appeared to have more power than previously because, in the struggle for the Treasurership, everybody from the Archbishop of Canterbury downwards was competing for her favour, 'since in fact she is very influential and well loved by the king'.[12]

There was never any question about the king's love for his wife, although it sometimes seemed strange to outsiders that there should be so much 'genuine reciprocal and exemplary goodwill' between them, considering their differences in temperament and religion. But Charles was not in the habit of talking politics with her and Senneterre, like everyone else, consistently overestimated the queen's ability to influence him. No ambassador ever seemed to grasp the fact that Henrietta, who saw everything in terms of personalities, was simply not interested in affairs of state unless, of course, one of her friends happened to be involved. She supported Francis Cottington because she liked him and found him an amusing and sympathetic companion. She worried intermittently about her mother, still holed up in Flanders, though here again she was unable to persuade Charles to grant her asylum, and she agreed to try to help Senneterre because she saw an opportunity to exert pressure on Richelieu to release the Chevalier de Jars.[13]

But while she made a conscientious effort to promote French interests – in September she was telling Senneterre that she thought the king would soon agree to the raising of the English troops for service with France and would also offer naval support – Henrietta had other, more congenial preoccupations in 1635. At the beginning of May the court was at Greenwich, where she was able to watch the finishing touches being put to the building of the Queen's House, or the House of Delights as

Inigo Jones's charming little domestic palace was sometimes known. Then, in June, came the announcement that the king would not be undertaking any long journeys that year because the queen was pregnant again – a piece of news which, according to Anzolo Correr, seemed to give their majesties and the whole court extraordinary pleasure.

The queen spent a quiet summer in the country, mostly at Oatlands and Hampton Court, amusing herself by 'getting her maids to perform pastorals and comedies and other pleasant diversions', while Charles went off on a curtailed progress. The unusually hot dry weather brought its inevitable crop of fevers and dysentery, and at the end of August the Prince of Wales went down with 'a slight fever' which brought his mother hurrying over to Richmond to see him. But fortunately the little boy recovered quickly and, as the fine weather continued into the autumn, it was November, a month later than usual, before the court returned to London for the season. Henrietta had suffered a good deal of discomfort during the early stages of her pregnancy but now, in the eighth month, she appeared to be in excellent health and was still going about and visiting the theatre. That autumn, too, there was the thrill of seeing the long-delayed arrival of Peter Paul Rubens' famous ceiling panels for the Banqueting House, which were shipped over from Antwerp in October.

Charles had by this time acquired an international reputation as an art collector and connoisseur. 'He takes great delight in sculpture and painting,' wrote Vicenzo Gussoni in his *Relation of England*, 'and he professes and indeed possesses a skilled and thorough knowledge of both.'[14] The king's artistic tastes had already been registered by the Vatican. The queen had asked Cardinal Barberini 'to use his interest' to persuade the fashionable and much sought-after sculptor Giovanni Bernini to make busts of the king and herself. Charles, too, was eager to purchase a statue of Adonis which he had heard was now in the Villa Ludovisi near Rome. Unhappily this proved to be impossible as the owner, another collector, refused to sell, but Barberini arranged to send Henrietta a selection of gifts which included 'an extraordinarily fine relic case' containing a bone of St Martina, virgin and martyr. The king expressed surprise and admiration over the beauty of the reliquary's workmanship and Barberini told Giulio Mazarin, nuncio at the French court, that he would not hesitate to rob Rome of her most valuable ornaments 'if, in exchange, we might be so happy as to have the King of England's name stand among those princes who submit themselves to the apostolic see'.[15]

Barberini's apparent belief that Charles could be lured back to Rome by such means may seem unduly simplistic, but in 1635 the possibility of reunion was being quite seriously discussed in some quarters. Gregorio Panzani may not have been very successful in bringing the Jesuits to heel, but he had helped to bring about a dramatic break-through on the diplomatic front. The question of a semi-official exchange of representatives between London and Rome – or rather between the Pope and his god-daughter the Queen of England – had been tentatively raised in conversation between Panzani and Francis Windebank as early as February. Cottington and Barberini became involved and the cardinal asked the queen's confessor, as someone with first-hand knowledge of the religious climate in England, to report on the feasibility of the project.

Father Philip was of the opinion that the king and several of his ministers 'were far from being averse to an union' but warned that it would be a very dangerous undertaking, pointing out that those who were most favourably inclined to the Catholic cause were often forced to give proofs of their zeal to the contrary 'for fear of notice', so that it was difficult to form a true idea of their feelings. (He may have been thinking of the late Lord Treasurer, who was rumoured to have died a Catholic.) He also felt bound to draw attention to the awkward fact that whenever there was a pressing need for money, the king was obliged, 'contrary to his inclination', to enforce the recusancy laws, as otherwise no money would be forthcoming from the Puritanical House of Commons and the government of England was such that no extraordinary levies could be granted without the consent of the people. Nevertheless, if a reciprocal agency could be set on foot, 'there might be some hopes of a reunion' and Father Philip proceeded to list the necessary qualifications for a successful papal agent.

The list was a formidable one. The chosen candidate must be neither too old nor too young – thirty-five seemed about right. He should be well-born, rich, handsome, affable in conversation but grave and reserved, at ease in the company of ladies but always careful to keep a proper distance, 'the king and queen being strictly virtuous and professed enemies to immodesty and gallantry'. Above all he must be tactful and patient, never blaming the king or his advisers for the severities sometimes practised against the Roman Catholics, nor must he appear too zealous to have them relieved from their hardships. He must make every effort to please the queen and cultivate the goodwill of the privy councillors, most, if not all of whom could be bought, or 'enticed with proper baits' as Father Philip put it. By employing this 'softly softly' approach the papal agent might hope to win a gradual relaxation of the penal laws and, by encouraging moderate Protestants to speak in favour of the Catholics, break down prejudice until a de facto liberty of conscience became generally accepted. Then, 'in a few years, the leading men of both houses [of Parliament] might be induced to think of an union'.[16]

The next step was to secure the king's agreement to the plan and this proved surprisingly easy, Charles stipulating only that he must himself nominate the man to go to Rome, and insisting that the matter be kept a close secret for the time being. After some delay, his choice of agent fell on Arthur Brett, a former gentleman of the bedchamber to King James; a Catholic who had seen military service abroad, he was a trusted favourite of the king and queen. Charles was anxious that it should be made absolutely clear that whoever went to Rome went as the queen's personal representative only with no mandate from himself, but all the same, in November, Brett received some private instructions from the king. Among other things, he was to try to persuade the Pope to lift his ban on the English Catholics taking the controversial Oath of Allegiance and also seek papal support for the restitution of the Palatinate to the king's nephew. If he was successful, then Charles indicated that he might after all agree to the appointment of a Catholic bishop in England, something he had so far flatly refused to consider.[17]

Underlying the changeable course of Charles's foreign policy there had always been the faint but persistent hope that some day, somehow, he might be able to prevail on someone to help him restore the fortunes of his sister and her family, conscious that his failure to do so remained a standing reproach among his subjects and, worse, a humiliating stain on his honour. The problem of the Palatinate was also now about to take on a special immediacy with the arrival, in time for Christmas, of the young Prince Palatine himself, sent by his mother who also cherished a persistent, if unrealistic hope that some day, somehow, her brother would be in a position to come to her rescue.

Charles Louis, the late Elector Frederick's eldest surviving son, was just eighteen, a dark-haired, rather melancholy youth, whose teenage years had been spent in a succession of fruitless attempts to recover his lost inheritance. His arrival in England was marred by a near-fatal mishap. A welcoming salute of guns was fired as, after a long and dangerous crossing, he entered Dover harbour, but, recorded Anzolo Correr, 'a badly aimed shot struck the Palatine's ship, killing five persons, including two German gentlemen, who were not more than a couple of paces from the Palatine himself'.[18] Having survived this daunting introduction, the prince came ashore to be greeted by the Earl of Arundel and was conducted ceremoniously up to London, where the king was waiting to receive him. The king was, in fact, not over-eager to receive his unfortunate young relative. To most Englishmen the prince personified the whole embattled Protestant cause and his coming would, as Correr remarked, 'certainly be greeted with acclamations from the general [public], with whom he is very popular because of his mother'.[19] But for his uncle, his presence would inevitably serve as an embarrassing reminder of his family's plight and of the king's inability to help them.

None of this could be allowed to appear, of course, and Charles and Henrietta welcomed the Palatine 'in a private manner, but most courteously' in the queen's apartments. Charles Louis was naturally on his best behaviour and his pleasing modesty and good manners made an excellent impression on the court. The king took to him at once, treating him with 'a familiarity and affection . . . that cannot be exaggerated' and there was talk of sending for his next brother, Rupert.

The Christmas season was now in full swing. 'Comedies, festivities and balls are the order of the day here', wrote Anzolo Correr, 'and are indulged in every day at court for the prince's sake, while all the greatest lords vie with each other in entertaining him.'[20] The festivities included the performance by the queen's ladies of a pastoral play in French for the benefit of the Palatine, although his command of English had turned out to be better than expected. Henrietta herself did not take part. She was now within days of her delivery which was planned to take place as usual at St James's Palace and where she duly gave birth to a daughter on 28 December, a cold wintry day with snow on the ground. The baby was christened five days later by Archbishop Laud and given the name Elizabeth as a compliment to her aunt, the Queen of Bohemia, the Prince Palatine standing godfather.

Henrietta was still lying-in when a consignment of works of art arrived for her from Cardinal Barberini – 'a far richer present for her Britannic majesty than he had formerly sent'. Panzani had been commissioned to deliver them to the queen and Henrietta ordered that they should be brought into her bedchamber. Charles, excited as a child on Christmas morning, came hurrying over to St James's and the pictures – works by Corregio, Veronese, da Vinci, Andrea del Sarto, and Giulio Romano among others – were unpacked there and then to the delight of the king and of Inigo Jones, who had accompanied him. Only the queen, finding no devotional subjects among them, was rather disappointed.[21]

There were no royal masques that year, owing to the installation of the Rubens ceiling in the Banqueting House and the queen's childbed. But Henrietta again made a quick recovery and Charles was able to go off to Newmarket at the end of January satisfied that she and the baby were both doing well. The Prince Palatine, however, was not at all well. He had been obliged to take to his bed immediately after the christening ceremony with a feverish attack caused, so Anzolo Correr believed, by a surfeit of hospitality, all the lords having insisted on wining and dining him every day without any regard to his health or digestion. He recovered enough to join his uncle at Newmarket in February, but then went down again with another quite severe fever. It was not known in London how serious it was, but the Venetians heard that in addition to his fever the prince was also

110

suffering from acute depression. 'This is unsuitable for his years', remarked Correr, who thought it was probably the result of natural disappointment and frustration, 'because the resolutions which he expected from this quarter move very slowly and are involved in difficulties.'[22] This was a studied understatement. Poor Charles Louis had yet to face the fact that all those lavish dinners, the theatricals, court balls and avuncular affability concealed a total inability even to begin to finance the sort of military force which would be needed to have the slightest chance of wresting the Palatinate from Hapsburg clutches. His brother Rupert had now arrived from Holland but, although the king received him 'with every sign of the warmest affection', he was not quite so welcome to the rest of the royal entourage who, remembering that the Queen of Bohemia still had several more hopeful and penniless sons growing up at the Hague, 'feared that by degrees they will all come and will take root'.[23]

It was a quiet, rather sad spring. The plague was threatening to become 1636 bad again and the king and queen had decided to spend the remainder of Lent out at Hampton Court instead of at Greenwich. The court was in mourning, too, for sixteen-year-old Charles Herbert, who had died of smallpox in Florence while on the Grand Tour. 'His Majesty feels it especially,' wrote Correr, partly because of the loss to the Earl of Pembroke, his Lord Chamberlain and one of his closest friends, 'and because the young man recently married a daughter of the late Duke of Buckingham, whose memory is deeply rooted in his affection.'[24]

Death was also to overtake Arthur Brett while on his way to Rome and a replacement had to be found. Gregorio Panzani noted that the matter was now being discussed quite openly, even by the Puritan faction, as if it were an ordinary embassy to any foreign court. Luckily, 'there was about the court one William Hamilton, a zealous Catholic, a young gentleman of about twenty-five years of age, nobly descended and allied to the royal family. His figure was fine; and in conversation he was agreeable and witty.' He seemed an excellent choice, though there were mutterings in some quarters about the wisdom of employing another Scot, two Scots in fact, since the papal agent was to be George Con, but 'by their majesties' joint consent' Hamilton was appointed to go to Rome.[25] He set out in May, carrying the same instructions as had been given to Brett, and reached his destination towards the end of June. At his first audience he made an elegant speech in the queen's name, declaring her intention of keeping one of her servants to reside in Rome in order that 'the state of the Catholics in England might be well understood there'. He touched briefly on the subject of a bishop for the English and concluded with 'a modest representation' of the Elector Palatine's case, which he hoped the Holy Father would consider, 'so that it might purchase ease to that distressed family and contribute to the general good of religion'. But since the Palatine family was well known to be of the Calvinist persuasion, it seemed rather unlikely that the Pope would consider its relief to be a priority. Urban replied 'with a great deal of good nature and sweetness of temper', while remaining noticeably non-committal, especially with regard to the Palatine. This, he indicated, was a very complicated case 'and the Roman see was seldom applied to in composing such differences'.[26]

The court had returned to town for Easter and one day in April, after doing a little shopping on Ludgate Hill, the king and queen went on to visit the Bethlem Hospital without Bishopsgate 'to see the mad folks, where they were madly entertained'. Unfortunately the occasion was somewhat marred by two of the female inmates, whose foul language so shocked their majesties that they and their attendants were 'almost frighted out of the house'.[27] At the beginning of May, Henrietta accompanied the Prince Palatine to a play at Blackfriars, but by the middle of the month the theatres were closing and Anzolo Correr reported that the court was once more planning to retreat to Hampton Court, 'so as not to be exposed to the plague which grows worse every day. . . . People foretell great destruction,' he went on gloomily, 'the evil being aided by the warmth of the season', and he feared that if the disease continued to spread the city would soon be deserted.[28] Correr saw the queen before she left and remarked that she seemed very nervous of the plague, telling him that she would certainly not allow anyone from an infected area to be admitted where she was staying.

With the coming of spring Franco-Spanish hostilities had resumed. On 23 June the Spanish army in Flanders had crossed the frontier into Picardy and a month later was over the Somme. Meanwhile, in England a vigorous campaign was being waged to persuade the king to join France in the war with Spain – a campaign which had brought some unlikely individuals into temporary alliance. These ranged from the queen herself, the Marquis de Senneterre and Walter Montagu, son of the Earl of Manchester and a recent convert to Catholicism, to the founders of the Providence Island Company, a group of Puritan sympathisers headed by Henrietta's old friend Lord Holland and his brother the Earl of Warwick, the Lords Brooke and Saye and Sele, John Pym and John Hampden. Providence Island in the Caribbean was a colonising venture originally intended as a sanctuary where Puritans could worship without interference, but memories of Drake and Hawkins were still green and the directors of the company soon began to dream of setting up a base from which godly privateers could prey on the Spanish silver fleets.

The arrival of the Prince Palatine had given added impetus to the anti-Spanish faction who were making every effort to induce the king to call parliament, urging the necessity of being well armed at sea while at the same time withholding the payment of ship-money. 'In the matter of the Palatine', wrote Anzolo Correr at the beginning of January, 'they go further, saying that it is impossible to do anything properly or seemly for this crown unless they take up arms resolutely.'[29] But although the ship-money contributions came in slowly and reluctantly, in the end everybody paid them 'to the bitter disappointment of those who hoped, by hanging back, to compel the king to convoke parliament'.[30]

The apparent alliance of the queen and the Puritans has been held to show that her so-called party or faction in the 1630s was not exclusively Catholic, but Henrietta had long had a number of non-Catholic friends – the principal qualities necessary for admission to her circle being aristocratic connections, courtly grace of manner and a talent to amuse. As a young woman, reported Panzani, she loved to gossip and hear 'lively stories and witticisms'. People with axes of their own to grind were naturally quick to make use of her name, but she herself seems to have done little more to further the aims of the Spanish war party than show hostility towards the Hispanophile Secretary Windebank and make fun of the Austrian ambassador.[31] Her concern was, as always, entirely personal – she welcomed a possible rapprochement with Richelieu if that would get de Jars out of prison and enable her mother to go home to France. When the Polish envoy begged her to use her influence to promote the match between his king and one of the Palatine princesses which was then under discussion, Correr remarked that 'she promised everything but has done little, as she is usually reluctant to interfere in matters of grave consequence, especially those which concern the interests of the state'.[32]

1636

July 1636 saw the arrival of George Con, the new papal agent, who landed at Rye on the 17th and was presented to the king and queen by Panzani. Their majesties, reported Anzolo Correr, 'received him with the greatest courtesy and it was particularly observed that the king seemed extraordinarily pleased at his arrival. This has much perturbed the lords and leading ministers, who fear this novel and free revival of confidential relations with the Holy See will in the end give rise to divisions and bitter hatred.'[33]

It was turning into another very hot dry summer and the king had been constantly on the move to avoid the plague which was still spreading through the southern counties, but Oxford was so far unaffected and at the end of August the whole court descended on the city for three days packed with Latin orations, sermons, sightseeing, play-going and dinners. The king and queen were greeted a mile out on the Woodstock road by Archbishop Laud in his capacity as Chancellor of the University and were escorted to lodgings at Christ Church by all the dignitaries of town and gown. Honorary degrees were conferred on the two Palatine princes and the royal party inspected the new quadrangle and library at Laud's own college of St John's before being entertained to a grand banquet at which the cooks had so contrived the baked meats 'that there was first the forms of archbishops, then bishops, doctors, etc. seen in order, wherein the king and courtiers took much content'. Several plays were put on during the course of the visit, one of which, *The Royal Slave*, pleased the queen so much that she asked to have the costumes and scenery sent to Hampton Court, 'that she might see her own players act it over again and see whether they could do it as well as it was done in the university'.[34]

George Con and Gregorio Panzani were also in Oxford for the royal visit. Con had been to have a look at the Bodleian which he thought very impressive though not, of course, anything to touch the Vatican Library, and he and Panzani were invited to the banquet at St John's. Con was in fact receiving a flattering amount of attention from the great and good. Already in his first six weeks in England he had been the guest of the Earl of Northumberland at Castle Ashby and had come to Oxford in the Marquis of Hamilton's party. His welcome into these exclusive circles was due in part to his nationality – as a Scot he would have found a number of influential compatriots at court – and, of course, it helped that he was himself very presentable, being well-bred, good-looking and good company. Most important, though, was the obvious fact that the king had taken an immediate fancy to this civilised and charismatic newcomer.

The exact nature of Con's mission remained a matter for speculation and rumours were already circulating that he had come to 'reconcile', that is to convert, his majesty – rumours which Charles dismissed as no more than malicious gossip. But Anzolo Correr was not so sure. Early in September he reported that he believed the Pope was cherishing the idea of rendering his name glorious to posterity by 'a work at once great, charitable and pious, in fine to bring the king himself over to the Roman faith. . . . No nation is made more of at Rome just now than the English,' he went on, adding that in London the priests had never enjoyed so much liberty, while the Catholics were not only able to hear mass at the queen's and embassy chapels without fear of arrest, but anyone who wished to have mass celebrated in his own house could do so with only a very little circumspection. 'This is all due to the connivance of the ruler', wrote Correr, 'and indicates if not a leaning to the rites of the Roman Church, at least an absence of aversion.'[35]

George Con had come to England well provided with gifts from both the Pope and Cardinal Barberini, whose secretary he had been, and had wasted no time in presenting the queen with a particularly beautiful diamond cross, the stones arranged in clusters in the form of bees, the badge of the Barberini family to which Pope and cardinal belonged. Henrietta had immediately fastened this round her neck and when she showed it to the king, he examined it with great interest, exclaiming 'is it possible, my heart, that the Pope has given you this?' When she said he had, Charles went on, 'I am very glad of it, because I shall change the opinion I have hitherto held that the priests of Rome are always ready to take, but never give anything away.' According to Correr, 'those present noticed that his Majesty uttered this jest with a very straight face without a smile. This is considered very remarkable, because they give the words "I shall change my opinion" a much more extensive and profound meaning.' Nevertheless, the Venetian thought that too much should not be made of it, as only time would bring the truth to light.[36]

Con had brought a picture of St Catherine, intending to have it framed before giving it to the queen, but 'declaring that she would take that trouble herself, she took away from me the tin case and the packthread with which it was tied and gave orders that the picture should be fastened to the curtains of her bed'. He also presented her with several rosaries of aloe wood, agate and one of buffalo horn 'curiously worked with cameo medallions'. He had not forgotten the Catholic ladies and maids of the household and rosaries were distributed among them by Father Philip in the queen's presence. When nearly all was finished, Con reported that the dwarf Geoffrey Hudson 'began to call out, "Madam, show the father that I also am a Catholic", with a manner and gesture that made all laugh. To the Marchioness of Hamilton, the Countess of Denbigh and the Countess of Holland, some trifle was also given.'[37]

The papal envoys found the Queen of England delightfully unspoilt. She blushed like a girl in the presence of strangers and Father Philip had told them that she was without sin, except those of omission. She was apparently never troubled by temptations of the flesh and 'when she confesses and communicates, she is so earnest that she surprises her confessor and all'. No one, it seemed, was ever admitted to her bedchamber except other ladies 'with whom she sometimes retires, and employs herself on light, but innocent matters'. In spite of her reputation for frivolity, she suffered from occasional bouts of melancholy, when she liked to be quiet and have 'recourse earnestly to God'. But Con had noticed that the queen 'thinks little of the future, trusting entirely to the king'. This was all very well, but if there was to be any hope of the king's conversion or, indeed, of a reunion with Rome, she would have to exert herself to play a more active part in affairs. 'She must endeavour more to gain the ministers of state, of whom, if she wishes, she may be the mistress.'[38]

Like the king, Henrietta had been spending the summer in the country, moving around to avoid the plague. In September, not long after the

Oxford visit, she was at Oatlands where a very alarming report reached her that a madman, Rochester Carr, brother of one of the Gentlemen of the Bedchamber, had escaped from his keepers, threatening that he would go to court to kill the king and marry the queen, 'not doubting that when he had achieved this he would be master of England'. The queen, now some twelve weeks into her sixth pregnancy, was so upset by this that her laces had to be cut 'to give her more breath'. Carr had been quickly recaptured but Henrietta, remembering perhaps those other assassins who had successfully struck down her father and the great Duke of Buckingham, remained in a state of acute anxiety until the king came in person to reassure her of his safety. 'He did this the more readily', reported Anzolo Correr, 'because she is known to be again enceinte with . . . more trouble than she is accustomed to experience, and he was afraid that she might be in some danger.'[39]

Although the plague had begun to subside with the onset of autumn, the epidemic was still serious enough to keep the theatres closed and the court out of London, but plans were going ahead for the grand opening of the chapel at Somerset House, now at last nearing completion, and the queen was back in town by early December in time to attend the first mass to be celebrated there. She was determined that it should be a memorable occasion and, according to Father Cyprien de Gamache, had given instructions that the service should be held 'with all possible pomp and magnificence'. The Capuchins had therefore approached François Dieussart, an eminent Flemish sculptor who had recently come to work in London and who designed a special stage set for them, displaying the Holy Sacrament in the centre of a Paradise of glory. Two pillars, forty feet in height, supported an arch in front of the high altar, with space on either side for the choir, organ and other instruments, and providing access for the priests coming from the sacristy to a portable altar set up beneath the arch. 'Behind the altar was seen a Paraclete, raised above seven ranges of clouds, in which were figures of archangels, of cherubim, of seraphim, to the number of two hundred, some adoring the Holy Sacrament, others singing and playing on all sorts of musical instruments, the whole painted and placed according to the rules of perspective.' Nine circles of decreasing size led the eye on to the Sacrament itself, which lay surrounded with red and gold and so skilfully lit 'that the painting seeming to vanish, there was left but the brilliancy of the lights, which caused that place to appear all on fire'. There were some four hundred lights altogether, as well as 'a great multitude of tapers ingeniously arranged upon the altar, which lighted the first circles'. As soon as the queen and her court were settled in their places, the curtains which had been hung to conceal the 'stage' were drawn back and simultaneously 'music, composed of excellent voices, set up an anthem, the harmony of which having no outlet but between the clouds and the figures of Angels, it seemed as if the whole Paradise was full of music, and as if the Angels were themselves the musicians'.

The effect of this *coup de théâtre* was stunning, even on an audience accustomed to the audio-visual sophistication of the court masque. Henrietta was seen to shed tears and Father Cyprien thought one must have a heart of stone not to be moved by the beauty and solemnity of this first pontifical high mass to be celebrated in England for nearly a hundred years. After dinner the queen came back to the chapel for vespers and her Grand Almoner brought the proceedings of that emotionally charged day to a close by preaching a 'very eloquent and very pathetic sermon', taking his text from the Psalms: 'This is the Lord's doing, and it is marvellous in our eyes.'[40]

The queen now retired but the packed congregation had some difficulty in forcing its way out 'on account of the crowd of people who were bent on forcing their way in to see the magnificence displayed there'. According to Father Cyprien the crush lasted so long that it was impossible to close the doors of the church till the third night, when the king ordered that it should be cleared of strangers so that he could come and see its wonders for himself. Charles stood for some time with his eyes fixed on Dieussart's composition, and then said aloud 'that he had never seen anything more beautiful or more ingeniously designed'. Throngs of sightseers, both Catholic and Protestant, continued to besiege Somerset House, and the queen gave orders that the chapel should be left with all its decorations until Christmas.[41]

Some sharp wintry weather having further reduced the incidence of plague, Charles and Henrietta decided it would be safe to go out to Greenwich to inspect the progress of the building work still going on around the Queen's House, and on their way down-river they stopped off to visit the Capuchins' austere living quarters adjoining Somerset House. They saw the sparsely furnished cells and the refectory, where they shared the friars' frugal supper, and those present reported that the king 'seemed to have enjoyed it very much'. The visit was an informal, spur of the moment affair prompted, so Anzolo Correr believed, by no more than the king's desire to please his wife and it would normally have attracted very little outside attention. But in December 1636 it gave rise to a good deal of talk. The arrival of a second papal envoy, together with the interest excited by the opening of the new chapel, had already roused Protestant suspicions, never very far below the surface. In particular, wrote Correr, 'those who claim the name of Puritans' were watching George Con with jealous eyes, noting his close relations with the queen's

1636

confessor and the Capuchins of her church, and saying 'that they may form conventicles and plots against the repose of the people and the general quiet of the realm. . . . Those also who for other reasons call passionately for the convocation of Parliament, increase their outcry . . . declaring that the excessive desire to avoid hurting the interests of the Catholics is leading to greater and more serious hurt to the crown.'[42]

Christmas that year was spent at Hampton Court and on Twelfth Night the king's company of players put on a production of *The Royal Slave*, the play which had been so much admired at Oxford. After a brief lull over the New Year period plague had broken out again in the capital, the result, so it was said, of the number of citizens returning to their unaired and infected houses, and soon a hundred deaths a week were being reported. Nevertheless, Henrietta insisted on coming back to town early in February, drawn more by superstition than any other reason, thought Anzolo Correr, 'as she is near her delivery and she imagines that it will not turn out well in any house but St James's'.[43] Certainly St James's had always proved lucky for her in the past and so this time, after only two hours' labour, the queen gave birth on 17 March to her third daughter and fifth surviving child. The baby was christened Anne after her paternal grandmother in a private family ceremony, the six-year-old Prince of Wales and the Princess Mary officiating as godparents.

Throughout the winter pressure had been mounting on the king to recall parliament, commit himself to a strict offensive and defensive league with France and declare war on the Hapsburgs. The Earl of Warwick went so far as to guarantee that if his majesty would indeed join with France in making war on the House of Austria for the recovery of the Palatinate, 'parliament would readily consent to supply him with all that he might desire to ask of it'. 'It now seems,' wrote the Venetian ambassador, 'that many of the leading men of the realm are determined to make a final effort to bring the forms of government back to their former state. They hold secret meetings for the purpose of achieving this result.'[44]

When, in January 1637, the Earl of Arundel came home empty-handed from a diplomatic mission to Vienna, it began to look as if Charles had finally made up his mind to come down off the fence. On 20 February Archbishop Laud told his friend and ally Thomas Wentworth that since it now appeared that no help for the Prince Elector could be expected from Spain, he verily believed 'it will in time grow into a war'.[45] A week later Charles himself wrote to Wentworth: 'Upon Arundell's return, I have perceived that directly, which heretofore I have much feared, to wit, the impossibility of restoring my sister and nephews by fair means, at least without threatening. This has made me fall in with France.'[46]

Negotiations with France continued through the spring and early summer and the terms of a treaty were drafted and discussed, but that was as far as it went. The French, who had now succeeded in driving the Spaniards back into Flanders, remained deeply suspicious of English good faith. 'They want things to suit themselves,' remarked Cardinal Richelieu, 'to avoid pledging themselves and do nothing while we do a great deal.' The English, for their part, complained about French bloodymindedness, and although Charles seems to have seriously considered the idea of undertaking a limited naval campaign independently of parliament he was still reluctant to sacrifice the country's valuable Spanish trade. In any case, according to the Venetians, he had 'not yet got his courage so high as to plunge right away into so great and costly a war'.[47] Henrietta, too, had begun to lose her initial enthusiasm for the project. The French ambassador de Poigny had died suddenly back in January and in July the Marquis de Senneterre returned disillusioned to France; the queen was being drawn more and more under the influence of George Con, who disapproved of her Puritan connections and, fairly or unfairly, was identified with Spanish interests.

Gregorio Panzani had gone back to Rome at the end of 1636, leaving Con securely established as a much sought-after member of London society. 'It is certainly a wonderful thing', wrote Anzolo Corror, 'to see in England a dependant of the Holy See not only living at liberty, but frequenting the court at all hours with so much confidence, and having such familiar access to the king's ear, as if he was one of his most intimate servants. . . . As a consequence of this even the most rigid and scrupulous Protestants esteem and honour him, visiting him frequently in his own house.'[48]

Charles appeared to have forgotten that the papal agent was supposed to be accredited only to the queen and the two men saw each other on an almost daily basis, both in public and private. But although they enjoyed a number of stimulating intellectual discussions on points of theology over cosy little dinners with the queen and Father Philip at Somerset House, Con soon came regretfully to the conclusion that there was little realistic chance of achieving a reconciliation. 'The king's conversion is more a matter to be desired than to be genuinely hoped for,' he told Barberini three months after his arrival, and reunion with Rome seemed an even more distant prospect. 'All is in the hands of God, especially the king's heart.'[49]

Con therefore concentrated his efforts on building up a dévot party round the queen, which would, he hoped, eventually become powerful enough to influence government policy, and the year 1637 was to be marked by a spectacular efflorescence of English Catholicism. 'The Catholics are no longer hated or persecuted with the old severity,' reported Anzolo Corror towards the end of May. 'The public services in

1637

the queen's chapel are most freely frequented by very great numbers, while those of the ambassadors are crowded, although the priests constantly celebrate mass in private houses without scruple.'[50]

George Con had opened a chapel in his rented house, where mass was said continually from morning till noon, while at Somerset House Father Cyprien de Gamache was able to boast that 'not a day passed without bringing some penitents to the confessional'. Here, too, mass was said every day from 6 a.m. until noon and on Sundays and festivals 'the throng was so great that one could not get in without great difficulty', people sometimes having to queue for as much as two or three hours to make their confessions.[51]

The Capuchins were now openly teaching the Catholic doctrine in English every Wednesday and Saturday, first catechising the children, 'who were very numerous', and then delivering a short discourse expatiating on the gratitude which those present owed to God for all the benefits they had received from him, 'and particularly for their vocation to the Catholic religion, as it was really true that there was no salvation for those who are separated from it, and die in that unhappy separation'. This, declared Father Cyprien, touched those Protestants who came out of curiosity but who would often return for further instruction and ask to be reconciled to the Catholic church 'which their forefathers had criminally forsaken'.[52]

The queen's Grand Almoner had also now joined in the battle for souls. The unassuming Abbé Duperron had recently been created Bishop of Angoulême (so Henrietta had a bishop in her household again after all) and, according to Anzolo Correr, had laid aside circumspection 'and seems to have openly undertaken not only the protection of the Catholics, but the increase of the Roman Catholic faith in every direction. He no longer has any scruple about frequenting openly the houses of the Protestants, and when there he takes the opportunity to dispute with them and with the women in particular.'[53]

Watching the crowds of worshippers flocking to mass, while the Pope's representative was being publicly petted by the king and queen and lionised by government ministers, Protestant Londoners could be forgiven for regarding all this new freedom as the not-so-thin end of a pretty sizeable wedge. In fact, although metropolitan Catholics, especially those having any connection with the court, were, temporarily at any rate, enjoying something very close to liberty of conscience, in the country at large Catholics attempting to practise their faith continued to be a disadvantaged minority very much at the mercy of the local authorities charged with enforcing the penal laws and, with the exception of those members of the aristocracy influential enough to overawe parish constables and churchwardens, finding that recusancy could still often be an expensive luxury.

But if the recusant Catholics and the priests who ministered to their needs remained public enemy number one in the eyes of most good English Protestants, by the 1630s the primate of the established church was coming under increasing attack from the Puritan party, who commonly called him 'the Pope of England'. William Laud was a fussy little man with an obsessive passion for good order and discipline (he would today no doubt be described as a control freak) and for restoring some at least of the old ceremonial and visual elements to Anglican worship. Among his most fiercely resented reforms was his insistence on the removal of communion tables from the body of the church and their replacement by railed-off stone altars attached to the east wall, as in pre-Reformation days. He was also known to favour auricular confession, bowing to the east and the reintroduction of candlesticks, images and other decorations so much deplored by Puritans, who worked themselves into a positive froth of indignation over 'the cringing and ducking to altars, the barking, roaring and grunting of choristers, and the silk and satin divines' of Laud's church.[54] To the radical pamphleteers all priests and bishops were little more than limbs of Antichrist, while the archbishop was accused in the crudest terms of not merely protecting the Catholics but of being himself a closet papist intent on preparing the Church of England for a Roman takeover.

This last was certainly unfair. Laud disapproved strongly of the latitude being allowed to the Catholics and was carefully avoiding any public contact with the papal agent, but felt powerless to act in view of the king's present attitude and the growing influence of the queen. As early as April 1637 he was writing gloomily to Wentworth: 'I conceive it most true that the party of the Queen grows very strong. And I fear some consequence of it very much.'[55]

Henrietta had never cared for Laud, the son of a tradesman who possessed none of the blue-blooded connections or social graces necessary for success at court. A confirmed bachelor, he was ill at ease in feminine company – 'I have no conversation with women' – and even his appearance was against him. A small, stout, bustling, red-faced man, he tended disastrously to look ridiculous in his archiepiscopal regalia, and with his 'hasty, sharp way of expressing himself' had an unfortunate talent for making enemies. He nevertheless enjoyed the king's confidence, Charles fully sharing his authoritarian views, and the queen's party was beginning to regard him as a potentially dangerous opponent.

The plague was still bad that spring and Anzolo Correr believed the summer progress would take the court further away than usual to avoid infection, but the king and queen were at Greenwich during June and paid a visit to town at the beginning of August for the marriage of the widowed Mary Villiers to the king's cousin James Stewart, Duke of Lennox. The ceremony was performed by Laud in the chapel at Lambeth Palace, Charles himself giving the young bride away. The king then went off hunting in the New Forest, while the queen spent the rest of the summer quietly at Oatlands or over at Richmond with the children.

These were the halcyon years of the Van Dyck portraits which depicted the ornamental little queen, curled, bejewelled and always most exquisitely presented. They were idealised portraits of course. Van Dyck was a court painter who knew his business, but he was also an artist of integrity and although Henrietta was certainly never beautiful in any classical sense, she had immense vitality and an instinctive flair for chic. Even more significantly, at this period of her life she possessed all the radiant serenity of a contented woman who knows herself to be greatly loved – 'I had a husband who adored me' – something which can give even the plainest a transforming bloom of happiness. As George Con had noticed, the queen was never one for looking into the future, but as she travelled the few miles through the Surrey countryside from Weybridge to Richmond to see her children (Van Dyck's famous portrait of them was painted in 1637), there was really no reason why she should have foreseen that this would be her last truly carefree summer. If she had heard the reports of a recent disturbance in the cathedral at Edinburgh they were not likely to have caused her any particular concern or even to have interested her very much.

By the end of September the plague had abated at last and the king was back at Hampton Court from where he and the queen and all the court journeyed down-river to Deptford 'to take part in the solemn function of launching and naming a very fine galleon, which has been building for some time by the most renowned craftsmen of the realm'.[56] This was the state-of-the-art *Sovereign of the Seas,* of over 1,500 tons burden, the first warship mounting three decks of guns and carrying more than ninety large cannon. Wonderfully carved and gilded and costing altogether more than £65,000, the *Sovereign* was to be the pride of the ship-money fleet and was intended to impress the continental powers with the King of England's mastery of the seas.[57] The King of England's own subjects might have been more impressed if the fleet had been seen to be doing more to justify its expensive existence than patrolling self-importantly up and down the Channel, harassing Dutch fishing boats and being pointedly ignored by the French. In the summer of 1637 its chief preoccupation appeared to be with escorting the Palatine princes back to Holland; although, to be fair, a squadron commanded by William Rainsborough which had been blockading the Moroccan pirate base of

Sallee did secure the release of a number of slaves and, for a while at least, curtailed the activities of the notorious Sallee rovers.

A third writ of ship-money had been issued in October 1636 and it was becoming increasingly clear to the more thoughtful members of the tax-paying classes that, as long as he could maintain himself by this and other dubious methods of fiscal feudalism, the king had no intention of ever calling another parliament. It was a worrying prospect and in the autumn of 1637 an intransigent Buckinghamshire squire insisted on having the legality or otherwise of his refusal to pay decided in open court.

John Hampden's famous ship-money test case opened in early November, by which time the king and queen were once more in residence at Whitehall where concern was growing over the number of Catholics, crypto-Catholics and their sympathisers surrounding the queen. These included Walter Montagu, Toby Mathew (he who had once acted as guide and interpreter to the young Henrietta Maria), Sir Kenelm Digby, son of one of the Gunpowder Plotters, Henry Jermyn and even the Secretary Francis Windebank, who had been drawn into the queen's circle by Con. And there were the ladies – the Duchess of Buckingham, who had fallen out of favour with the king since her remarriage to the Earl of Antrim, the Countesses of Arundel, Carnarvon and Portland, Lady Katherine Howard, Lady Anne Weston and Olive, née Boteler, a niece of the Duke of Buckingham and wife of the king's confidential Gentleman of the Bedchamber Endymion Porter.

Olive Porter in particular was a zealous proselytiser, specialising in the deathbed conversions of her relatives. When, in March 1637, she heard that her father was dangerously ill, she had descended on him, moved him to London, called in the priests and succeeded in 'reconciling' him in the nick of time. Later in the summer, her brother-in-law was also received into the church on his deathbed. Her next target was her cousin the Marchioness of Hamilton, who had been one of Henrietta's first English friends. In October Mary Hamilton lay dying of 'a wasting disease' and again, like a bird of ill omen, Olive appeared at the bedside, armed with controversial books and arguments. Whether she was successful on this occasion is open to question, for Lady Hamilton's conversion was never openly acknowledged. Then, in November, Olive's sister, the Countess of Newport, previously an apparently staunch Protestant, announced that she, too, had gone over to Rome. This caused a considerable political row, the king and the lady's husband in particular being 'bitterly displeased'. As Master of the Ordnance, a half-brother of Lord Holland and a member of the inner circle at court – he had been one of the masquers appearing in *The Temple of Love*, Lord Newport was an important man, at least in his own estimation, and he was seriously alarmed lest his position should be compromised by his wife's defection. He therefore appealed to William Laud, who seized on the opportunity to bring up the whole matter of the 'increasing Roman party' and the freedom being allowed to it at a meeting of the Privy Council. The archbishop singled out Montagu and Toby Mathew for special censure, both of them having been named by Lord Newport, together with George Con, as the instruments of his wife's conversion, or 'perversion' as Laud preferred to think of it, and he asked for them to be called to account.[58]

In fact, neither Montagu nor Mathew seem to have had anything to do with the matter which was more likely the work of Con and the Capuchins, but the king 'did use such words' of them that they were thoroughly frightened and found it prudent to lie very low for a while. Laud had hesitated to denounce George Con – as for Signor Con 'he knew not how he came to England or what he did there and therefore would say nothing of him'.[59] But other people were not so circumspect and some pretty harsh things were being said about the Pope's agent by those who had long been irked by his presence. More seriously, according to Anzolo Correr, 'by this stroke he has certainly lost much of his Majesty's favour, and if the king were not unwilling to offend the queen, he might possible take some resentful measures against him'. However, Correr had heard that 'if he continues to make similar achievements' his stay would not last much longer, and, in the ambassador's opinion, if England was ever to be brought back into communion with Rome, the Pope's representatives would be better employed disputing with the bishops and convincing them, rather than trying 'to profit by the simplicity of women, over whose weak minds the last impressions are always the strongest'.[60]

One woman who was not at all weak-minded and who remained a force to be reckoned with was, of course, the queen. She had heard all about Laud's attack on her friends at the Council table and did not attempt to conceal her displeasure. 'I doubt not but I have enemies enough to make use of this,' his grace wrote mournfully to Thomas Wentworth. 'But howsoever I must bear it, and get out of the briers as I can. Indeed, my Lord, I have a very hard task, and God (I beseech Him) make me good corn, for I am between two great factions very like corn between two millstones.'[61]

Repercussions of the Newport affair rumbled on till the end of the year and developed into a battle of wills between the archbishop and the queen over the issue of a proclamation 'Restraining the Withdrawing his Majesties Subjects from the Church of England and Giving Scandall in Resorting to Masses'. Con and Henrietta both worked hard to prevent its publication, or at least to ensure that the sting was drawn out of it first. The king stood firm up to a point, telling Con that 'by your good leave, I desire to show I am of the religion I profess', but he was not proof against his wife's persuasions and the proclamation, when it finally appeared on 20 December, amounted to very little more than a reminder to anyone seeking to win converts to 'the Roman superstition' that laws and penalties existed which his majesty could enforce whenever he saw fit.[62] The queen considered that she had won on points, and on Christmas Eve staged something very like a victory parade at Somerset House, attending midnight mass in the company of all the most recent recruits to 'the Roman superstition', with Anne Newport prominent among them. Afterwards she sent for Con, exclaiming triumphantly, 'you see the effect of the proclamation!' and the Venetians noted that everybody was now to be found gathering in the queen's apartments.[63]

There is no doubt that, under the hypnotic influence of the urbane Signor Con, Catholicism was becoming increasingly fashionable at court, particularly among the ladies – 'our great women fall away every day' – and especially since the opening of the queen's new chapel, of the visual and musical splendours of which one eye-witness remarked that 'Inigo Jones never presented a more curious Piece in any of the Masks at Whitehall'.[64]

After a two-year gap there were to be masques at Whitehall again and on 17 January the king presented *Britannia Triumphans*, scripted by William Davenant, sets and costumes as ever designed by Inigo Jones. In view of the on-going ship-money controversy (John Hampden's case was still being argued before the judges sitting in the Exchequer Chamber) the theme was a nautical one, with Charles cast as Britanocles, saviour of the western world,

> . . . thou treasure of our sight
> That art the hopeful morn of every
> day,

who has restored order to the seas and consequently brought the usual blessings of peace to his land, as the fleet 'with a prosperous gale entered the heaven'.[65]

The queen's masque, *Luminalia*, which followed on Shrove Tuesday, 6 February, was another typical Inigo Jones spectacular, representing the triumph of light over darkness, with Henrietta appearing as the goddess of brightness, haloed in 'a glory with rays'. Francesco Zonca, currently holding the fort at the Venetian embassy, found it 'a most pleasant entertainment', adding that 'it was noteworthy above all others presented for a long time past for the richness of the dresses and the subtlety of the inventions'.[66]

On the surface everything seemed much as usual, but when the king set out on his annual visit to Newmarket, Zonca reported that 'the greater part of the Council has gone with him, to assist in what may turn up', for it was no longer possible to ignore the firestorm spreading through Scotland. This had been sparked the previous July, when Charles and Laud, with their joint passion for order and conformity, had insisted on trying to foist a version of the English Book of Common Prayer – 'that fatal book', as Henrietta was later to describe it – on the Calvinistic Scottish kirk. The result had been an unseemly tumult in St Giles Cathedral, when a hail of stools and other missiles was directed at the unfortunate clergyman attempting to read the new liturgy, amid cries of 'the Mass is entered amongst us!' and 'Baal is in the church!' from the outraged congregation.[67] Resistance continued during the rest of the summer and autumn, becoming fiercer and more organised as the months passed. Exhortations emanating from London had no effect, the Scots repeatedly declaring 'orally and in writing that they will not obey the king's ordinances in the matter of the ceremonies and liturgies recently introduced', even protesting that they would go to mass at once 'rather than obey and conform to the present rites of England'.[68]

In February 1638 the king, astounded to discover that his royal wishes were not being attended to, issued a stern proclamation commanding his Scottish subjects to drop all opposition to the prayer book immediately, or be charged with treason. Within a matter of days a National Covenant had been drawn up in Edinburgh. This celebrated document was circulated throughout the country and signed by hundreds of thousands of Scots, not a few of them with their own blood, solemnly pledging themselves to defend the true reformed religion to the uttermost of their power against errors, corruptions and all innovations which had no warrant in the Word of God, and which plainly tended towards the re-establishing of popish tyranny and the subversion and ruin of the reformed religion.[69] The Scottish bishops, superimposed by King James on reluctant Presbyterians, were already beginning a prudent, if undignified, retreat over the border, while a worried Earl of Traquair, Treasurer of Scotland, on a visit to London begged the king not to drive his countrymen to despair, warning that if the English wanted 'that book' read in Scotland 'they must send an army of 40,000 men to defend the minister who must read it'.[70]

The queen was also now becoming worried about the situation, and Francesco Zonca heard 'from a very secret quarter' that she, too, had spoken to the king, begging him to satisfy the Scots, 'removing the fear of civil war, with danger to his royal person'. After all, she probably reasoned, it surely hardly mattered what form of heresy such hopeless cases chose to practise. Charles, however, had replied soothingly, telling her not to be alarmed and promising that 'when he wishes he can reduce those subjects to obedience as usual'.[71]

126

Thus reassured, Henrietta was able to turn her attention to making final preparations for the imminent arrival of the Duchesse de Chevreuse. The duchess, another long-standing enemy of Cardinal Richelieu, had been obliged to leave France in a hurry the previous September, taking refuge in Spain, and was now, she said, on her way to join the exiled Marie de Medici in Brussels. She landed at Portsmouth on 14 April to be greeted by Walter Montagu and Lord Goring, the queen's Master of the Horse. Arriving at Whitehall, she was at once conducted through the palace to the queen's Withdrawing Chamber, to be 'cheerfully welcomed with a kiss from both their Majestyes'. Henrietta, delighted to have this reunion with one of her girlhood friends, immediately offered her the tabouret – that is, the privilege of being seated in the royal presence – and the duchess was given lodgings 'richly furnished for her at the end of the Privy Garden next to King Street'. Her diet was also being provided at the rate of £40 a day, plus a further allowance of £200 a week for her petty expenses, and since she had arrived with only one maid and a couple of menservants, a supply 'of such as were necessary about her person (especially of women for her dressing etc.)' had to be hastily contrived out of the queen's own establishment.[72]

By no means everyone was happy about the attentions being lavished on Madame de Chevreuse who, as well as being a noted beauty and coquette, possessed a deserved reputation for mischief-making and intrigue. The recently arrived French ambassador in particular resented the fact that she had been granted the tabouret and he was vociferously, though unsuccessfully, demanding a similar honour for his wife, while the French government, afraid that the duchess might 'perform unfriendly offices' in London, was trying to persuade her to come home.[73]

The duchess, however, remained impervious to hints. 'Her departure for Flanders is postponed', wrote Francesco Zonca on 14 May, 'as she likes it here too much. . . . She has renewed her old acquaintances and is making new ones; all the lords pay her court and she passes the time merrily.' Among her previous acquaintances was her old flame Lord Holland and Zonca reported that she was already beginning to cause trouble, 'trying to convert the Earl of Holland to the Roman faith and win him for the Spanish party'. She was also, it seemed, 'artfully' throwing out suggestions about a possible marriage between the Princess Mary and the King of Spain's son, even pretending that she had the power to arrange it. Princess Mary was not yet seven years old, but while this was not necessarily too soon to be thinking about her future, memories of the last time an Anglo-Spanish marriage had been attempted did not inspire confidence and the Venetians were of the opinion that it would never come to anything.[74]

The royal children, though, were beginning to grow up. The Prince of Wales was approaching his eighth birthday, when he would have his own separate household with that 'fine gentleman' the Earl of Newcastle as his Governor, and on 19 May the court travelled down to Windsor to see the prince's installation as a knight of the Garter.

It was to be quite a year for family events, for in February had come the astonishing announcement that after twenty-three barren years the French queen was pregnant at last. Louis had written in his own hand to give his sister the joyful news and Henrietta responded at once with messages of congratulation. Writing to Mamie St Georges, she prayed that the pregnancy might continue (Anne had miscarried once before) and that it might produce a Dauphin. 'There will be work for Madame Peronne,' she went on. 'I must let her rest.'[75] That busy lady was not, as it happened, to be given much rest, for by mid-summer Henrietta knew that she was with child again.

By mid-summer, too, the great ship-money case had finally been brought to a conclusion, the judges pronouncing by a majority of seven to five that the king did indeed have the right to exact such payments from his subjects as he deemed necessary for the defence of the realm without recourse to parliament. Rex, in short, was Lex, 'for he is Lex Loquens, a living, a speaking, an acting law'.[76] Charles could not have put it better himself, but he had won a hollow victory and the ship-money grievances continued to fester, along with the general disquiet over his refusal to summon parliament, his repeated failure to assist the Palatine family, the frivolity and extravagance of his court and, most worrying of all, his tolerance – even, it sometimes seemed, encouragement – of the nest of papists surrounding his wife. But in the summer of 1638 it was the escalating crisis in Scotland which cast the longest shadow over public affairs.

Faced with the first serious challenge to his authority, the king's initial reaction had been his usual 'I mean to be obeyed,' but finding the Scots were not listening, he appears to have gone temporarily into denial – the Venetians could not understand his delay in moving 'to deal with a case of such importance'. At last, towards the end of May, he dispatched his kinsman, the Marquis of Hamilton, to treat with the Covenanters, who were now to all intents and purposes the ruling party in Scotland.

The marquis undertook his mission with reluctance, telling George Con that he had no hope in the world of doing any good, adding 'our countrymen are possessed of the devil'. His gloomiest forebodings were swiftly fulfilled and on 15 June he wrote to the king: 'I find most certainly that they [the Scots] will never disclaim nor give up the Covenant . . . alleging it to be warranted and to be justified by law, which is a tenet so dangerous to monarchy as I can not yet see how they will stand together.'

Hamilton was by now firmly convinced that the Covenanters would have to be suppressed by force of arms, but warned 'it will be a difficult work and bloody'.[77] Charles replied that he was preparing for war. 'I will only say that so long as this Covenant is in force . . . I have no more power in Scotland than as a Duke of Venice, which I will rather die than suffer.'[78]

But for all his brave words it was obvious that, in spite of his efforts to conceal it, the king was 'very distressed at heart'. Francesco Zonca reported that he was spending much less time than usual on his favourite pastime of hunting and had quite given up playing tennis. He had also drastically curtailed his summer progress, announcing that he meant to travel no more than twenty-five miles from London and would be back at Oatlands by the middle of August. Meanwhile, the Council was still very largely in the dark about his intentions. 'Various opinions are expressed about Scotland,' wrote Zonca in July. 'Some speak of orders to prepare artillery, arms and other implements of war, pointing to an inclination on his Majesty's part to use force to compel submission, but he lacks the chief nerve, namely the affection of his people and consequently money. . . . On the other hand the Scots have everything in order. They are united without any disagreements among themselves.'[79]

The queen was also at Oatlands that August, worrying about her husband and her mother. Marie de Medici, having finally outstayed her welcome in Brussels, had moved across the frontier into the United Provinces where she had been respectfully welcomed by the Prince of Orange, but her presence at the Hague quickly led to protests from the French ambassador and it was plain that she would soon have to move on again.

In September news came from France of the birth of a Dauphin. Henrietta was delighted. She had a Te Deum sung and bonfires were lighted, but the news from Scotland grew steadily worse. Charles had now been compelled to agree to a meeting of a General Assembly of the kirk but Lord Hamilton remained deeply pessimistic about the chances of restoring royal authority north of the border, 'the people being most obstinate about yielding a jot and ever more determined in their revolt'.[80]

In the circumstances it was particularly unfortunate that his majesty should now have been faced with the imminent prospect of a visit from his mother-in-law, something which he had been trying so hard to avoid for the past five years. This time, though, it looked as if no amount of discouragement was going to prevent the old lady from turning up on his doorstep, an expensive and certainly unwelcome guest. Archbishop Laud regarded her arrival as 'a miserable accident' and 'but a new beginning of evils'.[81]

1638

Marie de Medici landed at Harwich on 18 October and the king rode dutifully to meet her at Chelmsford, taking the young Duke of Lennox with him and escorted by the Gentlemen Pensioners. They returned to London on the 31st, to be greeted at Aldgate by the Lord Mayor and Aldermen in their scarlet gowns, and processed through streets decorated with banners and streamers and lined with the city trained bands and representatives of the livery companies.[82]

Henrietta was waiting with the children at St James's, where she had spent several weeks and a good deal of money preparing a suite of fifty rooms for her mother and that lady's hundred or so ramshackle and rapacious companions. The reunion of mother and daughter was an emotional occasion; falling into each other's arms they both shed tears, but Henrietta was certainly the only person to derive any pleasure from the dowager's arrival. Marie's reputation as a troublemaker had gone before her – her restless spirit being 'prone to embroil all wheresoever she came' – and the people 'were generally malcontent at her coming, and wished her farther off', especially when they discovered that it was costing £3,000 a month to supply her 'daily familiar needs'.[83] Nor did she endear herself to her hosts by 'maintaining the most rigid hauteur'. Giovanni Giustinian, the newly accredited Venetian ambassador, reported that when the Council went to pay its respects to the royal visitor 'she received it seated and responded in a few words. She did the same with the ladies and other great lords of the realm, being always very sparing with her courtesies. This has caused further murmurs, and increases the desire to see her out of the country.'[84]

There seemed little immediate prospect of this, King Louis remaining unmoved by all attempts to reconcile him with his wayward parent, and while Henrietta was earnestly assuring the murmurers that her mother's expenses would shortly be met by France, there seemed little sign of that happening either. The English ambassadors in Paris continued to urge that the queen-mother should be allowed to draw on her dower revenues, but Louis appeared quite content 'for the King of Great Britain to have the entire charge of this hospitality, although he did not invite his guest'.[85]

1638

The year ended in an atmosphere of gloom and anxiety. William Laud was never one to look on the bright side, but he probably summed up the prevailing mood pretty accurately when he wrote: 'It is not the Scottish business alone that I look upon, but the whole frame of things at home and abroad . . . and my misgiving soul is deeply apprehensive of no small evils coming on. God in Heaven avert them; but I can see no cure without a miracle, and I fear that will not be showed.'[86]

CHAPTER SIX

These Terrible Reformers

No glimpse of the sun was seen, as if darkness, confusion, and
deformity had possessed the world and driven light to heaven . . .
Salmacida Spolia, William Davenant

1639

The new year began badly for Henrietta. Her baby was due in January,
but with her mother now in residence there she was unable to lie in at
St James's and her superstitious affection for the old palace seemed
vindicated when her labour proved to be difficult and dangerous. The
baby, another girl, survived only just long enough to be baptised and
Henrietta herself was seriously ill. 'The physicians fear that the queen
may fall into a decline, as she has been reduced to a very weak condition
by her confinement,' reported the Venetian ambassador.[1]

Her recovery was slow and not helped by mounting anxiety over
the situation in Scotland, which continued to go from bad to worse. The
General Assembly, meeting in Glasgow in November, had abolished
the episcopacy and re-established the presbyterian system of church
government, something 'which neither our religion, justice, nor his
Majesty either with safety or honour can permit'. The Assembly was, in
short, denying the king's divinely conferred competence to regulate the
affairs of the kirk, and 'what then can be expected but a totall
disobedience to authoritie, if not a present rebellion?' demanded the
Marquis of Hamilton, whose own authority was being contemptuously
ignored by 'these most rigid and seditious Puritans'.[2]

At Whitehall that January the talk was all of war and the Earl of Essex, one
of the very few Englishmen of rank to have seen active service, was named
Lieutenant General of the army. Robert Devereux, the left-wing Protestant
son of Queen Elizabeth's favourite, would have been a popular appointment,
but its effect was largely spoilt when the queen begged the generalship of the
horse for her old friend, that well-known carpet knight Lord Holland, thus
causing considerable disgruntlement among the military men.[3]

Mobilisation continued through February and March. The northern
militia or trained bands were already on stand-by; the Lords Lieutenant
of the southern counties were ordered to supply their quota of additional
recruits, while the king had resurrected the ancient feudal custom of
requiring his tenants-in-chief to wait on him with their retainers. In this

way a force approximately 20,000 strong was cobbled together, though not without a good deal of foot-dragging and some outright resistance. The cause was not one calculated to appeal to the general public – indeed there was a strong undercurrent of sympathy for the Scots among the godly, and Scotland itself, being a poor country, offered little prospect of loot to encourage the others.

The king left for the north at the end of March, having parted 'very affectionately' from the queen. He had appointed a committee of senior councillors including Archbishop Laud, the Lord Treasurer Juxon, Lord Keeper Coventry, Secretary Windebank and the Earl of Northumberland to take charge in his absence and with special responsibility for the safety of his wife and children. The Privy Council was ordered to attend the queen every Sunday to keep her informed 'of all that takes place in the government of the country', and Giovanni Giustinian also heard that he had 'decreed under his own seal, that in the event of his death the queen shall have £40,000 a year as super dower, more than was customary with other widowed queens'.[4]

As the troops began to assemble at York their deficiencies in training, arms and equipment became distressingly apparent. The drafts from East Anglia, although 'good bodies of men and well clothed', were totally ignorant and without officers, and so were likely to be useless in the field; while Sir Edmund Verney wrote to his son that 'our army is but weak. Our purse is weaker; and if we fight with these forces and early in the year we shall have our throats cut, and to delay fighting long we cannot for want of money to keep our army together.'[5]

Want of money was, as always, the trouble. Without parliamentary support the king had been obliged to draw heavily on his own slender reserves and appeal to the generosity and/or patriotism of his wealthier subjects to make up the shortfall. The response was disappointing. Some cash came in from the clergy and individual lawyers and merchants, but the Inns of Court refused to make a joint contribution and the City of London, approached for a loan of £100,000, was equally disobliging. When asked to show their good will by supplying three thousand men for the present emergency, the aldermen refused that too, pointing out that the obligation of the people did not extend 'beyond the simple defence of London'.[6]

There was, however, one section of the community with a special interest in the preservation of the status quo, and special reason to be grateful for it. 'The queen', reported a contemporary writer of newsletters, 'has appointed a fast amongst the Catholic people every Saturday with a solemn service and sermons to be in her chapel, for the king's happy progression in his design, and for his safe return; the queen does appear in it to require the Catholic party to expend their liberal contribution towards the king's expenses in this expedition against the rebellious Covenanters.'[7]

In fact, plans to raise money for the war effort from the Catholic party had been in existence for several months, and on 11 April the superiors of the various orders issued a directive to the missionary priests urging them to solicit their parishioners 'as powerfully as you can to contribute chearfully and Bountifully upon this Occasion'.[8] A week later Henrietta added a personal touch in a letter drafted by her secretary Sir John Winter. 'We have so good a belief in the Loyalty and Affection of his Majesty's Catholick subjects,' it began, 'as we doubt not but upon this Occasion, that hath called his Majesty into the Northern Parts, for the Defence of his Honour and Dominions, they will express themselves so affected, as we have always represented them to his Majesty.'

As one who had so often in the past sought benefits for her fellow Catholics, the queen felt it was now time for her to ask them to show their gratitude by coming to his majesty's assistance with 'some considerable sum of money freely and chearfully presented'. She was, therefore, authorising John Winter to circulate copies of her appeal 'to the end that this our desire may be the more publick and the more authorised', and she went on to promise any waverers that she would endeavour in the most efficacious manner possible 'to remove any apprehension of Prejudice, that any who shall employ themselves towards the Success of this Business may conceive; by this they may be assured that we will secure them from all such objected inconveniences'.[9]

The actual task of organising the collection fell to George Con, assisted by a committee of court Catholics headed by Kenelm Digby and Wat Montagu, who sent out a letter to their co-religionists in the country, asking them to nominate 'such Persons as shall in your Opinions be agreed for the ablest and best disposed in every several County, not only to sollicit, but to collect such voluntary Contributions as every Bodies Conscience and Duty shall proffer'. The recipients of this communication were again reminded of the debt they owed the queen's majesty, 'to whose favourable Intercessions we must ascribe the happy Moderation we live under', and were urged joyfully to embrace this opportunity of showing their gratitude.[10]

The queen herself, reported Giovanni Giustinian early in May, was continuing to work her hardest to raise money and had written 'to all the gentry and ladies as well, earnestly begging for fresh help in these emergencies'. It was hoped, he went on, that her efforts would prove successful, 'as it is thought that no one will have the heart to refuse so just a request to so great a lady'.[11]

But although wealthy peers such as the Marquis of Winchester and the Earl of Worcester gave four-figure sums and in Henrietta's own immediate circle some ladies were persuaded to sacrifice their jewellery for the cause, the response in general was disappointing. Those members of the Catholic gentry who were already being pursued for recusancy fines were understandably reluctant to pay twice over. Nor were they entirely convinced by royal promises of protection from possible future consequences of their generosity and hesitated to draw down attention from the local authorities either to themselves or to the size of their incomes. Another unhelpful factor was the appearance of a mysterious letter, supposedly from the Pope, warning the Catholic community not to be too forward with money 'more than what Law and Duty enjoins them to pay', as this would have the effect of making them 'rather weaker Pillars of the Kingdom than they were before'.[12] The letter, addressed to George Con, appears to have been a forgery, but it had a wide circulation and was accepted as genuine by large numbers of relieved Catholics. In the end, about £14,000 was collected, considerably less than the first optimistic estimates of £40,000 and £50,000.

The political repercussions of the Catholic contribution were unfortunate, as it helped to reinforce growing suspicions that a 'popish plot' lay behind the unpopular Scottish war. 'We must needs go against the Scots for not being idolatrous and will have no mass amongst them,' declared one anonymous broadsheet, which accused the Pope's nuncio George Con, John Winter, 'whose kindred were some of the chief actors of the Gunpowder treason', and Toby Mathew of conspiring together to bring in popery.[13] It was also being said, in propaganda pamphlets distributed by the Scots, that the king was acting on the advice of pro-Catholic ministers, who 'under the pretence of reforming the liturgy of the churches of the two countries, proposed to introduce the mass as well, and to reduce these realms once more to subjection to the Roman court'.[14] No one had yet been bold enough to implicate the queen in any of these nefarious goings-on, not in print at least, but by allowing her name to be attached to the Catholic fund-raising campaign, Henrietta had become closely associated with them in the public mind, and she herself in later years was to tell her friend Madame de Motteville that Charles and Laud had been trying to transform religion in England and Scotland in order to prepare the way for its reversion to Catholicism.[15]

The so-called First Bishops War of 1639 was brief and inglorious. By the end of May the main body of the king's army was camped on the Tweed near Berwick, and on 3 June the Earl of Holland crossed the border with 300 horse and 3,000 foot. He got as far as Kelso where, having outstripped his infantry and believing himself to be outnumbered by the Covenanters, he lost his nerve and retreated 'with all speed and in some disorder'. Two days later the Scots, whose intelligence had been excellent throughout, judged the moment ripe to suggest a truce. Negotiations began on 11 June and on the 18th an agreement was reached, 'if that can be called an agreement in which nobody meant what others believed he did'.[16]

By the terms of the Pacification of Berwick, the armies were to be disbanded, those royal fortresses seized by the Covenanters restored and all other outstanding matters referred to a new General Assembly and a parliament to be convened at Edinburgh as soon as possible. The king had at first promised to come to Edinburgh himself, but soon changed his mind and on 1 August was being given a hero's welcome by the queen and court at Theobalds.

According to the Venetians, the peace at Berwick had been greeted with great joy by everybody, especially the Puritans, but already it was beginning to unravel. Having now discovered the extent of his majesty's weakness, reported Giovanni Giustinian at the end of July, the Scots had issued a new set of demands, 'at once insolent and seditious, in which they quite openly display their fixed intent to keep entire the authority they hold . . . leaving the king with the title and the mere shadow of authority'.[17] A week later he was writing again that affairs in Scotland showed no sign of improvement. 'The people are quite determined not to receive bishops . . . which means that they propose to sever themselves from obedience to this crown under this pretext.'[18]

In the circumstances it was unfortunate that the king's nephew should have chosen this particular moment to come back to England to try to persuade his uncle to finance another of his forlorn hope attempts to recover the Palatinate. 'In the present troubled state of affairs', observed Giustinian, 'and the very great scarcity of money it is not likely that his reasonable requests will meet with any response.'[19]

A more welcome arrival at court that August was the new papal agent, a good-looking and charming young Italian, Count Carlo Rossetti of Ferrara, who had come to take over from George Con. Con was now a sick man – his doctor had told him that he would not survive another English winter – and he was also a disappointed one. For all his success with the ladies, he had not been able to secure any major organisational breakthrough for the English Catholics, nor had he achieved his ambition of becoming a cardinal. He left for Italy at the end of the month, loaded with gifts from his many friends, and the queen insisted that 'a ship of the fleet should escort him to France as if he were an ambassador'.

Carlo Rossetti had presented his letters of credence and was received by the king and queen together as if he, too, were an ambassador, and he had offered compliments to his majesty on behalf of Cardinal Barberini much to the scandal of the Puritans. Rossetti spoke no English and did not have the advantage of Con's wide range of social contacts, but he formed a good working relationship with Francis Windebank and Father Philip and naturally gravitated towards his formidable compatriot at St James's Palace.

Marie de Medici, with her numerous undesirable hangers-on, her own well-furnished chapel and her Jesuit confessor, had now been expensively and provocatively entrenched at St James's for very nearly a year and seemed only too likely to become a permanent fixture there. Henrietta had sent Henry Jermyn over to France in the spring in an attempt to coax her brother into allowing their mother to go home with promises that she would in future agree to live in 'complete subjection' to him. But Louis and Richelieu were unimpressed and Marie stayed where she was, a persistent source of irritation to both English and French governments. 'French malcontents hold very frequent meetings in the house of the queen mother, constantly discussing schemes for making trouble for that crown,' reported Giustinian in July.[20]

Marie de Chevreuse was also still in London intriguing against Richelieu, and still promoting the idea of a Spanish marriage for Princess Mary. This, according to Giustinian, was most acceptable to the queen and, he added, 'they say freely at court that to facilitate it she allowed the Chevreuse to take the princess to the mass secretly'.[21] Henrietta had been obliged to waive the provisions in her marriage contract regarding the Catholic upbringing of her children but never entirely gave up hope of being able to influence their religious development; Panzani reported that she had begun to take the little Prince Charles to mass with her until the king put a stop to it.[22] As the heir, the prince was naturally an object of particular interest to Rome and George Con had gone to considerable trouble to cultivate his first tutor, Dr Duppa, and the aristocratic Earl of Newcastle, who was thought to be unsympathetic towards the Puritans.

At the beginning of September Giustinian wrote that 'the usual pleasures of the chase' were detaining his majesty in the country, but nothing much else went right for the king that autumn. Later in the month a Spanish fleet carrying an army destined for the Netherlands was waylaid in the Channel by the Dutch and forced to take shelter in the Downs. The Spanish and Dutch admirals then appealed, via their respective ambassadors, for English intervention which Charles, regardless of the prior undertakings made to his Spanish allies, proceeded to offer to the highest bidder, until the Dutch lost patience and attacked and severely mauled the Spaniards under the very noses of the great ship-money fleet. While this unsuccessful attempt at running a royal protection racket was still in progress the Prince Palatine had left for Germany, only to be arrested and imprisoned on his way through France. Cardinal Richelieu's own immediate plans for the future of the Rhineland did not include Charles Louis and he paid no attention to the angry protests which came from London.

The king's impotence abroad having been thus humiliatingly exposed, Giovanni Giustinian remarked in some exasperation how 'at the palace they have spent these days in continual dancing and other recreations, which occupy the attention of this idle court more than anything else'.[23] On the home front, however, things were moving. On 22 September the Lord Deputy had returned from Ireland, having been summoned by Charles to deal with that other troublesome outpost of empire, Scotland. Of all the king's servants Thomas, Viscount Wentworth, a tough, abrasive, ruthlessly efficient Yorkshireman, was undoubtedly the ablest and the most loyal, but his arrival on the Whitehall scene did not receive an unqualified welcome. The queen, in particular, was doubtful. Wentworth was known to be a close friend of William Laud, and Henrietta believed him to have shown little sympathy for the problems of the Irish Catholics – she had recently tried and failed to persuade him to have their ancient shrine at St Patrick's Purgatory in Ulster reinstated as a pilgrimage site. Nor did the Lord Deputy possess any of the courtier's social graces, although the queen was to remember that he had 'the most beautiful hands in the world'.

As winter set in attitudes on both sides of the border hardened. The parliament that met in Edinburgh at the end of August had immediately introduced legislation making the episcopacy unlawful within the Kirk and demanding what amounted to Home Rule, the Covenanters declaring that they would, in future, resist all attempts to govern them 'by orders and directions from the Council of England'.[24] A deputation headed by the Earls of Dunfermline and Loudon, which arrived in London in November with instructions, so the Venetians heard, 'to adhere pertinaciously to the measures taken by their parliament to the prejudice of the king's sovereignty', was coldly received. Indeed the king refused to receive it at all and both sides now began again to prepare for war.[25]

Thomas Wentworth, always an enthusiastic advocate of the policy of 'Thorough', had no doubt that the Scots must be taught to know their duty without delay and with all necessary force, but he insisted that this time the Westminster parliament must be called upon to supply the necessary finance, assuring the king that he would have no difficulty in managing the Commons as successfully as he had been managing its Irish equivalent. By early December he had carried his point and it was announced that elections would be held in the spring.

Wentworth, or the Earl of Strafford as he was about to become, was now established as the king's most trusted counsellor, and his new ascendancy had inevitably begun to arouse jealousy among his fellows and an 'unseasonable dislike and displeasure' on the part of the queen, who dreaded the possible appearance of another all-powerful favourite. When the old Secretary of State John Coke was dismissed, some thought because of his Puritan sympathies, Henrietta and James Hamilton pressed the claims of Sir Henry Vane, the Comptroller of the Household, 'a busy and a bustling man', a time-serving

courtier concerned only with his own advancement. Strafford detested Vane –
the feeling was mutual – and tried to have Coke kept in office, but 'by the
dark contrivance of the Marquis of Hamilton and by the open and visible
power of the Queen' Vane got the job, an appointment which, observed
Clarendon, 'afterwards produced many disasters'.[26]

In spite of the crisis situation once more building in the north, the king
and queen were busy with rehearsals for a Shrovetide masque. This was not as
irresponsible as it seemed, since the court masque had always provided a
valuable means of disseminating the official message that benevolent
autocracy brought the blessings of peace to a grateful nation, and *Salmacida
Spolia*, performed on three occasions in February 1640, was unmistakably
political in content. The curtain rose on a horrid scene of storm and tempest,
'as if darkness, confusion and deformity had possesst the world'. Discord, an
envious Fury wreathed with serpents, then appeared and summoned other
malignant spirits in an attempt to spread chaos through the tranquil realm.
These anti-masquers are put to flight by the entrance of 'Secret Wisdom' in
the person of the king, under the name of Philogenes or Lover of his People,
who reduces the threatening storm to calm as he ascends the throne of
Honour. The king and his attendant lords were in costumes of watchet blue,
white and silver, the colours of peace, patience and sweet reason:

> If it be kingly patience to outlast
> Those storms the people's giddy fury raise,
> Till like fantastic winds themselves they waste,
> The wisdom of that patience is thy praise.

In an unusual reversal of roles, the queen personated the chief
heroine, descending from heaven with her martial ladies, all in
Amazonian habits of carnation, with plumed helmets and baldricks with
antique swords hanging by their sides.

> All those who can her virtue doubt,
> Her mind will in her face advise,
> For through the casements of her eyes,
> Her soul is ever looking out.
> And, with its beams, she doth survey
> Our growth in virtue, or decay;
> Still lighting us in honour's way!
> All that are good she did inspire!
> Lovers are chaste, because they know
> It is her will they should be so;
> The valiant take from her their fire!

For the grand finale the scene changed to a great city, in the further part of which was 'a bridge over a river, where many people, coaches, horses and such like were seen to pass to and fro'. Then, from the heavens, came a cloud 'in which were eight persons richly attired representing the spheres; this, joining with two other clouds which appear'd at that instant full of music, covered all the upper part of the scene, and, at that instant beyond all these, a heaven opened full of deities, which celestial prospect . . . filled all the whole scene with apparitions and harmony'.

The king and queen were then serenaded by a chorus of all the masquers:

> All that are harsh, all that are rude,
> Are by your harmony subdu'd;
> Yet so into obedience wrought,
> As if not forc'd to it, but taught.
>
> Live still, the pleasure of our sight!
> Both our examples and delight,
> So long until you find the good success
> Of all your virtues, in one happiness.

After this, the spheres passed through the air and all the deities ascended again, 'and so concluded this Masque: which was generally approved of . . . to be the noblest and most ingenious that hath been done here in that kind'.[27]

Salmacida Spolia, which Inigo Jones is said to have considered his most inspired production, was the last of the Caroline masques, that peculiar genre, part pageant, part pantomime, part propaganda vehicle, and for Charles and Henrietta there would soon be no more harmony and no more happiness.

Writs for the elections to the new House of Commons had now gone out, 'causing extreme satisfaction everywhere' according to the Venetian ambassador. Everywhere, that is, except at court and in Catholic circles which were deeply apprehensive about the probable consequences. Carlo Rossetti in particular was alarmed, believing that his position as the Pope's agent would inevitably be threatened, and he begged the queen to impress on her husband the importance of protecting the Catholic community from renewed mistreatment. Henrietta, who was now nearly halfway through her eighth pregnancy, was naturally concerned for her friends, but there is nothing to indicate that, in the spring of 1640, she felt any disquiet on her own account. She was the queen and the Puritans, however hostile, were powerless to touch her.

1640

Parliament met on 13 April and the Commons, many of them newcomers to Westminster, spent the first few days gazing about them and 'upon each other, looking who should begin'. But all too soon the old familiar pattern started to reassert itself, the Crown demanding money with no questions asked, the Commons refusing to vote a single penny until their grievances had been redressed – and four days into the session the veteran member for Tavistock rose to enumerate those grievances.

John Pym was now in his mid-fifties, a man of family and substance owning considerable estates in north Somerset. Anti-Spanish and anti-Catholic by background and conviction, a lucid and cogent speaker, formidably intelligent, single-mindedly tenacious of purpose, with an unrivalled knowledge of the arcane mysteries of parliamentary procedure, Pym stood out as the natural leader of an inexperienced House of Commons. Some of the grievances he listed were old ones – the unchecked spread of popery, 'the taking of Tonnage and Poundage and divers other impositions without any ground in Lawe', monopolies 'whereby a burthen is laid not upon foreign, but upon native commodities as soap, salt, drinks etc.'. Others were more recent – the premature dissolution of the 1629 parliament, the demands for ship-money, fines for unwanted knighthoods and all the other petty aggravations of fiscal feudalism, the growing power of the church courts and of the Star Chamber. But there was one 'great grievance more which is the fountaine of all these and that is the intermission of Parliaments'. This was 'as prejudiciall to his Majestie as to the commonwealth, for by this meanes the union and love which should bee kept and communicated betwixt the King and his subjects is interrupted', and 'where the intercourse betwixt the head and the members is hindered, the body prospers not'.[28]

Pym spoke for two hours and when he sat down it was obvious that this parliament promised to be just as uncooperative as its predecessors. Unluckily for the king, the Earl of Strafford had not been present during its first week. He had gone back to Ireland in March in order to raise an army there and extract supplies from the Irish parliament. By the time he returned, having been delayed by an attack of dysentery, the Westminster proceedings were effectively beyond his power to control and an ill-judged attempt to go over the heads of the Commons with an appeal to the lords failed to drive a wedge between the two Houses – John Pym had made some useful friends among the left-wing peers as a result of his connection with the Providence Island Company. Nor was it possible to frighten the Commons with the rebellious Scots – many of them openly sided with the Covenanters – and even when, on Monday 4 May, an offer was made to do away with ship-money altogether in return for twelve subsidies paid over three years, it only succeeded in impressing the members with a sense of the king's desperation.

At a crisis Council meeting, held early on the following morning, Henry Vane gave it as his opinion that there was no hope of the Commons agreeing to grant a penny. Clarendon, writing with the benefit of hindsight, believed that in making a worse representation of the humour of the House than it deserved, Vane was acting maliciously 'and to bring all into confusion; he being known to have an implacable hatred against the earl of Strafford, whose destruction was then upon the anvil'.[29] Strafford himself, aware that he would be blamed for the failure of a parliament which had been his idea in the first place, wanted to go on trying to reach a compromise, but the majority, including the king, was against him, and later that day Charles went down to the House of Lords and dissolved what inevitably became known as the Short Parliament.

1640

The following weekend what the Venetian ambassador described as 'the irritation of the people' erupted into violent demonstrations on the part of the Londoners. Placards were posted up in conspicuous parts of the city' urging every class to preserve their ancient liberty and chase the bishops from the kingdom as pernicious men', and a mob several hundred strong and consisting mostly of apprentices, journeymen, seamen and dockhands marched with drums beating to attack Lambeth Palace, sending Archbishop Laud scuttling across the river to the safety of Whitehall.[30] Carlo Rossetti also sought sanctuary with Marie de Medici at St James's, but although the disorder lasted for several days no very serious damage was done and the only real casualty was the unfortunate young sailor who had tried to break down the archbishop's front door with a crowbar and was subsequently hanged and quartered.

All the same the city remained restless and angry and alive with rumours that the king was expecting to get money from Spain and that the Spanish ambassador, the queen-mother, the French exiles and the queen herself were all guilty of persuading him to dissolve parliament. Posters and broadsheets threatening papists and bishops with death continued to circulate and someone even managed to scratch a message on a windowpane in the king's own ante-chamber: 'God save the King. God confound the Queen with all her offspring. God grant the Palatine to reign in this realm.'[31]

It was perfectly true that the king had been negotiating an agreement with Spain whereby he would be paid generous amounts of Spanish gold in return for providing a naval escort to guarantee the safe passage of Spanish troopships through the Channel to Flanders. But that gold was still a distant, and problematic, prospect and in June 1640 Charles had no option but to try to gain time by opening fresh talks with the Covenanters. The queen, according to Giustinian, did not approve of these 'peaceful counsels'. In contrast to her previous attitude, it seemed that Henrietta was now doing her utmost to urge the king 'to pursue the war with spirit against the rebels until they are completely subdued. She not only intimates the hope of obtaining large contributions from the Catholics', continued Giustinian, 'but even of obtaining some help from the pope.'[32]

George Con had died in January, since when both Charles and Henrietta had been working to persuade the Pope to raise Charles's Catholic cousin, Ludovic Stuart d'Aubigny, to the cardinalate, and in the present emergency it was not surprising that Henrietta, encouraged by Rossetti, should have suggested asking her godfather for financial help as well. Given the political climate of the day it would be a high-risk strategy, but for the king, now at his wits' end for money, anything was worth trying and Rossetti was authorised to make an approach to Cardinal Barberini. The initial response was disappointing. Rome could hardly be expected to assist a heretical sovereign. Of course if the King of England were to convert things would be different, and both money and men would doubtless be forthcoming.

Henrietta meanwhile had retreated to Oatlands where, on 8 July, she gave birth to a healthy son with very little difficulty. 'The queen was never better nor so well of any of her children,' wrote Francis Windebank to Lord Conway, and William Laud travelled down to Oatlands for the last royal baptism he would perform. The baby was given the name Henry at a private family ceremony, with his two elder brothers and sister Mary as sponsors, and as a reward to his mother the king pardoned all the Catholic priests then in prison.

But although the safe arrival of the new prince, created Duke of Gloucester, was a cause of rejoicing to both parents, the king and queen had little else to give them pleasure that summer. The court stayed at Oatlands while desperate efforts continued to raise money to pay for the army. Once more refused a loan by the city fathers, the king was reduced to seizing bullion deposited in the Tower by the London merchants and threatening to debase the coinage. Then, on 20 August, the Scots, commanded by Alexander Leslie, a veteran of the German wars, crossed the Tweed at Coldstream. A week later they had reached the Tyne. On 28 August they comprehensively defeated an English force at Newburn, some four miles up-river from Newcastle. Two days after 'that infamous, irreparable rout' they entered Newcastle, to be warmly welcomed by the townspeople, and presently began to advance south towards Durham.

The king had left for the north, intending to lead his army in person, on the day the Scots crossed the border and was now at York where he was joined by Strafford. The situation looked sufficiently grim and in a moment of despair Strafford wrote to his friend George Radcliffe: 'Pity me, for never came any man to so lost a business. The army altogether necessitous. . . . Our horse all cowardly; the country from Berwick to York in the power of the Scots; an universal affright in all; a general disaffection to the king's service, none sensible of his dishonour.'[33]

Alarm and despondency were also prevalent among those members of the government left to guard the capital. The Covenanters had taken the precaution of issuing a manifesto justifying their invasion plans to their English brethren, asserting that 'the preservation or ruin of religion and liberty' was of vital concern to both kingdoms and calling for the king's evil councillors to be brought to justice by parliament, and in spite of vigorous official efforts to suppress it, *Information from the Scottish Nation* quickly became popular reading among Londoners. Giovanni Giustinian reported that the news of the Scots' victory at Newburn had been greeted with satisfaction by everyone and, he went on, 'although it is forbidden under severe penalties to speak in favour of the rebels, and many persons have been arrested for the offence, such devices are quite inadequate to restrain this free-spoken people within bounds, so powerful in them is the sentiment of liberty and the question of religion'.[34]

The free-spoken people were also expressing their feelings in 'cheap and senseless libels' scattered about the city, fixed on gates and other prominent places, attacking those in positions of 'highest trust and employment', while rumours of plots, Spanish, Irish and Popish, ran through the streets like rats. The Catholics were widely believed to have manufactured the Scottish crisis for their own purposes and Anne Hussey, an Irishwoman in London, swore that an Irish papist army was ready and waiting to overthrow the Protestant state – she had heard all about it from Marie de Medici's confessor.[35]

Of more immediate concern to the authorities was the fact that an influential group of left-wing peers, including the earls of Essex, Warwick and Bedford and the Lords Saye, Brooke and Mandeville, together with John Pym and other leading commoners, were known to be planning to exert pressure on the king to call another parliament and open peace negotiations with the Scots. 'The queen and ministers,' wrote Giustinian, 'having discovered full particulars of this daring resolution, conspiring with the most pernicious aims of the Scots, sent the news to the king with all speed, advising him to come quickly to this city to divert the serious mischief with which they are threatened if he is not disposed to summon parliament without a moment's delay. . . . In the Tower here they are preparing quarters for soldiers, and are hurriedly making many military preparations, with the object perhaps of providing, in the last resort, a refuge in that fortress for some minister or for the king himself.'[36]

The king did not immediately return to London. Instead he chose to revive a custom 'so old that it had not been practised in some hundreds of years', and called a Great Council of all the peers of the realm to attend him at York. This assembly, which met on 24 September, was greeted with the news that his majesty did indeed intend to summon parliament for the earliest possible date, in order, according to Clarendon, 'that the counsel might not seem to arise from them who were resolved to give it, and that the Queen might receive the honour of it, who, he said, had by a letter advised him to it; as his majesty exceedingly desired to endear her to the people'.[37]

Meanwhile, the problem of the Scots, now camped on the border between Durham and Yorkshire, had to be faced and any hopes Charles may have been cherishing that the peers would somehow provide him with the means to drive them out were quickly dashed. Anglo-Scottish talks began at Ripon in the first week of October and it was agreed that the Covenanters would continue to occupy Northumberland and Durham for the next two months and be paid a subsistence allowance of £850 a day. Further negotiations were to be transferred to London and, with the security of the forthcoming parliament, the city companies agreed a loan to keep the English army, such as it was, temporarily in being. If the First Bishops War had been inglorious, the second had ended in unmitigated disaster, but as Charles rode south at the end of October he did not appear to have realised that nothing would ever be the same again.

No one had yet gone so far as to attack the king himself, and blame for the whole sorry state of affairs was still being attributed to 'evil counsellors', headed by Strafford and Laud. Nor had anyone yet openly attacked the queen, although it seemed that the Scots commissioners at Ripon had spoken 'in confidence of the excess of the Queen's power, which, in respect of her religion and of the persons who had most interest with her, ought not to prevail so much upon the King as it did in all affairs'.[38]

Certainly the Catholics were looking forward to the parliament with the deepest misgivings. Giovanni Giustinian feared it would mean 'the total desolation of the Catholic faith in this country, with a notable diminution of the king's authority, and the final ruin of his most confidential ministers'.[39] The ambassador also believed that Count Rossetti and the queen-mother would be forced out, and three days before parliament met he reported that many Catholics were 'hurriedly selling their goods with the intention of going to live quietly in some other country until the present ill feeling has softened and the troubled state of this kingdom has altered'.[40]

On Tuesday 3 November the king went privately, almost secretively, to open his fifth and last parliament. There would be no question of a quick dissolution this time – not with the Scots army poised within a day's march of York – and the worst fears of the court party were soon realised as John Pym and his allies in both Houses moved in a well-orchestrated pre-emptive strike against their most dangerous adversary. On Wednesday 11 November

144

the Earl of Strafford was impeached by the Lords, arrested and committed to the temporary custody of the Gentleman Usher of the Black Rod, while detailed charges of high treason were prepared. Nor was Strafford the only victim. A month later the crypto-Catholic Secretary of State Francis Windebank fled abroad, closely followed by the Lord Keeper Sir John Finch, and on 18 December Archbishop Laud, 'chief incendiary and cause' of the Scottish wars, was also impeached. 'So that', wrote Clarendon, 'within less than six weeks . . . these terrible reformers had caused the two greatest counsellors of the kingdom, and whom they most feared and so hated, to be removed from the King and imprisoned under an accusation of high treason, and frighted away the Lord Keeper of the Great Seal of England and one of the principal Secretaries of State into foreign kingdoms for fear of the like.' By contrast, William Prynne, the ear-less Puritan martyr, was released from gaol and made a triumphant return to the capital.

Anti-Catholic feeling continued to run high, particularly in London, but its expression was now no longer confined to alehouse talk, inflammatory pamphlets and sporadic mob violence. Now it was being organised and channelled for political ends, and one of the first acts of the new parliament had been to appoint a committee to enquire into the state of religion and report on the numbers of dispensations and immunities granted to recusants by privy councillors. The papal agent, who was of course a natural target, received an unfriendly visit from three zealous city magistrates, accompanied by a posse of armed men, who hammered on his door at one o'clock in the morning shouting that they had a warrant to search his house for arms. Rossetti thought it more likely that they were hoping to find evidence of his relationship with the king, but he invited the justices inside and politely showed them round his chapel and picture gallery. Unnerved by the agent's elaborate courtesy, the would-be searchers retreated in some embarrassment, apologising for having inconvenienced him.[41]

Queen Elizabeth's Accession Day, 'the sacred seventeenth of November', which in her time had come to be celebrated as an unofficial Protestant holiday, was ordained by parliament as a day of prayer and fasting 'to implore the divine assistance in the present grave state of affairs', and on that day, reported Giovanni Giustinian, 'the ministers of the churches delivered from their pulpits seditious sermons stirring up the people to put down the Catholic religion entirely'. Thus encouraged, a hostile crowd assembled outside the queen's chapel and attacked the congregation with stones and weapons as they came out after mass.[42]

At the beginning of December the queen was told that she must dismiss the numerous English Catholics in her service who were thus being protected from prosecution. 'Justly incensed' at such an audacious demand, her majesty retorted that if she was forced to do without the

Catholics, she would dismiss her Protestant servants as well, 'and provide herself elsewhere with people of her faith.'[43]

Henrietta was on firm ground there, since her marriage contract ensured her right to a Catholic household, but it had said nothing about her right to have a resident personal envoy from the Pope and she was becoming worried about Rossetti's personal safety. All the same, she was very reluctant to let him go. Not only would that look like surrendering to the enemy, but it would also mean losing a vital channel of communication with Rome – Rossetti and Father Philip were still working to try to extract a loan from the papacy. In the end, after some discussion, it was agreed that the agent would stay, at least for the time being, although for greater security and to please the queen he agreed to move into St James's Palace.[44]

It had been a stressful and depressing year for the king and queen and it was to end with a family tragedy, when their three-year-old daughter Anne died at Richmond on 15 December of 'a suffocating catarrh'. Henrietta had lost two babies at birth but this was the first time she had experienced the sorrow familiar to so many parents of losing a child, and the Venetian ambassador reported that both their majesties were suffering intense grief. Theodore Mayerne, who performed a post-mortem examination on the princess, gave it as his opinion that from the disposition of her lungs and her extreme debility, she could not have been long-lived, 'and that a great part of her life has been at least as much owing to art as to nature'.[45]

But if Anne had been tubercular and Elizabeth also was rumoured to be delicate, the other four children continued to thrive – the Prince of Wales in particular displaying a sturdy resistance to the attentions of the medical profession, as appears from his mother's often-quoted early letter, written probably in 1638. 'Charles, I am sorry that I must begin my first letter with chiding you, because I hear that you will not take physic; I hope it was only for this day, and that tomorrow you will do it; for if you will not, I must come to you and make you take it, for it is for your health.'[46]

Henrietta was a normally concerned and affectionate mother by the standards of her day, but no royal parents would attempt to rear their offspring at court, and according to established custom the Stuart children had their own households of nursemaids, governesses and tutors, spending most of their time either at St James's or out at Richmond where they were visited at intervals by either one or both of their parents. George Con records one such occasion at Richmond in 1636, when the three elder children were allowed to join the king and queen at supper and he commented approvingly on the strong attachment which could be seen to exist between them.[47]

But fond though she might be of her children, for Henrietta her husband always came first and now, as his troubles gathered around him, she was preparing to go into battle. Giustinian had remarked that the king, destitute as he was of power and credit, 'must bow to necessity and wait until time affords him the means to restore his falling fortunes'. This was not good enough for the daughter of Henri le Grand. *Henry IV of France* 'The queen, who is full of generous spirit . . . shows that she feels very strongly at seeing her husband not only deprived of his most faithful ministers, but so effectively despised by his own subjects. For this reason she never ceases to urge him to throw himself into desperate courses, and it is to be feared that he may at last lose patience and listen to her.'[48]

Early in the new year Henrietta renewed her appeal to Rome. Writing *1641* personally to Cardinal Barberini she pointed out, reasonably enough, that her husband's present predicament was largely due to his past generosity to the English Catholics. The only remedy now, she went on, would be to buy off the Puritan leaders, but the disordered state of the country made it impossible to raise a large enough sum in England and she therefore begged the Pope for a loan of half a million crowns (£125,000), stipulating that this should be kept entirely secret and the money sent in small amounts by bills of exchange.[49] She was also appealing to France for financial and diplomatic support. There had been no French ambassador in London since the departure of Pompone de Bellièvre nearly a year ago and Henrietta was very anxious that a replacement should be sent as soon as possible.

While the queen naturally turned for help to the Catholic powers, in January 1641 the most hopeful source of foreign aid was to be found in a Protestant state. The idea of marrying one of the Stuart princesses into the Dutch ruling family seems to have been brought over originally by Marie de Medici and had at first been turned down as unworthy. But Frederick Henry, Prince of Orange, had persisted. He was a rich man, ambitious for his house and willing to pay handsomely to secure a royal bride for his son. Negotiations had continued intermittently over the next two years and in December 1640 Giovanni Giustinian reported the announcement that a marriage had been arranged 'between the second princess here and the eldest son of the Prince of Orange'. Soon though it was being rumoured that the bride would be the king's elder daughter and from the Orange point of view Mary certainly represented better value for money. At nine years old she was a more suitable age for the teenage Prince William than Elizabeth at barely six, and she also possessed a higher dynastic status – not that anyone in 1641 could conceivably have envisaged a day when Mary's son would become King of England. For Mary's parents, especially her mother who had once dreamed of seeing her married in Spain, it was a sad disappointment. But facts had to be faced. That optimistic matchmaker Marie de Chevreuse had finally left for Flanders and, in any case, with the Puritans in the ascendant, all hopes of a Spanish alliance had now evaporated. The Orange match would at least mean some desperately needed ready cash, the promise of a political alliance, perhaps even some military aid, so that when Frederick Henry began to make a point of asking for the senior princess the bargain was struck.

It was, though, the only gleam of light in an otherwise uniformly depressing landscape. Giustinian continued to report unrelenting severity against the Catholics and when a priest named Goodman, convicted and condemned for treason, was reprieved by the king at Henrietta's request, there was an immediate uproar. Parliament and the city 'both had recourse to the king to permit the sentence to be carried out, or else they assured him of the offence his people would take and that they would not grant him any subsidy in the future. They also threatened the queen with greater ills.' Charles hesitated, temporised and then gave way, remitting the case into the care of parliament, so that Giustinian feared the unfortunate priest would eventually suffer all the horrors of a traitor's death.[50]

The Commons, who remained deeply suspicious of the political activities of the queen and her friends, had now fastened on the ill-advised 'Catholic contribution' of 1639, and at the end of January Walter Montagu and Kenelm Digby were summoned to give an account of their part in its organisation and collection. Anxious to protect them and do something to moderate the temper of the House, Henrietta sent a conciliatory message to Westminster on 4 February, declaring that she had always been ready to use her best endeavours for the removing of all misunderstanding between the king and his people and would continue to do so, 'judging it the only way of happiness to the King, herself and [the] Kingdom'. She therefore promised that she would dismiss Count Rossetti 'within convenient time', understanding that his presence was distasteful to the country; and 'understanding likewise that exception hath been taken at the great resort to her Chapel', she also promised that she would in future be careful not to exceed 'that which is necessary for the exercise of her Religion'. As far as her attempt to raise money from the Catholics 'for the Assistance of the King in his Journey to the North' was concerned, the queen had been moved thereto 'meerly out of her dear and tender affection to the King, and the Example of other his Majesty's Subjects'. If she had done anything illegal, she could only plead ignorance of the law, promising to be more cautious hereafter. Her majesty, the message ended, 'being desirous to employ her own Power to unite the King and People, desireth the Parliament to look forwards, and pass by such Mistakes and Errors of her Servants as they may be guilty of formerly; and this your respect she promiseth, shall be repaid with all good Offices she can do to the House'.[51]

The Commons listened in stony silence as the queen's letter was read out by the Comptroller of her household and when Sir Hugh Cholmley, the member for Scarborough, moved a vote of thanks to her majesty, he found no support. Her majesty was now talking about going over to France, 'having need of her native air to restore her health'. This, observed Anzolo Correr at the embassy in Paris, 'may be true or merely a pretext to escape from some danger with which she may be threatened in the disturbances of England'.[52] More likely, the queen was already beginning to plan a trip abroad to seek military aid against the parliament, but if so she was to meet with a wounding rebuff. Cardinal Richelieu had not been entirely displeased by the recent turn of events across the Channel, which had at least removed any lingering danger of an offensive Anglo-Spanish league and, brother-in-law or no, he had not the slightest intention of allowing Louis to become involved in the affairs of the luckless King of England. His eminence therefore wrote to Henrietta 'in a confidential manner, persuading her to give up the idea of going to France, intimating that the Most Christian will not approve'.[53]

The Commons meanwhile had been busy passing the Triennial Act, which provided machinery for the summoning of parliament if the king failed to do so within three years of the previous dissolution. This had passed the Lords and received royal assent before the end of February 'amid universal rejoicings, though equally resented by his Majesty. At present,' reported Giustinian, 'nothing is left to him but the title and the naked shows of king.'[54] But although one concession after another was being forced out of him, Charles, sublimely confident of his God-given divine right, had by no means lost hope of confounding his enemies and was now working behind the scenes to try to build up a body of support among the more moderate peers. The Earl of Essex, temporarily displaced by Strafford, was once more commanding the army and there were plans to make the Earl of Bedford Lord Treasurer and the Earl of Hertford Lord Chamberlain, and there was even talk of offering John Pym the Chancellorship of the Exchequer in exchange for a secure and regular income, even perhaps for Strafford's life. The queen is said to have had a hand in these so-called 'bridging appointments' and to have conducted secret negotiations with Bedford and Pym.[55]

Henrietta may have been referring to this in her recollections of the hectic weeks leading up to Strafford's trial as told to Madame de Motteville; how she had arranged a series of late-night rendezvous, going alone down the backstairs by the light of a single taper to the apartments of one of her ladies, who was conveniently away in the country, in order to meet some of the 'most wicked' members of the opposition party; and how she had offered them 'toutes choses' in an attempt to save the king's clever and faithful minister (she had long since come to realise Strafford's worth) but all to no avail.[56]

It all sounds pretty implausible and Henrietta's memories may well have gained in dramatic colour over the years. More plausible, and more serious, was her encouragement of a scheme currently being discussed by a group of young officers, royalist MPs and courtiers. This group, or rather two loosely connected groups, one led by Henry Percy, the Earl of Northumberland's brother, Henry Wilmot and Jack Ashburnham, the other by George Goring, Governor of Portsmouth, Henry Jermyn and a couple of enterprising poets, John Suckling and William Davenant, were planning to stage a *coup* by bringing the remnants of the king's army down from York to occupy the city, intimidate the parliament and free Strafford from the Tower where he was now confined. This was just the sort of plan, with its promise of action and quick results, exactly calculated to appeal to Henrietta's restless, impatient nature. Unfortunately, though, the Army Plot (as it came to be known) owed a great deal more to wishful thinking than to the facts of life and indeed seems never to have progressed much beyond the talking stage. But the increased comings and goings of certain military men about the court and a general air of suppressed excitement among the queen's friends did not escape notice. Inevitably the amateur conspirators lacked both cohesion and discretion and it was not long before news of their intentions had been leaked to the enemy.

Strafford's trial opened on 22 March and the king and queen attended the proceedings in Westminster Hall on a daily basis in a deliberate show of solidarity with the accused, sitting in the private box provided for them, the queen listening intently and taking copious notes. The prisoner at the bar, the hate figure so carefully manufactured by the parliamentary propaganda machine, the oppressor of Ireland, the tyrant who had boasted that he would make 'the little finger of the King's prerogative heavier than the loins of the law', who had sought to overthrow the lawful government and introduce an arbitrary power, was now disconcertingly revealed as a stooped and shrunken, prematurely aged man (he was forty-eight), crippled with gout and suffering recurrent bouts of dysentery. His appearance, in fact, began to win him sympathy from the packed rows of spectators in the body of the Hall, but Strafford was not playing for sympathy and over the eighteen days of the trial defended himself with such skill and determination that the case against him showed every sign of collapsing. The nub of that case rested on Article 23 of the charges and on the interpretation of a single phrase taken from Henry Vane's roughly scribbled minutes of the Council meeting held on the day the Short Parliament was dissolved. The Scottish crisis had been under discussion and Strafford had apparently told the king, 'you have an army in Ireland you may employ here to reduce this kingdom'. Strafford naturally maintained that the kingdom in question was Scotland, then in open rebellion, and three other councillors who had been present at the meeting supported him, testifying that he had never advised using the Irish army against England.

It was at this point, faced with the likely failure of the impeachment, that John Pym suddenly changed tactics, and on 10 April he introduced a Bill of Attainder into the Commons. This obsolete but still deadly weapon, which merely decreed the guilt of an accused person by the will of the majority, was still before the House when the royal family's attention was temporarily distracted by the arrival from Holland of the Princess Mary's bridegroom.

Fifteen-year-old Prince William got a cool reception from his future mother-in-law. Henrietta, aware of raised eyebrows in Paris, had not yet quite been able to come to terms with the idea of a match she considered beneath the dignity of the daughter of a daughter of France, and William was also snubbed by another member of the family. The Prince Palatine, *1641* released from his French detention, had returned uninvited to England at the beginning of March with the sad persistence of the perennial poor relation, announcing that he hoped to take the opportunity of putting his case before parliament and adding to his uncle's problems by spreading it around that he had always been led to believe that his cousin Mary had been promised to *him*. Now he refused to pay the usual courtesy call on the bridegroom and sulked ostentatiously throughout the wedding festivities.

Not that the festivities amounted to much. In normal times the marriage of the king's eldest daughter would have been marked by court balls, masques and banquets for the great and good, bonfires, firework displays and free drink for the rest. In normal times, too, young Prince William, good-looking, well-mannered, Protestant and rich, would have been given a warm welcome by the people. But in the spring of 1641 times were far from normal – on 21 April, two days after William's arrival, the Commons had passed Strafford's attainder by a majority of 204 to 59 – and nobody was in the mood for partying. Beyond the palace walls the royal wedding passed almost unnoticed.

The ceremony itself, which took place in the chapel at Whitehall on Sunday 2 May, was a very low-key affair. The bride, in silver tissue and pearls, escorted by her two elder brothers and accompanied by her governess and a train of sixteen bridesmaids, 'young daughters of principal noblemen', was given away by her father, while her mother, grandmother and younger sister watched from a curtained recess in the gallery. The Bishop of Ely officiated, using the simple order of service set out in the Book of Common Prayer, 'for so the King had before directed', and the Bishop of Rochester preached the sermon. The ceremony was followed by a family dinner party and afterwards the queen and the young people walked in Hyde Park until supper-time. Later that evening the newly married couple had to go through the ritual of the public bedding. Mary was undressed by all the ladies in the queen's chamber and arranged in the state bed with its blue velvet curtains and gold and silver fringe. William, in dressing gown and slippers, was then led through the crowd by the king and the princes and, after kissing the princess, lay down beside her for a few minutes 'in the presence of all the great lords and ladies of England, the four ambassadors of the United [Dutch] States, and the distinguished personages who had attended him to London'. In order for the marriage to be pronounced officially 'consummated' the children's bare legs had to touch and when it was discovered that Mary's nightgown reached modestly to her ankles Geoffrey Hudson, the dwarf and licensed jester, produced a pair of shears to slit the garment amid much merriment from the bystanders.[57]

It would be the last light-hearted moment the court was to know. Next morning a large crowd of 'the most substantial' citizens gathered at Westminster, where the attainder was now before the Upper House, noisily demanding 'speedy justice from parliament and the head of the Lieutenant [Strafford], calling him traitor and enemy to the public liberty'. According to Giovanni Giustinian, they would not be appeased by mere words and threatened 'the most violent measures against the state and against His Majesty's own person and all the royal House'.[58]

Charles had already written to Strafford, promising 'upon the word of a king, you shall not suffer in life, honour or fortune', and he had told the Lords that nothing whatsoever would induce him to sign the earl's death warrant.[59] But he was steadily being driven into a corner. On 5 May John Pym, choosing his moment, revealed the existence of the Army Plot, informing a jittery House of Commons that 'he had great cause to fear there was at that time as desperate a design and conspiracy against the Parliament as had been in any age, and he was in [no] doubt persons of great quality and credit at court had their hands in it'.[60]

That night five of the 'plotters' fled ingloriously for their lives. They included Henry Percy, John Suckling, William Davenant and Henry Jermyn, the queen's Master of the Horse, 'who in addition to the crimes alleged against his fellows, is accused of too great an intimacy with the queen, so that even the honour of these unhappy princes is not safe from the slanderous tongues of their subjects'. Giustinian also reported that parliament, suspecting that the king was planning to go to the army at York and the queen to the fortress of Portsmouth, had sent a deputy to warn them not to leave London, on the pretext that they would be 'safer from the violence of the people under the eye of parliament than elsewhere'. Charles chose not to dignify this piece of audacity with a reply, but, continued the ambassador, the queen retorted 'with spirit' that she was the daughter of a father who had never learned to run away and she had no intention of doing such a thing herself.[61]

This was on Thursday 6 May. Next day a rumour started that the king and queen had made a treaty with France to bring ten regiments over to join up with the troops quartered at York and to employ that fabled monster the Irish army to reduce their subjects to obedience by force; and that in order to guarantee the safety of the French, who were apparently already at Dieppe waiting to embark, 'their Majesties had bound themselves to consign the fortress of Portsmouth to the Most Christian'. On hearing this report, which the more level-headed considered false, the Commons proceeded to give it credibility by at once dispatching four members to Portsmouth to investigate 'and to secure the place'.

Meanwhile the news had spread through the city, by now in the grip of something approaching mass hysteria – the French had taken the Channel Islands, a Spanish army was about to invade, the papists had set fire to the House of Commons – and on Saturday morning Giustinian heard that an armed mob was preparing to march on the palace to seize the persons of the king and queen. 'These on hearing the news and full of terror, made up their minds to leave this city without more ado.' They were on the point of starting when the Comte de Montreuil, the French official who had been minding the embassy since Bellièvre's departure, and some other 'confidential persons' hurried to Whitehall and managed to persuade their majesties to stay put. They also assured the leaders of the people that the king was ready to give them every satisfaction and that the rumours were entirely false. 'In this way', wrote Giustinian, 'the tumult was appeased and more serious disorder was diverted for the moment.'[62]

But only for the moment. On that same dreadful Saturday, a thin unhappy House of Lords, jostled and intimidated by the mob, bullied by the Commons and 'impelled by the implacable hatred against the Lieutenant of Ireland', passed the attainder by twenty-six votes to nineteen. They also passed an emergency measure rushed through by the Commons forbidding any dissolution or prorogation of the parliament without the consent of both Houses.

Strafford's life now lay in the king's hands and that night and all the next day Charles wrestled miserably with his conscience, while the mob now besieging Whitehall could clearly be heard baying for blood and justice, 'not without great and insolent threats and expressions, what they would do if it were not speedily granted'. The frightened Catholics in the palace confessed their sins and prayed. Old Marie de Medici, cowering at St James's, was given extra guards and the queen's Capuchins scattered to seek sanctuary in friendly houses round the city. Not even the foreign embassies felt secure and Giovanni Giustinian sighed devoutly for the time when he could leave 'the perils of this kingdom'. The palace, that rambling warren of courts, alleys and gardens, would have been impossible to defend if the rabble outside had once broken in and the members of the Privy Council, called together 'to advise what course was to be taken to suppress these traitorous riots', all urged the king to give his assent to Strafford's attainder, 'saying there was no other way to preserve himself and his posterity . . . and therefore that he ought to be more tender of the safety of the kingdom than of any one person, how innocent soever'. Finally, no less an authority than John Williams, the Archbishop of York, told him that there was a private conscience and a public conscience; that his public conscience as a king might oblige him to do that which was against his private conscience as a man and, in any case, the question now was not whether he should save the Earl of Strafford but whether he should perish with him, together with his wife and children who were all equally in danger.[63]

Strafford himself had written to his master, generously releasing him from his promise. 'To set your Majesty's conscience at liberty I do most humbly beseech your Majesty, for prevention of evils which may happen by your refusal, to pass this Bill.' By his own sacrifice the condemned man hoped the way would be cleared 'towards that blessed agreement which God I trust shall ever establish between you and your subjects', besides which, 'to a willing man there is no injury done'.[64]

So, at last, at nine o'clock on the Sunday evening, Charles gave in. Next morning his royal assent was conveyed to the House of Lords. 'My lord of Strafford's condition is happier than mine,' he said as he signed. But even now, it seems, he had not quite given up hope and on Tuesday he wrote a last abject appeal to the Lords to be merciful and commute the death sentence to one of perpetual imprisonment. 'This if it may be done without the discontentment of my people will be an unspeakable contentment to me.'[65] He must have known it was useless, but all the same he sent the letter to be delivered personally by the ten-year-old Prince of Wales.

Strafford was beheaded on Tower Hill on Wednesday 12 May in the presence of an exultant crowd more than 100,000 strong. 'And so', commented the Venetian ambassador, 'this minister lost his life whose admirable qualities certainly deserved a better age and a happier fate. The king, thus deprived of authority with the hatred of the people, which is even stronger against the queen . . . suffers the tortures of the deepest affliction.'[66]

The judicial murder, for such it had been, of Thomas Wentworth was an ugly business and for the king a bitter defeat and a betrayal for which he never forgave himself. Henrietta always remembered his distress and she, too, shed many tears. They both knew, she was to tell Madame de Motteville, that this death would some day take the life of one and the peace of mind of the other.[67]

CHAPTER SEVEN

A Subject Like Any Other

As to the rebels, neither their writings nor their threats shall ever
make me do anything . . . much less shall they frighten me.
Henrietta Maria to Charles I, 4 September 1642

If Charles and Henrietta had hoped that parliament would be appeased by
the sacrifice of Strafford, they were to be disappointed. 'The wisest freely
predict that this monarchy will soon be turned into a completely democratic
government,' wrote Giovanni Giustinian, 'and very solid foundations for
this have been laid by making Parliament perpetual.'[1] Certainly John Pym
and his cohorts were losing no opportunity to demonstrate their new
mastery. The king had been forced to agree to disband the Irish army, his
freedom to appoint his own nominees to government office was being
mercilessly curtailed and a Commons committee now sitting to investigate
the Army Plot had been given the fullest authority to examine witnesses
'and to make sure of every person without exception, which means their
Majesties themselves, if they appear guilty'.[2]

Since all outgoing mail was liable to be opened, the queen's
correspondence being especially targeted, Henrietta had been reduced
to begging the Venetian ambassador, whose diplomatic immunity was still
being respected, to forward a letter from her to Walter Montagu, now at
the French court. 'She charged me to use the utmost secrecy,' reported
Giustinian, who felt obligated to serve 'these afflicted princes' in their
time of need, and a week later he sent another of the queen's letters in
his packet for France.

Although Henrietta was still trying for help from France and her brother,
she had not given up hope of a papal loan, which she and Father Philip
were continuing to discuss with Rome through the agency of Carlo Rossetti.
But always the negotiations came up against the apparently insurmountable
obstacle of the king's religious scruples. His offer, passed on by the queen,
to grant his Catholic subjects full liberty of conscience and worship, when
once he had regained his own freedom of action, was not enough – a
similar undertaking, it was recalled, had been made and broken before.
Unless and until Charles agreed to convert or, at the very least, gave a sign
'certain though secret' of his intention to become a Catholic, the Holy See
would not move to help him and Cardinal Barberini could only urge the

queen to go on working for her husband's conversion, however difficult that might seem, as the only possible solution to his problems.[3]

It was becoming clear that Rossetti would not be able to remain at his post for much longer. By midsummer the clamour for his expulsion had grown increasingly menacing, and on 24 June he received a summons to appear before the House of Commons. Fearful of insult or even physical injury, he hurried round to the Venetian embassy for advice and protection, and Giustinian, who seems to have assumed the role of unofficial mediator between the opposing parties, contrived to arrange that 'without the shame of appearing in parliament he will be able . . . to leave this city honourably.'[4] Rossetti was also able to take his leave of the king and queen in a farewell interview during which, he reported, the king had spoken of religion more like a Catholic than a heretic and sent his thanks to the Pope and Cardinal Barberini for their compassionate understanding of his difficulties. After Charles had left the room, the queen told Rossetti that his majesty was certainly not averse to the Catholic faith, but he was so timid and so irresolute in action that it would be a long time before he would be able to bring himself to carry out such a holy resolution.[5]

For Henrietta the summer was rapidly turning into a nightmare. The departure of Walter Montagu with Kenelm Digby had marked the final break-up of her Catholic court circle and now parliament was demanding that her mother, too, must go, accusing her of having 'instilled evil counsels into her daughter'. But Marie was proving a good deal harder to dislodge than Rossetti had been. Not only had she no money for the journey – the king had been obliged to discontinue her allowance, so that she was having to sell her horses, plate and other possessions to meet her daily expenses – but she had nowhere to go, as none of the European powers was so far willing to grant her asylum.

Added to this, on 8 June the Commons committee on the Army Plot had produced its preliminary report, which made much of the queen's part in urging her friends to induce the army to march on London to release Strafford from the Tower; and of how her favourite Harry Jermyn had been ordered to go down to Portsmouth to 'secure that place for their Majesties, by intelligence with the governor, and then proceed to France to ask for help to support these efforts'. The report also revealed that it had been George Goring who, despite his promises of loyalty, had betrayed the details of the plan. 'The queen', wrote Giustinian, 'is tortured by cruel distress. . . . She fears that hate and temerity may induce parliament to take steps unbecoming her greatness and innocence.'[6]

A week later fresh disclosures made by the Earl of Northumberland in the hope of gaining immunity for his conspirator brother, now on the run, stirred the committee to renewed activity and led to further arrests. 'The end of this inquiry remains uncertain,' Giustinian reported on 18 June, 'and it keeps the whole court in a state of anxious expectation. Meanwhile, as they are searching ancient documents to find out what was done with other queens in like circumstances, the fear grows that parliament intends to force the queen to clear herself, and will possibly take steps even more injurious.'[7] It had, in fact, begun to look ominously as if Henrietta was being prepared to take the Earl of Strafford's place as public enemy number one.

On 24 June John Pym laid a list of Ten Propositions before the House of Lords for their consideration and agreement. These included a renewed demand that the court should be purged of all Catholic influence, that the queen's Capuchins should be expelled and her public chapel closed, and that in future all appointments to her household and to those of the royal children must be subject to parliamentary approval. The Commons' determination to 'uproot entirely the Catholic religion in this kingdom' was plain enough and the position of the Catholic minority had grown steadily more uncomfortable over the past six months, as it once more became a prime target for official harassment and hostility. The missionary priests, on whom the lay community depended, had been ordered to leave the country and in July Father William Ward, an elderly Franciscan, was executed at Tyburn after steadfastly refusing to renounce his faith. The Venetian ambassador's chaplain was also arrested, although Giustinian managed to rescue him and get him out of England, and in June Father Philip himself had been haled before the Secret Committee to be cross-examined about the Army Plot and confronted with one of his intercepted letters to Walter Montagu in which he had wondered how the King of France could stand by and allow his sister to be so ill-used: 'The Puritans if they dared would pull the good queen to pieces.'

At the beginning of July the new French ambassador, the Marquis de la Ferté Imbault, made his long-awaited public entry into London, an event which brought 'unspeakable consolation' to the king and queen, who were hoping that his presence might exert a restraining influence over parliament's violent career. On the evening of his arrival de la Ferté Imbault saw the queen privately and the following day, after his first official audience, he went again to her apartments, where they conferred in secret 'for quite four hours on end'.[8] The king was also present, but it is easy to imagine that it was Henrietta, pouring out the accumulated grievances of the past months, who did most of the talking.

The king was now planning a visit to Scotland. Charles had continued to give ground throughout the summer. He had graciously surrendered his right to levy tonnage and poundage, and assented to Bills abolishing the prerogative courts of Star Chamber and High Commission. He had dismissed Lord Newcastle, whose name had been mentioned on the fringes of the Army Plot, and given the prestigious post of Governor of the Prince of Wales to the Earl of Hertford. But no one, least of all John Pym, believed for a moment that he would regard these concessions as binding. Indeed, the queen had told Rossetti at his departure that according to the law of England anything granted by the king under duress was null and void.[9] The sudden death of the Earl of Bedford back in the spring had put an end to any hope of reaching a viable and lasting settlement of the differences between Crown and Commons – if, in fact, any such hope had ever really existed – and Charles was only waiting his chance to strike back, a chance he still felt confident would not be long in coming. His hopes were now centred on his northern kingdom. Aware that relations between the 'inflexible party' in the Commons and their brethren of Scotland were no longer quite so cordial, he seems to have convinced himself that a timely charm offensive in Edinburgh would be all that was needed to secure the gratitude of the Covenanters and persuade them to change sides.

For Henrietta the prospect of having to stay behind, alone among her enemies, was too horrible to contemplate and she made another attempt 'to seek a change of air for the sake of her health', being determined, she said, to cross the sea with her mother. Parliament had been forced to supply the money for Marie's travelling expenses and she was now only waiting for permission to pass through Holland on her way to Germany. Henrietta was also planning to take the Princess Mary to the Hague and deliver her to her husband. Prince William had gone home at the end of May, but Frederick Henry, who was paying good money for his son's bride, was known to be anxious that Mary should join her new family as soon as possible – understandably perhaps in view of the mob violence the Dutch had witnessed during their visit to London. Having seen the princess safely handed over, the queen, it was announced, would go on to Spa to take the waters, which were famous for their restorative properties.

The Commons, however, had other ideas. Suspecting an ulterior motive, especially when it was discovered that the queen intended to take a large quantity of valuable plate and jewels with her, they insisted on asking the royal physician some searching questions regarding her majesty's state of health. Theodore Mayerne confirmed that her majesty believed herself to be dangerously ill 'both in mind and body', but he did not consider that Spa water was the right treatment for her just yet, 'her body not being prepared'. In his opinion it was more important to satisfy her mind. 'Her mind being quieted, it would be much help to medicine in the cure.'[10]

Interpreting this to mean that there was nothing much the matter with the queen apart from temper, the Commons proceeded to petition the king to persuade his wife to change her mind about going abroad, promising to make every effort to ensure her personal safety and peace of mind during his absence. As to the Princess Mary, they really could not agree to her joining her husband until she was old enough to be a wife; and besides, what about the national ignominy that would ensue if the queen were to be seen taking her daughter to the Prince of Orange 'who in birth and other prerogatives is so inferior to this august house' – especially at a time when it would be impossible to provide the amount of state ceremonial which English greatness demanded.[11]

Henrietta tried to stick to her resolve. She was prepared to obey the king, she said, but not four hundred of his subjects, 'as this did not befit her spirit or her birth'. But when the four hundred subjects ordered the lady of the bedchamber entrusted with the custody of the queen's jewels 'to have them ready so that she may answer for them', and went on to threaten 'other and more violent measures should her Majesty persist in her original intention', her majesty was obliged to admit defeat. 'Under such vigorous pressure and moved by the strong arguments of the king and of the French ambassador she has finally yielded to what all desire,' wrote Giovanni Giustinian, 'and sent word to Parliament that on this occasion also she would give proof of her zealous desire to please the people.'[12] In her message Henrietta thanked both Houses for their care of her health and happiness, adding tartly, 'I hope I shall see the effect of it.'[13]

Parliament had also been making strenuous efforts to prevent the king from going to Scotland, but on this occasion Charles stood firm and set out on 10 August, taking the Prince Palatine with him. A week later Marie de Medici, too, set out for Dover on the first stage of her journey, accompanied by the Countess of Arundel and a number of English priests, leaving Henrietta in a mood of deep despondency. 'I swear to you that I am driven almost mad by the sudden change in my fortunes,' she wrote to her sister Christine. 'From the highest point of happiness I have fallen into despair. . . . Imagine what I feel to see the King's power taken from him, the Catholics persecuted, the priests hanged, the people faithful to us sent away and pursued for their lives because they served the King. As for myself, I am kept like a prisoner . . . with no one in the world to whom I can confide my troubles.'[14]

The plague was back in London with the hot weather and the queen left town for Oatlands, but the peace and quiet of the Surrey countryside was soon disturbed by a mysterious alarm, when a gentleman living nearby came to tell her majesty that he had received orders to have a number of his tenants armed and ready at midnight in the park, where he would find horsemen and officers who would give him further instructions. Believing this to be some evil design on the part of her enemies, Henrietta took what precautions she could, sending messages to her friends in London appealing for help, and also to George Goring, who she thought had now repented of his treachery, asking him to have relays of horses on the road in case she was forced to flee to Portsmouth. She then mustered the few men available at Oatlands, even down to the kitchen boys, arming them with such makeshift weapons as were to be found in the house and, as midnight approached, herself walked up and down outside 'showing no fear'. But midnight came and went and nothing happened – apart from some reports of a small band of roughly mounted men seen loitering on the boundaries of the estate.[15]

They may have been poachers. The whole incident may have been no more than a hoax intended to frighten the queen into leaving the neighbourhood, but it did nothing for her peace of mind. Nor was this improved by rumours reaching her from London that certain people had been heard speaking of the need to secure the persons of herself and the Prince of Wales should the king's activities in Scotland give cause for concern. The prince would, of course, be invaluable as a hostage and soon after parliament reassembled on 20 October the queen was visited by her old friend Lord Holland bringing a message from the House of Commons. The members, it seemed, were worried that the prince was spending too much time with his mother (and under her influence) while his father was away. They were afraid he must be neglecting his studies and therefore desired that he should be returned to 'make his ordinary abode' at Richmond under the care of his governor and tutors. Henrietta protested that he was only staying to celebrate his sister's birthday – Mary would be ten on 4 November – but, alone as she was, she dared not defy parliament's express commands and young Charles went back to the Marquis of Hertford, who was ordered not to let his charge out of his sight.[16]

The queen was finding her enforced passivity one of the hardest things she had to bear, telling Christine that she could only sit with folded hands waiting helplessly for her enemies to do their worst. In fact, she had been far from idle during those months spent at Oatlands. Charles had left her to guard his interests as best she could during his absence, working together with Edward Nicholas, one of the clerks of the Council and the only official he now trusted completely. But it was on Henrietta's judgement that he chiefly relied, telling Nicholas repeatedly to 'let my wife's direction guide you'. The queen was to concentrate her efforts on building up the strength of the king's party in the Lords, and by using her persuasive charm on the backwoodsmen, as well as on the younger, more frivolous element, cajole them into doing their duty by attending the House on a regular basis. This was especially important at a time when John Pym was intent on pushing through a measure to deprive the bishops – always a reliably royalist body of men – of their right to vote, and Henrietta was kept busy writing letters to all those peers who showed a regrettable tendency to disappear into the country at times of crisis or when, as now, the plague was bad.

At the end of October disturbing reports were filtering down from Scotland of an obscure conspiracy to kidnap the Earl of Argyll, leader of the Covenanters. The Incident, as it became known, almost certainly amounted to little more than careless talk among the king's less intelligent supporters but, like the Army Plot, provided another propaganda weapon which could be used to discredit him. Its implications were still being digested when, on 1 November, news of the outbreak of rebellion in Ireland was brought to the Commons. It was received in shocked silence. 'The accounts of this most serious event have aroused strong feelings everywhere here', wrote Giovanni Giustinian, 'and among the members of parliament in particular.' Ignorance of the admittedly abstruse complexities of Irish politics was profound among the Westminster cognoscenti, and any suggestions that the present disturbances could have had any connection with the removal of the strong hand of Strafford and the disbandment of his army were given no credence. Instead, 'the parliamentarians have conceived some suspicion that the queen may have given some encouragement to these movements in Ireland in secret ways'. Pym called for a list of all the queen's servants and her confessor was once more summoned to appear before the Commons. There is no reason to suppose that Father Philip knew anything about the Irish rebellion, but he had no desire to face questioning which might have revealed the fact that Henrietta was still in communication with Rome through Rossetti, now in Germany. He therefore refused to swear on a Protestant Bible and was promptly committed to the Tower. 'The true reasons which led them to examine this priest have not transpired', commented Giustinian, 'and this action causes well grounded anxiety to prudent people, since by the marriage treaty he enjoys full liberty as the queen's secretary.'[17]

The news from Ireland had, of course, redoubled 'the odium against the English Catholics' as well as their danger, and Henrietta, isolated as never before in an atmosphere solid with hostility and distrust, was finding the strain of her position well-nigh intolerable. She longed for Charles to return and wrote to him 'to hasten his coming'. Unfortunately her usual courier was sick and she appealed to Edward Nicholas to find her another safe messenger. 'Somebody that will be sure, for my letter must not be lost. . . . I am so ill provided with persons that I dare trust, that at this instant I have no living creature that I dare send. Pray do what you can to help me.'[18]

Nicholas, too, was anxious for the king's return, aware as he was of a new attack being mounted against him in the Commons, which 'reflects so much to the prejudice of your Majesty's government, as if your Majesty come not instantly away, I trouble to think what will be the issue of it'.[19]

This was the so-called Grand Remonstrance – a comprehensive list of every popular and parliamentary grievance, large and small, from the beginning of the reign to the present, followed by a demand that from now on the king should employ only those councillors and ambassadors 'as the Parliament might have cause to confide in' and that a general synod of the most grave, pious, learned and, by clear implication, Puritan divines should meet to consider the reformation of the church. This remarkable document, in effect a revolutionary manifesto which would have completed the work of destroying the king's authority by giving parliament the right of veto over his choice of advisers, control of the army and the government of the church was too much for a significant number of Commons members, and it was only after prolonged and heated debate that it was finally agreed by a narrow margin to send it up to the Lords.

The king, meanwhile, was on his way home, apparently satisfied that he had made his peace with the Scots and that they would support him in any future conflict with Westminster. He was greeted warmly by the people as he rode south. There had been definite signs that summer of a shift in public opinion – a general feeling that things had gone far enough. The tradition of reverence for the monarchy was deeply rooted in the English psyche – besides which the more thoughtful members of the property-owning, tax-paying class were beginning to have a nasty suspicion that parliament might well prove to be just as heavy-handed and expensive a master. There was also the all-important question of religion. The conservative majority was sincerely attached to the Church of England and the Book of Common Prayer. Suspicious though they might be of the king's high church tendencies and of anything that smacked of popery, they still preferred a bit of decent order and ceremony with their worship and were becoming seriously irritated by such uncontrolled excesses of Puritanism as the extempore prayers and hell-fire sermons spouted by any Bible-punching upstart who felt moved by the Lord to exhort his (or even sometimes her) social betters to repent.

The queen had gone out to meet her husband, taking the three elder children with her, and there was a happy family reunion at Theobalds on 24 November. Next day they entered the city, the king and the Prince of Wales on horseback, to find the streets decorated in their honour, the conduits running with wine and the people, who only six months earlier had been ready to form a lynch mob, cheering a loyal welcome. Richard Gurney, the royalist Lord Mayor, and his aldermen entertained the court to a civic banquet at the Guildhall and afterwards the king and queen rode back to Whitehall in something very like triumph. At St Paul's the choir came out to greet them with an anthem, and all along Fleet Street and the Strand more cheering crowds lit their way with torches flaring in the November dusk.[20]

The Venetian ambassador hoped this was a sign that the people, grown tired of so much violence, were contemplating a return to their old loyalty and devotion to his majesty and that he might yet be able to recover some of his authority.[21] But it was a delusory hope, for the decisive moment in the battle between King Charles and King Pym was now fast approaching. Charles was still being studiedly moderate in his public utterances, even when confronted with the Grand Remonstrance, but there were two issues on which he would make no concessions – control of the armed forces and any fundamental alteration to the doctrine and discipline of the church as established by Queen Elizabeth and his own father.

The day after their return to London the king and queen had left again for Hampton Court, intending to spend Christmas there, but a deputation of city aldermen, fearing the loss of trade which the court's absence during the winter season would mean, begged them to change their minds. Charles, well aware of the importance of the city's goodwill, gave way graciously, saying that he considered London to be the chief limb of his crown. He was prepared to do anything to further the interests of the citizens and, 'in the presence of the queen, as a token of regard, he knighted all the aldermen whom he afterwards sumptuously entertained'.[22]

So, three days later, on 6 December, the court came trundling back to town, where the atmosphere was not pleasant, especially for the queen. Father Philip had now, albeit reluctantly, been let out of the Tower and she still had her Capuchins, although they no longer wore their habits and were keeping a very low profile, but the many gruesome stories of atrocities against the Protestant settlers beginning to come in from Ireland had provoked a fresh outburst of anti-Catholic hysteria. The rumour factory was once more working at full stretch, and this time Henrietta was accused of being hand-in-glove with the Irish rebel chieftains. The capital was once more in an uproar and excited mobs, deliberately stirred up by the Puritans, or so Giustinian believed, roamed the precincts of Westminster and Whitehall, looking for trouble and shouting 'No bishops!' and 'No popish lords!' The king's attempt to replace the Lieutenant of the Tower with a militant royalist led to still further trouble and there were some ugly clashes between the royal officers and bands of city apprentices on the loose over the Christmas holidays when, for the first time, the opprobrious epithets of Roundhead for the crop-haired shop boys, and Cavalier, or caballero, were being flung around.[23]

Thus the old year ended, in disorder, bitterness and fear. The new year opened with a development long dreaded by the king and queen. It was an open secret that Charles had been preparing to launch a counter-attack on his tormentors in the Commons ever since his return from Scotland. 'At the palace they talk freely of changing many of the leading ministers,'

Giustinian had reported early in December, 'as well as servants of the court who . . . have publicly conspired against the intentions and interests of his Majesty.'[24] Now, in the aftermath of the recent riots, his majesty was making what appeared to some people preparations of an altogether more sinister kind. 'I never saw the court so full of gentlemen,' wrote Henry Slingsby to Admiral Pennington on 30 December; 'every one comes thither with their swords. This day 500 gentlemen of the Inns of Court came to offer their services to the King. The officers of the army since these tumults have watched and kept a Court of Guard in the Presence Chamber, and are entertained upon the King's charge.'[25]

The Commons reacted by demanding their own guard of trained bands under the command of the Earl of Essex but received only an evasive answer from the palace. On 1 January, therefore, they went into committee at the Guildhall, 'ostensibly for their security', and giving everyone the impression that there was a plot afoot against the liberty of parliament. 'Shut up there in long secret discussions', wrote Giustinian, 'they persuaded themselves that the king's action and his resentment were due to the advice of the queen. Accordingly they decided to accuse her in parliament of conspiring against the public liberty and secret intelligence in the rebellion in Ireland.'[26]

If the junta led by John Pym had intended to precipitate a crisis they could not have calculated it more exactly. Any threat to his wife touched the king on his most sensitive spot, and as soon as whispers of the committee's proceedings reached him he delayed his attack no longer, ordering the Attorney-General to bring charges of high treason against Pym and his four closest associates. The Commons, predictably, refused to surrender them, declaring the accusations to be an infamous libel and breach of privilege, 'thus casting shame on his Majesty's commands'. Next day, 4 January, staking everything on one desperate bid to regain the initiative, Charles descended on the House of Commons in his famous attempt to arrest the Five Members, encouraged, it is said, by the queen telling him to go and pull the rogues out by the ears or never see her face again.[27]

To Henrietta the situation was, and always had been, perfectly straightforward. It never, at any time, crossed her mind that the enemy might have had a valid point of view. In her eyes all those who, for whatever reason, challenged the king's authority were quite simply rogues, rebels and traitors to be destroyed without compunction by whatever means came closest to hand. Waiting at the palace that winter afternoon, anxiously watching the clock until she could contain her excitement and impatience no longer, she blurted out to her friend and confidante Lucy Carlisle, 'Rejoice, for at this hour the King, I hope, is master of the state and such-and-such are doubtless under arrest.' Lady Carlisle showed no emotion at this startling announcement but found an excuse to slip away and send a hasty message to *her* friend and confidant John Pym, so that the queen, who believed herself to have been the only person with prior knowledge of the intended *coup*, ever afterwards blamed her own indiscretion for the fact that when the king entered the Commons chamber at the head of his guards he found the birds, forewarned, had already flown.[28]

Actually the informant appears to have come from the French embassy, the ambassador having his own reasons for wishing to keep on good terms with parliament. In any case Charles had walked into a carefully baited trap and had now committed the ultimate folly of attempting a violent and unlawful act and failing. The moderate men who had been gradually gaining ground were confounded and the king himself had lost the last shreds of his credibility in the city, where all the shops were shut and the trained bands standing to arms in hourly expectation of an attack by bloodthirsty hordes of Cavaliers. Charles hung on for a week, trying to brazen things out. 'He has strengthened the garrison in the Tower', reported Giovanni Giustinian, 'and had the guns mounted, but as he is destitute of money, and perhaps of wise and loyal advice, the end of this thorny incident remains doubtful.'[29] The end came on 10 January, when the king and queen with their three eldest children and a handful of attendants suddenly bolted to Hampton Court – so suddenly that nothing was ready for them and the whole family, so Giustinian heard, had to spend an uncomfortable night all huddled together in one bed.

There followed an uneasy stand-off. Pym and his friends, who had returned to Westminster in triumph on the day after the king's flight, maintained that there had never been any question of impeaching the queen, and if her majesty would let them know who had given her this information, they would see that 'the authors of such reports' were suitably punished. The Commons also wanted the king to return to London – it would be more convenient to have him safely under their eyes – but Charles and Henrietta had now left Hampton Court, moving out to the greater security of Windsor, and showed no inclination to obey. The French ambassador went twice to the castle to offer his services as mediator, but de la Ferté Imbault had been a serious disappointment to their majesties, who believed him to be in complete sympathy with the opposite party 'and that France for her own ends wishes to encourage these troubles. Accordingly they limited their reply to generalities and gave the minister no opening to institute negotiations.' The Dutch ambassador, on a similar mission, had no better luck and returned from Windsor 'unsuccessful and ill-pleased'.[30] The king and queen, isolated and trusting no one, made their plans alone.

One thing had now become very clear. Henrietta must go abroad as soon as possible, for Charles would be hopelessly hampered in his dealings with the enemy while he feared for her safety. It was a hectic few weeks. As she later told Christine, Henrietta had so much to do before she left that it was a wonder she did not go mad. The parting from her husband and children had been terrible, but the violence of parliament against her was so great that her life had been in danger. They had not merely accused her of wishing to change the government and religion and of encouraging the Irish rebels, but had said publicly that a queen was no more than a subject and could be punished like any other. But it was not fear of death which had made her leave England, she went on, rather the thought of prison separating her from the king, which would have been worse than death; and besides, that would have ruined everything, for being at liberty she hoped to be able to continue to serve his cause.[31]

Baron van Heenvliet, the personal envoy of the Prince of Orange in England on a private visit, had already been asked to get the prince to make a formal request for Mary's departure to be expedited and on 7 February parliament was informed that being very much pressed to send the princess his daughter immediately into Holland, 'and being likewise earnestly desired by his royal consort the queen to give her majesty leave to accompany her daughter thither, [his majesty] hath thought fit to consent to both desires'.[32] This time the Commons made no objection – according to Giustinian they seemed now to think that the king would be more amenable to their demands with his strong-minded wife out of the way – and two days later the royal family left Windsor en route for Dover. They went first to Greenwich, where Henrietta collected the rest of her own and the king's personal jewellery. She was also able to make off with some other items which had escaped parliamentary vigilance. These included the Grand Sancy, acquired by James I and said to be the most valuable white diamond in western Europe, another huge diamond known as the Mirror of Portugal, which had belonged to Queen Elizabeth, and several gold collars, one set with rubies and pearls belonging to Henry VIII.[33] These were all crown property which the queen was planning to use to raise money for the rapidly approaching armed struggle.

The Venetian ambassador, who had gone down to Greenwich to pay his respects, was graciously received by Henrietta, but she told him positively that to settle affairs it would be necessary to unsettle them first, 'as she considered it impossible to re-establish her husband's authority in any other way'. Giustinian found the court 'much agitated over this unexpected departure of the queen, everyone being fearful of the object and of the results of this journey'. The Princess Mary, he reported, seemed pleased to be going to her husband, but the other princes were grieved at parting from their mother and sister, 'and so is the king also, whose love for the queen is beyond expression, and on this account he suffers greatly at seeing her go'.[34]

By 13 February the travellers had reached Canterbury, where they stayed
for three days while vessels for transporting the queen and her daughter,
with their baggage, servants and followers were still being hurriedly got
together. 'Things are done in such post haste that I never heard of the like
for the voyage of persons of so great dignity,' remarked one official
disapprovingly, and he did not see how they could be ready in time unless
the queen went without her coaches and horses. However, by 23 February
five ships had been collected and were waiting at Dover for the royal party
to embark. It was quite a small party by royal standards. Only three ladies
of honour were going with the queen, Mary Villiers, now Duchess of
Richmond, Susan Denbigh and the Countess of Roxburgh, and only two
lords, Arundel and Goring, the father of George. There was Father Philip,
of course, two of the queen's favourite Capuchins and the faithful dwarf
Geoffrey Hudson.

Sixteen years had gone by since the teenage Henrietta had first set eyes
on her disappointingly unimposing husband in the gloomy surroundings
of Dover Castle and had quarrelled with him over Mamie St Georges' place
in her carriage. Now, as he went with her down to the water's edge, they
clung together, conversing 'in sweet discourse and affectionate embraces'.
Both were in tears and many of their companions wept in sympathy. At last
Charles tore himself away. The queen went on board the *Lion* and the little
fleet stood out to sea, leaving the king to ride along the shoreline, waving
his hat in farewell until the sails faded from sight. The wind was favourable
and the voyage uneventful, at least until they reached the mouth of the
River Maas, when one of the baggage vessels sprang a leak and sank, taking
with it most of its crew, all the queen's chapel plate and the Duchess of
Richmond's wardrobe.

Prince William was waiting to welcome his bride and among the rest of
the quality who had come out to greet the Queen of England was that
other queen, whose misfortunes had cast such a long shadow over her
brother's foreign policy. The various shattering calamities and
disappointments suffered by Elizabeth of Bohemia would have destroyed
most women, but Elizabeth was a survivor and in spite of everything had
kept her unquenchable zest for life and 'wild humour to be merry'. Now,
as they sat together in the Orange state coach, she was doing her best to
make friends with her sister-in-law, although she disapproved of
Henrietta's Catholicism and thought her influence on Charles unhelpful:
'The queen is against an agreement with parliament but by war, and the
king doth nothing but by her approbation.'

The Queen of Bohemia was also accompanied by a daughter, eleven-
year-old Sophie, chosen from among her sisters because she was nearest in
age to the Princess Mary. Many years later when, as Duchess of Hanover,

she was writing her memoirs, Sophie could still vividly recall her surprise at finding the glamorous aunt from England, 'so beautiful in her picture', to be a rather scrawny little woman 'with long lean arms, crooked shoulders and teeth protruding from her mouth like guns from a fort'. Fortunately Henrietta had been tactful enough to say that she thought Sophie resembled the princess her daughter, which, since Mary was considered the beauty of the family, pleased the youngest Palatine so much that she was prepared to concede that her majesty was actually quite handsome, with 'beautiful eyes, a well-shaped nose and an admirable complexion'.[35] All the same, Henrietta was thirty-two now, and ten years of child-bearing and nearly two years of mounting anxiety and acute nervous strain had taken their toll on both her looks and her health.

The queen was given a polite, though not over-enthusiastic welcome at the Hague. The Prince of Orange received his daughter-in-law with pleasure and all the deference due to her exalted rank, but he had not bargained for having to entertain her mother as well and had, in fact, tried to discourage her visit. More to the point, the oligarchy of Dutch burghers who made up the States General of the United Provinces, of which Holland was the largest and richest, and who wielded the real power in an increasingly important trading nation were less than impressed by the grandeur of the English alliance. Sturdy Calvinist citizens stared suspiciously at her majesty from beneath their hat brims, sat down uninvited in her presence and sometimes just walked away without bowing or speaking. The High Mightinesses of the States General were predominantly republican in sympathy and, wrote an English resident at the Hague in a letter home, were 'studying all the wayes they can to gratifie and complie with your Parliament, not caring who they displease. I verily thinke the Queene will not trouble them long heere and that yee shall have her in England yet a good while before Easter.'[36]

But the queen, now installed in apartments in the New Palace in the Staedt-Straat, had begun to turn her attention to the serious purpose of her journey and showed no signs of being easily dislodged. She was anxious for news from Charles who, they had agreed, would go north to the provincial capital of York; but it was also imperative that he should make sure of the town of Hull, which was not only a valuable sea-port but contained all the arms and ammunition left after the Scottish campaigns. 'Hull must absolutely be had,' wrote the queen. It was vital to have an east coast port to which money, military supplies and letters could safely be sent. She was also worried about the security of the code in which she and Charles were to communicate. 'Take good care I beg of you, and put in nothing which is not in my cipher. Once again I remind you to take good care of your pocket, and not let our cipher be stolen.'[37] She was still waiting to know 'assuredly' where the king was when she wrote again. 'I hope this bearer will find you at York . . . and that if you find York well-affected, you will go to Hull, for we must have Hull.' She had heard worrying rumours that he was returning to London, but 'I believe nothing of it; and hope that you are more constant in your resolutions; you have already learned to your cost, that want of perseverance in your designs has ruined you.'

It was obvious that Henrietta placed very little reliance on her husband's standing firm without her beside him to stiffen his backbone. If he had really gone back to London with some idea of reaching an 'accommodation' with parliament, she told him flatly that she would have to leave him and retire into a convent, for she could never trust herself 'to those persons who would be your directors, nor to you, since you would have broken your promise to me'. She could hardly bring herself to believe that he would do such a thing, but confessed she was troubled almost to death for fear of the contrary: 'and I have cause, for if you have broken your resolutions, there is nothing but death for me'.[38]

While she was writing this letter she heard from Charles at Newmarket. It was disappointing, as she had been hoping he would surely be at York by this time, but she was so relieved to find he had not gone back to London that she did not reproach him, apart from reminding him that delay had never yet been to his advantage. For her part, she was losing no time, but had to admit that so far she had no money worth sending. She was having unexpected difficulty in pawning the more valuable jewels she had brought with her. It seemed they were too big and too expensive for the market at the Hague; also annoying doubts were being expressed about the queen's authority to pledge such large and important pieces.

At last, in mid-April, she received the news that the king had finally reached York and found the country 'well-affected', but he had still made no attempt to occupy Hull and Henrietta was furiously impatient with his excuses. 'As to what you write me, that everybody dissuades you concerning Hull from taking it by force, unless the parliament begins, – is it not beginning to put persons into it against your orders? . . . For you having Hull is not beginning anything violent, for it is only against the rascal who refuses it to you.' The queen could not understand her husband's reluctance to fire the first shot. It seemed to her that parliament was simply playing cat and mouse, and at this rate any money she succeeded in raising would be frittered away while he waited for them to declare war on him. Then 'there will be no further means of getting other monies, and thus you will be reduced to do what the Parliament shall please, and I shall be constrained to retire into a convent, or to beg alms'. Poor Henrietta's frustration was becoming almost unbearable, but afraid she might have said too much she apologised for her 'folly and weakness'. It was surely understandable though, for 'my whole hope lies only in your firmness and constancy, and when I hear anything to the contrary, I am mad'. Added to which she had such a bad toothache that she scarcely knew what she was doing.[39]

In her next letter the queen was able to report that 'after much trouble, we have at last procured some money, but only a little as yet, for the fears of the merchants are not yet entirely passed away. It was written from London that I had carried off my jewels secretly, and against your wish, and that if money was lent me upon them, that would be no safety for them.' However, now that she had received a 'power' signed by the king, it was easier to do business. But she had had to part with some cherished possessions, such as Charles's pearl buttons. 'You cannot imagine how handsome the buttons were, when they were out of the gold and strung into a chain. . . . I assure you that I gave them up with no small regret. Nobody would take them in pledge, but only buy them. You may judge', she wrote bitterly, 'now, when they know that we want money, how they keep their foot on our throat. I could not get for them more than half of what they are worth.' She had been advised to try to pawn the ruby collar at Antwerp, and was trying to interest the King of Denmark in the largest gold collar. 'This is all that concerns money,' she went on, 'but if we put all our jewels in pledge and consume them without doing anything, they would be lost, and we too.'[40]

Henrietta had been told that the Jews of Amsterdam might be willing to lend her money, and early in May the Prince of Orange escorted her there 'to note the marvels of the wealth of the city'. The Amsterdammers were well known for their republicanism and distrust of all royal pretensions, but they gave the Queen of England an elaborate welcome, which included a barge drawn by swans, pageants and 'triumphs' on the water. Unfortunately, though, the visit had to be cut short by a death in the Orange family, so the queen had no opportunity to open negotiations with the money-lenders.[41]

Back at the Hague, writing and enciphering her endless letters to Charles, she returned to the seemingly hopeless task of trying to prod him into action. The longer he delayed in seizing Hull, the worse his situation would be. If parliament, which now controlled the navy, were to send a fleet to remove the precious arsenal he would be powerless to prevent it, and 'if before that, you do not get the place, the folly is so great that I do not understand it'. She was afraid, too, that he might be pressured into ceding control of the armed forces. Perhaps he had already done so and was back at his old game of yielding everything. Henrietta was beginning to wish she had never left England. The whole point of her journey had been to leave the king free to act without fear of danger to her person, but if he was only going to sit at York and do nothing, she might just as well have stayed with him, and she ended by repeating her threat of retiring into a convent, 'for you are no longer capable of protecting any one, not even yourself'.[42]

Before this latest broadside could be dispatched, a messenger arrived from England with news of 'all that has passed at Hull'. It was not good. Apparently Charles had sent the eight-year-old Duke of York and the Prince Palatine to pay a 'friendly' visit to the town. They had been received, rather reluctantly, by the Governor, Sir John Hotham, and entertained to dinner, but when the king himself arrived a little later at the head of a troop of horse, the gates were shut and he was refused admission.

'You see what you have got by not following your first resolutions,' wrote the queen with pardonable exasperation. The Governor of Hull was a traitor who must be taken alive or dead, and Henrietta wished she could have been in young James's place. 'I would have flung the rascal over the walls, or he should have done the same to me.' There was no point in further reproaches, but 'Courage! I have never felt so much: it is a good omen.'[43]

She was keeping up a brave front for Charles – 'Go on boldly: God will assist you' – but with her old friend Mamie St Georges she could let down her guard. 'Pray to God for me, for be assured that there is not a more wretched creature in this world than I, separated far from the king my lord, from my children, out of my country, and without hope of returning there, except at imminent peril – abandoned by all the world, unless God assist me, and the good prayers of my friends. . . . Recommend me to the good Carmelites of Paris, I would fain, if it were possible, wish myself with them. . . . I assure you it is the only thing I think of with pleasure.'[44]

Spring turned into summer, and early in June Henrietta went with Mary to visit the Prince of Orange and his son with the Dutch army in camp near Utrecht and she was present at a grand military review. The queen had now begun to learn her way round the unfamiliar business of acquiring weapons of war, and on 4 June wrote to tell the king that she hoped soon to be able to send him 'six pieces of cannon, with one hundred barrels of powder, and two hundred pairs of pistols and carabines'.[45]

The task of gathering supplies became all the more urgent when, a few days later, a letter arrived from Charles bringing the not unexpected news that the arms and ammunition stored at Hull had now been removed to London by order of parliament. In her reply, Henrietta commented, with heroic restraint, that it would not be easy to find the money to make up for this loss. 'I must say', she went on, 'that if you had not delayed this going to Hull so long as you did, I think that you would

not have lost your magazine. . . . I am ever returning to the old point –
lose no time, for that will ruin you.' But, 'believe, my dear heart, that
I am moved to speak by no consideration in the world but by that of my
affection for you'.[46] Charles does not seem to have resented his wife's
plain speaking, for in a fragment of a letter written that summer
complaining there had been nothing from her in the 'weekly despatch',
he says sadly, 'I would rather have thee chide me than be silent.'

Exactly how much money and materiel Henrietta managed to collect
while she was in Holland remains unclear. Writing in July she enumerates
thirty thousand guilders received from the Prince of Orange, plus 'one
thousand saddles with all appurtenances, five hundred carabines, two
hundred firelocks, ten loads of powder', but does not say whether these
were part of or in addition to the earlier list.[47] Nor is it at all clear how
many of these precious supplies ever reached their destination.

Two of the Queen of Bohemia's soldier sons, the Princes Rupert and
Maurice, were now preparing to join their uncle and Henrietta proposed
to send a shipment of arms over with them. The Palatine princes, sailing
in the *Lion*, were driven back by bad weather, but their other ship, the 300-
ton *Providence*, managed to reach the Humber. According to the Venetian
ambassador, she brought 'cannons, gunpowder, arms, saddles and other
munitions of war', but was attacked by ships of the parliamentary fleet
which had been lying in wait. Fortunately, her master, Captain Strahan,
was not only 'full of zeal for the royal service', but also a skilful seaman
who evaded pursuit by running the *Providence* into one of the small sandy
creeks in the estuary, where her cargo was successfully unloaded.[48]

Others were not so fortunate for in a postscript to his next dispatch
Giovanni Giustinian reported: 'News comes at this moment that two ships
from Holland appeared off Uls [Hull], sent by the queen with munitions
to his Majesty. Falling in with the ships of the fleet they had to surrender,
with disadvantage to his Majesty's designs.'[49] There is mention, too, of
'a small Dutch ship, sent . . . towards York by the queen of England with
military provisions', which had to turn back to avoid capture by 'two large
Parliament ships'.[50]

But in August two ships did reach the king from Holland, carrying
'ammunitions, arms, money, and many English captains, who have fought
a long time in the armies of the Prince of Orange'. Giustinian does not
say so, but these were presumably part of the convoy escorting Rupert
and Maurice, who finally landed at Newcastle on 20 August, bringing with
them 'money, munitions and arms sent by the queen to his Majesty'. Two
more ships are mentioned in the Venetian dispatches as 'arriving in the
waters of Newcastle' during the autumn, one of them carrying
'a thousand sets of horse armour, 3500 muskets and other munitions';

but a third, bringing 'munitions, arms and 140 officers for the army', was forced to put in at Yarmouth, where it was seized by the enemy. 'A serious loss to the royal cause,' commented Giustinian.[51]

In one of her letters Henrietta speaks of having found a merchant who had assured her that he could deliver arms wherever she pleased, and there may well have been other anonymous little ships sailing out of the River Maas which managed to run the parliamentary blockade and slip unadvertised into the fishing ports of the north-east. But the cargoes such vessels could carry would have been extremely small, and the obstacles presented by wind, weather and hostile fleets must at times have appeared insurmountable. It was a disheartening business and the queen often felt quite crushed by it all. 'If you knew my unhappiness as it really is, you would pity me still more,' she told Christine. She was suffering acutely from migraine – 'I have almost always pains in the eyes, and my sight even is not so good as it was.' She didn't know whether this was caused by the air of Holland, by too much crying, or the strain of the amount of writing she was having to do.[52] She was worried about her children. Charles and James were with their father, but the two youngest, Elizabeth and Henry, who was still not much more than a baby, had been left behind at St James's when the family fled to Hampton Court and were now in the hands of parliament. That was bad enough, but worst of all was her constant nagging fear that the king might yet be pressured into coming to some dishonourable agreement with parliament, and find himself pardoning his enemies and forsaking his friends. 'You should take good care what you grant,' she wrote in September, 'for you are lost forever if you abandon your servants. . . . If you abandon your servants, it will be worse than your crown.' It would be the end of everything and she would have to retire to some place 'like a good country lady, where I can pray to God to take care of you, as he has assured me he will'.[53]

In spite of all these afflictions and anxieties – her uneasiness about what was going on at home, her headaches and continuing battles with tight-fisted Dutch pawnbrokers and money-grubbing arms dealers – Henrietta struggled valiantly on with her self-appointed task, sustained always by her fiercely protective love for her husband – 'there is nothing in the world, no trouble, which shall hinder me from serving you and loving you above everything in the world' – and her unshakeable belief in the justice of their cause. 'Justice suffers with us. Always take care that we have her on our side: she is a good army.'[54]

The queen was not, in fact, quite so friendless as she sometimes made out. The Prince of Orange had done what he could for his uninvited and importunate guest. He had allowed several royalist refugees such as Henry Jermyn, Lord Digby, Francis Windebank and the former Lord Keeper, Sir

John Finch, to join her at the Hague in spite of the ban imposed on them by the States General. He had also turned a blind eye, in defiance of the States' disapproval, to the shipment of arms from Dutch ports and had given a number of his more experienced officers leave to go and join King Charles. He was less eager to part with money, although he did offer himself as guarantor for the loans being made on the queen's jewels, even for 'the great collar' which, for some reason, no one would touch. Henrietta thought it must have some malediction on it.[55]

All this had not gone unnoticed in London and in August, to Henrietta's unspeakable fury, 'the rebels under the name of Parliament' had the impudence to send an envoy of their own to the Hague. The queen immediately registered a violent objection to his presence and the envoy, Walter Strickland, was not given official recognition, but the States 'have sent to the rogue in private to know what his commission was'. This appears to have been to protest about the assistance being rendered to the king, coupled with a warning that if nothing was done to put a stop to it, the English fleet would be obliged to regard all Dutch ships passing through the Channel as potential enemies. Henrietta told Charles that she intended to issue a statement setting out 'the things which the Parliament has done against you, and that you have done for Parliament', in order to show their malice and try to undeceive the Hollanders. She was so weary, having been talking all day and in such a passion about the envoy, that she was afraid her letter did not make much sense and Charles would have to get someone to help him decipher it. 'If I do not turn mad', she wrote, 'I shall be a great miracle.'[56]

The queen did not turn mad, but she was deeply hurt by rumours beginning to reach her from England that the king was dissatisfied with her efforts. She had been trying so hard to serve him and had been pathetically pleased by some of 'the pretty things' he had put in his letters, 'for you know I like to be praised'. But now it seemed she was being blamed for not trying hard enough, which was especially unfair considering that 'if everybody had done their duty, as I have', Charles would not be in his present predicament, and she wrote him a long self-justificatory letter listing the 'one thousand muskets, and as many pikes and swords', the two or three thousand pistols, another three thousand muskets and the thousand saddles so laboriously assembled and shipped during the past three months. The fact that many of them had failed to arrive was disappointing, but she could not be held responsible for contrary winds, nor was it her fault that the navy had so ungratefully gone over to the parliament, or that Hull had been allowed to remain in enemy hands. As for money, Charles knew the problems she had had in raising cash on their jewels, but she had sent him every sou left over from her expenditure on arms. She was still hoping to arrange some further loans, but it was no use trying to hurry the Dutch – 'the more they are hurried the less they do'. Besides which, 'these people here are so Parliamentarian that it is with great trouble we can get anything from them'.

Henrietta was convinced that deliberate mischief was being made by certain people close to her husband – 'base souls, as are many of those near you' – who were determined to reach a negotiated settlement with the enemy, 'and they have vilified me, knowing well that I should never consent to anything against your honour. . . . A long time ago', she went on, 'I was assured from London that there would be an accommodation in spite of me, if I would have nothing to do with it, and by those who were nearest to you . . . and they will persuade you that you are forced by want of arms.' If there were to be such an accommodation, she could not bear to return; but if not, 'let me come to you. I wish to share all your fortune, and participate in your troubles, as I have done in your happiness, provided it be with honour, and in your defence.'[57]

By this time – mid-September – the queen's anxieties had grown more acute, for on 22 August the king had finally raised his standard at Nottingham and England had slid confusedly, almost insensibly, into civil war. Communication was now more difficult than ever. Henrietta heard nothing from Charles for six weeks and news was reaching her only in disconnected snippets from anonymous sources. Holland, of course, was seething with rumours that the king had been defeated – 'for battles, there is not a day in the week in which you do not lose one', that he had been killed or captured, that the Prince of Wales was a prisoner, that the Palatine princes had been killed – there were men who claimed to have seen and touched their dead bodies. 'Such are the pastimes of this country and their tidings,' remarked Henrietta bitterly.[58]

She talked wistfully about coming home, but much as she longed to see Charles again – 'the only pleasure left for me in this world; for, without you, I should not wish to remain in it an hour' – she felt in duty bound to let him know that Louis was now offering her asylum in France. 'Wherefore consider well', she wrote, 'whether you would wish me to go there or not.' There were several things which should be thought of before deciding. 'Women cannot follow an army without great inconveniences, even for you. You may be sure too that the rebels will do all they can to prevent me from joining you, and to take me, believing that they will thus make a better bargain with you. If you were to chance to lose a battle, where would the poor women be? If by misfortune you were taken, I, being abroad, might yet serve you, whilst were I with you, all would be lost. . . . For my own part', she went on, 'you may imagine that my inclination leads me for England, but I entreat you not to think of that which will please me most . . . for I can bear much when your

[handwritten in margin: 1642]

service is concerned. . . . Only let me have a speedy answer, because the season is advancing, and I do not wish to stay in this country.'[59]

The answer, or at least an assurance that Charles wanted her to return whatever the risks involved, appears to have been brought by his cousin the Duke of Richmond, who visited the Hague at Michaelmas, for in her next letter Henrietta speaks of preparing for her journey as quickly as possible. Richmond had also been able to clear up a number of misunderstandings and to tell her of the king's courage and constant resolution against all the assaults made upon him. This cheered her up so much that she even ventured a little joke at the expense of the Puritans. 'I'll go pray for the man of sin that has married the popish brat of France, as the preacher said in London.'[60]

The queen had been planning, she said, to sail for home 'by All Saints' Day according to the style of England' – that is 1 November (O.S.). But the weeks passed and still she lingered. On 23 October the battle of Edgehill, the first major engagement of the war, had been fought, giving the king a rare opportunity for a rapid advance on London, and the Venetian Secretary at the Hague thought the queen was waiting in the hope of being able to go straight there with her court. If so, it was a vain hope. Charles was not quick enough and by the time his army reached the western approaches to London, the city was roused and ready. In the tense confrontation which took place among the orchards and market gardens of Turnham Green on 13 November it was the king who turned away, and by the end of the month he was settling into winter quarters at Oxford.

The queen had been in correspondence with the Earl of Newcastle, the royalist commander in the north, regarding her impending arrival in his territory, but York was now being threatened by Captain Hotham, son of the rascally Governor of Hull, and the earl had been forced to fall back to Durham. 'I have received letters from the Earl of Newcastle', wrote Henrietta at the beginning of December, 'by which he begs me not to come yet, for he is constrained to march into Yorkshire. Hotham is playing the devil. So that I shall wait the issue of his march. . . .'[61]

As always she found waiting the hardest part. She had a shocking cold and badly needed the air of England to cure it. However, as she repeatedly assured the king, she was not wasting her time. She had not given up hope of securing a loan from the merchants of the Dutch East India company, but the usual delays meant that the business would probably not be concluded before she left Holland – 'this country is too trying to the patience of persons who, like me, scarcely have any'. She was also continuing tirelessly to badger and cajole the other European princes, pointing out that it was in their own interests to support a fellow sovereign under attack from his own subjects. She had very little hope of

France, where they still suspected the King of England of pro-Spanish sympathies, but Denmark looked more promising. King Christian was, after all, Charles's uncle and the Danish ambassador had made some large, if rather vague promises of help during a recent visit to the Hague. And there was always the Prince of Orange. The suggestion of another Orange match, between the Prince of Wales and Frederick Henry's daughter, had first been made more than a year ago and Henrietta did not intend to let it drop. She herself could do no more. Her jewels were all in pawn by this time and she was virtually penniless. 'Adieu, my dear heart,' she wrote in the first week of the New Year, 'I am going to take my supper, and as it has cost money I must not let it be spoiled.'[62]

The Earl of Newcastle having regained control of the situation in Yorkshire, only a contrary wind now hindered the queen's sailing and on 19 January she was writing what she hoped would be her last letter from Holland. A final consignment of arms and ammunition had been loaded on to the waiting transports and the Dutch were providing an escort of eight warships. According to the Venetians, they were so anxious to see her off the premises that they were doing everything possible 'to render her departure comfortable and splendid'. The Queen of Bohemia, too, would not be sorry to say goodbye to her sister-in-law. Although they had remained on civil terms, Elizabeth had never been at ease with Henrietta. 'I find by all the queen's and her people's discourse that they do not desire an agreement betwixt his majesty and the parliament but that all be done by force, and rail abominably at the parliament,' she told her friend, the diplomat Sir Thomas Roe. Elizabeth was in a particularly difficult position with regard to parliament, being dependent on its good will for the payment of her English pension and quite literally could not afford to alienate the source of 'those necessary supplies'. She was therefore obliged to write conciliatory letters to the Speaker of the honourable House of Commons and deny that she had ever encouraged her sons to fight for her brother.

At long last, and to the enormous relief of all concerned, Henrietta took the road to Scheveningen, a short distance up the coast from the Hague, and on 2 February her fleet of eleven vessels put to sea. It was a voyage likely to be fraught with danger, for the parliamentary ships based at Yarmouth had been ordered to be on the look-out for the arrival of the queen and her popish army, and to be ready to open fire without ceremony. But whatever her other faults, Henrietta did not lack physical courage. She feared none but God, and 'as to the rebels, neither their writings nor their threats shall ever make me do anything . . . much less shall they frighten me, – God being my guide and my safeguard'.

On this occasion, however, it was the forces of nature rather than those of her earthly enemies which proved the greater danger. A fierce north-

177

easterly gale blew up and the queen and her escort were battered by one of the worst storms seen in the North Sea for many years. For nine hideous days and nights the hapless passengers remained tied to their cots in the chaotic darkness, noise and stench below decks, tended only by one of the Capuchin friars, an ex-Knight of Malta who, 'being habituated to a naval life', was the only member of the party not suffering from the miseries of seasickness. All expected death at any moment and the Catholics were frantically confessing their sins at the tops of their voices, any feelings of shame overcome by fear of imminent extinction. Henrietta herself is said to have quelled the general panic by reminding her companions that no Queen of England had ever yet been drowned, but all the same she made a vow to go on a pilgrimage to the shrine of Our Lady of Liesse and give it a silver ship if she were spared, and was later to tell the king that she had never expected to see him again.

Two ships managed to reach Newcastle and two more went down in the raging seas with the loss of eighteen men and twenty-three horses, but the rest staggered back to port at Scheveningen and the queen and the others on board the *Princess Royal* were carried ashore in varying degrees of prostration. Their clothes, stiff and sodden with sea water, vomit and excreta, had to be peeled off them and burnt, while the priest who gave thanks for their deliverance at the water's edge was unable to stand unsupported.[63]

Sensible men, like the Venetian resident at the Hague, thought the queen would now wait until the spring, or at least for better weather, but Henrietta, bruised, exhausted, seasick and 'stupified' from lack of sleep, had no intention of waiting. Nor was she impressed by all those well-meaning persons who 'do nothing but preach to me on the dangers I am incurring, and a strange conjunction of planets which will happen when I am at sea'. God had already saved her from one great danger and she did not expect him to abandon her now.[64]

She had to wait for ten days while the ships were repaired and refitted, using the time to convert a loan from the King of Denmark into specie and acquiring an additional supply of ammunition. At the last moment an incautious Dutch bureaucrat tried to arrest one of her transports on the grounds that the queen had not applied for a licence for the shipment of munitions it carried. The queen disputed this hotly. The munitions were for her own defence during her passage to England, and she addressed a furious protest to the States General over 'this notable injustice and indignity'. The States hurriedly gave way, two parliamentary ships lurking in ambush at the mouth of the Maas were warned off and the fleet set sail once more on or about 22 February. This time all went well. The sea remained calm and the voyage passed without incident, although it was known that half-a-dozen parliamentary ships were patrolling the waters off Newcastle. Here again Henrietta's luck held, for a last minute change of wind direction enabled the Dutch commander of the convoy to veer away to the south-west, making landfall in Bridlington Bay on the Yorkshire coast below Flamborough Head.

After waiting on board until a detachment of Lord Newcastle's forces had arrived from York, Henrietta went ashore and was put up in a cottage on the quayside of the little fishing village of Bridlington. But her adventures were not over yet. 'That night', she wrote to Charles, 'four of the Parliament ships arrived at Burlington [sic] without our knowledge, and in the morning about 4 o'clock, the alarm was given that we should send down to the harbour to secure our ammunition boats, which had not yet been able to be unloaded; but, about an hour after, these four ships began to fire so briskly, that we were all obliged to rise in haste, and leave the village to them: at least the women, for the soldiers remained very resolutely to defend the ammunition. . . . One of these ships had done me the favour to flank my house, which fronted the pier, and before I could get out of bed, the balls were whistling upon me in such style that you may easily believe I loved not such music.'

Dressed 'just as it happened' Henrietta and her ladies were bundled out into the street, but the queen suddenly realised that her pet dog had been left behind. Mitte was apparently an ugly beast but much loved by her mistress, who insisted on running back to fetch her. The ladies now went on foot to some distance from the village, to seek shelter in a ditch, 'like those at Newmarket' according to the queen. 'But before we could reach it', her account goes on, 'the balls were singing round us in fine style, and a serjeant was killed twenty paces from me. We placed ourselves then under this shelter, during two hours that they were firing upon us, and the balls passing always over our heads, and sometimes covering us with dust.' At last the Dutch admiral sent a message to the 'parliament ships' to say that if they did not stop, he would fire on them as enemies. Henrietta thought he had left this a bit late, 'but he excuses himself on account of a fog which he says there was'. At any rate, the bombardment now ceased and as the tide went out the larger ships were obliged to retreat out of range. The queen then returned defiantly to her lodgings, 'not choosing that they should have the vanity to say that they had made me quit the village', and she ended what she assured the king was a 'very exact relation of all that had passed' with the information that 'after this, I am going to eat a little, having taken nothing today but three eggs and slept very little'.[65]

Henrietta thought she could truly say that she had been in some danger by sea and by land, but God had protected her, as she had always believed he would in so just a cause, and now, undaunted, she was eager to take the road again for the longed-for reunion with Charles. 'As soon as I have arrived at York, I will send to you to ascertain how I can come and join you.'

CHAPTER EIGHT

Generalissima

There is nothing so certain as that I do take all the pains I can
imaginable to procure you assistance.
Henrietta Maria to Charles I, 18 November 1644

1643

News of the queen's arrival in Yorkshire was variously received. Sir Thomas Roe hoped that she would come 'as an angel and mediatrix of peace', while the king was naturally 'looking for her with tender affection'. But at the Venetian embassy, where Giustinian's secretary Gerolamo Agostini was now in charge, they heard that some of his majesty's 'good and loyal servants' who favoured a negotiated settlement with parliament were less than pleased, fearing that 'she may by her influence do considerable mischief in the successful conduct of affairs'.[1] Ferdinando, Lord Fairfax, parliamentary general in the north, wrote to offer her his protection if she would only refuse the attendance of those who, by the highest court, had been declared enemies of the state. He, too, expressed the hope that by the powerful influence of her presence and mediation with the king, 'this kingdom (that hath tasted nothing but war and misery since your departure) shall now be restored to the happy condition of peace'.[2]

Henrietta herself always maintained that she wanted peace more than anyone and with most reason, but since she regarded the dissolution of the 'perpetual parliament' as an essential pre-condition for any settlement, her chances of success as a mediatrix did not look promising. Parliament itself harboured no illusions about the violence of the queen's resentment towards it – a feeling it fully reciprocated – and, according to the Venetians, feared that 'her ardent French temper' would now inspire the king to more vigorous resolution. On hearing of her return, the Commons voted to send a message desiring her majesty's 'reparty to London, where she should be royally and lovingly entertained', but warning that if she refused this invitation, the parliamentary forces would do all they could, 'by open force of arms', to hinder her proceedings and oppose her march.[3]

Henrietta was delayed at Bridlington for several days by the difficulty of finding transport for the precious ammunition she had brought from Holland and eventually it was decided to leave half of Newcastle's men to protect the baggage train, while the other half escorted the queen to York. 'We have to do with enemies who are very vigilant,' she told

Charles, 'therefore we must be on our guard.' The danger that she might be snatched by the enemy was not imaginary. The Venetians had heard rumours of a kidnap plot involving, among others, her old enemy the Earl of Newport, and John Pym had reportedly hinted to certain members of the Lords who were pressing him for peace, that if they would only have a little patience 'they should see them get so good a pawn into their hands, that they might make their own conditions'.[4]

Happily, though, no hostage-takers were lying in wait on the road to York and by the second week of March Henrietta was safely installed in Sir Arthur Ingram's house, where she immediately plunged into the business of the war, conferring with James Hamilton and James Graham, Marquis of Montrose, about Scottish affairs and receiving visits from the local gentry. Prominent among these was Sir Hugh Cholmley, parliamentary governor of Scarborough, who rode into York at the head of a troop of horse for a parley with the queen and, after receiving certain assurances from her, agreed to defect to the royalist side, bringing with him not only the castle and useful little port of Scarborough, but also a ship laden with arms previously captured by the parliament.

All this was valuable, but Henrietta did not plan to stay in the north – 'I am in the greatest impatience in the world to join you' she had written to Charles from Bridlington; while he, for his part, wrote of his longing to have the happiness of her company and of his thankfulness at her escape from shipwreck. 'Indeed I think it not the least of my misfortunes that, for my sake, thou hast run so much hazard; in which thou hast expressed so much love to me, that I confess it is impossible to repay, by any thing I can do, much less by words.'[5]

Unfortunately communications between York and the king's headquarters at Oxford were proving almost as difficult as those between Oxford and the Hague. Letters were frequently interrupted and misunderstandings inevitably arose. The queen was particularly worried about talks currently being conducted at Oxford with a delegation of parliamentary commissioners and was, as usual, afraid that Charles might agree to some damaging concessions. He had written to explain that although the 'articles of cessation' proposed by parliament were quite unacceptable, he was nevertheless continuing the discussion process in order to show the people that it was not he who desired the continuance of the war but those who had caused and fostered rebellion. But this letter never reached its destination, and on 30 March Henrietta warned him that 'if you make a peace and disband your army, before there is an end to this perpetual parliament, I am absolutely resolved to go into France; not being willing to fall again into the hands of those people, being well assured, that if the power remain with them, it will not be well for me in England'.[6]

Disturbing rumours that the peace party with the king at Oxford was trying to persuade him not to speak of dissolving parliament, or of his intention to repeal the legislation it had passed, provoked another outburst from the north. If that were the case, and the present parliament remained, he would be no better off than before he had taken arms. 'Why then have you taken arms? You are betrayed! I will let you see it! Never allow your army to be disbanded, till it [the parliament] is ended, and never let there be a peace till that be put an end to . . . remember that you are lost if you consent to a peace unless that first be abolished.'[7]

Much to Henrietta's relief, the so-called Treaty of Oxford collapsed in April and parliament recalled its commissioners on the 14th. But that was not quite the end of the matter. Much as they detested the queen and everything she stood for, John Pym and the others had never underestimated the importance of her influence, believing that 'without her encouragement and aid the king would never have put himself in a position to resist'. His intercepted letters revealed that he had been consulting his wife over the proposed ceasefire and made it all too plain 'that nothing is to be done in that or other matters without her consent'. A discreet approach was therefore made to see if she would be willing 'to listen to a peace' and advise the king to re-open negotiations, promising that Essex's army (which had just occupied Reading) should not advance further until her reply had been received. 'I thought it fitting to show a desire for peace', wrote Henrietta demurely on 5 May, while at the same time taking advantage of the breathing space thus provided to get a much-needed consignment of gunpowder through to Oxford.[8]

It seems unlikely to have been coincidental that a couple of weeks later parliament should have abandoned all pretence in its dealings with her majesty. Her chapel at Somerset House had already been invaded and vandalised and her few remaining Capuchins unceremoniously bundled off back to France. Now, on 23 May, the Commons finally carried out its long-standing threat to impeach her. After long and serious debate, it was agreed that the queen was as liable to the censure of the law as any subject in the kingdom. After all, as the members reminded one another, she had never actually been crowned. The question then arose as to whether her pawning of the crown jewels in Holland, and her 'actual performances with her popish army' amounted to high treason, a question 'which was unanimously resolved by the whole house for the affirmative'.[9]

According to Gerolamo Agostini, 'when the resolution was voted some of the members threw aside all respect and even objected to giving her Majesty the title of queen of England', but they had been unable to find any way of avoiding the use of the name of Bourbon and thus offending the French royal family. Agostini was deeply shocked by the whole proceeding and could not bring himself to prophesy where 'this audacious presumption of subjects' might lead. 'The only thing clear', he went on, 'is the extreme feeling against the royal house and a line of conduct that indicates that the end of these affairs will not be reached without a change of the government or the total destruction of the kingdom.'[10] The queen herself was not greatly concerned. She had long ago accepted that her battle with parliament would be a fight to the death, but assured James Hamilton, in a letter written at the end of May, that she forgave the rebels from her heart for what they were doing to her.

From Henrietta's point of view, the most annoying thing the rebels were doing that spring was to delay her reunion with Charles, for they currently controlled a wide swathe of territory lying across the road to the south. Back in March the king had sent his nephew Rupert, now rapidly acquiring a formidable reputation as a cavalry general, to clear a passage for his wife. Rupert had taken Birmingham, a busy little Puritan town which made swords for the parliament, and laid siege to Lichfield, which fell to him on 21 April, but the loss of Reading and the consequent threat to Oxford had led to his hasty recall before the end of the month.

[margin note: Son of Sister ELIZABETH]

The royalists held most of the country north of the Humber, but Hull remained in enemy hands, and Fairfax and his son Thomas were a force to be reckoned with in the south and west of Yorkshire. In spite of her eagerness to join the king, Henrietta had become deeply involved with the northern campaign and her letters were beginning to read more and more like dispatches from the front. 'The rebels have quitted Tadcaster, upon our sending forces to Wetherby,' she told Charles on 30 March, 'but they are returned with twelve hundred men; we send more forces to drive them out.' And on 9 April: 'Our army is gone to Leeds, and at this time are beating down the town. God send us good success: our affairs are in very good condition in this country.'

A fortnight later the queen reported in more detail on the situation at Leeds, where Thomas Fairfax had now retreated. A council of war was called to decide 'whether the town should be forced by an assault, or rather by a siege'. The veterans, 'all the old officers from Holland', were of the opinion 'that an assault would be too dangerous . . . and also that a siege was impossible, as we were not enough to make lines of circumvallation, the town being of very large circumference, and the weather also being bad'. The 'fresh commanders', led by George Goring, were all for an assault, 'and I was with them', wrote the queen, but the voice of experience won the day and the army withdrew to nearby Wakefield. Henrietta now wanted to send a detachment of three thousand horse and foot, with some dragoons and cannon, to join the Earl of Derby in Lancashire 'and to clear out that country, which I hope can be done in ten or twelve days'. They could then rejoin her at Newark, 'whither I shall go from York with my regiment of foot and cavalry which consists of two thousand. I shall leave behind ten thousand men', she continued, 'who will, as I hope, soon have put an end to Fairfax.' These masterful plans were, however, being held up by the absence of Lord Newcastle. 'He is gone to bury his wife, who has died, and is not yet returned; and without him I can resolve on nothing. . . . He gives me to hope that he will be here tomorrow, but he has already written me that twice . . .'[11]

William Cavendish, first Earl of Newcastle, was a great nobleman of immense wealth and influence. A model of old-world courtesy and an acknowledged expert in every branch of the art of horsemanship, he had been perfectly suited to his former position of Governor to the Prince of Wales, but he was quite unfamiliar with the brutish demands of modern warfare and although he was certainly not lacking in physical courage it was sometimes hard to shake him out of his leisurely peacetime habit of lying in bed till eleven and taking an hour to dress. 'This army is called the queen's army', wrote Henrietta in one of her frequent moments of exasperation, 'but I have little power over it, and I assure you that if I had, all would go on better than it does.' When at last they were together again, she went on, Charles would say she was a good little creature and very patient, 'but I declare to you that being patient is killing me'.[12]

Still complaining of headaches and eyestrain – 'my sight is much weakened with writing' – the queen was nevertheless still tirelessly writing letters: to Charles; to Hamilton; to Montrose; to France, where her brother had just died; to Holland, where she was continuing to explore the possibilities of a marriage between the Prince of Wales and the Orange Princess Henriette; and to Denmark, where she believed she might be able to come to an arrangement with King Christian by offering him a post-dated promise to cede the Orkney Islands in exchange for present military aid, though of course this must be kept secret from the Scots, who would be bound to take offence.[13]

With Leeds and Hull still in enemy hands, the northern commanders were understandably reluctant to spare any of their forces to escort the queen on her way south, but on 18 May Henrietta was telling the king that 'our army is now to go to Leeds, Bradford and Halifax, which is only twenty miles from Manchester'. If Leeds were taken, Manchester, another Puritan stronghold and a wealthy town 'capable of arming six hundred men', would be the next objective and then 'all Lancashire is yours. . . . When that is done, all these counties on this side will be cleared, so that only garrisons in some places will suffice; and after that, the army may march where you will, all being clear behind them.'

As far as her own journey was concerned, it had been agreed that Newcastle would give her a regiment of foot, which she would arm, with six companies of horse and one park of artillery, all to be commanded by the volatile George Goring, whose previous treachery was now forgotten. One way and another, the queen was hoping to make up the numbers to at least 1,000 foot and 1,500 horse, 'and well armed I promise you'. However, to clinch the bargain with Newcastle, she had been obliged to give up some of the arms she had brought from Holland, 'so that I cannot bring the proportion which I expected, but believe that what I have done is well worth the arms; for, instead of an army which you should have had out of the north, you will have one in the north, and a little one which will go to you, and Lancashire regained, which would have been lost . . . I pray God that you may think this all right. It is all that I desire, or else I should not take the pains I do.'[14]

But before she could set out, the royalist cause in the north suffered two reverses. The Earl of Derby was defeated at Whalley Bridge and turned up at York, 'being no longer capable of defending himself, or of raising men, the rebels being too strong'; and on 24 May Thomas Fairfax broke out of Leeds and made a night attack on Wakefield, 'in which we have lost five hundred or six hundred men nearly, which is no small loss I assure you'. Newcastle was now begging her majesty to stay until he had taken Leeds, and to let him have what was left of the store of muskets and pistols she had been keeping for the king. It was not an easy decision to make but, thinking that if she refused and 'some new accident happened', she would get the blame, Henrietta felt obliged to acquiesce – but only on condition that the soldiers she was arming would be allowed to march with her when she went south. This was agreed, 'and thus we lose neither time nor arms; instead of arms I shall bring armed men'.[15] She herself now wanted to wait to see the fall of Leeds and asked the king's permission to stay. 'Although I am dying to join you, I am so enraged to go away without having beaten these rascals, that if you permit me, I will do that, and then will go to join you.'[16] But Charles, threatened by the presence of the Earl of Essex in the Thames valley, was not prepared to wait any longer and insisted that the queen – and her army – must leave at once. He also wanted Newcastle and his army to come south, an order which caused furious consternation in the northern camp and which the queen calmly ignored; 'I do not send it to you, since I have taken a resolution with you that you remain,' she told his lordship.[17]

Henrietta finally left York on 4 June with an escort of 4,500 horse and foot, reaching Newark on the River Trent by the 18th. She stayed there for two weeks, gathering more support and waiting in hopes that the Hothams, who had fallen out with the Fairfaxes and were showing signs of changing sides, might be ready to surrender Hull. 'Young Hotham having been put in prison by order of Parliament, is escaped, and hath sent to me that he would cast himself into my arms, and that Hull and Lincoln shall be rendered.' Unfortunately, though, young Hotham was recaptured and Hull remained in parliamentary hands.[18]

The queen dispatched her last situation report to Charles from Newark on 27 June: 'At this present, I think it fit to let you know the state in which we march.' She was leaving 2,000 foot, the wherewithal to arm five hundred more and twenty companies of horse for the defence of Nottinghamshire and Lincolnshire, but 'I carry with me three thousand foot, thirty companies of horse and dragoons, six pieces of cannon and two mortars'. Harry Jermyn was in overall command – George Goring had unfortunately been taken prisoner at Wakefield – while 'her she-majesty generalissima and extremely diligent' had a hundred and fifty baggage waggons to govern in case of attack.[19]

The journey proceeded in easy stages by way of Ashby-de-la-Zouch, Croxall, Walsall and King's Norton to Stratford-upon-Avon, and had taken on almost a holiday air. Henrietta was later to tell Madame de Motteville how, having got a fine army together, she had put herself at the head of her troops and marched towards the king, always on horseback, *sans nulle délicatesse de femme*, and living among the soldiers as she imagined the great Alexander must have lived with his; how she had picnicked with them outside in the sunshine, using no ceremony but treating them like brothers, and how they had all loved her in return.[20]

The generalissima's martial progress had not, of course, gone unremarked. A certain parliamentary colonel, one Oliver Cromwell, was urging that every effort should be made to intercept her, and Henrietta herself had asked for care to be taken 'that no troop of Essex's army incommodate us'. The Earl of Essex, who had been immobilised at Reading by an outbreak of typhus, was now advancing north towards Thame, only twelve miles from Oxford, but on 17/18 June Prince Rupert staged one of his brilliant cavalry forays which culminated in a short but bloody encounter in the cornfields at Chalgrove between Abingdon and Thame, where John Hampden, hero of the ship-money affair and most sympathetic of the parliamentary leaders, was mortally wounded.

Having achieved his object of scattering and unsettling the enemy and frightening Essex away from Oxford, Rupert was now free to meet the queen at Stratford, where she had spent a night at New Place as the guest of Shakespeare's grand-daughter, and to escort her the last few miles to the village of Kineton below Edgehill where, on 13 July, she was reunited with the king and the princes Charles and James. Husband and wife slept that first night at Sir Thomas Pope's house at Wroxton and the next day went on to Woodstock, before entering Oxford to a rousing welcome of church bells and cheering citizens.

Henrietta's great adventure had lasted for fifteen months and, despite her many protestations to the contrary, the impression somehow remains that she had rather enjoyed the challenge and excitement of it all. The absence of any systematic or official records makes it difficult to evaluate what she had accomplished in real terms, but even if her efforts had not been enough to make any difference to the final outcome of the war, they still represent an amazing achievement for a woman whose previous experience had been confined within the carefully ordered limits of one of the most civilised of European courts. The little queen immortalised by Van Dyck, looking as if her only possible function was to be ornamental, had proved herself quite capable of striking bargains with hard-nosed pawnbrokers and arms dealers. She had been undaunted by the prospect of shipwreck and showed cool courage under fire. Henrietta had made many mistakes in the past and would make more in the future, but no one could now deny her valiant spirit.

As if to reward all her hard work for her husband's cause, that summer of 1643 was to mark the zenith of the king's fortunes. While the queen was still on her way south Newcastle's forces had defeated the Fairfaxes at Adwalton Moor on the outskirts of Bradford. On 13 July, the very day when Charles and Henrietta were meeting under the shadow of Edgehill, the royalist cavalry was all but annihilating Sir William Waller's army at Roundway Down just north of Devizes, and before the end of the month Rupert had taken Bristol, the second port of the realm, thus consolidating the king's mastery of the south-west. But no amount of success in the north and west could compensate for the fact that parliament remained in undisputed control of the all-important south-east, or that the king had been driven out of his capital city and was now obliged to hold his court at Oxford.

The life of the university had been violently disrupted by the royal invasion. Scholars who had deserted their studies in droves to join the colours drilled in the college quadrangles, and troops of horse clattered noisily through the streets on their way to and from the outlying garrisons of Banbury, Wallingford and Abingdon. Fodder was now being stored in the Law and Logic Schools, New College had become a magazine and Magdalen College Grove an artillery park. Tailors stitched uniforms in the Music and Astronomy Schools and a mint had been set up at New Inn Hall. The king had taken over Christ Church as his headquarters and the queen now occupied the Warden's Lodgings at Merton, while other colleges were used to accommodate the lords and ladies, the army commanders, court officials and royal servants with their wives and families and hangers-on.

The queen's return had brought an influx of fashionable visitors and she and her friends were entertained with theatricals got up by the students in the romantic setting of the college gardens, while the king played tennis and still sometimes went hunting. There was music and dancing and gay little supper parties, and ladies, 'half-dressed like angels', amused themselves by teasing and scandalising the elderly dons. But beneath the surface feuding, faction and intrigue were rife. Henrietta's determination to re-establish herself as the king's mentor and confidante not surprisingly caused considerable resentment among those who had enjoyed unrestricted access to his majesty during her absence and who 'did not wish to see the court as it had been, or the Queen herself possessed of so absolute a power as she had been formerly'. For her part, the queen quickly became jealous of her husband's reliance on Prince Rupert. Nephew or no nephew, she thought him too young and self-willed for his advice to be taken seriously and strongly suspected him of leading a conspiracy to 'lessen her interest' with the king.[21] She also blamed him for persuading Charles to join the army now besieging Gloucester, thus leaving Oxford – and herself – dangerously exposed to attack. 'The king is gone himself in person to Gloucester,' she wrote crossly to the Earl of Newcastle in August, 'which gives no small dissatisfaction to everybody here, and with reason, too, to see him take such sudden counsel.'[22]

Gloucester, a Puritan bastion occupying a strategic position on the River Severn, was a prize worth taking. But the city stubbornly refused to surrender, giving parliament – which could hardly have survived another disaster – enough time to organise a rescue operation; a relieving force under the Earl of Essex arrived on the morning of 6 September to find the besiegers had withdrawn in the night. Rupert was planning to intercept Essex on the road back to London, and the armies clashed at Newbury on the 20th. But the terrain was unsuitable for cavalry and in the confused and bloody encounter which followed 'the loss on the king's side was in weight much more considerable and penetrating'. In the end nothing decisive was achieved; the royalists, their ammunition exhausted, had to break off the fight, leaving Essex, his army mauled but still in being, to resume his march. Both sides claimed a victory but the queen would admit to no doubt in the matter, sending Newcastle 'tidings of the victory we have gained over the rebels . . . although it has not been a total defeat, nevertheless it is a very great victory'.[23]

All the same, after the brilliant hopes of the summer, there was no denying that the campaigning season had ended badly. Casualties at Newbury had been horrendous and there was an atmosphere of despondency, a sense of great opportunities lost, in the royalist camp. Henrietta, who was not interested in the possibility of defeat, confessed that she was very weary 'not of being beaten, but of having heard it spoken of'.

For parliament, on the other hand, Newbury came as a much-needed bit of good news. In London especially, where the war had brought disruption of trade, high prices and shortages, morale had been getting dangerously low. August had seen some angry demonstrations of popular unrest, with a mob of women clamouring for peace at the very door of the Commons chamber, and the peace party in the Lords had felt brave enough to draw up a new set of propositions for a negotiated settlement.

At the end of the month half a dozen disillusioned and disgruntled peers, including the Earl of Holland, who had somehow become stranded on the wrong side of the political fence, defected to the king in a body. Their arrival in Oxford gave rise to further tensions and they got a chilly initial reception from those who had been loyal from the beginning. Lord Holland in particular presented a problem. According to Clarendon, he saw no reason to apologise for past errors, or even 'to have the least sense that he had committed any error', and expected, 'upon his first appearance . . . to have been in the same condition he was, in the bedchamber and in the Council, and in the King's grace and countenance'. The situation was made more awkward by the fact that he had apparently been given prior assurances to this effect by the queen, or at any rate by Harry Jermyn on her behalf; and Henrietta, perhaps because Holland was a reminder of happier days or because of his unrivalled courtly graces, would have given him what he wanted and 'trusted him herself as much as formerly'. But Charles was more reserved and Holland's old office of Groom of the Stole went instead to Lord Hertford, much to the queen's and Jermyn's annoyance.[24]

That autumn the court's attention was diverted from its internal squabbles by the prospect of receiving a new French ambassador. The Comte d'Harcourt landed at Dover (where his belongings were carefully searched by suspicious officials) at the beginning of October, but his arrival was marred by a sad misfortune to another of the queen's old friends. Walter Montagu had travelled in the ambassador's train, hoping to be able to rejoin her majesty at Oxford, but although heavily disguised he was spotted at Rochester by a sharp-eyed parliamentary captain and promptly arrested in spite of Harcourt's protests.

The ambassador, whose mission was to try to mediate a peace between the king and his rebellious subjects, suffered both discourtesy and inconvenience in wartime London. Henrietta had offered him the use of Somerset House, which would have been a suitably exalted lodging had parliament not stripped it of all its furniture, and he was obliged to wait about for a passport to visit Oxford. Even then he had some difficulty in leaving the fortifications and had to apply for a fresh order to get his baggage through without a search. 'Every time the ambassador surmounts obstacles and difficulties', observed Gerolamo Agostini, 'they [parliament] give him additional cause for offence here and show how little to their taste his mission is.'[25]

By contrast, when he did finally reach Oxford in the last week of October, he was warmly welcomed by the king and queen. Henrietta especially had been hoping for great things from France, where there had been sweeping changes during the past year. Those old antagonists Marie de Medici and Cardinal Richelieu had both died in 1642. Louis xIII had been succeeded by his five-year-old son and his widow Anne of Austria now reigned as queen regent with the support and assistance of another cardinal, the Italian Giulio Mazzarini, or Mazarin. But although the cast of characters had changed, government policy had not. What mattered to the French was still, first and last, the furtherance of French interests and, in spite of the civility he was receiving at Oxford, Harcourt was not greatly impressed by the situation he found there. The parliamentarians might be rude and uncouth, but as long as they continued to control the navy and London, the nerve-centre of power and trade, France would continue to keep at least on speaking terms with them. In any case there did not seem to be much he could do for the king, who showed no interest in his offers of mediation, although Agostini heard that the queen, 'through the influence of weariness of these troubles and hardships', had an intense desire for peace.

Harcourt returned to the capital in November, bringing with him a detailed statement of the king's grievances and demands which he presented to parliament for discussion, but the Venetians did not believe anything would come of it. For one thing, nothing could be done in London without the active approval of the Presbyterian Scots, with whom a treaty had recently been concluded. As the year drew to a close, spirits remained low in Oxford. Both Charles and Henrietta had lost friends in the fighting and there seemed no end in sight to a cruel war which was tearing the country apart. The queen, too, now had a special reason for her intense desire for peace, for by Christmas she knew that she was pregnant again.

The new year came in, and with it a new threat. John Pym had died of cancer in December, but he had left a deadly legacy in the shape of the treaty he had negotiated with the Scots. Parliament agreed to take the Covenant – something which would create serious problems for it in the future – as the price of immediate military aid, and the first Scottish regiments crossed the border in January. Bad weather delayed them, but by February they were laying siege to the town of Newcastle. Henrietta felt reasonably confident that her old friend and comrade-in-arms in the north would be able to deal with the invaders, and see that they did not get the chance to eat Yorkshire oatcakes, as she put it, but she was obliged to add an urgent postscript to a letter dated 15 March. 'Since my letter was written, we *1644* have tidings that Sir Thomas Fairfax is marching towards you to join the Scotch. Therefore lose no time and do not allow yourself to trifle, for if the Scotch pass the river Tees, I fear that there will be no more remedy.'[26] A week or two later Newcastle, now raised to the rank of marquis, took offence at some fancied slight in a message from Oxford, and the queen wrote again to his lordship in soothing mode. 'Do not imagine that we design to do or to believe anything to your prejudice. And if you accuse me of scolding you by this letter, remember what I told you when I was at York, that I only scold my friends, and not those whom I do not care about.'[27]

This was her last letter from Oxford, for Henrietta was now in no condition to take any further active part in affairs. She had been unwell during the winter with severe rheumatic pains and now she not only felt ill but very much afraid, telling Christine that she did not know where to go for safety in a country where there were no reliable strongholds. In Clarendon's opinion it was the queen's being with child 'which wrought upon her majesty's mind very much, and disposed her to so many fears and apprehensions . . . that she was very uneasy to herself', but it was true that Oxford, overcrowded and full of disease, was hardly suitable for a royal lying-in. It would also be very difficult to defend, and the news of William Waller's victory over a royalist force at Alresford in Hampshire on 29 March only served to confirm her majesty's fears and apprehensions. 'She heard every day of the good forces raised, and in readiness, by the Parliament . . . and that they resolved as soon as the season was ripe, which was at hand, to march all to Oxford. She could not endure to think of being besieged there, and, in conclusion, resolved not to stay there, but to go into the west; from whence, in any distress, she might be able to embark for France.' Edward Hyde, who had always disapproved of the queen and her interfering ways, clearly continued to believe that her present alarm was no more than a pregnant woman's natural fidgets, and the king 'heartily wished that she could be diverted'. However, 'the perplexity of her mind was so great, and her fears so vehement . . . that all civility and reason obliged every body to submit'.[28]

In fairness to the queen, a good deal of her panic was undoubtedly due to her conviction that there was nothing Charles would not have done, no concession, however damaging, he would not have made, had she been taken by the enemy, especially in her present condition. She left Oxford on 17 April with an escort of cavalry and accompanied by her husband and sons as far as Abingdon, where there was another sorrowful parting. She rested briefly at Bath, intending originally to go on to Bristol, but changed her mind and turned south-west for Exeter, where she moved into Bedford House, the Russell family's West Country headquarters. By this time she was feeling very ill indeed and on 3 May wrote pathetically to Theodore Mayerne begging him to come to her, 'having always in my recollection the care you have taken of me in my necessities'. It was a long way for an old man in such troubled times, but the king's famously desperate plea – 'Mayerne, for the love of me, go to my wife' – could not well be refused, and Sir Theodore set out for Exeter, taking his colleague Matthew Lister with him for support and a second opinion.[29]

The authorities in London had given permission for the doctors' journey, but were less receptive to a request for a midwife with a coach and six and three menservants. Fortunately, the queen regent of France came to the rescue, sending the ever-obliging Madame Peronne with a supply of baby clothes and a generous present of money. Anne of Austria also invited her afflicted sister-in-law to come to France if she thought the air would do her good, although the Venetians heard that Mazarin was less than enthusiastic at the prospect of having to grant asylum to the Queen of England, foreseeing that she would be a source of endless expense and diplomatic embarrassment.[30]

Mazarin, in fact, was at one with the English parliamentarians, who would certainly not have been inconsolable if Henrietta were to die in childbirth – an eventuality which she herself thought only too probable. Writing to Charles what would surely be her last letter before she was brought to bed, 'since I am now more than fifteen days in my ninth month', and perhaps the last letter he would ever receive from her, she told him that her state of weakness 'caused by the cruel pains I have suffered since I left you, which have been too severe to be experienced or understood by any but those who have suffered them, makes me believe that it is time for me to think of another world'. There were so many things she wanted to say but dared not commit to paper – 'the roads are so little sure' – only she begged the king to believe the messages which Jermyn and Father Philip would bring him.[31]

In spite of all this, Henrietta's baby, her ninth child and fourth daughter, arrived safely on 16 June – 'a lovely princess', according to M. de Sabran, the French envoy who had replaced Harcourt and who saw the queen a week after her delivery. The infant, although delicate, seemed likely to survive, but the mother's condition was still giving serious cause for concern. Henrietta had hoped she might feel better after her accouchement, but instead she was worse than ever, with 'a seizure of paralysis in the legs and all over the body' and such a constriction round the heart that she thought she would suffocate. 'At times I am like a person poisoned,' she told Charles. 'I can scarcely stir and am doubled up.' There was no feeling in one of her arms and her limbs were colder than ice. The disease had even risen to her head and she could no longer see out of one eye. On top of everything else, she was once more being threatened by the enemy. The Earl of Essex had come west again with the intention of relieving the siege of Lyme, and his army was now advancing towards Exeter.[32]

De Sabran, whose instructions were to try to persuade the queen to remain in England, had approached the parliamentary general to ask if he would give her a safe conduct to Bath, where she could take the waters and recover her health, only to be told grimly 'that the air of London would be even more healthy for her majesty'. But Henrietta had no intention of remaining anywhere within reach of men like Essex. Ill and exhausted though she was, she had already made up her mind that she must leave the country as soon as possible. 'I shall show you by this last action,' she wrote to Charles from her bed, 'that nothing is so much in my thoughts as what concerns your preservation . . . for as your affairs stand, they would be in danger if you come to help me, and I know that your affection would make you risk everything for that.'[33]

Two days later, leaving her baby daughter in the care of her trusted friend Anne Dalkeith, she set out for the coast with only three companions. 'The Queen is this day gone towards Falmouth, intending to embark herself for France,' wrote Henry Jermyn from Exeter on 30 June. 'The reason of this resolution is the apprehension of a siege here of which there hath been and is very much appearance, though no certainty.' It seemed that her majesty had not been able to overcome her dread of being 'shut up' in a siege, although Jermyn thought she was exposing herself 'to more dangers than those she could have undergone in this city in respect of her health and of the sea, if she persist in the desire of passing it'.[34]

Certainly the journey down to Cornwall was slow, painful and not without incident, at least according to later highly coloured French accounts which state, not very credibly, that the queen had been forced to lie hidden in a wayside but a few miles from Exeter, listening to bands of rebel soldiers passing on the road and boasting 'that they would carry the head of Henrietta to London as they should receive from the parliament a reward for it of 50,000 crowns'.[35] But Henrietta, who was being carried in a litter, with her party now increased by Jermyn, the ubiquitous dwarf Hudson and several more ladies, went on to reach Truro, where, on 9 July, she wrote a farewell letter to Charles – 'if the wind is favourable, I shall set off tomorrow' – and reminding him that 'I am giving you the strongest proof of love that I can give; I am hazarding my life, that I may not incommode your affairs. Adieu, my dear heart. If I die, believe that you will lose a person who has never been other than entirely yours.'[36]

A sympathetic gentleman, who had seen her as she left Exeter, told his wife that 'here is the woefullest spectacle my eyes ever yet beheld on: the most worn and pitiful creature in the world, the poor queen, shifting for one hour's life longer'. Even Theodore Mayerne, who was apt to dismiss many of the queen's symptoms as hysterical in origin, had prophesied that she would not live for more than another three weeks.[37] But yet again Henrietta was to prove her extraordinary resilience. Although it was known that a squadron of the parliamentary navy was lying in wait, she sailed with a small Flemish fleet which had been anchored in Falmouth bay. The parliament's ships, 'three of the best sailors we had', gave chase, but as most of the Flemings were able to use oars to increase their speed, the English, being 'more heavy far in burden', could not get the advantage of them. They still came close enough to 'bestow a hundred cannon shot' on their quarry, but the aim was high and scored no more than one hit. As the Channel Islands came in sight the Flemings gained the wind, drawing away from their pursuers, and when some French ships appeared on the horizon the English turned back, though it was later claimed that they had almost captured the queen and that she had had 'no other courtesy from England but cannon balls to convey her to France'.[38]

Henrietta had ordered the captain of her vessel to fire his powder magazine and destroy the ship rather than allow her to be taken – a heroic gesture which drew cries of protest from her companions and which she herself later regretted as having been an act of selfishness. Even now the ordeal was not over, for the weather turned nasty and after landing on the coast of Brittany the queen had to clamber over rocks and climb a steep cliff path to reach the rough shelter of a cluster of fishermen's huts. But after some initial hostility from the surprised fishermen, the daughter of Henri IV was given a warm welcome and the local dignitaries hastened to greet 'this princess who appeared more like the distressed heroine of a romance than a real queen', and to escort her to more suitable accommodation.[39]

Henry Jermyn was dispatched to Paris with letters for the queen regent, and the distinguished doctors who now arrived to attend the invalid decided that she should go straight to the royal spa at Bourbon l'Archambault, where they hoped the waters of the thermal springs would restore her to health. She was still very ill, feverish and in constant pain, with a toxic rash like measles all over her body and subject to uncontrollable fits of weeping. Everyone was shocked by her haggard appearance, but Henrietta was slightly cheered by the kindness she was receiving on all sides, 'from the greatest to the least', and on 10 August was able to report that, thank God, she was a little better, adding, with a flash of her old spirit, 'I am so well

1644

treated everywhere that if my lords of London saw it, I think it would make them uneasy'.[40] All the same, the journey across France in the summer heat took the best part of a month and almost the last of her strength. It was September before she could write again to Charles, by which time an abscess in her breast had been lanced, which had brought her some relief, and she was beginning to hope that she would not die.[41]

Towards the end of the month the physicians pronounced her well enough to travel and Gaston d'Orléans arrived to take her back to Paris. Brother and sister had not met since that long ago June day when they had ventured together in a little boat on the water of Boulogne harbour, and there was an affectionate reunion. On the road to Paris they were met by a messenger from England bringing three letters from Charles – the first news Henrietta had had since leaving Falmouth. Exeter had not, after all, come under siege. On the contrary, the king had entered the city himself on 25 July and made the acquaintance of his youngest 'and as they say prettiest daughter', who had been baptised with her mother's name in the cathedral. He had then advanced into Cornwall and comprehensively defeated the Earl of Essex at Lostwithiel on 31 August.

Henrietta was so excited by this that she managed to walk a few steps unaided for the first time since her illness, but she was still in a good deal of pain and worried that 'the weakness I have in my head' was preventing her from attending to any business. She could not yet manage to write in cipher and would have to leave that to Jermyn until she felt better. For the moment she could only tell the king that although everyone was being very kind she longed to return to England, for 'I have there what I have not here, that is YOU, without whom I cannot be happy, and I think I shall never have my health till I see you again'.[42]

She did, in fact, have a relapse after this, with another abscess and a high fever, and it was three weeks before she was able to resume her journey. So it was the beginning of November when she and Gaston finally arrived within ten miles of Paris, where they were met by Gaston's seventeen-year-old daughter by his first marriage to the Montpensier heiress. Since the new king had no sisters, Anne-Marie bore the official title of Mademoiselle, although she was more often known as La Grande Mademoiselle. A tall, gawky blonde, very conscious of her wealth and her importance, she noted condescendingly that while her unfortunate aunt had obviously taken great pains with her appearance, the result could inspire nothing but pity.[43] Nevertheless, the royal family was punctilious in showing Henrietta all the attentions due to a daughter of France. The queen regent, with the six-year-old Louis XIV and his four-year-old brother Philippe, had come out to greet her on the outskirts of the city and the sisters-in-law embraced affectionately before driving together in state through decorated streets to the palace of the Louvre, where the Queen of England was ceremoniously installed in apartments which she would occupy for the next eight years. She was also granted her childhood home of St Germain-en-Laye as a country retreat, and a pension of 30,000 livres a month.

In the early days of her marriage to Louis, Anne of Austria had been subjected to some unkind teasing by the young Henrietta and her mother, but she was a kind-hearted lady who bore no grudges, and she also provided her sister-in-law with a sympathetic friend and companion in the person of one of her own ladies-in-waiting, the young widow Françoise de Motteville. It was to Madame de Motteville that Henrietta later poured out the story of her adventures, and Madame de Motteville who recorded a description of the queen as she appeared in that winter of 1644. Although so much disfigured by the severity of her illness and misfortunes that no trace now remained of her past beauty, her eyes were still fine, her complexion admirable and her nose well-shaped, but her mouth, never her best feature, now appeared larger than ever in the thinness of her face. In spite of everything, she had not lost the vivacity and animation which was so much part of her charm. She was, says Françoise de Motteville, 'agreeable in society . . . living with those who had the honour to approach her without ceremony. Her temperament inclined her to gaiety; and even amid her tears, if it occurred to her to say something amusing, she would stop them to divert the company.'[44]

The queen's health was now definitely improving – perhaps the asses' milk prescribed by the physicians had been doing her good – 'Thank God I begin to feel like myself again,' she wrote on 18 November. She was still troubled by a numbness in her limbs but the drowsiness in her head bothered her less and less, so that she could at long last start attending to business again – to the unending, increasingly heartbreaking business of trying to prevail on the European powers to come to the aid of the beleaguered king of England. 'There is nothing so certain as that I do take all the pains I can imaginable to procure you assistance,' she told him.[45]

Her first rejection came from Cardinal Mazarin, who explained that, much as he would like to be able to help, it was impossible to spare any troops for England at present as France really did not have enough men for her own needs, having so much else on her hands in other places. The cardinal did not add that it suited him very well to see the English at one another's throats, thus leaving the French to pursue their various continental ambitions unhindered. However, he did remind the queen that the Duke of Lorraine had an army for hire, even giving her to understand that France might be prepared to foot the bill. This sounded like a promising lead, 'for it would be a benefit to France if they could get him [Lorraine] to withdraw from the service of Spain', and Henrietta wasted no time in following it up. Meanwhile, she advised the king to write himself to the queen regent and to Mazarin, who must be addressed as 'cousin'.[46]

Communications with England, which depended heavily on the good offices of the Portuguese agent in London and a handful of devoted postmen running the parliamentary blockade, were proving more than usually unreliable just then and in December Henrietta was complaining that it was more than a month since she had heard from Charles. 'It is a cruel anxiety to know nothing of you but by the London prints.' It was also making her task more difficult, for if people abroad began to suspect that the king did not trust her with up-to-date intelligence, she would lose all credibility with their governments.[47] She herself was beginning to have an uncomfortable feeling that her husband was keeping something from her, which was especially worrying since she had heard from Secretary Edward Nicholas that Charles was sending two emissaries to London with new terms for 'a reasonable peace' and was proposing to treat with the Westminster parliament, whose legitimacy he had repudiated after Pym's death. Hurt and disappointed that he had not taken her into his confidence – 'a thing very prejudicial to all your affairs here' – Henrietta wrote on 30 December urging him to take care of his honour, 'which is to remain constant in the resolutions that you have taken'.[48]

As the third year of the war began, there was an air of determined optimism in the royalist camp. Despite the loss of the north after Newcastle's defeat at Marston Moor and another inconclusive encounter at Newbury in the autumn, no one at Oxford would admit that the outlook was bleak. By contrast, the mood in London was one of gloom and recrimination. Although parliament now controlled approximately two-thirds of the country, its southern army was in a bad way after a long season's campaigning, and the soldiers, ill-clad, underfed, their pay in arrears and with sickness growing in their ranks, were showing an ominous disenchantment with the whole business of the war. At the same time the long-simmering dissension among the generals was reaching crisis point and in the first weeks of 1645 there were few signs that this would be the year of triumph for the New Model Army and Oliver Cromwell.

January was marked by the execution of poor old Archbishop Laud, who had been lying almost forgotten in the Tower for the past four years, and by the peace talks which became known as the Conference of Uxbridge. This prompted another flurry of anxious warnings from Henrietta. 'In my opinion religion should be the last thing upon which you should treat, for if you do agree upon strictness against the Catholics it would discourage them to serve you. And if afterwards there should be no peace, you could never expect succours either from Ireland or any other Catholic prince.'[49] Only half reassured by the king's promise 'that no danger or misery, which

I think much worse, shall make me do anything unworthy of thy love', Henrietta was horrified to hear that Charles might be going to London in person. 'For the honour of God, trust not yourself in the hands of these people. And if you ever go to London, before the Parliament be ended, or without a good army, you are lost. I understand that the propositions for the peace must begin by disbanding the army. If you consent to this, you shall be lost. . . . Above all, have a care not to abandon those who have served you, as well the bishops as the poor Catholics.'[50] And again, on 10 February, 'take care to preserve the bishops, and the sword that God has placed in your hands; that is not to quit it, till you are a KING'.

Letters from Charles were flowing more freely now and on the whole continued to be reassuring. 'As for trusting the rebels either by going to London, or disbanding my army before a peace, do no ways fear my hazarding so cheaply or foolishly.' The king had never expected the Uxbridge talks to come to anything. 'As for our treaty, there is every day less hopes than other, that it will produce a peace.' But he could absolutely promise Henrietta 'that if we have one, it shall be such as shall invite thy return. For I avow that, without thy company, I can neither have peace nor comfort within myself.' Whatever happened, she could be confident 'that in making peace, I shall ever shew my constancy in adhering to bishops, and all our friends, and not forget to put a short period to this perpetual parliament'.[51]

To Henrietta's relief – for she had continued to dread the possibility of a 'disadvantageous treaty' – and to no one's surprise, the Uxbridge conference ended in deadlock on 22 February, by which time the queen was busy in negotiations with the Duke of Lorraine who, she told the king, had sent her word that 'if his service be agreeable to you, he will bring you ten thousand men'. This was all very well but the difficulty was going to be transport and Henrietta had turned to her old ally the Prince of Orange, sending Dr Stephen Goffe, formerly one of the king's chaplains and more recently a royalist agent, on a mission to the Hague with instructions to ask the prince if he would provide an additional 3,000 troops as well as shipping and a naval escort for the Lorrainers, offering him the Prince of Wales as a son-in-law in return. But this time Frederick Henry, although polite, seemed strangely disinclined to become further involved with the importunate and expensive Stuarts. He was also sceptical about Lorraine's ability to deliver the number of men promised and, in any case, whatever his personal misgivings, the Hogens Mogens of the Dutch Estates were highly unlikely to agree to the use of Dutch ports and Dutch shipping for such a politically incorrect enterprise.

Charles suggested that the queen should try to arrange Lorraine's passage through France. 'If that of Holland be stuck at, it will much secure and facilitate the sea-transportation in respect of landing on the western coast, which I believe will be found the best.'[52] Henrietta therefore approached Mazarin to enquire if the expedition might embark at Dieppe, but the cardinal, whom Charles suspected of being privately in touch with parliament, made it clear that Lorraine would not be allowed entry to any part of France. Henrietta continued to worry at the problem with her usual persistence, but without success, until June when, no doubt fortunately for England, Lorraine himself settled the matter by going off with his mercenaries to fight for his old master, Spain.

The queen was still trying by every means she could to raise money, both to redeem her jewellery which was in danger of being sold off, and for the king. The sale of a shipment of tin from the Cornish mines helped a little, as did a private subscription raised among pious and sympathetic French Catholics after an appeal by Henrietta's old Grand Almoner, the Abbé Duperron, while she herself was sending every sou she could squeeze out of her French pension. On 21 March the Venetian ambassador in Paris noted that the Queen of England had remitted to her husband 36,000 crowns taken from the income assigned to her for her maintenance. 'Regarded as assistance it is little enough,' he remarked, 'but when one considers the needs of the one who receives and the effort of the other who stints herself, it seems great.'[53] It did not seem great to Henrietta, who happily dispensed with the ladies of rank, the maids of honour, the carriages, guards and running footmen who had surrounded her during her first months at the Louvre, and who would happily have starved rather than not send everything she could.[54] But however much she stinted herself, anything she sent would make no noticeable difference. Meaningful help must be measured in armies and all through the summer she and Charles continued vainly to pursue the chimera of help from Ireland.

Help from Ireland depended on the king's viceroy, James Butler, Marquis of Ormonde, being able to negotiate a lasting peace with the Irish rebels, or Confederates as they were more politely known, but the rebels, well aware of their superior bargaining power, were in no hurry to accept the terms offered. These were generous. The king promised – and commanded Ormonde to see it done – 'that the penal statutes against Romish Catholics shall not be put in execution, the peace being made, and they remaining in their due obedience'. He had also given the marquis full powers 'to conclude a peace with the Irish, whatever it cost, so that my Protestant subjects there may be secured, and my regal authority preserved'.[55]

These approaches to the Catholic rebels had, of course, to be kept very secret. Charles was keeping Henrietta fully informed, but felt it necessary to remind her that his letters were for her eyes only. 'For God's sake let none know the particulars of my dispatches.' This hurt her feelings very much. Did he really think her capable of showing his letters to anyone but Harry Jermyn, who deciphered them, her head not suffering her to do it herself? 'But, if it please you, I will do it, and none in the world shall see them. Be kind to me or you kill me. I have already affliction enough to fear, which without you I could not do; but your service surmounts all.'[56]

In spite of these occasional misunderstandings, their correspondence was vitally important to them both and in April Charles was begging his wife to write as often as she could, even if there was no business to discuss, just to let him know how she was and how she was spending her time, for 'believe me, sweetheart, thy kindness is as necessary to comfort my heart as thy assistance is for my affairs'.[57] But Henrietta was ill again that spring and it was the middle of May before she was strong enough to write again. 'My dear heart, this letter is only to assure you that God still pleased to leave me in this world to do you some service, and that, excepting a severe cold which my fever has left, and my old disease, I am tolerably well.' The doctors had promised that she would recover completely, and she hoped they were right, more because of the longing she had to see Charles again one day than any love she felt for the world. 'For all that troubled me during my illness, was that I was dying far from you. Otherwise, I did not care about it much.'[58]

She had also approved and sent on details of a scheme put to her by a Colonel Oliver FitzWilliam, who undertook, on the conclusion of a peace with the Confederates and the payment to himself of £10,000, to raise and equip a force of 10,000 Irish to be landed in Wales and paid according to the going rate in the royal army. They would fight as a self-contained unit with the colonel as their commander-in-chief and no other superior officers apart from the king and Prince Rupert.[59]

By this time the king had left Oxford to begin his summer campaign and had written to the queen on 12 May explaining that 'being now in my march, I cannot hope to hear so often from thee or thou from me so often as before'. The army was on its way first to the relief of Chester, so vital for the landing of Irish reinforcements, which had been under siege now for more than a year, and then to make a bid to recover the north. Charles was in optimistic mood. 'We all here think to be very hopeful,' he wrote from Droitwich on 14 May and again, from Daventry on 8 June, 'my affairs were never in so fair and hopeful a way'.[60]

Six days later at Naseby, midway between Daventry and Market Harborough, the battle 'of all for all' was fought, and the royalists were heavily defeated. By early afternoon on 14 June Rupert and the king with their 'broken troops' were in full retreat, leaving Thomas Fairfax and Cromwell in possession not only of the field, but also of between four and five thousand prisoners, the entire royal artillery train with its powder and ammunition, about eight thousand other weapons and a whole forest of colours.

Henrietta heard the news at St Germain, where she had gone to spend the summer. Kind Queen Anne had tried to soften the blow as much as possible but, reported Giovanni Nani from the Venetian embassy in Paris, 'here the event has made a great impression and they fear the consequences if parliament remains the sole master of the kingdom'.[61] Actual casualties at Naseby had been relatively light – a thousand or so on the royalist side, barely a hundred parliamentarians – but the king had lost all his baggage 'amongst which was his own cabinet, where his most secret papers were and letters between the Queen and him'. These letters, some of them going back to 1643, fatally revealed all those desperate efforts to raise money and armies from abroad, from Denmark and Holland, from France, from the Duke of Lorraine and, most damaging of all, from murderous papist Ireland. This was a honeyfall for any propaganda machine and the parliament not unnaturally made the most of it. By July the letters had been published under the gleeful title *The King's Cabinet Opened* and, by providing conclusive proof that he had been actively plotting to bring foreigners and papists into the country, were doing irreparable harm to his cause. As far as the queen was concerned, they merely confirmed everything her enemies had ever said or thought about her.

This did not bother the queen unduly. She was still looking towards Ireland – she had even spoken of going there herself – and had written to the Supreme Council of the Confederates to tell them of the great consolation she had received on hearing of their general desire to serve the king and make peace with those Protestants who were loyal to him. 'And I assure you,' she went on, 'that you shall lose nothing nor have any reason to repent of having acted in this manner.' The large powers which Charles had granted to his viceroy 'should be a sure pledge of his desire to make glad the heart of Ireland, and to leave you in peaceful enjoyment of all that is necessary to ensure your tranquillity.' She hoped to hear that their affection towards his majesty was maintained and also 'that you continue to forward the progress of the peace in his interest and your own, which are bound up together'.[62]

But Henrietta was finding the Irish frustratingly difficult to pin down and had already come to the conclusion that the Jesuit Father O'Hartigan, the Confederate agent in Paris, was not to be trusted. The situation was further complicated when the elderly Florentine Bishop of Fermo, Giovanni Rinuccini, arrived in France en route for Ireland, where he was being sent as papal nuncio. Rinuccini had instructions to assure the queen of his perfect goodwill to the kingdom of England and that he had no other object in the world than to sustain and propagate the

Catholic faith. At the same time, he was to urge her majesty to prevail on the Marquis of Ormonde to surrender Dublin to the Confederates and persuade her of the wisdom of giving them everything they asked for, pointing out that in present circumstances the English crown was likely to find its only resource in the assistance of the Irish Catholics.[63]

Henrietta, however, complained loudly to a member of Rinuccini's staff that the Irish were using the religious question as a pretext to throw off their allegiance to the king and were always adding new demands and petitions, each more exorbitant than the last. There was also the little matter of diplomatic protocol. The Vatican had not sought Charles's permission to send a nuncio to Ireland and the queen suspected that his real purpose was to attempt to set up an independent Catholic state. She therefore refused to grant him a public audience on the grounds that his title inferred sovereignty over the king's Irish subjects.[64]

But if Henrietta distrusted Rome's motives, Rome was equally suspicious of the queen, who appeared to be putting her husband's interests before those of her church, and Rinuccini, who had not forgiven her for snubbing him, went so far as to report that he could see nothing to corroborate her alleged affection for the Catholics, 'for not only is she surrounded by heretical counsellors, but she has spoken hardly of the Irish in this late rising, stigmatising them as rebels'. It was true that, in addition to the promised concessions to the Confederates, Charles had given his wife authority to promise in his name that he would revoke all the penal laws against the English Catholics as soon as he had the power to do so, but Rinuccini was not impressed: undertakings of this kind had, after all, been made all too often in the past. 'The English Catholics', he wrote, 'cannot hope that the King is either able or willing to favour them more than formerly' – unless, of course, they could be supported by an Irish Catholic army and made sufficiently powerful 'to serve the King, and at the same time to keep him in check and oblige him to make those concessions which, if left to himself, he would neither have the will nor power to grant'. With this long-term aim in view, Rinuccini was strongly in favour of concentrating all papal assistance on the Confederate Irish, for to divide it would, he believed, be to invite failure; besides which, any money sent directly to Henrietta for the king would be sure to be wasted by the bad management of the Protestants who surrounded him.[65]

Henrietta, meanwhile, had sent Sir Kenelm Digby as her own representative to Rome, but she was quickly to discover that the Roman establishment, not unlike the pawnbrokers of Amsterdam before them, could see her desperate need and had every intention of exploiting it. The new Pope, Innocent X, did agree to let the queen have a small subvention of 20,000 crowns (approximately £7,000) but it was made clear that any further aid would be conditional on Charles agreeing to what would indeed amount to the setting up of a virtually independent Catholic state in Ireland and also to the granting of complete freedom of worship to the English Catholics, together with the full restitution of their civil rights 'in such a manner that they may enjoy the properties, honours, liberty and prerogatives which are enjoyed by the other gentlemen of the kingdom'.[66]

The news coming from England during the late summer of 1645 was almost uniformly depressing. After Naseby, Charles had retreated temporarily into Wales, while Thomas Fairfax proceeded to cut a swathe through the once dependably loyal West Country. On 14 July the New Model Army defeated George Goring at Langport near Ilminster. Bridgwater fell on 23 July, Sherborne Castle on 14 August and on 10 September Rupert was forced to surrender Bristol, a calamity which caused 'a new earthquake in all the little quarters the King had left'. In September the king was once more on his way north, lured by the hope of being able to join up with the Marquis of Montrose, who had been conducting a spectacularly successful guerrilla war against the Covenanters in Scotland. But once again hope proved illusory. Montrose and his Highlanders and a handful of Irish were crushed at Philiphaugh on 13 September – the very day that Henrietta, now back in Paris, had ordered a Te Deum to be sung for his victories – and ten days later Charles and the remnants of his cavalry were themselves decisively beaten at Rowton Heath outside the walls of Chester. After that there was nothing for it but another retreat and while the king wandered across the Midlands looking for a safe haven, Fairfax and Cromwell were mopping up in the south. Basing House in Hampshire, the Marquis of Winchester's stronghold standing astride the road from London to the south-west, had withstood parliamentary attack since 1643 but was finally stormed and sacked on 14 October. Everything movable was seized by the victors, even down to the clothes on the backs of the vanquished and the great Inigo Jones, quite an old man now, who had been called in to advise on the fortifications at Basing, was carried out wrapped in a blanket to hide his nakedness.

Early in November the king returned to Oxford for what would be the last time, and it was now, with the royalist cause apparently on the point of collapse, that the French government moved to intervene – reflecting that a triumphant seafaring republic on the other side of the Channel might well become an inconvenient neighbour. Mazarin had, therefore, dispatched the diplomat Jean de Montreuil with instructions to try to broker a peace. But while Charles was still looking towards Ireland, the French, with their long tradition of friendship with Scotland, turned north in the hope of arranging an alliance between Charles and the Covenanters against the English rebels. Thus, they reasoned, the balance of power between king and parliament might be redressed and some sort of compromise solution arrived at. Unfortunately, however, this perfectly sensible, rational plan came up against the king's obstinate, irrational refusal even to consider surrendering the Church of England to Presbyterian discipline as demanded by the Covenanters.

The French, and Henrietta in particular, found this difficult to understand. Given their present predicament, the queen had little patience with what seemed to her a mere quibble over different forms of heresy, although in his letters from Oxford that winter Charles tried hard to make her see his point of view. 'The difference between me and the rebels concerning the church is not bare matter of form or ceremony which are alterable according to occasion, but so real, that if I should give way as is desired, here would be no church, and by no human probability ever to be recovered; so that, besides the obligation of mine oath, I know nothing to be an higher point of conscience.' After all, with what patience would Henrietta herself listen 'to him who should persuade thee, for worldly respects, to leave the communion of the Roman church for any other?' Moreover, this was not, as she seemed to think, a mere temporary expedient, 'whether I should lay by the bishops for a time', but a question of whether he should betray the religion he had been bred in and which he had sworn a sacred oath to maintain and defend at his coronation.[67]

In spite of her husband's awkward scruples of conscience, Henrietta had not given up trying to help him by whatever means she could. 'The queen . . . is the same woman she was, and is resolved to her power to manage the business for the continuance of the wars here,' a parliamentary newswriter commented sourly, and on 1 January she appealed to Gaston to approach the regent and the cardinal to see whether it might be possible to detach some of the French troops now entering winter quarters and send them off to England. 'If that were feasible,' she wrote, 'I should owe you obligations which no words could express. I refer to you to judge of the time proper for speaking of this affair; I entreat you not to lose it – we are very near our end.'[68]

Towards the end of January the Venetians heard that 'the queen of England has at last obtained leave to enlist 3,000 infantry in Brittany' and Charles at once began to make plans to march into Kent with 2,000 horse and dragoons to meet up with them somewhere near Hastings. By mid-February their numbers had grown: 'For God's sake, as thou lovest me, see what may be done for the landing of the 5,000 men . . . and with them as much money as possible thou canst.'[69] But no Frenchmen were enlisted in 1646 to sail for Hastings or anywhere else, and this plan, like so many others, vanished into smoke.

At the beginning of February any last lingering hope of help from Ireland had also vanished with the fall of Chester, and on 21 March the veteran Cavalier Jacob Astley, on his way to Oxford with a scratch force of newly recruited Welsh foot soldiers, was defeated at Stow-in-the-Wold. The Welsh recruits surrendered *en masse* and Astley and his second-in-command were taken prisoner, as were most of the other officers who were not killed, 'and the few who escaped were so scattered and dispersed that they never came together again, nor did there remain from that minute any possibility for the King to draw any troops together'.[70] On 9 April Exeter surrendered, bringing the war in the west to an end, and as Fairfax began to advance on Oxford, Charles had to make up his mind what he was going to do – try to escape abroad, or trust himself to the Scots in the very forlorn hope that he might yet be able to reach an accommodation with the Covenanters.

On 22 April he wrote his last letter from Oxford, telling Henrietta that he intended, by the grace of God, to get privately to the east coast port of Lynn and either go by sea to Scotland to join Montrose, still at large somewhere in the Highlands, or else to Ireland, or France, or even Denmark, 'but to which of these I am not yet resolved; desiring if it may be, to have thy judgement before I put to sea, to direct my course by. In the meantime,' he went on, 'I conjure thee, by thy constant love to me, that if I should miscarry (whether by being taken by the rebels or otherwise), to continue the same active endeavours for Pr. Charles as thou hast done for me, and not whine for my misfortunes in a retired way, but, like thy father's daughter, vigorously assist Pr. Charles to regain his own.'[71]

Five days later, at three o'clock in the morning of 27 April, the king, that sensitive, fastidious little man, always so careful of his precious dignity, slipped out of Oxford disguised as a servant, riding over Magdalen Bridge and on up Headington Hill behind his only two companions, his friend John Ashburnham and his chaplain Michael Hudson. After more than a week of aimless wandering, during which time it became increasingly obvious that escape by sea was going to be impossible, he came at last to the Scots' camp at Newark, relying on a vague, verbal promise conveyed by Montreuil that they would receive honourably and not seek to make him act against his conscience. He had no choice but to hope they meant it.

CHAPTER NINE

The Widow

I have lost a king, a husband and a friend, whose loss I can never
sufficiently mourn.

Henrietta to Madame de Motteville

Some five weeks before that ignominious exit from Oxford, the king had
written to his wife that his chief security would be the knowledge that their
eldest son was with her in France, and on the same day, 22 March, he also
wrote to young Charles 'hoping that this will find you safe with your
mother'.[1] Young Charles, in fact, was then still at St Mary's on the Scilly
Isles. He had been sent down to the West Country the previous spring
when it no longer seemed wise for father and son to be together in the
same place, and given his own mini court and council and the nominal
command of the armies of the Western Association. At the beginning of
March 1646, when the collapse of the royalist cause in the west was plainly
imminent, his advisers-cum-guardians had hurried him away to temporary
refuge on the Scillies, but Henrietta was not at all happy about this. 'I shall
not sleep in quiet, until I shall hear the Prince of Wales shall be removed
from thence,' she told Edward Hyde, a leading member of the prince's
council. She hardly needed to remind him 'of what importance to the
king and all his party the safety of the prince's person is', for if he were to
fall into rebel hands 'the whole would thereby become desperate'.[2]

It was true that the Scillies, poor, primitive, insufficiently fortified and
impossible to defend against any sustained attack, were quite unsuitable for
a prolonged stay and it was agreed to transfer the prince's precious person
to Jersey – the Channel Islands now being pretty well the last solidly loyal
territory anywhere in the kingdom. The move took place in mid-April, but
the anxious parents were still not satisfied and on the 15th the king wrote
again from Oxford, urging Henrietta, if the prince were not yet with her, to
send 'mine and thine own positive commands to him to come unto thee'.[3]

A month later the prince was still in Jersey and on 17 May the queen
sent him a copy of Charles's letter, 'by which you may see the king's
command to you and to me . . . therefore make all the haste you can to
show yourself a dutiful son, and a careful one, to do all that is in your
power to serve him'. She added a warning that now the king had left
Oxford 'the Parliament will, with all their power, force you to come to

them. There is no time to be lost; therefore, lose none but come speedily.'[4] She had written by the same messenger to John Culpepper, another member of the prince's entourage: 'There is no longer time to delay; the life of the king, the good of my son, and of the kingdom depend on it; therefore, there must be no more dispute upon it.'[5]

There was, however, a good deal more dispute upon it, as Edward Hyde and some of the others were very reluctant to see the Prince of Wales go as a refugee to France, where he would not only become the dependant of a foreign power and identified with its interests, but would also come under the exclusive influence of his mother and her friends with all sorts of possibly undesirable results. But the king and queen were not to be denied and on 28 May the king, who had been taken up to Newcastle by his Scottish hosts-cum-captors, addressed yet another urgent appeal to Henrietta. 'I think not Pr. Charles safe in Jersey; therefore send for him to wait upon thee with all speed (for his preservation is the greatest hope for my safety), and in God's name let him stay with thee till it be seen what ply my business will take, and for my sake let the world see that the queen seeks not to alter his conscience.'[6] This prompted yet another letter from an increasingly impatient Henrietta to the prince. 'Considering of what high importance your safety is, as well to the king's person and his affairs, as likewise to your own interest . . . I must positively require you to give immediate obedience to his majesty's commands.'[7] She went on to promise that he would be given an honourable reception by the French government, with full liberty either to stay or go at his pleasure. As for herself, she pledged her word that whenever his council 'should find it fit for him to go out of France', she would not oppose it; nor would she interfere in any matters of importance which might concern him. He could discuss and resolve them with his council as freely as if he were still in England or Jersey.[8] Meanwhile, all that mattered was that he should make all possible haste to join her, and she sent Harry Jermyn and George Digby to add their personal persuasions.

The result was a heated argument between the pro- and anti-French factions which dragged on over three days, until the prince himself put a stop to it, announcing that he was 'resolved to comply with the commands of the Queen and forthwith to remove into France'. He sailed for St Malo on 25 June not yet aware that he was now the only one of the king's sons still at liberty, for with the surrender of Oxford two days earlier his brother James had joined the princess Elizabeth and young Henry of Gloucester as wards of parliament. Even the baby of the family, the little Princess Henriette, had been trapped in Exeter when the city fell to Thomas Fairfax in April, but so far her devoted governess had been able to keep control over her.

The French authorities, having agreed to grant asylum to the Prince of Wales, had no great desire to advertise the fact and since he was officially travelling incognito they were able to treat his arrival as a private family affair. It had, however, caused a considerable flutter of interest in court circles, where there was much anxious discussion about the correct protocol to be observed – whether or not the prince should be seated in the king's presence, whether he should occupy the place of honour on Louis' right-hand and be given a chair with arms. It was several weeks before these important details had been settled to everyone's satisfaction, but when at last sixteen-year-old Charles was introduced to his French relatives he seems to have made a favourable impression. Madame de Motteville remarked on his big black eyes, his excellent figure and general air of grace and dignity, while La Grande Mademoiselle, meeting her young cousin at Fontainebleau in August, thought him tall for his age, with a fine head of hair, brown complexion and tolerable figure. 'I saw in a moment', she recorded in her Memoirs, 'that the Queen of England much wished me to believe that he was in love with me,' for Henrietta, with her usual unquenchable optimism, was already busy matchmaking, seeing in Anne-Marie d'Orléans, heiress to an immense fortune and reputedly the richest woman in Europe, a matrimonial prize worth every effort to secure. Anne-Marie herself listened politely to her aunt singing her son's praises – 'he was almost the only subject of her conversation' – but remained unresponsive. The great heiress, who had her eye on the recently widowed Hapsburg Emperor Ferdinand, most definitely did not consider a penniless English exile as suitable husband material; another quite serious drawback was his surprising inability either to speak or to understand French. But, she wrote, 'I think that, had he pleaded his own cause, he would have been equally unsuccessful. I know that I did not much value what they told me on the part of a man who could say nothing for himself.'[9]

Would say nothing was more likely. Charles at sixteen already possessed a firmer grasp of political realities than his mother, and while he probably found the buxom, highly coloured, overdressed Anne-Marie physically unattractive, he could see that in present circumstances publicly to commit himself to a Catholic ally would surely spell the final ruin of his father's cause. At the same time he had been repeatedly ordered by his father to obey his mother in all things – except, of course, religion – and he knew better than to risk a scene with his volatile parent on whom he was also now financially dependent. He therefore took the path of least resistance, a technique he was to perfect during his years in the wilderness, and played the part of attentive but silent admirer, handing Mademoiselle to her carriage whenever she visited his mother and always remaining uncovered in her presence, so that 'his civilities appeared in everything'.

If her eldest son was proving less cooperative than she had hoped, the unexpected reunion with her youngest daughter early in August brought the queen unalloyed delight. Realising that she would soon be forced to surrender her charge, Lady Dalkeith, the two-year-old Henriette's governess and guardian, had made up her mind somehow to smuggle the child over to France. Taking only two trusted servants into her confidence, she disguised herself in a shabby gown and cloak, with a bundle of rags stuffed into one shoulder to give a hunchbacked appearance. Posing as a Frenchwoman and accompanied by a French *valet de chambre* as her 'husband', Anne Dalkeith (she had been born Anne Villiers, a niece of the murdered Buckingham) set out to walk from Oatlands to Dover carrying the little princess, who was passed off as a boy called Pierre. They had three days' start, but there was no attempt at pursuit. It seems most probable that the parliamentary authorities were frankly relieved to be spared the responsibility and expense of yet another royal child and the travellers were able to go on their way unhindered – their only anxiety being caused by the little Henriette, who insisted on informing all and sundry that her name was not Pierre but princess and that the rough clothes she was wearing were not her own. On reaching the port, they went on board the ordinary cross-Channel packet for Calais, arriving without incident. A message was sent to the queen and, according to the Capuchin Father Cyprien de Gamache, carriages were quickly sent to fetch them 'and the *gouvernante*, with all her train, reached Paris in safety, and respectfully placed in the hands of her Majesty the precious deposit, which she had so happily preserved amidst so many awful dangers. O, the transports of joy! O, the excessive consolation to the heart of the Queen! She embraced, she hugged, she kissed again and again that royal infant. . . . Many thanksgivings did she render to God for this mercy; and, regarding the princess as *un enfant de bénédiction*, she resolved, with the grace of God, to have her instructed in the Catholic and Roman religion.'[10] Henrietta had previously been inclined to blame Lady Dalkeith for not removing the princess from Exeter before it fell, which Edward Hyde thought most unfair, but now the valiant *gouvernante* became quite a heroine and everyone in Paris was charmed by the 'pretty romance' of her story.

But genuinely delighted though she was to have her baby restored to her, nothing could for long distract Henrietta from her husband's unhappy situation in Scottish hands. 'I never knew what it was to be barbarously baited before,' he had written in June. '. . . for, upon I know not what intelligence from London, nothing must serve but my signing the Covenant, declaring absolutely, and without reserve, for Presbyterian government . . . I answered them', he went on, 'that what they demanded was absolutely against my conscience, which might be persuaded, but would not be forced by anything they could speak or do.'[11]

The battle for the king's conscience went on all summer, but although he ducked and dived, played for time and offered marginal concessions, neither threats, persuasions nor 'fair promises' from the Scots, the French, the Westminster parliament, and his wife and her friends could induce him to agree to abandon the church he had been bred in, or accept a doctrine which 'never came into any country but by rebellion' and breathed nothing but treason. To Henrietta he wrote that all the comfort he had was her love and a clear conscience, but as she continued to urge him to come to terms with the Scots and win their support by whatever means necessary to satisfy them, he was finally driven to tell her that she would break his heart 'if she any more undertake to obtain my consent for Presbyterian government'.[12] In October he was still trying to make her understand that he was not being unreasonable or 'wilful', but that 'the absolute establishing of Presbyterian government would make me but a titular king . . . for they [the Presbyterians] intend to take away all the ecclesiastical power of government from the crown, and place it in the two houses of parliament. Moreover, they will introduce that doctrine which teaches rebellion to be lawful, and that the supreme power is in the people, to whom kings (as they say) ought to give account and be corrected when they do amiss.'[13]

To Henrietta the army was of far greater importance than the Anglican bishops, for, as she pointed out, 'if you are lost, so are they without resource'; but, 'if you can put yourself again at the head of an army, we shall replace them. . . . Keep the militia, and by that everything will return.'[14]

Charles did not agree. 'I am still of the opinion that, unless religion be preserved, the militia will not be much useful to the crown. . . . For though it be most true, that the absolute grant of the militia to the parliament dethrones the king, yet the keeping of it is not of that importance as is thought . . . because the militia here is not, as in France and other kingdoms, a formed powerful strength . . . and certainly if the pulpits teach not obedience, the king will have but small comfort of the militia.'[15]

The queen reluctantly accepted his scruples. 'Touching the pulpits, and Presbyterian government etc., I will not any more enter into dispute with you, finding that arguments of that nature have neither done you nor your business any good.'[16] Nevertheless, she was horrified to learn that Charles had granted control of the militia to parliament for ten years, 'which is as much as to say, that we shall never see an end to your troubles. For as long as the Parliament lasts you are not king; and as for me, I shall not again set my foot in England. And with the granting the militia, you have cut your own throat; for having given them this power, you can no longer refuse them anything, not even my life if they demand it from you; but I shall not place myself in their hands.' Poor Henrietta could hardly contain her rage and disappointment. 'Do you think that

Costume designs by Inigo Jones for Henrietta: as the Amazon Queen in Salmacida Spolia *(left) and as Bellesa in* The Shepherd's Paradise. *(Devonshire Collection, Chatsworth. Reproduced by permission of the Duke of Devonshire and the Chatsworth Settlement Trustees. Photograph: Photographic Survey, Courtauld Institute of Art)*

Inigo Jones, drawing by Van Dyck. (Devonshire Collection, Chatsworth. Reproduced by permission of the Duke of Devonshire and the Chatsworth Settlement Trustees. Photograph: Photographic Survey, Courtauld Institute of Art)

Charles I in 1631, by Daniel Mytens. (By courtesy of the National Portrait Gallery)

Henrietta Maria. (By courtesy of the National Portrait Gallery)

The five eldest children of Charles and Henrietta, pictured by Van Dyck in 1637. (The Royal Collection © 2000. Her Majesty the Queen)

Henrietta Maria's arrival in Holland, 1642. (Ashmolean Museum, University of Oxford)

Henrietta Maria's landing at Bridlington, February 1643. (The Royal Collection © 2000. Her Majesty the Queen)

The cottage at Bridlington where the queen is reputed to have lodged. (Bridlington Museum)

Oliver Cromwell, by Peter Lely.
(Birmingham Museums & Art Gallery)

Prince Rupert, attributed to Honthorst.
(By courtesy of the National Portrait Gallery)

William Cavendish, Duke of Newcastle.
(Mary Evans Picture Library)

Mon cousin pay resen ūū lettre par persons: auec la
relation de tout ce qui sest passe a newcastell et suis
bien ayse que vous nayes pas encore mange les rats
pour veu que les escossois ne mange point des yorkshire
oate cakes tout yra fort bien jespere que vous je eloerne
ves ordre:

or fordle 15º mars

Ūū fidelle et bien bonne amie

HENRIETTE MARIE R

Letter from Henrietta to the Duke of Newcastle. (Reproduced by permission of the British Library)

Charles I at his trial. (The Royal Collection © 2000. Her Majesty the Queen)

Henrietta as a widow. (British Museum Department of Prints & Drawings)

when I see you so resolute in the affair of the bishops, and so little in that which concerns yourself and your posterity, that I am not in great despair, after having so often warned you as I have done, and it avails nothing.'[17]

Paris was very gay that winter season, and while she continued to write impassioned letters to Charles, begging him on no account to give anything more away to parliament – '*voici pour la derniere fois que je vous dirai encore, que si vous accordes d'avantage, vous estes perdu*' – Henrietta was still in hot pursuit of La Grande Mademoiselle, with her son still in obedient, if speechless, attendance. 'One day,' recalled Mademoiselle, 'when I was going to an assembly at Madame de Choisy's, the Queen of England, who wished to dress my hair and to adorn me herself, came to my residence and took every care to see that I was well attired, the Prince of Wales holding the flambeau near me to give light.' The prince, wearing her colours of carnation, white and black, arrived at the party ahead of her, ready to hand her from her coach, and when she paused in an ante-room to arrange her skirts and titivate, he was there again holding the candlestick. At the end of the evening, he followed her home, waiting to see her safely inside, so that 'his gallantry thus openly shown, occasioned much talk in the world'. Another time, Henrietta insisted on lending her niece her few remaining pieces of jewellery to wear at a grand fête held at the Palais Royal, where Mademoiselle, already positively dripping diamonds, sat in state on a raised throne overlooking the dance-floor with the Prince of Wales lounging at her feet. But gazing on him, '*de haut en bas* with my heart as well as my eyes', she could only regard him as an object of pity.[18]

This was scarcely surprising in view of the unrelievedly depressing nature of the news coming from England. France's latest efforts at mediation having failed, Mazarin had all but abandoned the Stuart cause and Pompone de Bellièvre, sent over in the summer to reinforce Montreuil, was asking to be recalled. The Scots had also now come to accept that the king's conscience was indeed unpersuadable and were in somewhat acrimonious discussion with parliament about his future. According to one of the regular reports forwarded from London to the Venetian embassy in Paris: 'The English maintain that the disposal of his Majesty belongs to them alone. The Scots prove that it belongs to both kingdoms to exercise it by common consent. While the life and dignity of the king are being hawked about amid strange opinions, he is at Newcastle as usual, waiting for what time may bring.'[19]

This was at the end of November. A month later, on Saturday 2 January 1647, Charles wrote to his wife: 'Deare Hart, I must tell thee that now I am declared what I have really beene ever since I came to this army, which is a prisoner.'[20] At the end of January, having finally agreed satisfactory terms with Westminster, the Covenanters handed him over to

1647

a delegation of parliamentary commissioners and prepared once more to cross the border in consideration of the sum of £400,000 for services rendered during the past three years. The fishwives of Newcastle pursued them with brickbats and cries of 'Judas!' and Charles, with a rare flick of sardonic humour, reproached them with having sold him too cheap. He was now escorted south as far as Holdenby, where, eleven years before, he had entertained George Con and Henrietta had pinned a picture of St Catherine to her bed-curtains.

Although he was allowed to walk in the grounds and even ride over to nearby Althorp to play bowls, all pretence that he was anything but a closely guarded prisoner had been dropped and his correspondence with Henrietta, made possible by the French during his time at Newcastle, ceased abruptly. Not that the queen stopped writing, and in April a Major Bosvile [Boswell?] 'in rustic disguise' did manage to smuggle in a packet from her to the king. The gallant major was subsequently arrested and questioned but denied knowing anything of the packet's contents.[21] Nevertheless, it was not long before the Venetian newsletter reported that parliament was planning to move his majesty nearer to London in order to facilitate the peace negotiations, 'and it is coming to be known that the despatches from the queen, put into the king's hands secretly some weeks ago, urged him to accept any terms'.[22]

In her increasing anxiety for Charles's survival, Henrietta appears at last to have given up all thought of her own future in England and her mental distress during those early months of 1647 was acute. Giovanni Nani in Paris heard that 'the Queen of England with bitter tears has lamented to the Regent the condition of herself and her husband, and that the long delayed hopes which have been held out of peace have reduced them to the utmost extremity, in which they are languishing at present'.[23]

In March Henrietta had turned back to Ireland, sending an envoy over to try to broker a fresh treaty between the Marquis of Ormonde and the Confederate Supreme Council. Ormonde had succeeded in patching up an interim agreement with the Confederates in March of the previous year, but as it contained no commitments about religion, the papal nuncio Rinuccini, supported by the clergy, had persuaded them to repudiate it. Rinuccini still cherished dreams of creating a united, independent and Catholic Ireland under the personal protection of the Pope, but the embattled Ormonde, responsible for the lives and property of the Protestant settlers and loyalist Irish, was dealing with reality and in June he was forced to accept the inevitable. He negotiated a treaty with the parliamentary commissioners and surrendered Dublin into their hands.

Meanwhile, in England, the king was becoming a pawn in the developing conflict between the authoritarian Presbyterian faction which dominated parliament and the so-called Independents, who favoured greater freedom and decentralisation of church government and who formed a majority of the army. Nervous of the army's size and strength and the popularity of its victorious generals, parliament was now attempting to embark on a programme of cut-price demobilisation, but soon discovered that the formidable instrument it had created was not so easily disposed of. Soldiers who were owed up to nine months' back pay were not going to go quietly, and late in the evening of 3 June a businesslike troop of horse under the command of Cornet Joyce arrived unheralded at Holdenby to take possession of the king. In what amounted to a military *coup d'état* Oliver Cromwell and the New Model Army had effectively seized power, although they were no nearer to reaching any decision about the future.

For the king the future had begun to look brighter – he had always hoped that the inevitable dissensions among his enemies would one day work to his advantage – and the present was a definite improvement. Comfortably installed at Hampton Court and treated with respect, even deference, he had the freedom to hunt in Richmond Park, to worship as he pleased for the first time since leaving Oxford, to write letters and receive and entertain visitors. Better still, he was able to see his children. Elizabeth, who was now eleven, Henry and thirteen-year-old James were spending the summer at nearby Syon House under the guardianship of the Earl of Northumberland, and came over regularly to play in the gardens at Hampton Court.

On 23 July the army presented Charles with their conditions for his reinstatement. These Heads of Proposals were fundamentally the same as the Newcastle Propositions put forward by parliament the previous summer in that they aimed at transferring executive power from the crown to an elected parliament, but they did not require anyone to take the dreaded Covenant and the king's more sensible friends urgently advised him to accept them. Unhappily, though, Charles had convinced himself that in the last resort neither the army nor parliament could do without him and, cheered by the signs of reviving royalist sentiment which he had seen on his journey south, plus the flattering attention he was currently receiving from the various contending parties, he continued stubbornly to pursue his unwise and ultimately fatal policy of attempting to play both ends against the middle – he was also talking to the Scots commissioners in London led by the Earl of Lauderdale.

By the autumn the army's patience was beginning to wear distinctly thin, while the radical elements in its ranks were becoming harder to control. In November the king, alarmed by the increased security around him and reports that the radicals, or 'Levellers', were demanding to have him brought to justice, managed to escape from Hampton Court, ending up on the Isle of Wight in the belief, mistaken as it turned out, that the

Governor there was sympathetic to his cause. He continued to conduct his clandestine correspondence with the Scots, who were also nervous of the army's growing power and influence, and at Christmas signed a secret treaty whereby he undertook to sanction the establishment of Presbyterianism for a limited trial period, to suppress the scandalous doctrines and practices of the Independents and appoint 'a considerable and competent number of Scotsmen' to his Privy Council. In return, the Scots 'engaged' to restore him to his throne, by force if necessary.

In the New Year his circumstances changed again, this time for the worse. Exasperated by his double-dealing, both parliament and the army broke off negotiations and Charles once more became a close prisoner, confined in Carisbrooke Castle. In Paris Henrietta heard the news with tears, as once more all channels of communication with her husband were blocked. Letters addressed to 'a gentlewoman in the castle, or in her absence to Mistress Mary who has relation to her' were intercepted, but, reported the *Weekly Intelligencer*, they were mostly written in the queen's 'cabalry and mystical lock of numbers' to which no one apparently possessed a key. However, 'in the end of her letters she writes outright in full letters, and imploreth the mercy of God for the preservation of his majesty and his power for the destruction of his adversaries'.[24]

And it looked as if the mercy of God would indeed be the king's only resource. Kenelm Digby in Rome had been told by the Pope that 'there was not one Cardinal who advised him to contribute to his majesty', while it was painfully obvious that not one of the other European powers was prepared to lift a finger either. The single remaining ray of hope now came from Scotland and soon Henrietta was back at her familiar task of trying to raise money for military supplies, sending Sir William Fleming to Amsterdam to sell the last of her jewels still in pawn.

True to their promise, the Engagers, as they were known, led by James, now Duke of Hamilton, and the earls of Lauderdale and Lanark, had begun recruiting for an invasion force, although hampered by the hostility of the hard-line Covenanters who were not satisfied by the king's half-hearted attitude. At the beginning of June the queen called a meeting of the most senior English refugees now gathered in Paris, at which it was agreed that the Prince of Wales should join the Scots army. Then, towards the end of the month, came the encouraging news that a number of ships of the parliamentary navy had defected to the royalists. So, instead of Scotland, the prince sailed for the Dutch port of Helvoetsluys, where he found both the disenchanted mariners and his brother James, who had recently made a dramatic escape from captivity disguised in girl's clothes.

After her son's departure, Henrietta had retreated temporarily to the Carmelite convent in the Faubourg St Jacques, partly in order to pray for his success and partly, it seems, to economise, money as usual being in desperately short supply. Madame de Motteville, who went with a friend to call on the queen, found her busy writing and closing up dispatches which were, she assured her visitors, 'of the greatest importance'. She had gone on to complain about her poverty and showed them a little gold drinking cup, saying sadly 'that she had not another piece of gold, coin or otherwise in her possession'.[25]

Henrietta was still in the convent on 8 July, when the Duke of Hamilton crossed the border in pouring rain – it was the wettest summer anyone could remember – with a large but untrained and ill-equipped army. His invasion had been intended to coincide with a series of royalist uprisings in Essex, Kent and South Wales, but these had erupted prematurely and the so-called Second Civil War turned into a brief but bloody fiasco, culminating in Cromwell's annihilation of Hamilton at Preston in the third week of August. Prince Charles, who had sailed as far as the Downs and who might possibly, if all had gone well, have been able to rescue his father, now had no choice but to return ingloriously to Holland.

For the rest of the year a variety of schemes of varying degrees of impracticality involving Ireland and/or the Channel Islands were discussed by the royalist expatriates, while on the Isle of Wight a parliamentary delegation was making a last-ditch attempt to reach an agreement with the king which would have preserved the monarchy, albeit in a severely emasculated form, and curbed the power of the generals. But Cromwell and the General Council of the Army had now come to the conclusion that there was only one way to deal with 'Charles Stuart, the Man of Blood'. At the end of November they brought him over to the mainland and lodged him at Hurst Castle, a gloomy little fortress built by Henry VIII on a spit of sand and shingle overlooking the Solent. Five days later a detachment of regular troops replaced the City militia at the approaches to the Houses of Parliament while Colonel Thomas Pride, said to have started his career as a brewer's drayman, supervised the forcible exclusion of all those members of the Commons regarded as opponents of the army. On New Year's Day 1649 the survivors of Pride's Purge – a body known to history as the Rump – passed an ordinance for the trial of Charles Stuart 'the now King of England' on a charge of treason. Charles had been transferred to Windsor just before Christmas and on 19 January he came back to the capital which he had last seen almost exactly seven years before.

1648

1649

Across the Channel Henrietta waited in a state of agonised suspense. France was just then distracted by the Wars of the Fronde, a succession of civil disturbances born out of general resentment against the power of central government and in particular against the dominance of Cardinal Mazarin over the regent. In the winter of 1648/9 Paris was in the hands of

Louis XIV

the insurgents and Queen Anne and her young son had retreated to St Germain, but the Queen of England insisted on remaining at the Louvre, believing that news from London would reach her more quickly there. Her situation was acutely uncomfortable. Her pension had not been paid for several months and now, with the royal family absent and the city in a state of siege, the Parisian shopkeepers were refusing to extend her credit any further. The weather had turned very cold and with no money for fuel, she and the little Henriette shivered in their fireless apartments.

All this, though, was as nothing to her mental anguish. Apart from the occasional precariously smuggled letter, it was nearly a year since she had heard from Charles or had any reliable news of him. Nor did she know how many of her own letters were getting through; early in January she had written, using an employee of the mysterious Major Boswell as messenger, 'expressing her deep sense, and sorrow for his Majesties condition, with whom she saith, she bears an equal share, and wishes to die for him; nor will she live without him'.[26]

At about the same time, 'being struck to the heart with amazement and confusion upon the report what the Parliament intended', she also wrote to the Lord General Thomas Fairfax and both Houses of Parliament begging to be allowed the consolation of going to her dearest lord the king. These letters were entrusted for delivery to Pierre de Bellièvre, sieur de Grignan, the present French ambassador in London, together with a covering note from the queen: 'I have specified nothing to the Parliaments and to the general, but to give me the liberty to go see the king my lord. . . . You must know then, that you are to ask passports for me to go there, to stay as long as they will permit me. . . . I will send a list of those that I wish shall attend me, in order that if there are any in the number of them that may be suspected or obnoxious, they may be left behind. . . . I dare not promise myself that they will accord me the liberty of going,' she went on. 'I wish it too much to assure myself of it at a time when so little of what I desire succeeds; but if, by your negotiation, these passports can be obtained, I shall deem myself obliged to you all my life.'[27] But although the ambassador faithfully presented the queen's letters, they were never answered. They were not even read (they were discovered more than thirty years later, still sealed, among a bundle of old papers stuffed into someone's desk) and the sad responsibility of saying goodbye and recording her father's last messages fell to the Princess Elizabeth, now just turned thirteen.

The king's trial took place in Westminster Hall between 20 and 27 January, and after sentence had been passed – 'that the said Charles Stuart as a Tyrant, Traitor, Murderer and Public Enemy shall be put to death by the severing his head from his body' – they took him back to St James's for the last two days of his life. He had asked to see his children, and Elizabeth and Henry were brought up from Syon House on the afternoon of Monday the 29th. He kissed them both and gave them his blessing and then turned to Elizabeth, who was already in tears. 'He told me he was glad I was come, and although he had not time to say much, yet somewhat he had to say to me.'

Elizabeth's recollection of his words, set down immediately after the event, still has the power to move: 'He wished me not to grieve and torment myself for him, for that it would be a glorious death that he should die, it being for the laws and liberties of this land, and for maintaining the true Protestant religion. . . . He told me, he had forgiven all his enemies, and hoped God would forgive them also, and commanded us, and all the rest of my brothers and sisters to forgive them. He bid me tell my mother that his thoughts had never strayed from her, and that his love should be the same to the last. Withal he commanded me and my brother to be obedient to her, and bid me send his blessing to the rest of my brothers and sisters, with commendation to all his friends.'[28]

'Sweetheart, you'll forget this,' said Charles to his weeping daughter. '"No" (said she) "I shall never forget it while I live." The king then took the little Duke of Gloucester on his knee and said, "Sweetheart, now they will cut off thy father's head. Mark, child, what I say. They will cut off my head, and perhaps make thee a King. But mark what I say, you must not be a King, so long as your brothers Charles and James do live; for they will cut off your brothers' heads (when they can catch them) and cut off thy head too at the last; and therefore I charge you, do not be made a king by them." At which the child, sighing, said "I will be torn in pieces first".' These words, according to the account printed in the *Eikon Basilike*, 'falling so unexpectedly from one so young' – Henry was still only eight – 'made the King rejoice exceedingly.'[29]

Charles gave the children some of his few remaining pieces of jewellery and told them once more not to grieve for him, 'for he should die a martyr'. He kissed them both again before turning away to go into his bedroom. But a fresh outburst of grief from Elizabeth brought him back for one last embrace. 'Most sorrowful was this parting,' wrote an eyewitness to the scene, 'the young princess shedding tears and crying lamentably, so as moved others to pity that formerly were hardhearted; and at opening the bed-chamber door the King returned hastily from the window and kissed them and blessed them; and so parted.'[30]

News of the king's execution took nearly a fortnight to reach his widow. According to Madame de Motteville, Henrietta heard a rumour that Charles had actually been rescued on the steps of the scaffold by a mob of outraged Londoners and had half believed it, knowing 'how dearly the king was beloved by many who were ready still to sacrifice life and fortune in his service'. But at last the truth had to be told. Father Philip, her old friend and confessor, had died in the autumn, so it was Cyprien de Gamache who was warned to stay behind after saying grace at dinner 'and not to leave her Majesty, but stop and comfort her, upon the sad tidings which were likely to be brought her'. The task of actually breaking the news was undertaken by Henry Jermyn and, says Father Cyprien, the queen was so deeply shocked that she stood motionless as a statue, silent and tearless. 'The words and the reasons that we employed to rouse her, found her deaf and insensible.' At last, he went on, 'we were obliged to desist and to remain about her in silence, some weeping, others sighing, all sympathising with her extreme grief'.[31] It was not until evening, when the Duchesse de Vendôme, wife of her illegitimate half-brother and a friend from childhood days, came in weeping to kiss her hand and talk gently to her that Henrietta's frozen stupor finally melted in a great gush of tears.

Two days later, when Madame de Motteville came to pay a visit of condolence, the widow took the opportunity to send an urgent message to the regent. 'She commanded me to tell my queen,' remembered Françoise de Motteville, 'that King Charles her lord, whose death had made her the most afflicted woman on the wide earth, had been lost because none of those in whom he trusted had told him the truth; and that a people, when irritated, was like a ferocious beast, whose rage nothing can moderate . . . and that she prayed God that the queen regent might be more fortunate in France than she and King Charles had been in England. But above all she counselled her to hear the truth, and to labour to discover it; for she believed that the greatest evil that could befall sovereigns was to rest in ignorance of the truth, which ignorance reverses thrones and destroys empires. . . . Pressing my hand, she said, with a burst of grief and tenderness, "I have lost a king, a husband and a friend, whose loss I can never sufficiently mourn, and this separation must render the rest of my life an endless suffering".'[32]

In the first agony of bereavement Henrietta had sought refuge again with the Carmelites, but although she often said that she never expected to survive her terrible loss and looked forward to a lifetime, which she hoped would be short, of nothing but poverty and desolation, the great cause which had occupied her thoughts and energies to the exclusion of pretty well everything else for the best part of the last ten years, still had to be served; so that when Father Cyprien came to the convent to remind her that her family needed her, she roused herself to return to the field of battle. She might have lost one king, but now there was another to support and fight for, advise and admonish, and soon the indomitable little figure, dressed in the deep mourning which she would wear for the rest of her life – 'on her person and in her heart' – was back at her desk, writing to

Montrose, now exiled in Denmark; to the new Duke of Hamilton, whose brother had been executed after Preston; and to the envoy she was sending to her 'dearest son', who at the time of his father's death was still in Holland. La Grande Mademoiselle, calling to see the widow after her return to the Louvre, thought her less grief-stricken than might have been expected, considering how much her husband had loved her and the horrific manner of his end. But perhaps, reflected Mademoiselle, God grants special powers of endurance at times of great affliction, to enable one to submit to his will with resignation.[33] Undoubtedly Henrietta drew much inner strength and spiritual consolation from her religion, but the daughter of Henri le Grand was also undoubtedly driven by a strong earthly desire for victory and revenge. She had once remarked that her husband would never be a king until he had hanged every member of parliament!

In the spring of 1649 the queen favoured the idea of sending young Charles over to Ireland where, having seen off the meddlesome Rinuccini, Ormonde and the royalists had once more come to terms with the Confederates and were having some success against the parliamentary forces. First, though, Henrietta wanted the new king back in France, so that plans and preparations could be made. Meanwhile, she had resumed her matchmaking activities – now more than ever her son needed a rich wife – and sent the ever-useful Harry Jermyn to Mademoiselle to make her 'many fine protestations on the part of the King of England'. Mademoiselle herself remained doubtful. However, on the June day when the royal family were to meet the new king at Compiègne, she got up early to have her hair curled, something she seldom bothered to do, and prepared to offer her bashful suitor a limited amount of encouragement. But although he was apparently quite willing to talk, in French, to eleven-year-old Louis about hunting, as soon as they were left alone together after dinner he became obstinately monosyllabic again and made no attempt at all to please her with pretty speeches. No, decided Mademoiselle, he would never do. 'My son is too poor and too unfortunate for you,' said Henrietta sourly.[34]

At their first meeting, mother and son had shed tears together over their shared loss and Henrietta had written to Christine in July to tell her that 'the King my son lives with me in the greatest affection possible. You, who have a son who treats you in the same way, can judge what that means to a mother.'[35] But as the weeks passed she found that her son was not prepared to discuss his plans with her. On the contrary, he told her plainly 'that he would always perform his duty towards her with great affection and exactness, but that in his business he would obey his own reason and judgement, and did as good as desire her not to trouble herself in his affairs'. This was not at all the sort of thing Henrietta had been expecting, but tears and reproaches had no effect. If she made a scene, Charles simply walked out of the room – 'finding her passions strong,' observed Edward Hyde, 'he frequently retired with some abruptness'.[36] Relations became increasingly strained, so when it was decided that the king should go back to the Channel Islands to await developments – news that Oliver Cromwell had just landed near Dublin in command of a large, well-equipped expeditionary force had not been encouraging – the queen made no attempt to detain him and he left for Jersey towards the end of September, taking the young Duke of York with him, for no other reason than to annoy his mother, thought the Venetian ambassador in Paris, adding that there was little love lost between them.[37]

By the end of that disastrous year Cromwell's ruthless suppression of all Catholic and royalist resistance, notably at Drogheda and Wexford, had put paid to any ideas of establishing a bridgehead in Ireland and, as once before, the only remaining gleam of hope came from the north. The Scots had taken serious umbrage over the arbitrary manner in which the English had tried, condemned and executed the king without reference to his Scottish subjects, and they had proclaimed his son Charles II at the Mercat Cross in Edinburgh in a deliberate snub to the new rulers in London. Now it appeared that they were prepared to offer their support – on certain conditions; and although there was considerable doubt among his advisers as to the wisdom of trusting the Scots, Charles really had very little choice. He travelled over to Holland in the spring of 1650 and at the beginning of June set sail for his kingdom of Scotland.

1650

The first year of the new decade brought no joy for Henrietta; her last birthday had been her fortieth and her health was poor. She had never fully recovered from her serious illness in 1644, which appears to have been rheumatic fever complicated by childbirth, and although she still went every year to Bourbon for the waters she told Madame de Motteville that she rarely had a day free from pain. Now her eldest son had vanished, literally, into the northern mist to be as barbarously baited as ever his father had been and the queen shed tears of bitter mortification when she heard that Charles had not only subscribed to the Covenant, but had sworn 'to do his endeavour to extirpate the common prayer books, with many other horrid particulars, by which she said the King of England had renounced and deserted his own Religion and so justly exasperated and incensed all popish princes . . . that he could not expect any assistance from them, nay, she herself was hereby disabled to serve him'. When it was pointed out that she was believed to have encouraged him to come to an agreement with the Scots, she retorted angrily 'God forbid that I should have had a hand in persuading him to sacrifice his honour or conscience.'[38]

Two distinct and feuding factions, both competing for control of the king, now divided the exiled royalists. The queen's party, usually referred to as 'the Louvre', included Henry Jermyn, George Digby and Lord Henry Percy. The other group, which had gathered round the then Prince of Wales during his first sojourn in Jersey and later in Holland, was led by Edward Hyde and Edward Nicholas and, after 1651, the Marquis of Ormonde. Henrietta, of course, blamed them for her son's hurtful refusal to confide in her or to listen to her advice, while they maintained that nothing would be more prejudicial to his cause than a general perception that he was governed by his mother and 'the Louvre'.

It was Jermyn, created 1st Baron Jermyn in 1643, who attracted the strongest hostility from the king's party. 'I hold Lord Jermins counsells and designes as pernicious and destructive as ever,' Edward Nicholas had written in the spring of 1648, 'and his power as vast and exorbitant.'[39] Rumours that he and Henrietta were lovers had been circulating intermittently ever since the days of the Army Plot, and rumours that they were secretly married continued to circulate during the years of her widowhood. But no evidence to support either of these allegations was ever produced, nor is it credible that Henrietta, whose religious principles and pride of caste were so deeply ingrained, would ever have contemplated any relationship other than that of mistress and trusted factotum. Far more credible is the belief, widespread among the exiles, that plump, comfort-loving Jermyn was consistently lining his pockets at the queen's expense. Madame de Motteville, a shrewd observer of human nature, thought 'the favourite' a pleasant enough individual of limited ability, with a mind 'more fitted for petty matters than great ones'. She considered him a loyal servant, but 'he wanted money before all else to meet his expenses, which were large'. No doubt the queen placed too much confidence in him, she went on, but it was not true that he controlled her completely, for she often disagreed with him and supported her opinions with strong reasons.[40] Royal favourites, though, are seldom popular with other members of the family and, in the course of one of their numerous quarrels that summer, the Duke of York did not hesitate to accuse his mother of loving Lord Jermyn more than all her children.[41]

Henrietta was having problems with her second son. James, left to kick his heels in Paris, was both bored and resentful of maternal authority, and like most bored and resentful teenagers was making a nuisance of himself. Finally, at the beginning of October, he ran away to Brussels, then part of the Spanish Netherlands. This was especially embarrassing for Henrietta, since France and Spain were still at war and she was obliged to write an apologetic letter to Cardinal Mazarin, confessing her 'small influence' over her son. He had chosen to go against her wishes and without telling her what he meant to do, but had promised her not to take up arms against France. 'I ought to be ashamed to avow to any one this affair between the

Duke of York and myself,' she wrote, 'but with you I wish to use the freedom in all my own affairs, of which I have always made profession to you.'[42] Dependent as she was on French hospitality, she had very little choice.

The autumn brought another sorrow. News of Charles II's arrival in Scotland had caused a flurry of alarm in Whitehall, where executive power now rested in the hands of a Council of State, and as a precaution it was decided that 'the two children of the late king . . shall be sent out of the limits of the Commonwealth'. Elizabeth and Henry had spent the past year in the care of the Countess of Leicester at Penshurst in Kent, but now orders were sent to the Governor of Carisbrooke Castle that he and his wife were to collect the children from Lady Leicester and escort them over to the Isle of Wight. They landed at Cowes on 13 August, but Elizabeth's stay on the island was destined to be short. Less than a month later she was dead, reportedly of 'a malignant fever', but Henrietta had no doubt as to the real cause of death. Her daughter, she told Christine, had died of grief 'at finding herself taken to the same castle where the king her father had been kept prisoner, and in a place where she had no assistance in her malady'.[43] In fact, it seems pretty certain that the fourteen-year-old Elizabeth, who had never been strong, was already in the terminal stages of tuberculosis when she came to Carisbrooke.

The year ended with yet another death, this time of Mary's husband the young Prince of Orange, who had succeeded his father in 1647. Henrietta particularly regretted the loss of her son-in-law for she had been counting on his help in achieving the king's restoration. It really seemed as if God was trying to show her that she should detach herself altogether from the world and its troubles.

In the circumstances it was understandable that she should be turning more and more to the solace of her religion, but the realisation that she intended to bring up her youngest child, her *enfant de bénédiction*, in the Catholic faith was the cause of much disquiet in the rest of the family. Charles himself had attempted to tackle his mother on the subject before his departure for Jersey, but this had only resulted in another scene from which he had hastily retreated, leaving the unpleasant task of speaking freely with the queen to Edward Hyde. Poor, faithful, pompous, conscientious Ned Hyde did his best, 'as well as I could have done had it been to save my life', he wrote plaintively to Edward Nicholas. 'I told her the evil it might do the king by making his own religion suspected, the damage and prejudice it would bring her in the affections of England, and the irrecoverable ruin it would be to the princess.'

But Henrietta, who detested Hyde anyway, proved unpersuadable. The late king of sacred memory had himself given her permission to raise her last child in her own faith, she declared. 'In a word, she was resolved, and it should not be in any body's power to hinder her.' Faced with so much 'passion and resolution', Hyde, too, retreated, only extracting a promise that the queen would not seek to put her daughter in a nunnery. That was easily given – Henrietta had more ambitious plans for the little Henriette, now known as Henriette Anne as a compliment to the queen regent.[44]

It was obvious that nothing could be done, for the present at least. Charles was in no position to provide a home for his sister, even if it had been possible to take her away from her mother and Hyde could only counsel patience, pointing out that it would be several years before the child was capable of understanding much about religion. Here, though, he underestimated the efforts of Father Cyprien, to whom the princess's religious instruction was entrusted, and who found her an exceptionally apt and eager pupil.

Ironically, Henrietta now found herself being accused of protecting heretics and showing 'want of zeal in her religion'. The Protestant members of her household had been accustomed to attend daily prayers in a basement room at the Louvre, but in 1650 orders had arrived from the regent forbidding the practice of any religion other than Roman Catholicism in any of the royal palaces. Handling the situation with unusual tact, Henrietta told Hyde that she was surprised and troubled by this decree, which she blamed on the influence of Walter Montagu, who had recently entered the priesthood, and added that she greatly regretted the loss of her old confessor, Father Philip, who had always urged her to live amicably with those Protestants 'who deserved well from her and to whom she was beholden'. Nevertheless, she had no choice but to obey the regent and in future Dr Cosin, the Anglican chaplain, would have to hold his services in the house of Sir Richard Browne, the resident ambassador.[45]

Henrietta had a particular reason for wanting to keep on good terms with her sister-in-law just then, for she needed her help over a project very close to her heart. She had long wanted to found her own religious house and had managed to acquire a small, rather run-down property at Chaillot, then on the northern outskirts of Paris, which had once belonged to her old friend the Maréchal de Bassompierre and which since his death had become a rather shady place of entertainment. An anonymous donor had guaranteed the purchase price, but there had been a lot of tedious legal problems with the Maréchal's creditors and heirs (one of whom was another old friend, the Comte de Tillières), objections from the local magistrates and opposition from the Archbishop of Paris. In the end, though, the regent had a word with the archbishop and in June 1651 Henrietta had been able to install a dozen nuns of the Order of the Visitation, founded by St Francis de Sales especially to meet the needs of ladies of gentle birth. The queen had her

223

own suite of rooms looking out over the Seine towards Paris, but the sisters declared their quarters to be far too luxurious and insisted on sleeping in the attics until the more ornate furnishings which Henrietta had had brought down from the Louvre were taken away. But at last everyone was happy; Queen Anne came to attend the inaugural mass in the convent chapel and Chaillot became the widowed Queen of England's 'beloved and most delicious retiring place', where she would often stay for several weeks at a time.

Throughout this period she continued to watch anxiously for news from Scotland. The previous summer Cromwell, fresh from his triumphant campaign in Ireland, had taken the army north in a pre-emptive strike and comprehensively defeated the Scots at Dunbar on 3 September. Then, at the beginning of 1651, Charles had finally been crowned King of Scotland with Bruce's golden circlet in a ceremony at Scone Abbey. Helped by the prestige this conferred and his own personal popularity – his mother heard that all the Scots were united for him – he had managed to recruit an army roughly 20,000 strong for an invasion of England but no one was very enthusiastic about the idea and it was early August before they crossed the border at Carlisle.

The king's plan had been to cut Cromwell's lines of communication (he and the army were still in Scotland, occupying Edinburgh and most of the south-east), and then make for London in a desperate bid to regain the throne. It was a plan which relied heavily on the assumption that the English royalists would rise in sufficient numbers to overwhelm the enemy, but in 1651 the English royalists were a spent force and in no mood to rise – especially not for a king leading an army of Scots. Failure to attract any meaningful support, plus the fact that Cromwell was now storming down from the north, put an end to any hope of reaching London and Charles had no alternative but to continue his march on through the West Midlands. His army, by this time much reduced by sickness and desertion, arrived at the loyal city of Worcester on 22 August and there, some ten days later, it was destroyed. The battle of Worcester marked the end of the Great Civil War, which had lasted for nine years and cost an estimated 190,000 English lives. For Oliver Cromwell it was the crowning mercy; for King Charles, now a fugitive with a price on his head, it looked like the end of the line.

Conflicting rumours of events in England were crossing to France and the Low Countries. Elizabeth of Bohemia heard that the king's advance towards London continued apace, and Henrietta believed that it was Cromwell who had been defeated. But then news of Worcester began to filter through, prompting an agitated note from the queen to the Reverend Mother Prioress at Chaillot. 'Mother, I cannot go today to Chaillot as I intended . . . on account of the bad news from England, which nevertheless I hope is not quite so unfortunate as it is represented. My uneasiness renders me unfit for anything, until I receive the news which will arrive tonight. Pray to God for the king, my son.'[46]

For six weeks there was silence. 'All the world went to console the Queen of England', remarked La Grande Mademoiselle, 'but this only increased her distress, for she knew not whether her son was a prisoner or dead.'[47] Then, in the third week of October, a tired, desperately shabby young man, with close-cropped hair and deeply tanned complexion, turned up in Rouen, begging for money and some clothes from a couple of English merchants in the town.

The king's seemingly miraculous preservation naturally led to an outburst of rejoicing among the exiles and the queen was said to be 'constantly wonderful merry', but although his escape had given everyone 'a new seed of hope for future blessings', there could be no denying the fact that his cause appeared all but lost. England was now officially a commonwealth; Ireland and Scotland were both subdued; 'the royal and loyal party lay grovelling and prostrate'; even Jersey had surrendered by the end of the year.

Meanwhile, Henrietta, never one to take no for an answer, had resumed her dogged pursuit of Mademoiselle. 'My son is incorrigible, he loves you more than ever,' she told her niece, and Mademoiselle certainly found him much improved, in spite of his bizarre new hairstyle and growth of beard. For one thing he had become quite chatty, regaling her with stories about the horrors of life in Scotland, where people thought it sinful to play a musical instrument, and with a carefully fictionalised account of his amazing adventures after Worcester.[48]

But while he was now behaving in a more satisfactorily lover-like fashion, even making some pretty speeches in perfectly adequate French, Mademoiselle remained unconvinced. When Henrietta began to press her for a decision, painting a rosy, and quite untruthful picture of his prospects of regaining his throne, she replied evasively. She was so content with her present situation that she had never thought of marriage, and although treating this proposal with all proper respect she really needed more time to think about it. In fact, she was beginning to feel trapped and when she heard that Lord Jermyn was going round openly saying that as soon as the marriage contract was signed they would cut down her establishment and start selling off her estates, she hesitated no longer in putting an end to the affair. 'It was a little brusque I admit,' she wrote, 'but such is my humour.'[49]

As it turned out, Mademoiselle soon had other things to think about, for the Wars of the Fronde, which had been rumbling on intermittently for most of the past four years, now flared up again into the so-called

[margin note: daughter of Gaston]

christine = sister of Henrietta (daughter of Henry IV)
now Princess of Piedmont - duchess of Savoy

Princely Fronde – a resumption of the old conflict between the court and the princes of the blood, Gaston d'Orléans, Condé and the Duke of Lorraine against Mazarin, the queen regent and the thirteen-year-old king. By the spring of 1652 sporadic fighting between the rival factions was going on all over northern France and life in Paris had become both difficult and dangerous. Early in May Henrietta told Christine that one hardly dared venture outside the gates of the city for fear of the soldiers, thieves and ruined peasants who preyed on passers-by. It was true, she wrote, that after all she had been through, she ought not to be afraid of anything and certainly she did not fear death, only the manner of it and its coming unexpectedly.[50] A month later she wrote again from Chaillot. 'I think that God wishes to afflict our family, for if the war continues this poor country will be ruined. . . . You would imagine,' she went on, 'that God means to humiliate all kings and princes. He began with us in England; I pray that France will not follow the same path.'[51]

That summer Condé's army entered Paris and there was fierce fighting in the streets between the Frondeurs and the monarchists. The Hotel de Ville was burned down and the mob threatened to attack the Louvre, so that Charles was obliged to escort his mother and little sister under cover of a wet August night out of the city to St Germain, where the French royal family had already taken refuge. There Henrietta attempted to offer advice, based on her own experience of civil unrest, only to be severely snubbed by the harassed regent, who asked if she wanted to be Queen of France as well as England. No, retorted Henrietta, but since she was now nothing, she thought she should at least try to help her sister-in-law remain something. Given the present crisis, it was inevitable that tempers and nerves should have become frayed, but in general relations between the two queens were amicable enough, considering the humiliating dependence of the one on the other. Happily for the Stuarts and the Bourbons, the king's army, commanded by Marshal Turenne, won the day and on 21 October young Louis and his mother were able to return to the capital to cries of *Vive le roi*, but La Grande Mademoiselle, who had sided enthusiastically with Condé, was in deep disgrace and found it prudent to retire into the country. *her father*

Since the Louvre was now needed for Louis, who had recently attained his official majority, Henrietta, with Charles and eight-year-old Henriette Anne, had to move into the Palais Royal, once the residence of Cardinal Richelieu. The restless James had finally found a satisfactory outlet for his energies in the French army, serving as a colonel on Turenne's staff, but no such career option was open to Charles, who was forced to go on living under his mother's roof, unemployed, disregarded and financially dependent. It was a wretched situation and not surprisingly he was

226

sometimes said to be 'very sad and sombre'. More and more, though, as time went by he learnt to conceal his inner despair behind a façade of apparently carefree indifference, to sing for his supper and take his pleasures where he could find them.

Money, or the lack of it, remained a constant nagging preoccupation for all the exiles. Henrietta's own pension had been paid irregularly or not at all during the Fronde years and when Charles was at last granted a separate allowance from the French government, he found that he owed most of it to his mother for his board. The queen's temper had not been improved by adversity and penury, nor was the atmosphere in the household improved by her freely expressed dislike of Hyde and Edward Nicholas, her son's principal councillors, while their distrust of Jermyn continued to be an open secret. No wonder, therefore, that relations were frequently strained to breaking point.

1653

At the beginning of 1653 the authorities in London decided that 'Henry Stuart, the son of the late King, should be sent out of the realm, for lessening the charges for his keeping by the Commonwealth'. A more compelling reason may have been recent indications of an upsurge of royalist interest in the Duke of Gloucester, who was said to be showing signs of exceptional promise. Accordingly, in March, 'little Mr. Harry' arrived in Holland, accompanied by his tutor Richard Lovell. The widowed Princess of Orange was delighted to see him and wanted to keep him with her, offering to provide for him and give him a good education. But from Paris came pathetic pleas from the queen for a reunion with the son she had not seen since he was a baby. It was difficult to refuse and Charles rather reluctantly agreed that his brother might come for a visit. Now rising thirteen, Gloucester proved to be a good-looking boy with plenty of Stuart charm. He was an immediate success with the French and Henrietta wrote to Christine on 12 June that she had received so many visits from people who wanted to see '*ce petit cavalier*' that she had had no time for anything else.[52]

James

There was quite a family gathering in Paris that summer, for the Duke of York was home on leave from the army, but to the queen's acute distress France had now recognised the republican regime in England and was beginning to move towards a closer understanding with it. Consequently, by the following spring, Cardinal Mazarin let it be known that he felt it was time for Charles to find another refuge and Henrietta told Christine that if an ambassador were to come to Paris from that scoundrel [Cromwell], it would be the culmination of all her misfortunes. But, 'affairs everywhere and particularly in France are so changeable that one has to be prepared for almost anything,' she went on. It had been explained to her that Cromwell, now dignified by the title of Lord Protector, had already concluded an advantageous treaty with Holland; other European powers were likely to follow and France could not afford to let Spain get in ahead of her. 'These reasons of state are terrible,' lamented Henrietta, 'and I swear that I do not understand them, perhaps because they are always against me.' It was a comfort, though, to be able to pour out her troubles to a sympathetic sister, who sent her elegant little gifts of perfume and a beautiful pair of gloves which arrived just in time for her to wear at King Louis's coronation.[53]

Charles, meanwhile, was making preparations for departure, not at all sorry to be leaving the increasingly poisonous atmosphere of the Palais Royal – his mother had been getting more and more impossible just lately. He really could not accuse himself of having used her so ill as she says he has, he told Jermyn. And anyway, who were those enemies of hers 'that he makes so much of and trusts so absolutely?'[54] He was not happy about having to leave young Harry in her care and had asked her with unusual earnestness to promise not to try to convert him. 'It is not in my thought that any such attempt should be made,' she replied.[55]

Charles also asked his mother to make her peace with Edward Hyde before they left. Henrietta agreed, but with a very bad grace, telling the Chancellor, in a loud angry voice, that 'she had been contented to see him, and to give him leave to kiss her hand, to comply with the King's desires, who had importuned her to it', but he had no reason to expect to be welcome to her. His disrespect towards her was obvious to everyone and everyone knew that he never came near her, although they were living under the same roof. When she paused for breath Hyde pointed out that whatever his faults he had never been in Bedlam and was not such a fool as deliberately to provoke the late king's wife, and all this in France 'where he was a banished person and she at home'. He begged the queen to tell him what he had done to earn so much displeasure, but Henrietta, 'with her former passion', merely repeated her objections to Hyde's credit with the king and his endeavours to lessen that credit which she herself ought to have with him, concluding 'that she should be glad to see reason to change her opinion'. Whereupon, carelessly extending a hand to be kissed, her majesty swept out of the room.[56]

Charles finally departed on 18 July, making for Spa where he was to meet the Princess of Orange. Brother and sister then went off on holiday together, visiting Aix-la-Chapelle, Cologne and Dusseldorf, until the beginning of October, when Mary had to leave for home. Charles returned to Cologne to spend the winter, only to be greeted by letters informing him that the Duke of Gloucester was about to be received into the Catholic church.

This news sent alarm bells ringing all round the exiled royalist community and Charles, roused for once to real anger – 'so full of passion that he cannot express himself' – wrote to his mother that he could only suppose she neither believed in nor wished for his restoration; to his brother that he need never think to see England or him again if he changed his religion and to Jermyn that if the queen's attempt to seduce Gloucester was not stopped immediately the breach between them could never be made up. He also dispatched the Marquis of Ormonde to assess the situation on the spot and bring Gloucester away. Ned Hyde had never seen his master 'in so great trouble and perplexity . . . nor show such quickness and sharpness in providing against the mischief'.[57]

Ormonde reached Paris on 20 November to find that Gloucester had been separated from his tutor, a mild-mannered individual easily intimidated, and sent to Pontoise, an abbey just outside the city, where that bird of ill-omen Walter Montagu was in charge, and that plans were already well advanced to have him transferred to the Jesuit college at Clermont. Ormonde saw the queen on the day after his arrival but could make no impression on her. She listened to what he had to say but replied only that her conscience obliged her to have her son reformed of his errors. She did not believe any harm would come to the king as a result – these ideas had been put into his head by other people. Reminded of her promise not to try to convert Gloucester, she said that this extended only to not using violence. Ormonde then remarked that dismissing his tutor, sending him into the country where no one could have free conference with him and 'the purpose of sending him to the Jesuits' could not be regarded as anything but very strong compulsion. Henrietta became evasive. She did not consider the dismissal of Mr Lovell as being of any great importance, and in any case he had wanted to go. On the contrary, retorted the marquis, Lovell absolutely denied that he had asked to leave. Cornered, the queen 'retracted that part of her answer, and cut off the discourse by promising to think of what had been said'. She added that Ormonde need not trouble to go to Pontoise, as the duke would be returning to Paris in a day or two.[58]

But James Butler, soldier, aristocrat and great man, was not so easily put off. Next day he went down to Pontoise unannounced and was able to see Gloucester in private, finding the boy distressed but resolute. Theological argument was beyond him, but the memory of that dreadful January day at St James's five years ago, when he had leant against his father's knee and heard him speak of maintaining the true Protestant religion, had armoured him against any emotional or moral blackmail which could be exerted by his mother or his mother's priests.

Ormonde now took him back to Paris and the Palais Royal and nearly a week passed, during which the marquis became aware of how deeply the French royal family were involved in the campaign to persuade the duke

1654

to 'turn'. Then, on Saturday 28 November, Henrietta called her son to her and 'pressed him, as she said for the last time, to go to the Jesuits and conform to her pleasure', giving him the rest of the day to think it over. But when Gloucester saw his mother again that evening, he told her that although deeply afflicted to find the king's and her commands so opposed that he could not obey both, 'the former were more suitable to his inclinations and his duty'. Realising that she had lost the battle, Henrietta proceeded to lose her temper and her self-control. 'I will no longer own you as a son,' she screamed and ordered him to get out of her sight. Ormonde could provide for him in future, she said, and when he knelt to ask for her parting blessing, she refused to give it. Next day Ormonde removed him to the house of a sympathetic royalist in the town and set about the depressing business of raising money for their journey back to Cologne.[59]

This sorry episode has always been cited as damning evidence of Henrietta's religious bigotry, and certainly her treatment of her youngest son was both foolish and unkind. But it should perhaps be remembered in her defence that she was herself under a good deal of pressure from the queen regent and Walter Montagu, now her almoner, both of them powerful influences; and, apart from her concern for his spiritual welfare, she may well have been genuinely convinced that Gloucester's best, perhaps his only, chance of an honourable career lay with the Catholic church.

1654

Now, in the winter of 1654, she was not only estranged from two of her sons but was having to come to terms with the fact that France was negotiating a commercial treaty with the arch-enemy, the abominable traitor Cromwell. Nothing since the death of her lord the king had touched her so nearly as this, she told Christine. It seemed like killing his memory.[60] Further humiliation was to come, for when Cardinal Mazarin approached his new friend in an optimistic attempt to extract payment of the widowed Queen of England's dower income, the response was an unambiguous negative. Since Henrietta had refused to be crowned she had no legal status as queen consort and consequently no right to receive anything from the state. The outraged widow's reaction was to enquire that if she was not recognised as the wife and consort of the late king, what had she been? But if the king her nephew was content to allow a daughter of France to be thus insulted and treated *en concubine*, then she must submit, being perfectly satisfied herself with the respect which had always been paid to her as queen by her husband and his loyal subjects.[61]

Apart from her religion, Henrietta's only real solace during this period, perhaps the bleakest of all her exile, was in seeing her youngest daughter grow up. Henriette Anne, devout, obedient, affectionate and, in spite of her smallness and air of fragility, showing promise of developing into a beauty, was everything a mother's heart could desire, and Henrietta was beginning to dream of a glorious future for her *enfant de bénédiction*. The little princess had already begun to make occasional appearances at court, and at the age of nine had been honoured with a part in a ballet given at a grand fête celebrating the marriage of one of Mazarin's nieces. This remarkable production, which featured King Louis in what was to become his favourite role of Apollo, had been a great critical success, with the Princess of England's performance as Erato, muse of love and poetry, being singled out for special notice. Less successful was a private party given by the queen regent when the teenage Louis caused much embarrassment by refusing to dance with his cousin, saying sulkily that he did not like little girls.[62]

1655

In November 1655 the Princess of Orange announced that she was planning a trip to Paris to visit her mother, a prospect greeted with dismay by her brother's advisers, who pointed out that in view of the new Anglo-French entente and the fact that the king was currently negotiating an alliance with France's enemy Spain, this was hardly a suitable moment for his sister to appear at the French court. Charles himself tried to persuade her at least to postpone her journey, but since he had been obliged to borrow the money from her to finance his embassy to Spain, he was hardly in a position to dictate her actions and in any case Mary was not to be deflected. This would be a purely private family affair. She had not seen her mother since she was a child and Henrietta had written so kindly pressing her to come 'that truly if I should deny her majesty it were very barbarous in me'. It seems rather more likely that the princess, who had not been well, was yearning for a taste of the sophisticated delights of Paris and a brief escape from her humdrum home life. She had always disliked Holland and the Dutch, more especially since the Estates had forbidden her to receive her brothers on Dutch soil, and she was also now involved in a long-running acrimonious dispute with her in-laws over the guardianship of her small son, another William, born in the week following his father's death.

Socially the visit was an undoubted success. She arrived at the beginning of February 1656, in time for the carnival season, and Lord Jermyn told Charles that 'the great balls and the masque were reserved for her, and much of the good company of the place resolved to pay her all sorts of respects and civilities'.[63] Mary was, after all, a grand-daughter of France and first cousin to Louis XIV, and she certainly had nothing to complain of in the warmth of her reception. 'She pleases all here, from the greatest to the least,' wrote her mother on 4 February. 'She has been today so overwhelmed with visitors that I am half-dead with fatigue.'[64]

1656

A dazzling succession of balls and ballets, masques and banquets filled the next few weeks and although, according to the rules of etiquette for widows observed by the queen regent, Mary was not able to take part in the dancing, it was noticed that Anne of Austria showed the Princess of Orange every courtesy, even to the extent of inviting her to sit on a chair with arms, a privilege usually reserved for crowned heads.

Mary was still only twenty-four, an attractive and very eligible widow, so there was naturally a good deal of speculation about her possible remarriage. Back in 1652 there had been a minor scandal in the family when the irresponsible young Duke of Buckingham, son of the murdered Steenie, had pursued her with a 'wild pretence' of marriage and Henrietta, horrified, had exclaimed that if she thought for a moment that her daughter was contemplating the idea of so base a *mésalliance* 'she would tear her in pieces with her own hands'.[65] Now it was being rumoured that the princess's real purpose in coming to Paris had been to set her cap at King Louis, but Mary was not thinking of marriage, saying that as soon as her brother Charles was settled in one place, she meant to go and make her home with him. But while the Princess of Orange may not have been thinking of a new husband, romance was nevertheless in the air, for it was at this time that the Duke of York and Ned Hyde's daughter Anne, who had come to France in Mary's train, first became lovers – a fact they were both very careful to conceal from their relatives.

Mary's stay in Paris prolonged itself into the summer and in July she and Henrietta and a large company of ladies and gentlemen drove out to visit La Grande Mademoiselle at her chateau at Chilly. Mademoiselle, accustomed as she was to look down on the dispossessed Stuarts, was quite impressed by the Princess of Orange who, she remembered, 'wore the most beautiful diamond earrings I ever beheld, very fine pearls, clasps, and large diamond bracelets, with splendid rings of the same'. The princess's mother evidently considered this display rather vulgar. 'My daughter of Orange', she told Mademoiselle, 'is not like me; she is very lofty in her ideas, with her jewels and her money. I tell her she ought to save. Once I was as she is – even more so. But look at me now!' Henrietta could not resist mentioning Charles. 'And the poor King of England! You are so unfeeling as not to enquire for him? Alas, he is so foolish as to love you still.'[66]

It was autumn before Mary finally tore herself away, going home by way of Bruges in the Spanish Netherlands where Charles was now established, having signed a treaty with Spain, whereby Philip IV agreed to work for his restoration in return for a promise of future help against France. Young Gloucester was with him and he had summoned James to join them, since it was no longer possible for him to continue to serve in the

French army. Henrietta, left alone with little Henriette, was house-hunting again. She had begun to feel the need of a modest home of her own in the country, but not too far from Paris, of course, and after some looking round the outlying villages, found what she wanted at Colombes, some half a dozen miles to the north-west of the city, which she was able to buy with the help of the queen regent. But she still spent most of her time at the Palais Royal. Henriette Anne was growing up. She was thirteen in the summer of 1657 and must be launched into society in a proper manner if she was to make a suitably grand marriage. *1657*

Meanwhile, the queen continued to worry about the international situation. England and Spain were now at war and in the previous March France and the Protectorate had signed a defensive alliance, with England undertaking to provide 6,000 men and a fleet to join with the French in a campaign in Flanders. All three Stuart brothers were engaged on the Spanish side and in September Charles was rumoured to have been wounded at the defence of Mardyke, prompting a letter from his mother dated in December 1657. 'I am very glad that the report which has been carried is not true,' she wrote. 'It is not, however, altogether unreasonable that I should beg of you to be more careful of yourself than you are. Although I do not doubt that God is reserving you for better times, yet you also should not tempt him, and should take care of yourself; my prayers too will not be wanting, if they are worth anything.'[67]

A surprise visitor had turned up literally on Henrietta's doorstep that winter, when the Palatine Princess Louise, one of the Queen of Bohemia's numerous offspring, left the Hague without warning to enter the Catholic church. She had gone first to the English Carmelites at Antwerp and from there to the queen *Henrietta* at Chaillot – hardly a tactful choice in the circumstances. Henrietta wrote promising to care for the defector as if she were her own child and begging her afflicted sister-in-law's forgiveness and understanding. But Elizabeth was furious. After all, how would Henrietta have felt 'if she had had the same misfortune' and her daughter had run away from home to become a Protestant?[68] The Winter Queen, as she was sometimes known, had suffered all too many misfortunes over the years *Charles I* and was living now in dire poverty – her violent reaction to her brother's murder having led to the withdrawal of her English pension. Her family was widely scattered. The princes Rupert and Maurice, driven out of England after the fall of Oxford, had taken to a life of adventure and freelance privateering on the high seas. The Prince Palatine, on the other hand, had spent several years living in London as the guest of the parliament, apparently hoping that they might decide to offer him his uncle's throne, and only returning to Holland, and an uncomfortable interview with his mother, after the king's execution. Now, with the Thirty

Years War over at last, he had been able to go back to Heidelberg and a greatly reduced portion of his ancestral Rhineland territory.

Charles Louis might have been able to go home but, as another year ended, any prospect of his cousins enjoying similar good fortune seemed as far away as ever. In the spring of 1658 Henrietta paid her usual visit to Bourbon, where she was joined by Gaston and his family. She was back in Paris in June to hear news of the Battle of the Dunes and the fall of Dunkirk to the combined Anglo-French forces. The Dukes of York and Gloucester had fought bravely on the losing side and were said to have only narrowly escaped being taken prisoner. 'I have been in the greatest possible apprehensions for your brothers,' Henrietta wrote to Charles on 21 June, 'and I spend my time ill enough here, seeing all that passes. . . . I hope that the good God will at length put an end to our misfortunes, and will re-establish us in spite of all the world, and will yet grant me time enough to see for myself that happy day.'[69]

Then, in September, came the news that Oliver Cromwell, that great beast and murderer, had died – seven years to the day since his victory at Worcester. In a very secret meeting at the Hague, George Downing, the Protectorate's ambassador to the States General, knelt before King Charles to ask pardon for past offences and the Queen of Bohemia told Charles Louis that 'all the French court went to congratulate this monster's death with the queen my sister' – even Cardinal Mazarin himself had been heard to refer to his late ally as 'this viper'.[70]

But although in some places there was dancing in the streets at noon-day, where 'the Devil is dead' was the language at every turn and 'the entertainment of the graver sort is only to contemplate the happy days approaching', Henrietta's reaction seemed oddly muted. Replying to a letter of congratulation from Madame de Motteville, she wrote: 'In truth I thought you would hear with joy of the death of that wretch; yet, whether it be because my heart is so wrapped up in melancholy as to be incapable of receiving any, or that I do not as yet perceive any good advantages likely to accrue to us from it, I will confess to you, that I have not felt myself any very great rejoicing, my greatest being to witness that of my friends.'[71]

There had been so much sorrow, so many disappointments, that perhaps it was natural that she could not, indeed dared not, let herself believe that happy days might now at last be approaching.

CHAPTER TEN

Maddam La Mère

> Her Majesty had a great affection for England, notwithstanding the
> severe usage that she and hers had received from it. Her discourse . . .
> was much in praise of the people and of the country.
>
> *Memoirs of Sir John Reresby*

The burst of elation with which the exiled community had greeted the
news of Cromwell's death quickly subsided, for it seemed that after all
nothing had changed. Oliver's son Richard was proclaimed as his lawful
successor. The city and the armed services accepted him without a
murmur. 'Foreign princes addressed their condolences to him, and
desired to renew their alliances; and nothing was heard in England but
the voice of joy, and large encomiums of their new Protector.' Charles,
alone and virtually penniless in Brussels, remained a shadow king and
Edward Hyde thought his condition had never appeared so hopeless, so
desolate.[1] His mother was told that he had nothing to propose for the
moment, but 'when you command me in anything for your service,' she
wrote from Paris on 4 October, 'you shall find me as ready as I have ever
been. . . . We must wait opportunities to avail ourselves of them. I assure
you I will let none slip.' Jermyn, who had gone north to confer with the
king, evidently returned with a tactful warning not to do anything hasty,
for Henrietta wrote again, promising to be careful and to do nothing
'which could in any possible manner be prejudicial to you. Believe this,
I beg you.'[2] The previous summer she had written to Charles, 'I only wish
we were in a condition to be able to meet all together', but that happy day
looked as far away as ever, and meanwhile she could only wait and pray.

The new year brought a prospect of peace between France and Spain,
the recent French success in Flanders having marked a lull in the
seemingly unending Franco-Spanish struggle for European supremacy.
It would also lead to a realisation of Anne of Austria's long-cherished
ambition of seeing her son married to her niece, the Spanish Hapsburg
Infanta Maria Theresa. Negotiations continued throughout the summer
and the Treaty of the Pyrenees was finally signed in November 1659.

The French court had gone south with the intention of returning with
the peace and the Infanta, and the exiled King of England was also paying a
private visit to Spain, or at least to the frontier town of Fuenterabbia where

the peace talks were being held, in the faint hope of picking up support from one side or the other. But Mazarin refused even to see him and the Spaniards, although polite, offered nothing but fair words. Henrietta too, scenting a possible opportunity, had sent Henry Jermyn and Walter Montagu down to Toulouse to try their luck with Mazarin, but according to the Venetian ambassador, the cardinal told them openly that 'in the present state of affairs he could do nothing for the advantage of King Charles'.[3]

On his way back to Brussels in December, King Charles stopped off to visit his mother at Colombes. Mother and son had not met for five years – not since her unfortunate conversion attempt on the Duke of Gloucester – but now they embraced affectionately, past differences apparently forgotten. Charles was also able to renew his acquaintance with his little sister. At fifteen Henriette Anne was apparently fulfilling all her early promise of beauty and virtue. Her hair was 'of a bright chestnut hue', wrote an enthusiastic Frenchwoman, 'and her complexion rivals that of the gayest flowers. . . . Her eyes are blue and brilliant, her lips ruddy, her throat beautiful, her arms and hands well made.' She was gentle, obliging and kind-hearted, danced with incomparable grace, sang like an angel, 'and the spinet is never so well played as by her fair hands'. Although not reckoning her beauty of the most perfect order, Madame de Motteville also admired the princess's sparkling eyes, delicate 'roses and jasmine' complexion and her excellent teeth; while old Father Cyprien joined in the chorus, praising his former pupil's rare beauty, sweet temper, noble spirit and religious devotion.[4]

Allowing for an expectable measure of flattery – there had at one time been a rumour that 'the amiable and accomplished Princess of England' was being considered as a possible bride for the King of France – Henriette Anne was undoubtedly an attractive and talented young woman. She was not, in fact, strictly beautiful. One shoulder was slightly higher than the other, although this defect was so cleverly camouflaged that few people were aware of it, and she remained painfully thin – 'the bones of the Holy Innocents' as Louis once described her. But she possessed an irresistibly appealing ethereal quality and Charles, that well-known connoisseur of female charms, was immediately captivated, giving her the private pet-name of Minette, or 'little puss', and during the ten days or so that he stayed at Colombes the foundations of an enduringly loving relationship were laid between brother and sister.

Charles had been warned to move on by a message from Mazarin, but with the removal of Cromwell's iron hand some English travellers were now venturing to visit Henrietta's little court at the Palais Royal, where they were given a warm welcome. 'The Queen commanded me to be there as often as I conveniently could,' remembered the Yorkshire baronet John Reresby. Her majesty, he went on, 'had a great affection for England, notwithstanding the severe usage that she and hers had received from it. Her discourse . . . was much in praise of the people and the country . . . and would excuse all their miscarriages in relation to unfortunate effects of the late war as if it were a convulsion of some desparate and infatuated persons, rather than from the genius or temper of the kingdom.' Although the French court was very splendid, Reresby believed that there was greater resort to the Palais Royal, 'the good humour and wit of the Queen Mother of England and the beauty of the Princess her daughter' offering better entertainment than the stiff Spanish formality of Queen Anne.[5]

Another winter had closed in and Charles, back in Brussels for Christmas, was reduced to eating his one meal a day off a pewter dish, having been forced to part with the last of his plate. But he was no longer without hope, for across the Channel the miracle was beginning to happen. The Protectorate had come to an end in April 1659 when Richard Cromwell was removed from office and had retired thankfully back into private life. There had followed nine months of mounting disarray among the various contending interest groups and when, in February 1660, General George Monck, commander of the army of occupation in Scotland, entered the capital with two regiments of horse and three of foot, no one knew for certain what he meant to do. The so-called Rump, the forty-odd survivors of the 1648 purge of the original Long Parliament, was sitting again at Westminster and fighting a determined rearguard action, but after the shambles of the past year the tide of public opinion was running high and strong for a free parliament. Before the end of the month Monck had begun to show his hand, demanding the reinstatement of the 'secluded' members – that is, all those expelled in Pride's Purge – and on the 21st young Samuel Pepys watched as the first batch of about twenty was admitted to Westminster Hall. That night he wrote 'it was a most pleasant sight to see the City from one end to the other with a glory about it, so high was the light of the bonfires'.[6] Church bells rang out from every steeple and for the first time men could be seen drinking the king's health in public 'without any fear'.

Events now began to take on a momentum of their own – Pepys could hardly believe the greatness and suddenness of it all. On 16 March the Long Parliament finally agreed to dissolve itself, after a record nineteen years, and writs were issued for an election. The new free or Convention Parliament which met in April proceeded to declare that, after all, the government of England properly consisted of King, Lords and Commons and, having received a conciliatory message from Charles, begged him to come home. He and his brothers sailed from the Dutch port of Scheveningen, landing at Dover on 25 May (O.S.), where they were greeted 'with all imaginable love and respect. . . . Infinite the crowd of people and the gallantry of the horsemen, citizens and noblemen of all sorts.' And it was the same as the royal party travelled in a stately coach on the road to Canterbury. 'The shouting and joy expressed by all' was past imagination.[7] It seemed like the very best kind of fairy-tale happy ending.

News of the king's safe arrival reached his mother at Colombes, and she wrote from there at five o'clock in the morning of 9 June: 'You may judge of my joy and if you are torn to pieces in England with kindness, I have my share of it also in France. I am going this instant to Chaillot to hear the Te Deum sung, and from thence to Paris to have bonfires lighted.'[8] The joy seemed universal and Henrietta was kept busy from morning till night receiving visits of congratulation, as well as petitions from exiles who were now beginning to emerge from corners all over western Europe. All were sad and deserving cases which obliged her to trouble the king with letters more often than she would have liked, but 'so many people come to beg me to recommend them to you whom I cannot refuse, being old servants'.[9]

To Christine, to whom she had so often in the past poured out her troubles, she could now write that at last '*le bon Dieu* has looked on us in his mercy, and has wrought, as one must say, a miracle in this restoration, having changed the hearts of a people in an instant from the greatest hatred to the greatest possible love and submission marked with demonstrations of unparalleled joy'. She was not yet certain of her own plans, although her son was pressing her to return to England and she naturally hoped once more before she died to see all her family reunited 'and no longer vagabonds'.[10]

The queen had a particular reason for putting off a decision about her return to England. The French court was now on its way back to Paris after nearly a year's absence. The coming season promised to be especially brilliant, and with her daughter to be creditably established this was no time to be going off to London. Young Henriette's prospects had of course been transformed by the Restoration and, although Louis himself might now be married, a strong rumour was current that his younger brother Philippe intended to make an offer for the English princess. Sure enough, on 24 August, Henrietta received a *visite en cérémonie* from Queen Anne bringing a proposal of marriage on behalf of her son, and she immediately wrote off to Charles with the great news. An ambassador would shortly be sent over to London to arrange the details, but in the meantime Henrietta saw no reason why the king should not give her permission to say that he approved. 'I assure you,' she went on, 'that your sister is not at all displeased about it; and as to Monsieur, he is violently in love and quite impatient for your reply.'[11]

On the following day the queen-mother of England and her daughter stood with the queen-mother of France at the windows of the Hotel

Beauvais in the rue St Antoine to see Louis XIV and his Spanish bride make their state entrance into the capital, with nineteen-year-old Philippe riding a white charger close behind the queen's carriage and looking extremely handsome. Two days later he came with the king and queen to call on Henrietta and her daughter and when, early in September, Cardinal Mazarin gave one of his splendid parties, Philippe arrived not with the French royalties but escorting the English queen and princess. For the second time that year congratulations flowed into the Palais Royal and, as she looked into the future of her precious *enfant de bénédiction*, Henrietta was probably happier than at any time since her troubles had begun nearly twenty years before.

It certainly seemed to be another fairy-tale happy ending for the dispossessed Stuarts, especially for the Cinderella princess who, until very recently, had had so little value on the international marriage market that Louis had told his brother: 'You will marry the princess of England, for nobody else wants her.' As the king's brother, Philippe wore the courtesy title of Monsieur and would soon be created Duc d'Orléans – Henrietta's own brother Gaston having conveniently died that spring. Henriette Anne would therefore become not only the Duchesse d'Orléans but Madame de France, first lady in the land after the queen. Then, too, she would not, like her mother and sister, be banished to a foreign land to live among strangers. This fortunate bride would be able to stay at home in familiar surroundings, married to a cousin she had known from childhood. Nor would she ever have to contend with the religious differences which had caused her mother so much distress in the past. Henrietta could now congratulate herself on the determination and foresight which had ensured her daughter's upbringing as a good Catholic and, in case there should be any lingering doubts about this in anyone's mind, Father Cyprien was encouraged to publish his *Exercices d'une Ame Royale* which recorded the instruction he had given the little English princess.

On 9 September Henrietta was writing again to Christine and after recommending a wonderful new remedy for colds – 'it is tea, a certain leaf which comes from India' – went on to confirm the reports of the engagement, promising to keep her sister fully informed of developments. 'As for our affairs in England,' she ended triumphantly, 'these are going so well that there has never been a king more absolute than my son.'[12]

Sadly, though, it appeared that God did not intend her to be entirely content, for early in September the Venetian resident in London heard that the Duke of Gloucester was ill in bed and was not expected to recover soon, as smallpox had declared itself. However, 'it does not seem to be of the worst kind, and as all the signs are good, they hope that his Highness is in no danger'.[13] But Henry's condition suddenly worsened and on the 13th the handsome, high-spirited boy who had once so famously defeated his mother's priests was dead at the age of twenty-one. The news came as a dreadful shock to everyone. The king was said to be much distressed 'for he loved his brother tenderly', and the queen would now never have the opportunity of becoming reconciled with her youngest son, from whom she had parted in anger and bitterness six years before.

Family bereavement was swiftly followed by family scandal. By early October rumours that the child being all too visibly carried by Anne Hyde had been fathered by the Duke of York and – worse – that the couple were secretly married. Henrietta was outraged. 'To crown my afflictions,' she told Christine, 'the Duke of York has married without my knowledge or that of his brother the king to a young woman who was already with child. God grant that it is his; a girl who will give herself to a prince will easily abandon herself to another man.'[14] The queen had intended to postpone her return to England until the spring, but now she was preparing to set out immediately on a mission to 'unmarry' James and 'prevent with her authority so great a stain and dishonour to the crown'.[15]

She and her daughter, with an entourage that included Henry Jermyn, now Earl of St Albans, Walter Montagu, Father Cyprien and Prince Edward Palatine (another of the Queen of Bohemia's sons who had married a French aristocrat and converted to Catholicism), set sail from Calais on a sea so glassily calm that the crossing took two days. They were escorted by an impressive English fleet commanded by the Duke of York in his capacity as Lord High Admiral, and were met at Dover by the king, the Princess of Orange and Prince Rupert. Thus the family reunion which Henrietta had so long desired took place in the gloomy old castle where she had spent her first night in England all those years ago, and when the company sat down to supper that evening history began to repeat itself with uncanny exactitude. 'The king's chaplain blessed the viands after the Protestant fashion,' recorded Father Cyprien. 'Immediately afterwards I did the same, according to the Catholic . . . and, extending my arms, made the sign of a large cross over the dishes which had been set on the table. The Puritans, the Independents and Quakers, of whom the town of Dover is full, and who are sworn foes to the ceremonies of the Church and particularly to the sign of the cross, were highly astonished at the liberty which I took to make it thus publicly at the table of the Protestant king. They were much more astonished on the following day, when we said mass in a very large apartment, with all the doors open, in the presence of an innumerable concourse of people.'[16]

Henrietta arrived in London in the dusk of a November evening, 'coming very private, Lambeth-way'. Nevertheless the Thames was so

240

crowded with boats waiting to see her cross the river to Whitehall stairs that Samuel Pepys, who had paid a sculler sixpence to take him there, could not get close enough even to catch a glimpse of the royal party. According to the Venetian resident, the queen 'was acclaimed with the utmost joy and affection' and in the area round the palace complex church bells were rung and bonfires lit at every corner along the Strand as far as Ludgate, but Pepys says he observed no more than three illuminations in the city itself that night, which confirmed him in his opinion that the queen's coming 'do please but very few'.[17]

For the queen herself, the return to Whitehall was an intensely emotional experience and the sight of the royal apartments which held so many memories, together with the realisation that she was so close to the spot where her husband had met his death, caused her to break down in a flood of tears, calling herself '*la reine malheureuse*'. By the next day, however, she had recovered her composure and was ready to receive a congratulatory address from 'all the privy council in a body' headed by Edward Hyde, now Lord Chancellor and lately raised to the peerage as Baron Hyde of Hindon.

Her majesty greeted his new lordship, in public at least, with a cheerful countenance and 'many gracious expressions'. It is not likely that she had been impressed by accounts of his acute shame and distress over his daughter's deceitful behaviour, but she was somewhat mollified by James who, it seems, had been listening to the stories being spread by the Chancellor's enemies that Anne was a loose woman, notoriously free with her favours, and who was now apologising to his mother for having 'placed his affection so unequally'. He told her that he was not married and had now 'such evidence of her [Anne's] unworthiness that he should no more think of her'.[18]

This sounded satisfactory and Henrietta felt able to turn her attention to approving the financial and political arrangements currently being made for her daughter's marriage. These appeared to be proceeding smoothly, and indeed the special envoy charged with settling the formalities reported on 8 November that he regarded it rather as a family and domestic matter than an affair of state. 'The king talks about it so publicly every day, and sees so clearly all its advantages that there is scarcely any doubt to be entertained about it.'[19] Everyone was curious to get a look at the Princess Henriette and on 22 November Samuel Pepys and his wife were admitted to the Presence Chamber to see the royal family at dinner. The queen he dismissed as 'a very little plain [that is, plainly dressed] old woman', with nothing in her appearance to distinguish her from any ordinary woman. Pepys was disappointed, too, in the princess who, although very pretty, was much below his

1660

expectation, and he disapproved of the way her hair was frizzed up short over her ears.[20]

Henrietta had intended to leave for France again before the end of November, but as the king would be needed in London for the forthcoming dissolution of the Convention Parliament, it was agreed that her departure should be put off to the new year and plans were being made for a memorable Christmas, with a revival of all those good old customs suppressed under the Commonwealth. Meanwhile, the queen took her daughter away on a brief visit to Tunbridge Wells.

On their return, Henrietta discovered to her fury that the Duke of York had been going to see Anne Hyde and her baby, now a month old; worse, it appeared that they were indeed married, the ceremony having been performed by the duke's chaplain, very privately but quite legally in the presence of witnesses, and that all those tales about the new duchess had been nothing but wicked slanders. The king, who seems to have been the only person to have behaved throughout with generosity and common sense, took the attitude that since the business was done they must all make the best of it, but Henrietta remained implacably hostile, announcing 'that whenever that woman should be brought into Whitehall by one door, her majesty would go out of it by another door and never come into it again', and ostentatiously cutting James dead whenever he appeared. By this time people were becoming more than a little tired of the situation and were looking for ways of bringing it to an end. However, when it was suggested that perhaps the Lord Chancellor might make a conciliatory approach to the queen, that prudent individual, with his past experience of her majesty in a rage, 'absolutely refused to make the least advance towards it, or to contribute to her indignation by putting himself into her majesty's presence'.[21]

Matters were thus at a standstill when, in the week before Christmas, the Princess of Orange, who had been ailing ever since her arrival in England in the autumn, fell seriously ill. Smallpox was diagnosed and five days later she too was dead. In the twenty-nine years of her life the second Mary Stuart had known little personal happiness and made no lasting impression on the history of her times, but that Christmas of 1660 she left behind a shocked and darkened court and a sorrowing family. Over in Holland her ten-year-old son surprised everybody by the intensity of his grief and the Queen of Bohemia mourned the loss of her dearest niece. 'I shall never forget her memory,' she wrote. 'We lived almost twenty years together and always loved one another.'

Mary was buried in the family vault in Westminster Abbey on 29 December, by which time preparations were well advanced for the journey of the queen and Princess Henriette. The princess had been

242

hurriedly moved away to the healthier air of St James's as soon as her sister's rash appeared, but frantic appeals were now arriving from France from Monsieur who, fearing the loss or – worse – disfigurement of his fiancée, was imploring the queen to bring her out of the danger zone without further delay. Henrietta, who had also been excluded from the vicinity of the sickroom for fear that she might attempt a deathbed conversion, was equally anxious to be gone, 'declaring roundly that if she stays in England she will soon end her days'; according to the Venetians, 'neither the king nor anyone else tries to detain her'.[22]

It looked as if 'the duke's affair' was going to be left under 'the renunciation and interdiction of a mother' until almost the last moment, when her majesty's mood suddenly lightened, the sun came out and she began to treat James 'with her usual kindness', telling him that she realised his marriage which had so offended her had now gone too far to be remedied 'and therefore that she would trouble herself no further in it, but pray to God to bless him and that he might be happy'. She was even, apparently, speaking graciously about her old enemy Chancellor Hyde, and saying that she wanted to be good friends with him.[23]

An explanation of this surprising *volte-face* was presently provided by Walter Montagu, who came to tell Hyde that the queen had recently received a letter from Cardinal Mazarin 'in which he had plainly told her that she would not receive a good welcome in France if she left her sons in her displeasure, and professed an animosity against those ministers who were most trusted by the king'. He had consequently advised her 'to be perfectly reconciled to her children, and to those who were nearly related to them' and had done so 'in so powerful a style and with such powerful reasons, that her majesty's passions were totally subdued'.[24]

As a practical man of affairs, Mazarin had no intention of allowing Anglo-French relations to be put at risk by a foolish family quarrel. There was also the financial aspect. Henrietta's dower lands had been sold off during the Commonwealth and were now so 'wasted' and divided up that it hardly seemed worth the trouble of trying to recover them. It had therefore been agreed by parliament the previous summer that she should be granted an annual income of £30,000 in compensation, and the king had agreed to add a further £30,000 pension from the Exchequer. The Princess Henriette had also been voted a dowry of £40,000 to which her brother was adding £20,000 in jewellery and cash. All this had been promised but had not yet materialised. Charles was notoriously easygoing in such matters, but Hyde was not. As Lord Chancellor, Hyde had become very powerful and Mazarin, who had been obliged to support the Queen of England and her daughter during the years of their exile, was clearly having horrid visions of the possible consequences of offending him and insulting his daughter.

It is equally clear that, once they had been pointed out to her, Henrietta shared the cardinal's misgivings, for her capitulation was complete. She asked James to bring his wife to see her, and on 1 January 1661 received the former Anne Hyde 'without the least show of regret, or rather with the same grace as if she had liked it [the marriage] from the beginning' and made her new daughter-in-law sit down beside her. One eye-witness to the scene, which took place in the queen's bedchamber, remarked that there was such a crowd and so much noise that it was impossible to hear what was said, but the duchess was very humble, kneeling on both knees, and the queen had kissed her.[25]

Later that evening Henrietta had an interview with the Chancellor, rising from her chair to greet him. Dismissing the ladies and other bystanders, she told him that if, in her passion, she had said anything of him which he had taken amiss, he must put it down to the great provocation she had suffered. However, she now knew that he had had nothing to do with contriving this unfortunate marriage and had indeed been equally offended by it. 'Therefore, as she was receiving his daughter as her daughter, and heartily forgave the duke and her, and was resolved ever after to live with all the affection of a mother towards them; so she resolved to make a friendship with him, and hereafter to expect all the offices from him, which her kindness should deserve.' It seemed a fair bargain and Edward Hyde was moved to reflect that the attempt of those who designed to bring shame and dishonour upon himself and his family had, by God's good pleasure, turned instead to their shame and reproach, and to the increase of his own greatness and prosperity.[26]

Next day the queen and princess set out for Portsmouth, where they were to embark for France, stopping off at Hampton Court which Henrietta had last seen on that night almost exactly nineteen years before, when she and the king had fled from Whitehall through an angry mob. The journey to the coast now continued via Guildford, where the royal party was given a warm welcome and presented with a silver basket filled with sweetmeats, and on 9 January mother and daughter went on board the *London* to sail for Le Havre but were almost immediately overtaken by Henrietta's usual ill-luck at sea. Within a few hours a storm had blown up, the *London* ran aground on the Horse Sand and was forced to return to harbour. To add to everyone's distress, the princess Henriette had fallen ill with a high fever and for several dreadful days it was feared that she might become yet another victim of the smallpox epidemic which had been raging at court. 'This news do make people think something indeed,' observed Mr Pepys, 'that three of the Royal

244

Family should fall sick of the same disease.' However, it was decided that the princess was suffering from no more than a bad attack of measles, although some of her attendants believed she owed her recovery to her sensible refusal to allow the physicians to bleed her to excess.

It was the end of the month before they could set out again, but this time all went well. The French royal family was waiting to welcome the travellers at Pontoise and Father Cyprien described the reunion between the engaged couple in glowing colours. Monsieur, it seemed, 'fancied himself in Paradise on seeing Madame Henriette . . . looking steadfastly at her, he scarcely knew whether he ought to believe his eyes, so delighted was he to behold her again, and so overcome that he could hardly speak when he kissed her'.[27]

There was some delay before the wedding date could be fixed. The papal dispensation necessary for a marriage between first cousins did not arrive until the beginning of March. Then Cardinal Mazarin died and the court went into mourning for a fortnight. Monsieur grew increasingly restless and impatient and was further exasperated by the antics of the Duke of Buckingham, who had insisted on attaching himself to the party in England. This optimistic individual, who had once caused a brief scandal by his pursuit of the Princess of Orange, was now declaring himself hopelessly in love with the princess Henriette. None of the English took him seriously, but Monsieur was not amused. He sulked and complained to his mother. Representations were made to London and Buckingham departed, dolefully protesting his undying devotion. It was not usual to celebrate marriages in Lent and the bride's family were still in mourning but, in view of the bridegroom's state of nervous agitation, the two queen-mothers agreed that it might be wiser not to wait any longer and the wedding took place very quietly on 30 March in Henrietta's private chapel in the Palais Royal. The new Madame was only going as far as Monsieur's apartments in the adjacent Tuileries, but when the moment of parting arrived both mother and daughter were in floods of tears. The sympathetic Father Cyprien believed nothing could be more painful than the separation of persons who had a perfect love for one another and 'there was general mourning in the Palais Royal; the sighs, the tears and sobs of the Queen and Madame made some weep, melted the hearts of others and pained all'.[28]

Henrietta now retired to Colombes to recover from the emotional excesses of the past few months and, after a brief honeymoon, the newly-weds joined the court at Fontainebleau, where Henriette Anne, making her debut in society as a married woman, scored an immediate and triumphant personal success. Everyone was enchanted by her. 'Never has France had a princess as attractive as Henriette d'Angleterre,' exclaimed that accomplished courtier and man of the world, the Abbé de Choisy.

'Never was there a princess so fascinating and so ready to please all who approached her.' Another courtier who knew her well at this time, remarked on the sweetness and gentleness which no one could resist. 'When she speaks to you, she seems to ask for your heart at once, however trifling are the words that she has to say.' Madame de Motteville observed that 'she was so lovable in herself that she could not fail to please' and even La Grande Mademoiselle, who had been accustomed to regard the Princess of England as a little girl to whom no attention need be paid, felt bound to admit that she was extremely amiable. 'There was a peculiar grace in all her actions and she was so courteous that everyone who approached her was charmed.'[29]

Everyone, that is, except her husband, whose ardour had been more that of an avid collector of desirable objects than a genuine human emotion and who was later to confess that his love for his wife had lasted exactly a fortnight. But then, as another contemporary remarked, 'the miracle of inflaming his heart was not in the power of any woman in the world'. All the same, while the novelty of the situation lasted, Monsieur could still derive satisfaction from the praise being lavished on Madame, and congratulate himself on his own perspicacity in discovering and acquiring such a treasure before the rest of the world had begun to appreciate her.

The whole court was in holiday mood that summer. Louis, free at last from the tutelage of Mazarin, was determined to enjoy himself and the days were filled with hunting parties, bathing parties, picnics and *fêtes-champêtres*, the nights with banquets and balls, ballets and masquerades, and always in the thick of the fun was Madame, her beauty, gaiety and radiant charm quite eclipsing the king's dull, lethargic Spanish wife, who seemed to care for nothing but eating, going to church and playing cards.

Like everyone else, Louis had been taken aback by the startling transformation of the shy, skinny child he had once refused to dance with and it was not long before people began to notice that the king admired Madame; how it was always Madame who rode or drove with him on excursions, Madame who was singled out for his gallantry, Madame who accompanied his majesty on long moonlight walks in the forest. They exchanged witty little notes in verse and planned the next day's entertainments together. Inevitably people began to talk. Louis' wife might be dull, but she was not stupid and she resented the amount of time the king was spending with his sister-in-law.

Out at Colombes, Henrietta had heard enough to make her uneasy and in June she wrote to Madame de Motteville: 'I saw some ladies yesterday who came from Fontainebleau and who tell me that you are always with the queens, and that one cannot have access to you. . . . If you have much noise where you are, I have here much silence, which is more suitable for remembering one's friends, and I beg you to believe yourself one of mine. . . . You have with you another little edition of myself, who is, I assure you, very much your friend. Continue to be hers. I have said enough . . .'[30]

Françoise de Motteville took the hint and had a quiet word with Madame, who listened with her usual grace, but 'her natural sentiments were opposed to prudence'. She 'heard with the ear the counsels I gave her,' wrote de Motteville, 'but the impulses of her heart rejected them'.[31] Madame, in short, saw nothing wrong in her friendship with the king and is said later to have told one of her confidantes that although constantly teased about Louis' attachment to her, she had never considered it to be closer than was justified by their family relationship. Louis, though, had scented danger and began to transfer his attentions to Louise de la Vallière, one of Madame's maids of honour, while Madame herself soon acquired a new admirer in the Comte de Guiche, a handsome soldier and courtier and a favoured member of Monsieur's circle.

Henrietta was now beginning to make plans for returning to England, her financial settlement having been made on the understanding that she would live and spend her income there. First, though, she wanted to see her daughter safely through her first pregnancy. Madame was not at all well, thinner than ever and suffering from a persistent cough. It was also obvious that her marriage was already going seriously wrong – rumours had even reached London that 'Monsieur is very jealous of Madame and makes her a very bad husband'. Her child, a girl, to the bitter disappointment of both parents, was born in March 1662 and not long after she emerged from her lying-in the 'affaire de Guiche', which had followed the classic pattern of indiscreet letters and clandestine meetings, was betrayed to her husband, who took his complaints to his mother-in-law.

To what extent Henrietta was aware of Monsieur's homosexuality is not clear, although she must certainly have known about his cross-dressing and other suspiciously effeminate tendencies – these were encouraged at court, as no one wanted another Gaston making trouble for the royal family. Philippe d'Orléans's other, more disagreeable tendencies, were not as yet so apparent, or not at any rate to Henrietta. He was her godson as well as her son-in-law and they had always been on affectionate terms. Now she came to see her daughter 'and scolded her a little, telling her all that Monsieur knew for certain, so that she might confess to him just this much and no more'. Monsieur and Madame then had 'a great explanation' and Monsieur 'took such pleasure in his position of authority, having Madame confess to him things that he knew already, that his acrimony melted away; he embraced her and retained but a slight grudge against her'.[32] De Guiche had been posted to a command in Lorraine, a mischief-making maidservant dismissed and, on the surface at least, everything seemed to have been happily resolved, so that by midsummer Henrietta felt free to set out for England. She was, as she told Christine, eager to make the acquaintance of her latest daughter-in-law, for Charles was married at last, to the Portuguese princess Catherine of Braganza, who had brought a handsome dowry of £500,000, together with the ports of Bombay and Tangier and the right of free trade with Portugal's far-eastern colonies.

Monsieur and Madame accompanied the queen-mother as far as Beauvais, where there was another tearful farewell, and on 28 July Samuel Pepys noted her arrival, coming up-river from Gravesend as high as Woolwich. She was bound at first for Greenwich, her old home Somerset House, which had been left empty and neglected during the Interregnum, being not yet ready for occupation. Everyone seemed glad to see her and Charles, writing to his 'dearest Minette' early in September, hoped she had been pleased with her welcome. 'I am sure I have done all that lies in my power to let her see the duty and kindness I have for her. The truth is', he went on, 'never any children had so good a mother as we have, and you and I shall never have any disputes but only who loves her best, and in that I will never yield to you.'[33]

His majesty had not always felt so warmly towards his mother, but Henrietta appears now to have been on her best behaviour, anxious 'to live with the least offence imaginable to any sort of men'. She was delighted with the new queen and told Christine that her son was being so kind and affectionate that she could not wish for more. 'Our affairs are going as well as possible and the king has more power than any of his predecessors have had; the queen my daughter-in-law is the best creature in the world who shows me the greatest goodwill, and I have the joy of seeing that she and the king are very much in love.'[34]

In fact, of course, the unfortunate Catherine, whom Mr Pepys thought had 'a good, modest and innocent look', was doomed to suffer all the long-drawn-out humiliation of her husband's serial infidelity, but Henrietta remained determined to look on the bright side. 'I am entirely satisfied with my son,' she wrote in November, 'and I believe that God once more wishes to give me some happiness in this world.' As for her daughter-in-law, she was a saint and very religious. 'I am truly blessed in her.'[35] It was Christmas now and the king was urging his mother to come and see some of the ballets being performed at court. She normally made it a rule not to appear at large public entertainments, but on this occasion she really thought she would have to go and she was also present at a grand reception for the ambassadors from the Emperor of Russia which took place in the Banqueting House on 29 December.

She was back in residence at Somerset House by this time and living in considerable style. Indeed it was being said that the queen-mother's court offered more amusing hospitality and drew greater crowds than Queen Catherine's. Old Henry Jermyn, plumper and more prosperous than ever, was still at her side as her Lord Chamberlain or Steward or, as some still said, husband. Rumours that they were secretly married had revived and even improved. Henrietta was now said to have borne her major-domo a son, or was it a daughter, somewhere in France. Pepys heard all the gossip, but 'how true God knows!' Abraham Cowley, the poet-secretary to whom Jermyn had delegated most of the drudgery of coding and decoding the queen's voluminous correspondence, was also still on the strength, as were the de Ventelets, husband and wife, who had been with the queen ever since her first arrival in England. Other old friends now back at Somerset House included Sir John Winter, her secretary in pre-war days and Walter Montagu, her Grand Almoner. Another great Catholic, Lord Arundell of Wardour, was her Master of the Horse and her ladies were still led by the Duchess of Richmond, once Mary Villiers, Susan Denbigh and Anne Newport, whose conversion had created such a to-do back in the thirties. And then there were the gentlemen ushers, who were paid £130 a year with diet, the footmen and pages of the backstairs, the liveried bargemen, the bedchamber women, laundresses and seamstresses, a physician and an apothecary, the officers of the pantry, ewery, cellar and buttery – not to mention a guard of four-and-twenty gentlemen kitted out in black velvet cassocks and golden embroidered badges, ready with their halberds to wait on her majesty when she was getting into her sedan, or at chapel, or at meals, or driving out in one of her four coaches and six – all the appurtenances, in short, of a very great household.[36]

Her majesty was now in her fifty-fourth year, but had lost neither her vivacity nor her power to charm and it had become the fashion, particularly among the younger set, to visit Maddam la Mère, that tiny, wizened, black-robed personage who had known and seen so much, and who could remember all those legendary figures of what now seemed a bygone age – Buckingham and Strafford, Bishop Laud and even John Pym himself. But while Henrietta was undoubtedly enjoying this unexpected Indian summer holiday of grandeur and popularity, she never forgot her other obligations. Inigo Jones's beautiful chapel, so comprehensively trashed by the parliamentary soldiers at the beginning of the war, could not be fully restored to its former glory, but all traces of the French Protestant community which had been using it were removed and before long her faithful Capuchins were once more preaching there and celebrating mass. According to Cyprien de Gamache the news soon spread among the local Catholics, who came flocking back to receive communion, to confess and to have their children baptised, so that more priests had to be hurriedly summoned over from France. The queen-mother was also acquiring quite a reputation for good works, 'bestowing good sums of money quarterly to charitable uses, particularly to the releasing of poor prisoners, that lay in for small debts, or for fees in the prisons in and about London'. This gave the Capuchins an unexceptionable excuse for prison visiting and for attending executions 'to reconcile those that died to the church of Rome'.[37]

Although she was now proceeding more discreetly than in the past, Henrietta continued to welcome any opportunity for making converts and was offered an especially unusual candidate one day, when a vessel put into the port of London with a cargo of luxury goods from the East Indies which included 'a little Chinese lad, fourteen or fifteen years old, of a gentle disposition, well made and of good figure'. Someone, remembering perhaps her fondness for pets, dwarfs and other rarities, decided he would make a good present for the queen-mother and Henrietta immediately welcomed the boy and took him into her household. Discovering that he had already learned to speak English, she handed him over to Father Cyprien to be made into a Christian and a Catholic. She herself stood godmother at his baptism and co-opted the Duke of Richmond's brother to be godfather. Thus, wrote Father Cyprien, 'the young Chinese, so far distant from his country, deprived of his own father and mother, sustained a lucky loss, since he was made by the grace of baptism a real heir of Paradise, and had on earth for his spiritual father one of the most illustrious gentlemen in England and for mother a mighty Queen, who designed to secure to him an honourable subsistence'.[38]

Aside from her philanthropic efforts, Henrietta was principally occupied just then with plans for enlarging and improving Somerset House. Inigo Jones was dead by this time, but his drawings for a new river frontage, made to her order back in 1638, were still in existence. There was to be a gallery with full-length windows overlooking the Thames and an Italian garden with paved walks leading down to the water. This ambitious and expensive project was put in hand early in 1663 and in May Mr Pepys made a special journey by water to the Strand to view the work in progress.

The king and queen paid a visit to Tunbridge Wells that summer, but Henrietta restricted her excursions to day trips. She went to have a look at Richmond, now crumbling into decay, and on another occasion spent an afternoon out at Deptford visiting John Evelyn at Sayes Court, where she accepted a collation and stayed on till quite late in the evening. She seems to have been in excellent form and kept the company entertained with 'many observable tales of the sagacity of various dogs she had formerly possessed'.[39]

The queen-mother was also busy embellishing the interior of her palace and the months passed pleasantly enough, but she was finding the cold damp English winters increasingly trying. Her catarrh was definitely getting worse and by early 1665 she was beginning to think seriously about going back to France – not permanently, of course, but for long enough to pay a therapeutic visit to Bourbon and to see her daughter again. Madame had been safely delivered of her second child, a boy this time, but the news of her general health and the state of her marriage was not good, and Anne of Austria, too, was now seriously ill with breast cancer.

In spite of all this, Henrietta, in the words of Father Cyprien, 'wavered long irresolute', worried that she would be deserting the English Catholics, her presence being 'advantageous to the service of their religion'. The religious settlement enacted by the Cavalier parliament in 1661, which had re-established the Church of England and the bishops, had on the whole been harder on dissenters of the Presbyterian complexion than on the Catholics; due largely to the influence of the king, who could not forget the vital part they had played in his escape after Worcester, the Catholics were so far being left more or less alone. But the penal laws remained in place and anti-Catholic feeling still simmered only just beneath the surface. Ominously, on Christmas Eve, placards threatening 'the extirpation of popery' had appeared on the walls of the queen-mother's chapel. However, the king reassured her, promising that the chapel would be kept open during her absence, although she warned the eight Capuchin friars who were to remain behind that, while labouring for the assistance of the Catholics and the conversion of heretics, they must be especially careful 'not to afford any cause of complaint to the Protestant bishops and ministers, and to our enemies the Puritans'.[40]

By early summer, hastened by an alarming increase in reported cases of plague in the capital, Henrietta was making preparations for departure and Samuel Pepys, happening to call at Somerset House on 29 June, found them all packing up, 'the Queen-mother setting out for France this day; and intends not to come [back] till winter come twelvemonths'.[41] The king escorted his mother as far as Gravesend and the Duke of York saw her down to Dover.

She found Henriette-Anne at Versailles recovering from the birth of a dead baby and as soon as she was strong enough mother and daughter left together for Colombes, where they stayed until the end of August. The international situation was now causing considerable concern to both women. Anglo-Dutch relations had been growing increasingly strained for the past year, as the commercial rivalry between two expanding maritime powers competing worldwide for trade and territory grew fiercer, and there was 'a great appetite for war' in England, especially among the 'Parliament men'. Charles himself had some old scores to settle with the Dutch republicans but he was worried about

Louis' attitude, as France had an offensive and defensive treaty with Holland and his letters to his sister frequently referred to his desire for 'a strict friendship with France' – something which he felt sure would be best achieved through her good offices. 'There is nobody so fit to make a good correspondence and friendship between us as yourself,' he had written in the summer of 1664 and Madame was eager to assure him in return how much that friendship was wished for in France. 'Profit by this, in God's name, and lose no time in obtaining the King's secret promise that he will not help the Dutch. You understand that he cannot bind himself publicly, owing to his engagements with them, although we all know these are only worth what he chooses to make them.'[42]

In fact, Louis, who had designs of his own on the Spanish Netherlands, was anxious to keep out of the approaching conflict if at all possible and when England finally declared war on Holland in the spring of 1665, he did his best to find a peaceful solution. In this he was supported by both his aunt and his sister-in-law, as the English ambassador, Denzil Holles, reported on 22 August. Holles had gone to Colombes to take his leave of Henrietta before she left on her visit to Bourbon and was still there when Louis himself arrived. 'The King of France and the Queen-mother went alone into her bedchamber and our Princess, Madame, went in after they had been there at least an hour.' Holles later saw Henrietta again and 'took the boldness to ask her how she found things. She said they had been all the time within talking over these businesses of Holland and that the King of France told her he had made King Charles some propositions, which were very fair ones, which if he refused he must take part with the Hollanders.'[43]

But parliament remained in a belligerent mood, the French propositions were turned down and in January 1666 Louis came into the war on the side of the Dutch, protesting that he did so reluctantly and only because he was bound by his treaty obligations. Henrietta told him that 'she was sorry he was engaging in an enterprise wherein she could not go along with him in her prayers', but at the same time she continued her efforts for peace. Working in conjunction with the Dutch ambassador in Paris she was ready to offer Charles, ostensibly on her own initiative, a plan which would provide a possible basis for negotiation, only to have her 'projected intervention' absolutely rejected by that monarch on the grounds that any mediation attempted by his mother would be distrusted by the English, because she was French and too fond of living in that country. According to the Venetians, it was the Chancellor who principally objected to the queen's involvement, but it is clear enough that both Charles and Hyde – now elevated to the earldom of Clarendon – were determined to marginalise her and were now trying to persuade her to return to England.[44]

Henrietta, though, was never easily discouraged. Two meetings of interested diplomats were held at Colombes under her auspices around the Easter holidays and Louis, who was fond of his aunt and valued her contribution to the peace process, visited her more than once during the summer. 'The king knows her to be worthy and necessary to his allies and to this kingdom, and very competent and helpful for negotiations,' reported the Venetian ambassador in September. 'Accordingly the queen, as if on her own motion, has despatched to England my lord Germen [sic], her major domo, who has been employed on similar affairs on other occasions.'[45]

But although Jermyn wrote at the end of November of London's inflexibility, the war was in fact beginning to come to an end. The English had, on the whole, had the best of it, with two notable naval victories, but Charles had no means of financing another campaign. The ships were having to be mothballed and their unpaid crews – those who had not already deserted – were rioting in the streets. The Dutch, too, by and large had had enough. They did, however, manage to have the last word when Michiel de Ruyter led a daring raid up the Medway as far as Chatham in June 1667. By this time Charles and Louis had quietly come to terms in an unadvertised correspondence carried on via Colombes. Louis was now free to concentrate on his long-planned invasion of Flanders, while Henrietta spent a good deal of the summer visiting her daughter at St Cloud, the delightful country house on the banks of the Seine which had become Madame's favourite retreat.

Madame badly needed her mother's support just then, for she had recently known the grief, all too familiar to parents in every walk of life, of losing her little son, who had died of convulsions at two years old, said to be due to teething. She was now pregnant again but miscarried in July and for a few days was desperately ill. She continued to ail for the rest of the year and Henrietta anxiously applied remedies both spiritual and medical. Like many ladies of a certain age she did not entirely trust the new generation of doctors, but had never lost her confidence in the abilities of the now-deceased Theodore Mayerne and remembered a certain never-failing prescription of his, so that Charles, writing to his sister the following spring, wondered if her recovery should be ascribed to 'Mam's masses or Mr de Mayerne's pills'.[46]

Henrietta's own health was becoming increasingly poorly and the Bourbon waters no longer seemed to help very much. Louis had granted her the grand Hotel de la Bazinière in Paris as a town residence, but she was living very quietly now, dividing her time between Colombes and Chaillot. She had outlived nearly all her contemporaries: Christine had died five years ago and Anne of Austria in 1666, but at Chaillot she could enjoy the company of Madame de Motteville, who had left the court after the death of her mistress Queen Anne and was living in retirement at the convent. The two friends sat together peacefully talking over old times and Françoise de Motteville, who was planning to spend her leisure writing her memoirs, suggested that the queen should do her the honour of dictating some of her reminiscences of the English revolution.

Henrietta was showing no signs of returning to England. In her present state of health she really could not be expected to face the rigours of another sea crossing. But Charles was seriously short of money and his advisers, looking round for possible economies, reminded him that his mother was still drawing her £60,000 a year, money which was supposed to be spent on English goods and services – and in any case, living as she was in almost complete seclusion, she surely could not be spending all of it. Towards the end of 1668, therefore, the Secretary of State Lord Arlington wrote to the Earl of St Albans informing him that his majesty would be reluctantly compelled to reduce the queen's income by one-fourth.

1668

If either Charles or Arlington expected Henrietta to accept this sudden sharp loss of income without protest, they quickly discovered their mistake. Arlington's letter, she told her son, had surprised her to a degree that she found very difficult to express, 'it not having entered into my imagination that you would have wished to retrench me, since you knew well yourself, I had come down as near to economy as I could for my subsistence. . . . I feel assured that when you have reflected, you will change your opinion, and will not wish to render the rest of my days, which will be short, unfortunate by the debts for which I stand engaged, on your word, always putting confidence in what you promised me; and I assure you what touches my heart most is that people see that your saving extends to your mother. . . . I hope to have news from you promptly, in order to determine what I am to expect and what is to become of me. . . . I end by conjuring you again to think well of it and to give me a speedy answer.'[47] To Arlington she wrote that she could not conceive how anyone could imagine that it would be possible for her to subsist with such a retrenchment, especially as she had already, with no little trouble, reduced her expenses to the exact amount of her revenue. It was hard enough for her to overcome the losses and debts of past years without this final, unlooked-for blow, and the outraged widow felt certain that his lordship would find her 'so based upon right and justice' as to give her the benefit of his good offices.[48]

The argument rumbled on into the summer. 'Here is a great clamour at the Queen Mother's about the King's stopping her money,' wrote the ambassador Ralph Montagu to Arlington in July 1668. 'They say she must be forced to go into a monastery if the King does not pay her, and they think the King will be ashamed to let his mother be driven to that necessity.' But the general feeling in Paris seems to have been that Henrietta was making altogether too big a fuss. 'All the French think it ridiculous, at a time when we are thought so poor in England, to have so much money spent abroad.' Even Madame told Montagu that she thought the queen should be able to manage quite well with what she had, 'notwithstanding all the King stopped', and they had had a falling out over it.[49]

But Madame was always likely to take Charles's side in any dispute, and besides brother and sister had weightier matters on their minds just then than Mam's unreasonableness over her money. The king had continued to rely on Minette to act as his unofficial ambassador and was now engaged on some very private business with Louis in which she was proving invaluable as a go-between. The two kings were, in short, planning a mutually advantageous, if distinctly unethical arrangement by which Charles (who had significantly now dispensed with the services of his faithful Lord Chancellor) would, at a convenient moment, announce his conversion to Catholicism and grant full freedom of worship to all his Catholic subjects. In return, he would receive an annual subsidy from France, hopefully large enough to make him independent of parliamentary interference, plus, if need be, enough French troops to ensure the suppression of any consequent civil unrest. He would also undertake to assist Louis in a projected French dismemberment of the Dutch empire in return for a share in the spoils.

The preliminary stages of this enterprising programme had, of course, to be kept very quiet indeed and it is not clear how much, if anything, the queen-mother knew about it. Her friend and Master of the Horse, the devoutly Catholic Lord Arundell, was certainly in the secret – he was employed as courier. Henry Jermyn appears to have known, or guessed, a good deal and several other people connected with the household at Colombes strongly suspected that something unusual was in the air. If, as seems highly probable, Henrietta did know at least that the king her son was seriously contemplating converting to her faith and there was a chance that England might after all become reconciled to Rome – the seemingly unattainable ideal she had prayed for so earnestly for so long – then it must surely have gladdened what were to be the last months of her life.

She had had an attack of bronchitis in the spring and appeared to recover well, in spite of being bled repeatedly, but during the summer her chronic insomnia, recurrent fevers and fainting fits were giving increasing cause for concern. According to the devoted Father Cyprien, she showed 'none of those ill tempers which are common with ailing women', but continued 'to exhibit an agreeable serenity and a majestic cheerfulness as if she had enjoyed perfect health. I have frequently heard her say', he went on, 'that complaints in illness were useless, or, if they served for anything, it was to show the great weakness and the little resolution of the persons who complained. She laughed at those ladies who scream, who weep, who lament, about a touch of headache or toothache.'[50]

Henrietta had once told Madame de Motteville that she was afraid of death and preferred not to think about it, but the last time they met she had said that she was planning to retire to Chaillot in order to die there. She was not going to bother any more with doctors and their remedies but think only of her soul. However, when she visited St Cloud in August to see her daughter, who was approaching the end of her fifth pregnancy, she allowed herself to be persuaded to agree to a consultation with some of the royal physicians. Accordingly, Messieurs Vallot, Esprit and Yvelin arrived at Colombes on 8 September to be received by Henrietta who described her various symptoms with such clarity and detail that her own doctor, M. Duquesne, was left with nothing to add but 'his mode of treatment and the medicines he had employed'. Vallot, who was Louis's doctor and leader of the visiting posse, approved everything which had been done and gave it as his opinion that her majesty's ailments, although painful and distressing, were not likely to prove fatal and suggested only that she should take three grains of laudanum to help her sleep. Henrietta at once objected, saying that sedatives disagreed with her and 'the famous English physician M. de Mayerne, had warned her never to take any'. But Vallot answered 'with great respect, that the grains which he proposed were of a particular composition, and that he would not have been so ill-advised as to propose them had he not known to a certainty that they would be conducive to her health'.[51]

The next day was Sunday, 'the festival of the nativity of the most blessed Virgin', and Henrietta had a long spiritual conversation with her confessor to prepare herself for taking the sacrament on the Monday. She was in specially good form that evening, and ate a hearty supper, laughing and talking 'as if nothing ailed her'. She went to bed at her usual time of ten o'clock and there was some discussion as to whether she should take Dr Vallot's recommended sleeping draught, but she was thought to be 'in too much heat . . . and the resolution was taken not to give it at all'. An hour or so later, realising that she was not going to sleep naturally, she asked for Duquesne to be summoned and told him that she would take the laudanum after all. He demurred, or said he did, but the queen insisted and he gave her the dose mixed with the yolk of an egg. Soon she was asleep but the doctor, sitting by the bed, 'perceiving her to sleep too profoundly, and her pulse to alter, endeavoured by all the means he could to wake her and bring her to herself'. The room quickly filled with light and noise and a sense of panic, as people ran to and fro, fetching things, shouting orders, crying and lamenting; as the priests frantically exhorted the small, still figure in the bed 'to contrition of her sins, to the love of

God and confidence in his mercy', beseeching her to make some sign that she understood. But Dr Vallot's 'luckless grains' had done their work too well. Henrietta's drugged sleep would be her last, and at some time between three and four o'clock in the morning of Monday 10 September 1669 she slipped quietly away without ever regaining consciousness. The great adventure which had begun at Boulogne all those years ago was over.[52]

A messenger was sent off at once to break the news to the French royal family, while Henry Jermyn sat down to write to King Charles to tell him that his mother was dead. Madame, whose baby, another disappointing girl, had been born at the end of August, was still lying-in, but Monsieur *(St Albahs)* came hurrying over to Colombes, where he found the grieving household in a state of shock and confusion and fury against Dr Vallot. Discovering that Henrietta appeared not to have made a will, he immediately ordered everything to be put under seal. According to French law, he said, the property of anyone dying intestate automatically belonged to any of their children living in the country and he therefore considered that his wife should be her mother's sole heiress. Jermyn, however, thought that the mere fact of the queen's dying in France did not alter what would have been the case if she had died in England, 'which is that the king is her sole heir'.[53]

Ralph Montagu's account of the matter is rather different. Writing to Lord Arlington on 11 September, the ambassador complained that he had only heard of the queen's death by chance and, 'supposing my Lord St Albans would seize upon all she left, and for that reason did not send me word', had himself asked the French authorities to have her possessions sealed until the question of inheritance was settled. 'I am sure without this my Lord St Albans would not have left a silver spoon in the house.'[54]

This may have been unfair, but my Lord St Albans did seem to be much preoccupied with finance. What was he to do about money, he asked in a series of plaintive letters to London. There was mourning to be provided for everyone in the house, the servants' wages to be paid and 'somewhat besides to give to the poorer sort, to carry them home to England'. Then there was the burial, which would have to be suitably grand. What did the king want him to do about that, and who was going to pay for it?[55]

Gradually things were sorted out. Louis decreed that his aunt, as a daughter of France, was to have a state funeral which the state would pay for. This took place in the abbey of St Denis in the presence of the princes and princesses of the blood, of the members of the Paris Parlement, the diplomatic corps and all the late queen's household officers. The Archbishop of Rheims celebrated the mass, assisted by four bishops, and Henrietta's tiny coffin was ceremoniously lowered into the

the IX th

royal vault to lie with her father the Great Henry, but her heart was taken to Chaillot enclosed in a silver casket engraved with the inscription: Henrietta Maria, Queen of England, France, Scotland and Ireland, daughter of the King of France Henry IV the Victorious, wife of Charles I the Martyr and mother of the restored Charles II.[56]

Philippe d'Orléans did not succeed in his attempt to seize the queen's property. Madame herself had, with no little difficulty, persuaded him to drop his claim which, as Ralph Montagu commented, 'might have proved very troublesome, and have brought in the Duke [of York] and the Prince of Orange, too, with their pretensions'.[57] After some representations made by his lawyers, King Charles was duly adjudged to be his mother's sole heir. He ordered that all the furniture in her rooms at Chaillot should be left there for the nuns to dispose of as they wished and Madame later persuaded him to make a gift to the convent to finance the building of a chapel in their mother's memory. An inventory was taken at Colombes and, with the exception of such pictures as were not fixed to the walls, Charles made the house and its contents over to his sister for her sole use and benefit, adding a note in the margin of the inventory that 'what Madame cares not to have to be distributed among the Queen's women'. There does not seem to be any record of what happened to the little box containing a miniature of Charles I and 'two rings which are believed to be the Queen's wedding rings'.

The household was now broken up. The Duchess of Richmond and the Earl of St Albans returned to England, the duchess to take up a position as lady of the bedchamber to Catherine of Braganza and Henry Jermyn to enjoy another fifteen years of good eating, card playing and property speculation, despite his gout and increasing blindness. Henrietta's chapel at Somerset House was finally closed in November and the survivors of the little community of Capuchin friars, who had stayed faithfully at their post through the years of plague and fire, came back to France. Cyprien de Gamache found a haven in Madame's family, where he stayed till his death, and Madame also took over responsibility for James's daughter, the four-year-old Princess Anne of York, who had been staying with her grandmother while having treatment from a Paris eye specialist.

King Charles is said, naturally, to have been greatly afflicted by his mother's death, but privately he may have been a little relieved. The relationship had always been a difficult one and nowadays, apart from being a source of expense and possible political embarrassment, she principally represented a reminder of a past which the king would have preferred to forget. It was Henrietta's *enfant de bénédiction* who mourned her most and felt her loss most grievously for, as La Grande Mademoiselle remarked, Madame 'had always relied on Queen Henrietta to reconcile her with her husband, as she usually lived on uneasy terms with him'. It was Madame who organised a memorial service for Henrietta at Chaillot, inviting the famous preacher Jacques Bossuet, Bishop of Condon, to give the address. The convent chapel, heavily draped in black, was packed to bursting point for the occasion and a wax effigy of the late queen was displayed in the centre of the choir, lying on a bier covered in black velvet and embroidered in gold with her armorial bearings.

Bossuet had been provided with a potted biography of his subject by Madame de Motteville and proceeded to enthral his audience with the details of Henrietta's amazing story. 'You will see in a single life all the extremities of things human; happiness without bound as well as misery; the long and peaceful enjoyment of one of the most noble crowns in the universe; all that which can render birth and position most glorious heaped upon one head, and then exposed to the outrages of fortune; the good cause at first followed by good success, and then sudden reverses and changes unprecedented. . . . There is the lesson', declared Bossuet, 'which God gives to kings; thus does he show to the world the worthlessness of its pomp and grandeur.'[58]

To her own contemporaries Henrietta tended to appear either as a tragic heroine – *la reine malheureuse* – or as a dangerous and determined enemy, according to point of view. Later predominantly male and Protestant historians have seen her as a thoroughly bad influence, frivolous and extravagant, a tiresome, hysterical, interfering woman who ruled her weak, vacillating husband to his serious disadvantage. This was also an opinion held by not a few men at the time. But Françoise de Motteville, an intelligent and perceptive witness, who knew Henrietta personally for twenty-five years, remarked that although many persons attributed the fall of King Charles to the bad advice of his queen, she herself was not inclined to agree, since the queen so candidly avowed the faults and mistakes she had actually committed. And certainly, while Charles would not appoint a gentleman of the bedchamber without seeking his wife's approval, it is noticeable that he seldom if ever took her advice on matters of state.

Intensely feminine in outlook, Henrietta remained the product of her background and upbringing, and it is surely unreasonable to blame her for not being a serious, high-minded liberal intellectual, guiding the king along the paths of political correctitude. Passionate in her loves and hates, Henrietta could be both insensitive and wrong-headed, but in spite of her many all-too-obvious faults and mistakes there can be no denying the courage and steadfastness of this ardent, warm-hearted, devoted, fiercely protective little creature, who had once told her husband, 'there is nothing in the world, no trouble, which shall hinder me from serving you and loving you above everything in the world'.

HENRIETTA'S ENGLISH FAMILY

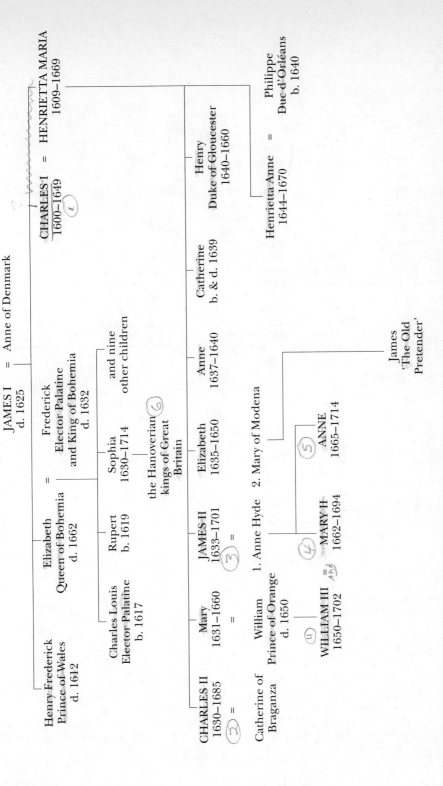

Notes

CHAPTER ONE

1. Sir Henry Wotton, *Life and Death of George Villiers, Duke of Buckingham*, 1642. Harleian Miscellany, Vol. 8, pp. 615–16; *Letters of Charles I*, ed. Sir Charles Petrie, Cassell, 1935, pp. 7–9; *Autobiography of Lord Herbert of Cherbury*, ed. Sidney Lee, London, 1886, pp. 239–42.
2. I.A. Taylor, *The Life of Henrietta Maria*, Hutchinson, 1905, pp. 1–2, 6; E. Hamilton, *Henrietta Maria*, Hamish Hamilton, 1976. p. 2.
3. *Life and Death of Henrietta Maria de Bourbon*, 1685, reprinted 1820, pp. 3–4.
4. F. de Bassompierre, *Mémoires*, ed. Marie LaCropte, Paris, 1870, Vol. I, p. 273.
5. *Life and Death of Henrietta Maria de Bourbon*, p. 4.
6. Lucy Crump, *Nursery Life 300 Years Ago*, Routledge, 1929, pp. 28–32.
7. M.A.E. Green, *Letters of Henrietta Maria*, London, 1857, pp. 3–4.
8. *Life and Death of Henrietta Maria*, p. 4; K.A. Patmore, *The Court of Louis XIII*, Methuen, 1909, pp. 29–42.
9. Hamilton, *Henrietta Maria*, p. 21.
10. Leveneur de Tillières, *Mémoires*, ed. M.C. Hippeau, Paris, 1863, pp. 23–4.
11. *Life and Death of Henrietta Maria*, p. 4.
12. De Tillières, *Mémoires*, p. 25 et seq.; Patmore, *The Court of Louis XIII*, pp. 97–8.
13. *Narrative of the Spanish Marriage Treaty*, ed. and trans. S.R. Gardiner, Camden Soc., No. 101, 1869, pp. 298–303.
14. Ibid., pp. 196–7.
15. Ibid., pp. 274–5; de Tillières, *Mémoires*, pp. 52–7.
16. Calendar of State Papers Venetian, Vol. 18, p. 182, Zuane Pesaro to the Doge and Senate, 5 January 1624.
17. *Cabala: Mysteries of State*, 1654, p. 290, Viscount Kensington to the Duke of Buckingham.
18. Ibid., p. 287, Kensington to Prince Charles.
19. Ibid., p. 288, same to same.
20. Ibid., p. 287, same to same.
21. Ibid., p. 291, Kensington to Secretary Conway.
22. Ibid., pp. 293–4, Kensington to the Duke of Buckingham.
23. Ibid., p. 286, same to same.
24. Hardwicke State Papers, Vol. I, pp. 535–6, Lord Carlisle to Prince Charles, 7 October 1624.
25. R. Lockyer, *Buckingham*, Longman, 1981, p. 203; Charles Carlton, *Charles I*, Routledge, 1995, p. 55; Hardwicke S.P., Vol. I, pp. 523–5, Secretary Conway to Lords Carlisle and Holland, 12 August 1624.
26. Cal. S.P. Venetian, Vol. 18, p. 438, Marc Antonio Morosini to the Doge and Senate, 13 September 1624.
27. Hardwick S.P., Vol. I, pp. 536–7, Lord Carlisle to Secretary Conway, 18 October 1624.
28. Cal. S.P. Venetian, Vol. 18, p. 486, Morosini to the Doge and Senate, 16 November 1624.
29. Cal. S.P. Venetian, Vol. 18, p. 504, Zuane Pesaro to the Doge and Senate, 6 December 1624.
30. Quoted in Lockyer, *Buckingham*, p. 209.
31. Cal. S.P. Venetian, Vol. 18, pp. 455–6, Zuane Pesaro to the Doge and Senate, 11 October 1624.
32. Cal. S.P. Venetian, Vol. 18, pp. 523–5; Charles Dodd, *Church History*, ed. M.A. Tierney, London, 1843, Vol. V, pp. 155–6; Hardwicke S.P., pp. 546–7.
33. Hardwicke S.P., Vol. 1, pp. 552, 554, Lord Carlisle to the Duke of Buckingham, 16 February 1625.
34. Cal. S.P. Venetian, Vol. 18, p. 610, Zuane Pesaro, 14 March 1625; p. 615, Zuane Pesaro, 21 March 1625.
35. *Salvetti Correspondence* (Manuscripts of Henry Duncan Skrine) H.M.C. 11th Report, App. I, HMSO, 1887, p. 3.

36. Green, *Letters of Henrietta Maria*, p. 7.
37. Cal. S.P. Venetian, Vol. 19, p. 44, Morosini to the Doge and Senate, 16 May 1625; Hamilton, *Henrietta Maria*, pp. 48–9.
38. Lockyer, *Buckingham*, p. 236.
39. Hardwicke S.P., Vol. 1, pp. 571–2; Cal. S.P. Venetian, Vol. 19, p. 59, Morosini to the Doge and Senate, 25 May 1625.
40. Lockyer, *Buckingham*, pp. 238–9.
41. Letter printed in Cardinal Richelieu, *Mémoires*, Société de l'Histoire de France, Paris, 1907–31, Appendix to Vol. V, pp. 275–81.
42. Cal. of State Papers Domestic, Charles I, 1848, Vol. 1, p. 41, Mayor of Dover to Secretary Conway, 9 June 1625.
43. *Cabala: Mysteries of State*, p. 302, Sir Toby Mathew to the Duchess of Buckingham, 9 June 1625.

CHAPTER TWO

1. Cal. S.P. Venetian, Vol. 19, p. 87, Zuane Pesaro to the Doge and Senate, 27 June 1625; de Tillières, *Mémoires*, pp. 89–90.
2. Thomas Birch, *Court and Times of Charles I*, 1848, Vol. I, pp. 30–1.
3. De Tillières, *Mémoires*, p. 90.
4. *Life and Death of Henrietta Maria*, p. 7; J. Rushworth, *Historical Collections*, Vol. I, p. 170; Edmund Ludlow, *Memoirs* (1751), Vol. III, pp. 305–9.
5. Birch, *Court and Times*, Vol. I, p. 31.
6. De Tillières, *Mémoires*, p. 90.
7. Birch, *Court and Times*, Vol. I, p. 31; de Tillières, *Mémoires*, p. 91.
8. Henry Ellis, *Original Letters*, Series I, Vol. 3, pp. 196–7 and 199.
9. James Howell, *Familiar Letters*, p. 238.
10. Birch, *Court and Times*, Vol. I, pp. 30–1 and 23.
11. S.R. Gardiner, *History of England*, Longmans Green, 1884, Vol. 5, p. 317.
12. *Salvetti Correspondence*, H.M.C., 11th Report, App. I, pp. 6–7, 25 April 1625.
13. Lucy Hutchinson, *Memoirs of . . . Col. Hutchinson*, p. 46.
14. Rushworth, *Historical Collections*, Vol. I, p. 172.
15. Birch, *Court and Times*, Vol. I, p. 33.
16. Cal. S.P. Venetian, Vol. 19, p. 99, Zuane Pesaro, 4 July 1625; *Salvetti Correspondence*, pp. 22–3, 4 July 1625; Birch, *Court and Times*, Vol. I, p. 35, John Chamberlain to Dudley Carleton, 25 June 1625.
17. Cal. S.P. Domestic, Charles I, Vol. I, p. 16; Cal. S.P. Venetian, Vol. 19, p. 98, Zuane Pesaro, 4 July 1625; *Salvetti Correspondence*, p. 24, 4 July 1625.
18. *Salvetti Correspondence*, p. 25, 11 July 1625; Birch, *Court and Times*, Vol. I, p. 40.
19. De Tillières, *Mémoires*, pp. 92–5.
20. Cal. S.P. Venetian, Vol. 19, pp. 141–3, Zuane Pesaro, 21 August 1625; pp. 146–7, 26 August 1625; *Salvetti Correspondence*, pp. 29 and 31, 19 August and 15 September 1625; Rushworth, *Historical Collections*, Vol. 1, p. 194.
21. De Tillières, *Mémoires*, pp. 99–100.
22. Birch, *Court and Times*, Vol. I, pp. 50 and 52; *Salvetti Correspondence*, p. 38, 26 November 1625; de Tillières, *Mémoires*, pp. 101–4; Cal. S.P. Venetian, Vol. 19, p. 145, Marc Antonio Morosini, 22 August 1625; p. 177, Zuane Pesaro, 7 October 1625.
23. De Tillières, *Mémoires*, pp. 105–6; Cal. S.P. Venetian, Vol. 19, pp. 189–90, Zuane Pesaro, 25 October 1625.
24. De Tillières, *Mémoires*, p. 107.
25. Sir Charles Petrie, *Letters etc. of King Charles I*, p. 40.
26. Ibid., pp. 40–1.
27. Ibid., p. 42.
28. *Salvetti Correspondence*, p. 45, 13 February 1626.
29. Cal. S.P. Venetian, Vol. 19, p. 311, Zuane Pesaro, 5 February 1626.
30. Ellis, *Original Letters*, Series I, Vol. 3, pp. 212–13 and 220.
31. De Tillières, *Mémoires*, pp. 118–20; Cal. S.P. Venetian, Vol. 19, p. 327, Zuane Pesaro, 20 February 1626.
32. Cal. S.P. Venetian, Vol. 19, pp. 328–9, Zuane Pesaro, 20 February 1626; de Tillières, *Mémoires*, pp. 121–2.
33. De Tillières, *Mémoires*, p. 127.
34. Birch, *Court and Times*, Vol. I, p. 121, John Pory to Reverend J. Mead, 1 July 1626; Cal. S.P. Venetian, Vol. 19, p. 545, Simon Contarini, Paris, 22 September 1626.
35. *Salvetti Correspondence*, p. 47, 6 March 1626; Birch, *Court and Times*, Vol. I, p. 85; *The Chamberlain Letters*, ed. E. McClure Thomson, p. 359.

36. Cal. S.P. Venetian, Vol. 19, App. I, p. 605.
37. Gardiner, *History of England*, Vol. 6, p. 62.
38. Rushworth, *Historical Collections*, Vol. I, p. 215; Gardiner, *History of England*, Vol. 6, p. 77.
39. Rushworth, *Historical Collections*, Vol. I, pp. 216–17 and 225.
40. Birch, *Court and Times*, Vol. I, p. 113.
41. De Tillières, *Mémoires*, p. 129.
42. Ibid., p. 135; Cal. S.P. Venetian, Vol. 19, p. 494, Andrea Rosso, 31 July 1626.
43. Cal. S.P. Venetian, Vol. 19, p. 495, Andrea Rosso, 31 July 1626.
44. Ludlow, *Memoirs*, Vol. III, pp. 305–9.
45. Cal. S.P. Venetian, p. 497, Andrea Rosso, 7 August 1626.
46. De Tillières, *Mémoires*, pp. 137–8.
47. *Salvetti Correspondence*, p. 57, 17 April 1626.
48. Cal. S.P. Venetian, Vol. 19, p. 517, Simon Contarini, Paris, 21 August 1626; Birch, *Court and Times*, Vol. I, p. 121.
49. Ludlow, *Memoirs*, Vol. III, pp. 305–9.
50. *Salvetti Correspondence*, p. 81, 31 July 1626; Cal. S.P. Venetian, Vol. 19, Andrea Rosso, 7 August 1626; de Tillières, *Mémoires*, p. 142.
51. *Salvetti Correspondence*, p. 82; Cal. S.P. Venetian, Vol. 19, p. 506, Antonio Rossi, 14 August 1626; Ellis, *Original Letters*, Series I, Vol. 3, pp. 238–9, John Pory to Joseph Mead; Hamilton, *Henrietta Maria*, p. 78; see also Gardiner, *History of England*, Vol. 6, p. 135, notes 1 and 2.
52. Ellis, *Original Letters*, Series I, Vol. 3, pp. 238–9.
53. Cal. S.P. Venetian, Vol. 19, pp. 506–7, Antonio Rossi, 14 August 1626.
54. Birch, *Court and Times*, Vol. I, pp. 136 and 138; Ellis, *Original Letters*, Series I, Vol. 3, pp. 240–1; Cal. S.P. Venetian, Vol. 19, p. 508, Antonio Rossi, 14 August 1626.
55. Ellis, *Original Letters*, Series I, Vol. 3, pp. 244–6.
56. Birch, *Court and Times*, Vol. I, p. 136; de Tillières, *Mémoires*, p. 251.
57. De Tillières, *Mémoires*, pp. 252–3; Comte de Baillon, *Lettres Inédites de Henriette Marie*, 1884, pp. 3–6.
58. De Baillon, *Lettres*, p. 6.

CHAPTER THREE

1. Cal. S.P. Venetian, Vol. 19, p. 520, Alvise Contarini to the Doge and Senate, 28 August 1626; p. 525, same to same, 4 September; p. 542, same to same, 18 September.
2. De Bassompierre, *Mémoires*, Vol. 4, pp. 257–8.
3. Ibid., pp. 259–60; Cal. S.P. Venetian, Vol. 19, p. 573, Alvise Contarini to the Doge, 16 October 1626.
4. Bassompierre, *Mémoires*, pp. 264–5; Hugh Williams, *A Gallant of Lorraine*, 2 vols, London, 1921, Vol. 2, pp. 476–9 and notes; Cal. S.P. Venetian, Vol. 19, p. 582, Alvise Contarini to the Doge, 23 October 1626.
5. Bassompierre, *Mémoires*, pp. 265–6.
6. Ibid., pp. 266–7.
7. Brief Discourse of the Embassy of Marshal Bassompierre, Harl. MS 1323, printed in *Memoirs of the Embassy of the Marshal de Bassompierre to the Court of England in 1626*, John Murray, 1819, App. 6, pp. 136–40.
8. Ibid., App. 7, p. 146.
9. Bassompierre, *Mémoires*, p. 270.
10. Williams, *A Gallant of Lorraine*, Vol. 2, p. 489.
11. Bassompierre, *Mémoires*, pp. 271–2.
12. Ibid., p. 273.
13. Birch, *Court and Times*, Vol. I, p. 166, to Joseph Mead, 10 November 1626; *Salvetti Correspondence*, H.M.C., 11th Report, App. 1, pp. 94–5.
14. Birch, *Court and Times*, Vol. I, p. 169, Joseph Mead to Sir Martin Stuteville, 11 November 1626.
15. Cal. S.P. Venetian, Vol. 20, p. 82, Giorgio Zorzi to the Doge and Senate, 7 January 1627.
16. *Salvetti Correspondence*, pp. 99–100.
17. Cal. S.P. Venetian, Vol. 20, pp. 68–9, Alvise Contarini to the Doge, 25 December 1626.
18. Birch, *Court and Times*, Vol. I, p. 206, to Joseph Mead, 16 March 1627.
19. Cal. S.P. Venetian, Vol. 20, p. 184, Alvise Contarini to the Doge, 16 April 1627.
20. Lockyer, *Buckingham*, p. 371.
21. Birch, *Court and Times*, Vol. I, p. 226, to Joseph Mead, 16 May 1627.
22. Cal. S.P. Venetian, Vol. 20, pp. 247–8, Alvise Contarini to the Doge, 6 June 1627; p. 298, same to same, 23 July 1627.
23. Green, *Letters of Henrietta Maria*, p. 11, to Marie de Medici.
24. Carola Oman, *Henrietta Maria*, White Lion Publishers, 1976, p. 55 note; Cal. S.P. Domestic, 1627/28, p. 283.

25. Cal. S.P. Domestic 1627/28, p. 276.
26. Cal. S.P. Venetian, Vol. 20, p. 342, Alvise Contarini to the Doge, 27 August 1627.
27. Hardwicke S.P., Vol. 2, Charles to Buckingham, 13 August 1627.
28. George Ballard, *Memoirs of British Ladies*, London, 1775, p. 194.
29. Gardiner, *History of England*, Vol. 6, p. 181.
30. Ibid., pp. 197–9.
31. Cal. S.P. Venetian, Vol. 20, p. 499, Alvise Contarini to the Doge, 2 December 1627; Birch, *Court and Times*, Vol. I, p. 278, to Joseph Mead, 16 November 1627.
32. Cal. S.P. Venetian, Vol. 20, p. 497, Alvise Contarini to Zorzi, 1 December 1627; Birch, *Court and Times*, Vol. I, p. 291, to Joseph Mead, 23 November; p. 281, Mr Pory to Joseph Mead, 2 November 1627.
33. Cal. S.P. Venetian, Vol. 20, pp. 542–3, Alvise Contarini to the Doge, 2 January 1628.
34. Rushworth, *Historical Collections*, Vol. 1, p. 476.
35. *Salvetti Correspondence*, p. 154.
36. Birch, *Court and Times*, Vol. I, p. 367, Joseph Mead to Sir Martin Stuteville, 29 June 1628.
37. Lockyer, *Buckingham*, p. 439; Birch, *Court and Times*, Vol. I, p. 368, Joseph Mead to Sir Martin Stuteville, 29 June 1628.
38. Cal. S.P. Domestic, 1627/28, p. 573.
39. Cal. S.P. Venetian, Vol. 21, p. 213, Alvise Contarini to the Doge, 7 August 1628.
40. *Salvetti Correspondence*, p. 161, 25 August 1628.
41. Ellis, *Original Letters*, Series I, Vol. 3, pp. 256–8, Lord Carleton to Henrietta, 23 August 1628.
42. Clarendon, *History of the Rebellion*, ed. W. Macray, Oxford, 1888, Vol. I, p. 37; Cal. S.P. Venetian, Vol. 21, p. 262, Alvise Contarini to the Doge, 2 September 1628; p. 283, same to same, 12 September 1628; Birch, *Court and Times*, Vol. I, p. 396, Joseph Mead to Sir Martin Stuteville, 20 September 1628.
43. Birch, *Court and Times*, Vol. I, p. 391, Lord Dorchester to Sir Isaac Wake, 2 September 1628; *Salvetti Correspondence*, p. 165, 20 October 1628.
44. Cal. S.P. Venetian, Vol. 21, p. 283, Alvise Contarini to the Doge, 12 September 1628; Birch, *Court and Times*, Vol. I, p. 394, Joseph Mead to Sir Martin Stuteville, 13 September 1628.
45. Birch, *Court and Times*, Vol. I, p. 399, Joseph Mead to Sir Martin Stuteville, 19 September 1628.
46. Gardiner, *History of England*, Vol. 6, p. 369.
47. Cal. S.P. Venetian, Vol. 21, p. 287, Alvise Contarini to Giorgio Zorzi, 14 September 1628; pp. 310–11, same to same, 26 September 1628.
48. Cal. S.P. Domestic, 1628/29, p. 393, Thomas Carey to the Earl of Carlisle, 24 November 1628.
49. Ibid., p. 412, same to same, 21 December 1628; Birch, *Court and Times*, Vol. I, p. 417, Joseph Mead to Sir Martin Stuteville, 31 October 1628.
50. Cal. S.P. Venetian, Vol. 21, p. 310, Alvise Contarini to Zorzi, 26 September 1628.
51. Ibid., pp. 375 and 377, same to same, 3 November 1628.
52. Ibid., p. 539, same to same, 16 February 1629.
53. Ibid., p. 493, same to same, 20 January 1629.
54. W. Notestein and F.H. Relf, *Commons Debates for 1629*, Univ. of Minnesota, 1921, p. 267; Birch, *Court and Times*, Vol. II, pp. 11–12, Mr Isham to Paul D'Ewes, 5 March 1629; Sir Simonds D'Ewes, *Autobiography*, ed. J.O. Halliwell, 2 vols, London 1845, Vol. 1, p. 402.
55. Cal. S.P. Venetian, Vol. 21, pp. 589–90, Alvise Contarini to the Doge, 23 March 1629.
56. Cal. S.P. Venetian, Vol. 22, p. 38.
57. Cal. S.P. Venetian, Vol. 21, p. 593, Alvise Contarini to Zorzi, 23 March 1629.
58. Cal. S.P. Venetian, Vol. 22, p. 61, Alvise Contarini to the Doge, 18 May 1629; p. 68, Alvise Contarini to Zorzi, 25 May 1629; p. 65, Francesco Corner to the Doge, 19 May 1629; Birch, *Court and Times*, Vol. II, pp. 13–14, Mr Beaulieu to Sir Thomas Puckering, 13 May 1629.
59. Birch, *Court and Times*, Vol. I, pp. 355–6, Mr Beaulieu to Sir Thomas Puckering, mis-dated 20 May 1628; Sir Simonds D'Ewes, *Autobiography*, p. 411; Cal. S.P. Venetian, pp. 68–70, Alvise Contarini to Girolamo Soranzo, 25 May 1629.

CHAPTER FOUR

1. Francis Cottington to Thomas Wentworth,
   7 August 1629, quoted in Hamilton,
   Henrietta Maria, p. 97.
2. Gardiner, *History of England*, Vol. VII, p. 106.
3. Cal. S.P. Venetian, Vol. 22, p. 177, Giovanni
   Soranzo to the Doge and Senate,
   7 September 1629; p. 169, same to same,
   24 August 1629.
4. Cardinal Richelieu, *Mémoires*, ed.
   R. Lavollee, Paris, 1907–31, Vol. X, pp. 240–7.
5. Green, *Letters of Henrietta Maria*, pp. 14–16,
   to Marie de Medici.
6. Cal. S.P. Venetian, Vol. 22, pp. 315–16,
   Giovanni Soranzo to the Doge and Senate,
   5 April 1630; Cal. S.P. Domestic, 1629/31,
   pp. 217–18, 20 March 1630; Birch, *Court and
   Times*, Vol. II, p. 70, Joseph Mead to
   Sir Martin Stuteville, 27 March 1630.
7. Birch, *Court and Times*, Vol. II, pp. 301–2.
8. Birch, *Court and Times*, Vol. II, pp. 67–9,
   John Beaulieu to Sir Thomas Puckering,
   18 March 1630; Joseph Mead to Sir Martin
   Stuteville, 20 March; Cal. S.P. Domestic
   1629/31, p. 209; Cal. S.P. Venetian, Vol. 22,
   pp. 304–5, Giovanni Soranzo to the Doge
   and Senate, 22 March 1630.
9. Cal. S.P. Venetian, Vol. 22, p. 308, Giovanni
   Soranzo to the Doge and Senate, 29 March
   1630; Birch, *Court and Times*, Vol. II, p. 76,
   Joseph Mead to Sir Martin Stuteville,
   24 April 1630.
10. Birch, *Court and Times*, Vol. II, pp. 67–9 and
    p. 77, Joseph Mead to Sir Martin Stuteville,
    24 April 1630; Cal. S.P. Venetian, Vol. 22,
    p. 309, Giovanni Soranzo to the Doge and
    Senate, 29 March 1630; *Diary of John Rous*, ed.
    M.A.E. Green, Camden Soc., 1856, pp. 49–50.
11. Birch, *Court and Times*, Vol. II, p. 63, Joseph
    Mead to Sir Martin Stuteville, 6 March 1630;
    Cal. S.P. Venetian, Vol. 22, p. 638, Vicenzo
    Gussoni, Ambassador in England, to the
    Doge and Senate, 23 July 1632.
12. Cal. S.P. Venetian, Vol. 22, p. 353, Giovanni
    Soranzo to the Doge and Senate, 14 June
    1630; Ellis, *Original Letters*, Series 2, Vol. 3,
    p. 259, Lord Dorchester to Mr de Vic,
    Chargé d'Affaires in Paris, 27 May 1630.
13. Ibid., p. 262, same to same, 20 May 1630;
    Life and Death of Henriette Marie de Bourbon,
    pp. 10–11.
14. Cal. S.P. Venetian, Vol. 22, pp. 349–51,
    Giovanni Soranzo to the Doge and Senate,
    14 June 1630.
15. *Life and Death of Henriette Marie de Bourbon*,
    p. 10; Peter Heylyn, *History of the Life and
    Death of William Laud*, London, 1671, p. 198.
16. Birch, *Court and Times*, Vol. II, p. 306.
17. *Ceremonies of Charles I, The Note Books of John
    Finet*, ed. A.J. Loomie, Fordham U.P., New
    York, 1987, pp. 88–90; Cal. S.P. Venetian,
    Vol. 22, pp. 368–9, Giovanni Soranzo to the
    Doge and Senate, 5 July 1630; p. 372, same
    to same, 12 July 1630.
18. Green, *Letters of Henrietta Maria*, pp. 17–18,
    Henrietta to Madame de St Georges, no
    date.
19. Cal. S.P. Venetian, Vol. 22, p. 439, Vicenzo
    Gussoni to the Doge and Senate,
    11 November 1630.
20. Ibid., p. 448, Giovanni Soranzo to the Doge
    and Senate, 20 December 1630.
21. Ibid., p. 527, same to same, 18 July 1631;
    Birch, *Court and Times*, Vol. II, p. 123, John
    Pory to Sir Thomas Puckering, 16 June
    1631; Cal. S.P. Domestic, 1631/33, p. 68;
    Gardiner, *History of England*, Vol. VII, p. 186.
22. Cal. S.P. Venetian, p. 538, Giovanni Soranzo
    to the Doge and Senate, 29 August 1631;
    p. 544, same to same, 19 September 1631.
23. Ibid., p. 545.
24. Ibid., p. 359, 21 June 1630.
25. *Clarendon's History of the Great Rebellion*,
    ed. W. Macray, Oxford, 1888, Vol. 1, p. 62.
26. Cal. S.P. Venetian, Vol. 22, p. 464, Giovanni
    Soranzo to the Doge and Senate, 24 January
    1630.
27. Ibid., p. 554, same to same, 17 October
    1631.
28. Hamilton, *Henrietta Maria*, pp. 103–4; Ben
    Jonson, *Works*, ed. C. Herford and
    P. Simpson, Oxford, 1925–52, Vol. X;
    J. Harris, S. Orgel and R. Strong, *The King's
    Arcadia*, Arts Council, 1973, p. 169.
29. Green, *Letters of Henrietta Maria*, pp. 17–19,
    to Madame St Georges, no date.
30. Birch, *Court and Times*, Vol. II, p. 140, Sir
    George Gresley to Sir Thomas Puckering,
    9 November 1631.
31. *The King's Arcadia*, p. 170; Aurelian
    Townshend, *Poems and Masks*, ed.
    E.K. Chambers, Clarendon Press, 1912,
    Albion's Triumph, p. 57 et seq.

32. Cal. S.P. Venetian, Vol. 22, p. 592, Giovanni Soranzo and Vicenzo Gussoni to the Doge and Senate, 27 February 1632.
33. Hamilton, *Henrietta Maria*, pp. 109–10; Townshend, *Poems and Masks, Tempe Restored*, p. 81 et seq.; *The King's Arcadia*, pp. 171–2.
34. Green, *Letters of Henrietta Maria*, p. 19.
35. Birch, *Court and Times*, Vol. II, pp. 308–10.
36. Birch, *Court and Times*, Vol. II, p. 208, John Pory to . . ., 13 December 1632.
37. Birch, *Court and Times*, Vol. II, p. 205, John Pory to Lord Brooke, 6 December 1632; Cal. S.P. Venetian, Vol. 23, p. 47, Vicenzo Gussoni to the Doge and Senate, 17 December 1632.
38. Birch, *Court and Times*, Vol. II, p. 214, John Pory to Sir Thomas Puckering, 3 January 1633.
39. *Documents Relating to Proceedings Against William Prynne*, ed. S.R. Gardiner, Camden Soc., 1877, pp. 1–11; Birch, *Court and Times*, Vol. II, p. 222, J. Paget to James Harrington, 28 January 1633; p. 224, Sir George Gresley to Sir Thomas Puckering, 31 January 1633.
40. Gardiner, *History of England*, Vol. VII, pp. 328–33.
41. Cal. S.P. Domestic, 1633/34, pp. 3, 4, 11, 12 and 14.
42. Cal. S.P. Venetian, Vol. 23, p. 100, Vicenzo Gussoni to the Doge and Senate, 29 April 1633.
43. Ibid., p. 127, same to same, 15 July 1633.
44. Ibid., p. 131, same to same, 5 August 1633.
45. Green, *Letters of Henrietta Maria*, p. 22, Henrietta to Madame St Georges, September 1633.
46. Cal. S.P. Venetian, Vol. 23, p. 160, Vicenzo Gussoni to the Doge and Senate, 4 November 1633.
47. James Shirley, *Dramatic Works and Poems*, ed. W. Gifford and A. Dyce, John Murray, 1833, Vol. 6, pp. 257–85; *The King's Arcadia*, pp. 165 and 173; Hamilton, *Henrietta Maria*, pp. 116–17; Cal. S.P. Venetian, Vol. 23, p. 195, Vicenzo Gussoni to the Doge and Senate, 17 February 1634.
48. *The Poems of Thomas Carew*, ed. Rhodes Dunlap, 1949, pp. 151–85 and 273–83; *The King's Arcadia*, p. 176; Hamilton, *Henrietta Maria*, p. 118; Erica Veevers, *Images of Love and Religion*, C.U.P., 1989, pp. 197–9.
49. Cal. S.P. Venetian, Vol. 23, p. 251, Francesco Zonca to the Doge and Senate, 28 July 1634.
50. Sir John Goring to John Coke, July 1633, quoted in Carlton, *Charles I*, p. 124.
51. Henrietta to Madame de Motteville, quoted in Oman, *Henrietta Maria*, p. 72.
52. Cal. S.P. Venetian, Vol. 23, p. 284, Francesco Zonca to the Doge and Senate, 8 October 1634.
53. Ibid., p. 286, same to same, 13 October 1634.
54. Gordon Albion, *Charles I and the Court of Rome*, Burns Oates & Washbourne, 1935, p. 117 et seq.
55. Ibid., p. 148.

CHAPTER FIVE

1. Cal. S.P. Venetian, Vol. 23, p. 321, Anzolo Correr, Ambassador in England, to the Doge and Senate, 12 January 1635; Gregorio Panzani, *Memoirs*, trans. Joseph Berington, London, 1793, pp. 133–4.
2. Panzani, *Memoirs*, pp. 135–9.
3. Ibid., pp. 161–2.
4. Ibid., pp. 149–50.
5. Ibid., pp. 155–60.
6. Cal. S.P. Venetian, Vol. 23, p. 323, Anzolo Correr to the Doge and Senate, 19 January 1635.
7. William Davenant, *Dramatic Works*, ed. J. Maidment and W.H. Logan, London, 1872–4, Vol. I, pp. 281–316; Erica Veevers, *Images of Love and Religion*, pp. 134–5; *The King's Arcadia*, p. 177; Cal. S.P. Venetian, Vol. 23, p. 334, Anzolo Correr to the Doge and Senate, 23 February 1635, and Note.
8. Gardiner, *History of England*, Vol. VII, p. 368; Cal. S.P. Venetian, Vol. 23, p. 314, Anzolo Correr to the Doge and Senate, 5 January 1635.
9. Cal. S.P. Venetian, Vol. 23, p. 325, Anzolo Correr to the Doge and Senate, 5 January 1635.
10. Ibid., p. 335, same to same, 23 February 1635.
11. Ibid., p. 531, same to same, 21 March 1636.
12. R.M. Smuts, *The Puritan Followers of Henrietta Maria in the 1630s*, E.H.R., Vol. 93, 1978, p. 35, note 4.
13. Cal. S.P. Venetian, Vol. 23, p. 363, V. Gussoni, Relation of England, 13 April 1635; Quentin Bone, *Henrietta Maria, Queen of the Cavaliers*, p. 95.

14. Cal. S.P. Venetian, Vol. 23, p. 363, V. Gussoni, Relation of England, 13 April 1635.
15. Panzani, *Memoirs*, pp. 196–7 and 194.
16. Ibid., pp. 186–9; Albion, *Charles I and the Court of Rome*, p. 152.
17. Panzani, *Memoirs*, p. 206; Albion, *Charles I and the Court of Rome*, pp. 154–6.
18. Cal. S.P. Venetian, Vol. 23, p. 483, Anzolo Correr to the Doge and Senate, 7 December 1635.
19. Cal. S.P. Venetian, Vol. 23, p. 483, Anzolo Correr to the Doge and Senate, 26 October 1635.
20. Ibid., p. 491, same to same, 21 December 1635.
21. Panzani, *Memoirs*, pp. 250–1; Albion, *Charles I and the Court of Rome*, p. 395.
22. Cal. S.P. Venetian, Vol. 23, p. 509, Anzolo Correr to the Doge and Senate, 1 February 1636; pp. 505–6, same to same, 18 January 1636; pp. 514–15, same to same, 15 February 1636.
23. Ibid., p. 519, same to same, 22 February 1636.
24. Ibid., p. 527, same to same, 7 March 1636.
25. Panzani, *Memoirs*, p. 233; Albion, *Charles I and the Court of Rome*, p. 157.
26. Panzani, *Memoirs*, p. 252.
27. Birch, *Court and Times*, Vol. II, p. 244, Mr E.R. to Sir Thomas Puckering, 13 April 1636.
28. Cal. S.P. Venetian, Vol. 23, p. 560, Anzolo Correr to the Doge and Senate, 9 May 1636.
29. Ibid., p. 500, same to same, 11 January 1636.
30. Ibid., p. 515, same to same, 15 February 1636.
31. Smuts, *The Puritan Followers of Henrietta Maria*, pp. 30 and 38.
32. Cal. S.P. Venetian, Vol. 24, pp. 11–12, Anzolo Correr to the Doge and Senate, 27 June 1636.
33. Ibid., p. 39, same to same, 13 August 1636.
34. William Laud, *Works*, Oxford, 1860, Vol. V, pp. 148–53; Charles Carlton, *Archbishop William Laud*, Routledge, 1987, pp. 141–3.
35. Cal. S.P. Venetian, Vol. 24, p. 69, Anzolo Correr to the Doge and Senate, 18 September 1636.
36. Ibid., p. 70, same to same, 18 September 1636.
37. Green, *Letters of Henrietta Maria*, pp. 30–1.
38. Ibid., p. 32.
39. Birch, *Court and Times*, Vol. II, p. 250, Mr E.R. to Sir Thomas Puckering, 28 September 1636; Cal. S.P. Venetian, Vol. 24, p. 77, Anzolo Correr to the Doge and Senate, 2 October 1636.
40. Birch, *Court and Times*, Vol. II, pp. 311–13, Memoirs of Father Cyprien de Gamache.
41. Birch, *Court and Times*, Vol. II, pp. 311–13.
42. Cal. S.P. Venetian, Vol. 24, pp. 120–1, Anzolo Correr to the Doge and Senate, 2 January 1637.
43. Ibid., p. 143, same to same, 13 February 1637.
44. Ibid., p. 125, same to same, 16 January 1637.
45. Laud, *Works*, Vol. VII, p. 319, Laud to Thomas Wentworth.
46. *Earl of Strafford's Letters and Despatches*, ed. W. Knowler, 1739, Vol. II, p. 53, cited in Smuts, *The Puritan Followers of Henrietta Maria*, p. 38, note 8, Charles I to Thomas Wentworth, 28 February 1637.
47. Cal. S.P. Venetian, Vol. 24, p. 191, Alvise Contarini, ambassador in France, to the Doge and Senate, 28 April 1637; p. 187, Anzolo Correr to the Doge and Senate, 17 April 1637.
48. Ibid., p. 218, Anzolo Correr to the Doge and Senate, 29 May 1637.
49. Albion, *Charles I and the Court of Rome*, p. 248.
50. Cal. S.P. Venetian, Vol. 24, p. 217, Anzolo Correr to the Doge and Senate, 29 May 1637.
51. Birch, *Court and Times*, Vol. II, p. 134.
52. Ibid., p. 315.
53. Cal. S.P. Venetian, Vol. 24, pp. 149–50, Anzolo Correr to the Doge and Senate, 20 February 1637.
54. Albion, *Charles I and the Court of Rome*, p. 219.
55. Laud, *Works*, Vol. VII, p. 334, Laud to Wentworth, 5 April 1637.
56. Cal. S.P. Venetian, p. 282, Anzolo Correr to the Doge and Senate, 9 October 1637.
57. James Scott Wheeler, *The Making of a World Power*, Sutton, 1999, p. 36; C. Carlton, *Charles I the Personal Monarch*, Routledge, 1995, p. 177.
58. Laud, *Works*, Vol. III, Diary, pp. 229–30.
59. *Strafford's Letters*, Knowler, Vol. II, pp. 125 and 128.

60. Cal. S.P. Venetian, Vol. 24, p. 319, Anzolo Correr to the Doge and Senate, 13 November 1637.
61. Laud, *Works*, Vol. VII, p. 380, Laud to Wentworth, 1 November 1637.
62. Rushworth, *Historical Collections*, Vol. II, p. 453; Cal. S.P. Venetian, Vol. 234, p. 359, Francesco Zonca to the Doge and Senate, 22 January 1638.
63. Albion, *Charles I and the Court of Rome*, pp. 226–8; Cal. S.P. Venetian, p. 350, Francesco Zonca to the Doge and Senate, 15 January 1638.
64. *Strafford's Letters*, Knowler, Vol. I, p. 505, cited in Veevers, *Images of Love and Religion*, p. 168.
65. *The King's Arcadia*, pp. 179–80; Veevers, *Images of Love and Religion*, p. 202.
66. Cal. S.P. Venetian, Vol. 24, p. 374, Francesco Zonca to the Doge and Senate, 19 February 1638.
67. Clarendon, *History of the Rebellion*, Vol. I, pp. 144–5; Gardiner, *History of England*, Vol. VIII, p. 314.
68. Cal. S.P. Venetian, Vol. 24, p. 316, Anzolo Correr to the Doge and Senate, 6 November 1637.
69. Gardiner, *History of England*, Vol. VIII, pp. 330–1.
70. Cal. S.P. Venetian, Vol. 24, p. 379, Francesco Zonca to the Doge and Senate, 5 March 1638.
71. Ibid., p. 395, same to same, 9 April 1638.
72. Finet, *Note Books*, pp. 245–6.
73. Cal. S.P. Venetian, Vol. 24, p. 414, Anzolo Correr, ambassador in France, to the Doge and Senate, 23 May 1638, p. 405, same to same, 4 May 1638.
74. Ibid., p. 410, Francesco Zonca to the Doge and Senate, 14 May 1638, p. 417, same to same, 28 May 1638, p. 424, same to same, 18 June 1638.
75. Green, *Letters of Henrietta Maria*, p. 23.
76. Gardiner, *History of England*, Vol. VIII, p. 278.
77. *The Hamilton Papers*, ed. S.R. Gardiner, Camden Soc., N.S. 27, 1850, pp. 9 and 12.
78. Gilbert Burnet, *Lives of the Hamiltons*, 1852, p. 59.
79. Cal. S.P. Venetian, Vol. 24, pp. 435–6, Francesco Zonca to the Doge and Senate, 16 July 1638.
80. Ibid., p. 448, Giovanni Giustinian to the Doge and Senate, 17 September 1638.
81. Laud, *Works*, Vol. VII, p. 494, Laud to Wentworth, 8 October 1638; p. 497, same to same, 22 October 1638.
82. Finet, *Note Books*, pp. 253–4.
83. Rushworth, *Historical Collections*, Vol. II, p. 724.
84. Cal. S.P. Venetian, Vol. 24, p. 471, Giovanni Giustinian to the Doge and Senate, 19 November 1638.
85. Cal. S.P. Venetian, Vol. 24, p. 480, Anzolo Correr to the Doge and Senate, 21 December 1638.
86. Laud, *Works*, Vol. VII, p. 456, Laud to Wentworth, June 1638.

CHAPTER SIX

1. Cal. S.P. Venetian, Vol. 24, p. 497, Giovanni Giustinian to the Doge and Senate, 11 February 1639.
2. *Hamilton Papers*, Gardiner, pp. 60–1.
3. *Strafford Letters*, Knowler, Vol. II, p. 276, Northumberland to Wentworth, 29 January 1639; Cal. S.P. Domestic, Charles I, 1638–9, pp. 362 and 378.
4. Ibid., March 1639, p. 506; Cal. S.P. Venetian, Vol. 24, p. 525, Giovanni Giustinian to the Doge and Senate, 15 April 1639.
5. *Hamilton Papers*, Gardiner, p. 74; *Letters and Papers of the Verney Family*, ed. J. Bruce, Camden Soc., 56, 1853, p. 228.
6. C.V. Wedgwood, *The King's Peace*, Collins, 1955, p. 229; Cal. S.P. Venetian, Vol. 24, p. 509, Giovanni Giustinian to the Doge and Senate, 18 March 1639.
7. Quoted in Caroline Hibbard, *Charles I and the Popish Plot*, Univ. of North Carolina Press, 1983, p. 103.
8. Albion, *Charles I and the Court of Rome*, App. IX, p. 421; see also Hibbard, *Charles I and the Popish Plot*, pp. 101–4.
9. Rushworth, *Historical Collections*, Vol. II, p. 820; Green, *Letters of Henrietta Maria*, pp. 24–5.
10. Rushworth, *Historical Collections*, Vol. II, pp. 822–3.
11. Cal. S.P. Venetian, Vol. 24, p. 539, Giovanni Giustinian to the Doge and Senate, 13 May 1639.

12. Rushworth, *Historical Collections*, Vol. II, p. 821.
13. Hibbard, *Charles I and the Popish Plot*, p. 126.
14. Cal. S.P. Venetian, Vol. 24, p. 536, Giovanni Giustinian to the Doge and Senate, 6 May 1639.
15. *Mémoires de Madame de Motteville*, ed. M. Petitot, Paris, 1824, p. 190.
16. Clarendon, *History of the Rebellion*, Vol. I, p. 162.
17. Cal. S.P. Venetian, Vol. 24, p. 561, Giovanni Giustinian to the Doge and Senate, 5 August 1639.
18. Ibid., p. 563, same to same, 12 August 1639.
19. Ibid.
20. Ibid., p. 557, same to same, 15 July 1639.
21. Ibid., p. 543, same to same, 27 May 1639.
22. Gardiner, *History of England*, Vol. VIII, p. 137.
23. Cal. S.P. Venetian, Vol. 24, p. 594, Giovanni Giustinian to the Doge and Senate, 18 November 1639.
24. Gardiner, *History of England*, Vol. IX, pp. 54 and 74–5.
25. Cal. S.P. Venetian, Vol. 24, p. 595, Giovanni Giustinian to the Doge and Senate, 25 November 1639.
26. Clarendon, *History of the Rebellion*, Vol. I, pp. 165–6.
27. Davenant, *Dramatic Works*, Vol. 2, pp. 310–26.
28. *Proceedings of the Short Parliament*, ed. E.S. Cope and W.H. Coates, Camden 4th Series, Vol. 19, 1977, pp. 254–9.
29. Clarendon, *History of the Rebellion*, Vol. I, p. 182.
30. Cal. S.P. Venetian, Vol. 25, p. 47, Giovanni Giustinian to the Doge and Senate, 25 May 1640.
31. Hibbard, *Charles I and the Popish Plot*, p. 151; Albion, *Charles I and the Court of Rome*, p. 339.
32. Cal. S.P. Venetian, Vol. 25, p. 52, Giovanni Giustinian to the Doge and Senate, 15 June 1640.
33. Strafford to George Radcliffe, 1 September 1640, quoted in Gardiner, *History of England*, Vol. IX, p. 195.
34. Cal. S.P. Venetian, Vol. 25, p. 75, Giovanni Giustinian to the Doge and Senate, 14 September 1640.
35. Clarendon, *History of the Rebellion*, Vol. I, pp. 187–8; Hibbard, *Charles I and the Popish Plot*, p. 156.
36. Cal. S.P. Venetian, Vol. 25, p. 77, Giovanni Giustinian to the Doge and Senate, 15 September 1640.
37. Clarendon, *History of the Rebellion*, Vol. I, p. 202.
38. Ibid., p. 205.
39. Cal. S.P. Venetian, Vol. 25, p. 79, Giovanni Giustinian to the Doge and Senate, 21 September 1640.
40. Ibid., p. 93, same to same, 9 November 1640.
41. Albion, *Charles I and the Court of Rome*, p. 341.
42. Cal. S.P. Venetian, Vol. 25, p. 97, Giovanni Giustinian to the Doge and Senate, 30 November 1640.
43. Ibid., p. 103, same to same, 14 December 1640.
44. Albion, *Charles I and the Court of Rome*, p. 347.
45. M.A.E. Green, *Lives of the Princesses of England*, 1855, Vol. 6, p. 394.
46. Green, *Letters of Henrietta Maria*, p. 28.
47. Green, *Lives of the Princesses*, Vol. 6, p. 103.
48. Cal. S.P. Venetian, Vol. 25, p. 96, Giovanni Giustinian to the Doge and Senate, 24 November 1640; pp. 111–12, same to same, 11 January 1641.
49. Albion, *Charles I and the Court of Rome*, p. 360 and note 2.
50. Cal. S.P. Venetian, Vol. 25, p. 119, Giovanni Giustinian to the Doge and Senate, 8 February 1641.
51. Rushworth, *Historical Collections*, Vol. II, pp. 823–4.
52. Cal. S.P. Venetian, Vol. 25, p. 124, Anzolo Correr to the Doge and Senate, 19 February 1641.
53. Ibid., p. 127, Giovanni Giustinian to the Doge and Senate, 1 March 1641.
54. Ibid.
55. Gardiner, *History of England*, Vol. IX, p. 273; Kevin Sharpe, *The Personal Rule of Charles I*, Yale U.P., 1992, pp. 947–8; Clarendon, *History of the Rebellion*, Vol. I, pp. 280–1.
56. Madame de Motteville, *Mémoires*, p. 98.
57. Finet, *Note Books*, pp. 310–12; Green, *Lives of the Princesses*, Vol. 6, pp. 114–18; Quentin Bone, *Henrietta Maria, Queen of the Cavaliers*, Peter Owen, 1973, p. 126.
58. Cal. S.P. Venetian, Vol. 25, pp. 147–8, Giovanni Giustinian to the Doge and Senate, 16 May 1641.

59. Gardiner, *History of England*, Vol. IX, p. 340.
60. Clarendon, *History of the Rebellion*, Vol. I, p. 329.
61. Cal. S.P. Venetian, Vol. 25, pp. 149–50, Giovanni Giustinian to the Doge and Senate, 17 May 1641.
62. Ibid., p. 150, same to same, 24 May 1641.
63. Clarendon, *History of the Rebellion*, Vol. I, pp. 337–8.
64. C.V. Wedgwood, *Thomas Wentworth, a Revaluation*, Cape, 1961, p. 373.
65. Gardiner, *History of England*, Vol. IX, pp. 367–8.
66. Cal. S.P. Venetian, Vol. 25, pp. 151–2, Giovanni Giustinian to the Doge and Senate, 24 May 1641.
67. Madame de Motteville, *Mémoires*, p. 105.

CHAPTER SEVEN

1. Cal. S.P. Venetian, Vol. 25, p. 152, Giovanni Giustinian to the Doge and Senate, 24 May 1641.
2. Ibid., p. 153, same to same, 31 May 1641.
3. Albion, *Charles I and the Court of Rome*, pp. 365–6.
4. Cal. S.P. Venetian, Vol. 25, p. 175, Giovanni Giustinian to the Doge and Senate, 6 July 1641.
5. Gardiner, *History of England*, Vol. IX, pp. 404–5.
6. Cal. S.P. Venetian, Vol. 25, p. 163, Giovanni Giustinian to the Doge and Senate, 21 June 1641.
7. Ibid., p. 166, same to same, 28 June 1641.
8. Ibid., pp. 175–6, same to same, 12 July 1641.
9. Gardiner, *History of England*, Vol. IX, p. 404.
10. Green, *Letters of Henrietta Maria*, Mayerne's Report, pp. 39–40.
11. Cal. S.P. Venetian, Vol. 25, p. 186, Giovanni Giustinian to the Doge and Senate, 2 August 1641.
12. Ibid., pp. 183 and 187, same to same, 26 July and 2 August 1641.
13. Rushworth, *Historical Collections*, Vol. 1, Pt. 3, p. 350.
14. H. Ferrero, *Lettres de Henriette Marie à sa Soeur Christine*, 1881, pp. 57–8, 8 August 1641.
15. Madame de Motteville, *Mémoires*, pp. 106–7.
16. *The Nicholas Correspondence, J. Evelyn, Diary and Correspondence*, Vol. 4, ed. W. Bray, 1852, p. 105; Cal. S.P. Venetian, Vol. 25, p. 241, Giovanni Giustinian to the Doge and Senate, 15 November 1641.
17. Ibid., pp. 240–1, same to same, 15 November 1641.
18. *Nicholas Correspondence*, p. 118, Henrietta Maria to Edward Nicholas, 10 November 1641.
19. Ibid., p. 117, Edward Nicholas to Charles I, 8 November 1641.
20. Rushworth, *Historical Collections*, Vol. IV, p. 429; Cal. S.P. Venetian, Vol. 25, p. 254, Giovanni Giustinian to the Doge and Senate, 7 December 1641.
21. Ibid., p. 251, same to same, 29 November 1641.
22. Ibid., p. 261, same to same, 20 December 1641.
23. Clarendon, *History of the Rebellion*, Vol. I, p. 456.
24. Cal. S.P. Venetian, Vol. 25, p. 262, Giovanni Giustinian to the Doge and Senate, 20 December 1641.
25. Cited in Gardiner, *History of England*, Vol. X, p. 124.
26. Cal. S.P. Venetian, Vol. 25, pp. 275–6, Giovanni Giustinian to the Doge and Senate, 17 January 1642.
27. Gardiner, *History of England*, Vol. X, p. 136.
28. Madame de Motteville, *Mémoires*, p. 109.
29. Cal. S.P. Venetian, Vol. 25, p. 277, Giovanni Giustinian to the Doge and Senate, 17 January 1642.
30. Ibid., p. 283, same to same, 31 January 1642.
31. Ferrero, *Lettres de Henriette Marie*, pp. 59–60, 4 April 1642.
32. Green, *Lives of the Princesses*, Vol. 6, pp. 124–5.
33. R. Marshall, *The Intrepid Queen*, HMSO, 1990, p. 94.
34. Cal. S.P. Venetian, Vol. 25, p. 295, Giovanni Giustinian to the Doge and Senate, 21 February 1642.
35. Sophia, Electress of Hanover, *Memoirs*, trans. H. Forester, 1888, p. 13.
36. Ellis, *Original Letters*, Series 2, Vol. 3, p. 295.
37. Green, *Letters of Henrietta Maria*, pp. 52–4, Henrietta to Charles, 17 March 1642.
38. Ibid., pp. 55–7, same to same, March 1642.
39. Ibid., pp. 60–1, same to same, 16 April 1642.

40. Ibid., pp. 63–5, same to same, May 1642.
41. Cal. S.P. Venetian, Vol. 26, pp. 59 and 64, Zuanne Zon to the Doge and Senate, 19 and 26 May 1642; Green, *Lives of the Princesses*, Vol. 6, p. 131.
42. Green, *Letters of Henrietta Maria*, pp. 68–9, Henrietta to Charles, 11 May 1642.
43. Ibid., p. 70, same to same, 11 May 1642.
44. Ibid., pp. 72–3, Henrietta to Mme St Georges, 28 May 1642.
45. Ibid., p. 77, Henrietta to Charles, 4 June 1642.
46. Ibid., pp. 78–80, same to same, 9 June 1642.
47. Ibid., p. 92, same to same, 24 July 1642.
48. Cal. S.P. Venetian, Vol. 26, p. 103, Giovanni Giustinian to the Doge and Senate, 18 July 1642.
49. Ibid., p. 109, same to same, 25 July 1642.
50. Ibid., p. 138, Zuanne Zon to the Doge and Senate, 3 September 1642.
51. Ibid., pp. 142, 162, 178 and 189, Giovanni Giustinian to the Doge and Senate, 5 September, 26 September, 17 October and 31 October 1642.
52. Ferrero, *Lettres de Henriette Marie*, p. 61, 23 June 1642; Green, *Letters of Henrietta Maria*, p. 91, Henrietta to Charles, 23 July 1642.
53. Green, *Letters of Henrietta Maria*, pp. 110–11, Henrietta to Charles, 13 September 1642.
54. Ibid., p. 109, same to same, 11 September 1642.
55. Ibid., pp. 93–4, same to same, 31 July 1642.
56. Ibid., pp. 101–3, same to same, 8 September 1642.
57. Ibid., pp. 112–17, same to same, 19 September 1642.
58. Ibid., pp. 123 and 147, same to same, October and 8 December 1642.
59. Ibid., p. 126, same to same, 6 October 1642.
60. Ibid., pp. 128–30, same to same, 11 October 1642.
61. Ibid., p. 145, same to same, 1 December 1642.
62. Ibid., p. 153, same to same, 8 January 1643.
63. Madame de Motteville, *Mémoires*, pp. 113–14; Birch, *Court and Times*, Vol. II, p. 350; *A True Relation of Her Majestie's Return out of Holland*, Oxford, 1643; Cal. S.P. Venetian, Vol. 26, p. 241, Zuanne Zon to the Doge and Senate, 19 February 1643.
64. Green, *Letters of Henrietta Maria*, p. 163, Henrietta to Charles, 13 February 1642.
65. Ibid., same to same, pp. 166–8, 25 February 1643; Madame de Motteville, *Mémoires*, p. 114.

CHAPTER EIGHT

1. Cal. S.P. Venetian, Vol. 26, p. 240, Gerolamo Agostini to the Doge and Senate, 13 February 1643.
2. Lord Fairfax to Henrietta Maria, *Kingdom's Weekly Intelligencer*, 14 March 1643, printed in Green, *Letters of Henrietta Maria*, p. 170.
3. Green, *Letters of Henrietta Maria*, p. 171.
4. *Mercurius Aulicus*, 17 January 1643, printed in Green, *Letters of Henrietta Maria*, pp. 165–6; Cal. S.P. Venetian, Vol. 26, p. 236, Gerolamo Agostini to the Doge and Senate, 5 February 1643.
5. *The King's Cabinet Opened*, Harleian Miscellany, Vol. VIII, p. 567, Charles to Henrietta Maria, 13 February 1643.
6. Ibid., p. 561, Henrietta Maria to Charles, 30 March 1643.
7. Green, *Letters of Henrietta Maria*, p. 182, Henrietta Maria to Charles, 8 April 1643.
8. Ibid., pp. 193–4, same to same, 5 May 1643.
9. *The Perfect Diurnal*, 29 May 1643, printed in Green, *Letters of Henrietta Maria*, p. 214.
10. Cal. S.P. Venetian, Vol. 26, p. 280, Gerolamo Agostini to the Doge and Senate, 5 June 1643.
11. Green, *Letters of Henrietta Maria*, pp. 188–91, Henrietta Maria to Charles, 23 April 1643.
12. Ibid., pp. 200–1, same to same, 14 May 1643.
13. Ibid., pp. 209–10, same to same, 27 May 1643.
14. Ibid., pp. 204–5, same to same, 18 May 1643.
15. Ibid., pp. 208–9, same to same, 27 May 1643.
16. Ibid., p. 212, same to same, 27 May 1643.
17. Ibid., p. 219, Henrietta Maria to Newcastle, 18 June 1643.
18. *The King's Cabinet Opened*, p. 563, Henrietta Maria to Charles, 27 June 1643.
19. Ibid., same to same, 27 June 1643.
20. Madame de Motteville, *Mémoires*, Vol. II, p. 115.
21. C.V. Wedgwood, *The King's War*, Collins, 1958, p. 207.
22. Green, *Letters of Henrietta Maria*, p. 225, Henrietta Maria to Newcastle, 13 August 1643.
23. Ibid., p. 227, same to same, 23 September 1643.

24. Clarendon, *History of the Rebellion*, Vol. III, pp. 194–5.
25. Cal. S.P. Venetian, Vol. 27, p. 37, Gerolamo Agostini to the Doge and Senate, 6 November 1643.
26. Green, *Letters of Henrietta Maria*, p. 238, Henrietta Maria to the Marquis of Newcastle, 15 March 1644.
27. Ibid., p. 239, same to same, 5 April 1644.
28. Clarendon, *History of the Rebellion*, Vol. III, pp. 341–2.
29. Green, *Letters of Henrietta Maria*, p. 243, Henrietta Maria to Theodore Mayerne and Charles to Mayerne, May 1644.
30. Cal. S.P. Venetian, Vol. 27, pp. 99 and 101, Gerolamo Agostini to the Doge and Senate, 13 and 20 May 1644.
31. Green, *Letters of Henrietta Maria*, p. 244, Henrietta Maria to Charles, 18 June (sic) 1644.
32. Ibid., pp. 247–8, same to same, 28 June 1644.
33. Ibid., pp. 246 and 248; Cal. S.P. Venetian, Vol. 27, p. 116, Gerolamo Agostini to the Doge and Senate, 15 July 1644.
34. Cal. S.P. Domestic, Charles I, 1644, p. 318, Henry Jermyn to George Digby.
35. Agnes Strickland, *Lives of the Queens of England*, 1845, Vol. 8, p. 113.
36. Green, *Letters of Henrietta Maria*, p. 249, Henrietta Maria to Charles, 9 July 1644.
37. Ibid., p. 250.
38. Ibid., pp. 250–1.
39. Madame de Motteville, *Mémoires*, Vol. II, pp. 116–17.
40. Green, *Letters of Henrietta Maria*, p. 253, Henrietta Maria to Charles, 10 August 1644.
41. Ibid., p. 255, same to same, 7 September 1644.
42. Ibid., p. 258, same to same, 24 September 1644.
43. *Mémoires de Mlle. de Montpensier*, ed. A. Chereul, Paris n.d., Vol. I, pp. 98–100.
44. Madame de Motteville, *Mémoires*, Vol. II, pp. 126–7.
45. Green, *Letters of Henrietta Maria*, pp. 263–5, Henrietta Maria to Charles, 18 November 1644.
46. Ibid., p. 269, same to same, 3 December 1644.
47. Ibid., p. 273, same to same, 23 December 1644.
48. Ibid., p. 277, same to same, 30 December 1644.
49. *The King's Cabinet Opened*, p. 562, Henrietta Maria to Charles, January 1645.
50. Ibid., p. 563, same to same, 17/27 January 1645.
51. Ibid., p. 549, Charles to Henrietta Maria, February 1645.
52. Ibid., p. 547, same to same, 27 March 1645.
53. Cal. S.P. Venetian, Vol. 27, p. 178, Giovanni Nani to the Doge and Senate, 21 March 1645.
54. Montpensier, *Mémoires*, Vol. 1, p. 100.
55. Charles Petrie, *Letters etc. of Charles I*, Cassell, 1935, pp. 151–2, Charles to the Marquess of Ormonde, 18 January 1645; *The King's Cabinet Opened*, pp. 554–5, same to same, 27 February 1645.
56. *The King's Cabinet Opened*, p. 563, Henrietta Maria to Charles, 13 March 1645.
57. Ibid., pp. 550–1, Charles to Henrietta Maria, 9 April 1645.
58. Green, *Letters of Henrietta Maria*, pp. 301–2, Henrietta Maria to Charles, 17 May 1645.
59. *The King's Cabinet Opened*, pp. 557–8.
60. Ibid., pp. 551 and 554, Charles to Henrietta Maria, 14 May and 9 June 1645.
61. Cal. S.P. Venetian, Vol. 27, p. 196, Giovanni Nani to the Doge and Senate, 14 July 1645.
62. *The Embassy in Ireland of Monsignor G. Rinuccini*, trans. A. Hutton, Dublin, 1873, p. 553.
63. Ibid., pp. li–lii.
64. Cal. S.P. Venetian, Vol. 27, p. 194, Giovanni Nani to the Doge and Senate, 20 June 1645.
65. Rinuccini, *Embassy*, pp. 28–40.
66. Ibid., p. 573.
67. *Charles I in 1646*, ed. John Bruce, Camden Soc., 63, 1856, pp. 6–7 and 19, Charles to Henrietta Maria, 11 January and 19 February 1646.
68. Green, *Letters of Henrietta Maria*, p. 309, Henrietta Maria to Gaston, Duke of Orléans, 1 January 1646.
69. Bruce, pp. 14–15 and 20, Charles to Henrietta Maria, 1 and 19 February 1646.
70. Clarendon, *History of the Rebellion*, Vol. IV, p. 191.
71. Bruce, pp. 38–9, Charles to Henrietta Maria, 22 April 1646.

CHAPTER NINE

1. Clarendon, *History of the Rebellion*, Vol. IV, p. 171.
2. Ibid., p. 170, Henrietta to Edward Hyde, 5 April 1646.
3. *Charles I in 1646*, Bruce, p. 36, Charles to Henrietta, 15 April 1646.
4. Green, *Letters of Henrietta Maria*, p. 316, Henrietta to Prince Charles, 17 May 1646.
5. Ibid., p. 317, Henrietta to Lord Culpepper, 17 May 1646.
6. *Charles I in 1646*, Bruce, p. 42, Charles to Henrietta, 28 May 1646.
7. Green, *Letters of Henrietta Maria*, p. 319, Henrietta to Prince Charles, 20 June 1646.
8. Clarendon, *History of the Rebellion*, Vol. IV, p. 195.
9. Montpensier, *Mémoires*, Vol. 1, pp. 127–8.
10. Birch, *Court and Times*, Vol. II, p. 410.
11. *Charles I in 1646*, Bruce, pp. 45–6, Charles to Henrietta, 10 June 1646.
12. Ibid., p. 62, same to same, 31 August 1646.
13. Ibid., p. 71, same to same, 17 October 1646.
14. Green, *Letters of Henrietta Maria*, p. 326, Henrietta to Charles, 9/19 October 1646.
15. *Charles I in 1646*, Bruce, p. 79, Charles to Henrietta, November 1646.
16. Green, *Letters of Henrietta Maria*, p. 332, Henrietta to Charles, December 1646.
17. Ibid., pp. 335–6, same to same, December 1646.
18. Montpensier, *Mémoires*, Vol. 1, pp. 137–40.
19. Cal. S.P. Venetian, Vol. 27, p. 292, Advices from London, December 1646.
20. *Charles I in 1646*, Bruce, p. 99, Charles to Henrietta, 2 January 1647.
21. Cal. S.P. Venetian, Vol. 27, p. 314, Advices from London, 25 April 1646.
22. Ibid., p. 320, Advices from London, 6 June 1647.
23. Ibid., p. 301, Giovanni Nani to the Doge and Senate, 12 February 1647.
24. *The Weekly Intelligencer*, 15 February 1648, cited in Green, *Letters of Henrietta Maria*, p. 345.
25. Madame de Motteville, *Mémoires*, Vol. II, p. 414.
26. *Life and Death of Henriette Marie de Bourbon*, p. 19.
27. Green, *Letters of Henrietta Maria*, pp. 349–50, Henrietta to M. de Grignan, 6 January 1649.
28. Green, *Lives of the Princesses*, Vol. 6, p. 369.
29. Ibid., pp. 370–1.
30. Ibid., p. 370 note; T. Herbert, *Memoirs of the last Two Years of King Charles*, 1813, p. 122.
31. Birch, *Court and Times*, Vol. II, p. 383.
32. Madame de Motteville, *Mémoires*, Vol. III, pp. 204–7.
33. Montpensier, *Mémoires*, Vol. 1, pp. 210–11.
34. Ibid., pp. 224–5.
35. Ferrero, *Lettres de Henriette Marie*, p. 74, 22 July 1649.
36. Clarendon, *History of the Rebellion*, Vol. V, p. 50.
37. Cal. S.P. Venetian, Vol. 28, p. 119, Michiel Morosini, ambassador in Paris, to the Doge and Senate, 28 September 1649.
38. *The Nicholas Papers*, ed. G. Warner, Camden Soc., N.S. 40, 1886, Vol. 1, p. 173.
39. Ibid., p. 116.
40. Madame de Motteville, *Mémoires*, Vol. II, p. 128.
41. *Nicholas Papers*, Vol. 1, p. 196.
42. Green, *Letters of Henrietta Maria*, p. 368, Henrietta to Cardinal Mazarin, 3 October 1650.
43. Ferrero, *Lettres de Henriette Marie*, p. 89, 21 October 1650.
44. Green, *Lives of the Princesses*, Vol. 6, pp. 417–18.
45. Clarendon, *History of the Rebellion*, Vol. V, pp. 166–8.
46. Green, *Letters of Henrietta Maria*, p. 373.
47. Montpensier, *Mémoires*, Vol. 1, p. 319.
48. Ibid., pp. 320–1.
49. Ibid., pp. 325 and 332.
50. Ferrero, *Lettres de Henriette Marie*, p. 99, 9 May 1652.
51. Ibid., pp. 99–100, 13 June 1652.
52. Clarendon, *History of the Rebellion*, Vol. V, pp. 336–7; Ferrero, *Lettres de Henriette Marie*, p. 104, 12 June 1653.
53. Ferrero, *Lettres de Henriette Marie*, p. 107, 1 April 1654; p. 110, 29 June 1654.
54. Cal. S.P. Clarendon, ed. W.D. Macray, Oxford, 1869, Vol. II, p. 348.
55. Thurloe State Papers, 1742, Vol. II, p. 180.
56. Clarendon, *History of the Rebellion*, Vol. V, pp. 341–2.
57. Cal. S.P. Clarendon, Vol. II, pp. 419–20 and 426.
58. Ibid., p. 428.
59. Ibid., p. 433.

60. Ferrero, *Lettres de Henriette Marie*, p. 112, 3 September 1654.
61. Strickland, *Lives of the Queens of England*, Vol. 8, pp. 197–8; Madame de Motteville, *Mémoires*, Vol. IV, p. 415.
62. Madame de Motteville, *Mémoires*, Vol. IV, pp. 369–40.
63. Green, *Lives of the Princesses*, Vol. 6, p. 246.
64. Green, *Letters of Henrietta Maria*, p. 383, Henrietta to Charles II, 4 February 1656.
65. Cal. S.P. Clarendon, Vol. II, p. 124.
66. Montpensier, *Mémoires*, Vol. II, pp. 435–6.
67. Green, *Letters of Henrietta Maria*, p. 386, Henrietta to Charles II, 21 December 1657.
68. C. Oman, *Elizabeth of Bohemia*, Hodder & Stoughton, 1938, pp. 397–401.
69. Green, *Letters of Henrietta Maria*, p. 388, Henrietta to Charles II, 21 June 1658.
70. *Letters of the Queen of Bohemia*, ed. L.M. Bakar, Bodley Head, 1953, p. 278.
71. Green, *Letters of Henrietta Maria*, p. 388, Henrietta to Madame de Motteville, 18 September 1658.

CHAPTER TEN

1. Clarendon, *History of the Rebellion*, Vol. VI, p. 98.
2. Green, *Letters of Henrietta Maria*, p. 389, Henrietta to Charles II, 4 October 1658; p. 390, same to same, 18 October.
3. Cal. S.P. Venetian, Vol. 32, pp. 95–6, Francesco Giustinian, Venetian ambassador in France, to the Doge and Senate, 29 November 1659.
4. Julia Cartwright, *Madame*, London, 1894, pp. 49–50; Madame de Motteville, *Mémoires*, Vol. 5, p. 110; Birch, *Court and Times*, Vol. II, p. 414.
5. *Memoirs of Sir John Reresby*, ed. Andrew Browning, R.H.S. 1991, pp. 28 and 30.
6. Samuel Pepys, *Diary*, ed. Lord Braybrooke, 1858, Vol. 1, p. 26, 21 February 1660.
7. Ibid., p. 74, 25 May 1660.
8. Green, *Letters of Henrietta Maria*, p. 398, Henrietta to Charles II, 9 June 1660.
9. Ibid., p. 399, same to same, 18 June.
10. Ferrero, *Lettres de Henriette Marie*, p. 121, 4 June 1660.
11. Green, *Lives of the Princesses*, Vol. 6, p. 429, Henrietta to Charles II, 25 August 1660.

12. Ferrero, *Lettres de Henriette Marie*, pp. 122–3, 9 September 1660.
13. Cal. S.P. Venetian, Vol. 32, p. 196, Francesco Giavarina, Venetian Resident in London, to the Doge and Senate, 17 September 1660.
14. Ferrero, *Lettres de Henriette Marie*, p. 124, 28 October 1660.
15. *The Life of Edward, Earl of Clarendon, written by Himself*, Oxford, 1827, Vol. 1, p. 384.
16. Birch, *Court and Times*, Vol. II, p. 417.
17. Pepys, *Diary*, Vol. 1, p. 119, 2 November 1660.
18. Clarendon, *Life*, p. 387.
19. Green, *Lives of the Princesses*, p. 437.
20. Pepys, *Diary*, Vol. 1, p. 125, 22 November 1660.
21. Clarendon, *Life*, p. 394.
22. Cal. S.P. Venetian, Vol. 32, p. 235, Francesco Giavarina to the Doge and Senate, 7 January 1661.
23. Clarendon, *Life*, p. 395.
24. Ibid., p. 396.
25. Guizot de Witt, *The Lady of Lathom*, London, 1869, p. 260.
26. Clarendon, *Life*, pp. 402–4.
27. Birch, *Court and Times*, Vol. II, p. 423.
28. Ibid., p. 424.
29. Cartwright, *Madame*, pp. 88–9; Madame de Motteville, *Mémoires*, Vol. 5, p. 110; Montpensier, *Mémoires*, Vol. III, p. 527.
30. Madame de Motteville, *Mémoires*, Vol. 5, pp. 126–7.
31. Ibid., p. 125.
32. Marie Madeleine de la Fayette, *The Secret History of Henrietta, Princess of England*, trans. J.M. Shelmerdine, London, 1929, pp. 60–1.
33. Cartwright, *Madame*, p. 121.
34. Ferrero, *Lettres de Henriette Marie*, p. 126, 28 October 1662.
35. Ibid., p. 128, 26 December 1662.
36. *Life and Death of Henrietta Marie de Bourbon*, pp. 25–7.
37. Ibid., p. 33.
38. Birch, *Court and Times*, Vol. II, pp. 437–40.
39. Oman, *Henrietta Maria*, p. 308.
40. Birch, *Court and Times*, Vol. II, pp. 453–4.
41. Pepys, *Diary*, Vol. II, p. 254, 29 June 1665.
42. Cartwright, *Madame*, p. 117, Henriette Anne to Charles II, 28 November 1664.
43. Ibid., p. 222.
44. Cal. S.P. Venetian, Vol. 34, p. 280, Marc Antonio Giustinian, ambassador in France, to the Doge and Senate, 6 April 1666.

45. Ibid., Vol. 35, p. 63, same to same, 7 September 1666.
46. *My Dearest Minette*, ed. Ruth Norrington, Peter Owen, 1996, p. 151, Charles II to Madame, 7 May 1668.
47. Green, *Letters of Henrietta Maria*, pp. 412–13, Henrietta to Charles II, 9 December 1668.
48. Ibid., pp. 413–14, Henrietta to Lord Arlington, 9 December 1668.
49. Hist. MSS. Comm. Report, Buccleugh and Queensberry, HMSO, 1899, Vol. 1, p. 432, Ralph Montagu to Arlington, July 1669.
50. Birch, *Court and Times*, Vol. II, p. 465.
51. Ibid., pp. 465–6.
52. Ibid., pp. 466–8; Green, *Letters of Henrietta Maria*, pp. 416–17, Earl of St Albans to Charles II, 10 September 1669.
53. Green, *Letters of Henrietta Maria*, p. 418, St Albans to Lord Arlington, 11 September 1669.
54. Hist. MSS. Comm., Buccleugh and Queensberry, p. 440, Montagu to Arlington, 11 September 1669.
55. Green, *Letters of Henrietta Maria*, pp. 417–18, St Albans to Lord Arlington, 11 September 1669.
56. Rosalind Marshall, *Henrietta Maria*, p. 146.
57. Hist. MSS. Comm., Buccleugh and Queensberry, p. 444, Montagu to Arlington, 26 October 1669.
58. Cited in Bone, *Henrietta Maria, Queen of the Cavaliers*, p. 252.

Select Bibliography

(Place of publication London unless otherwise stated)

Albion, Gordon, *Charles I and the Court of Rome*, Burns Oates, 1935

Ballard, George, *Memoirs of British Ladies . . . Celebrated for their Writings or Skill in the Learned Languages, Arts and Science*, 1775

Bassompierre, Marechal de, *Journal de ma Vie: Mémoires*, 4 vols, Société de l'Histoire de France, Paris, 1870–7

Birch, Thomas, *The Court and Times of Charles I*, 2 vols, 1848

Bone, Quentin, *Henrietta Maria, Queen of the Cavaliers*, Peter Owen, 1973

Buisseret, David, *Henry IV*, George Allen & Unwin, 1984

Cabala, sive scrinia sacra: Mysteries of State and Government, 1691

Calendar of Clarendon State Papers, 3 vols, ed. W.D. Mackay, Oxford, 1869

Calendar of State Papers, Domestic, of the Reign of Charles I, 1625–1649, 23 vols, ed. John Bruce and others, 1858–97

Calendar of State Papers, Venetian, 38 vols, ed. Allen B. Hinds and others, 1864–1940

Carlton, Charles, *Charles I – The Personal Monarch*, Routledge, 2nd edn, 1995

——, *Archbishop William Laud*, Routledge & Kegan Paul, 1987

Cartwright, Julia (Mrs Henry Ady), *Madame, A Life of Henrietta Daughter of Charles I and Duchess of Orleans*, 1894

Clarendon, Edward, Earl of, *History of the Rebellion and Civil Wars in England*, 6 vols, ed. W.D. Mackay, Oxford, 1888

Life of Edward, Earl of Clarendon, Written by Himself, 2 vols, Oxford, 1827

Crump, Lucy, *Nursery Life 300 Years Ago*, Routledge & Kegan Paul, 1929

Davenant, Sir William, *Dramatic Works*, 1872

Dodd, Charles, *Church History of England*, ed. M.A. Tierney, 5 vols, 1839–43

Ellis, Henry, *Original Letters Illustrative of English History*, 3 series, 11 vols, 1824–46

Evelyn, John, *Diary and Correspondence*, ed. W. Bray, 4 vols, 1852

Finet, John, *Ceremonies of Charles I (The Notebooks of John Finet)* ed. A.J. Loomie, N.Y. Fordham U.P., 1987

Fraser, Antonia, *Cromwell Our Chief of Men*, Weidenfeld & Nicolson, 1973

——, *King Charles II*, Weidenfeld & Nicolson, 1979

Gardiner, S.R., *History of England 1603–1642*, 10 vols, Longmans Green, 1884

——, *History of the Great Civil War – 1642–1649*, 4 vols, Windrush Press edition, 1987

——, *History of the Commonwealth & Protectorate 1649–1656*, 4 vols, Windrush Press, 1988

Goodman, Godfrey, *The Court of King James*, 2 vols, 1839

Green, M.A.E., *Lives of the Princesses of England*, 6 vols, 1855

Hamilton Papers, ed. S.R. Gardiner, Camden Soc., N.S. 27, 1880

Hamilton, Elizabeth, *Henrietta Maria*, Hamish Hamilton, 1976

Hardwicke State Papers (Philip Yorke, 2nd Earl of Hardwicke), 2 vols, 1778

Havran, Martin J., *The Catholics in Caroline England*, OUP, Oxford, 1962

Herbert of Cherbury, Edward, Lord, *Autobiography*, ed. Sidney Lee, 1886

Heylin, Peter, *Cyprianus Anglicus, History of the Life and Death of William Laud*, 1671

Hibbard, Caroline, *Charles I and the Popish Plot*, Univ. of North Carolina Press, 1983

Select Bibliography

Hist. MSS Commission, *Report on the MSS of the Duke of Buccleuch and Queensberry*, 3 vols, HMSO, 1899–1926

Howell, James, *Familiar Letters*, 3 vols, 1903

The King's Arcadia – Inigo Jones and the Stuart Court: Quatercentenary exhibition catalogue, John Harris, Stephen Orgel and Roy Strong, Arts Council of Great Britain, 1973

The King's Cabinet Opened, Harleian Miscellany, Vol. VII, 1811

Laud, William, Archbishop, *Works*, 7 vols, ed. J. Bliss & W. Scott, Oxford, 1847–60

Selection of the Letters of John Chamberlain, ed. E. McClure Thomson, John Murray, 1966

Letters, Speeches and Proclamations of King Charles I, ed. Sir Charles Petrie, Cassell, 1935

Letters of King Charles I to Queen Henrietta Maria, ed. John Bruce, Camden Soc., series I, 63, 1856

Lettres Inédites de Henriette Marie, le Comte de Baillon, Paris, 1884

Lettres de Henriette Marie de France à sa Soeur Christine, Duchesse de Savoie, ed. Hermann Ferrero, Turin, 1881

Letters of Henrietta Maria, ed. M.A.E. Green, 1857

The Life and Death of Henrietta Maria de Bourbon, 1685

Life and Times of Anthony a Wood, abridged from Andrew Clarke's edition with an introduction by Llewelyn Powys, 1932

Lockyer, Roger, *Buckingham: The Life and Political Career of George Villiers, 1st Duke of Buckingham, 1592–1628*, Longman, 1981

Mackay, Janet, *Little Madam – a Biography of Henrietta Maria*, G. Bell & Sons, 1939

Marshall, Rosalind, *Henrietta Maria, The Intrepid Queen*, HMSO, 1990

Marvick, Elizabeth Wirth, *Louis XIII: the Making of a King*, Yale U.P., 1986

Memoires de Madame de Motteville, 4 vols, Collection des Mémoires Relatifs à l'Histoire de France, 2nd series, Vols 37–40, ed. M. Petitot, Paris, 1824

Memoir by Madame de Motteville of the Life of Henrietta Maria, ed. M.G. Hanotaux, Camden Misc., Camden Soc., N.S. 31, 1863

Memoires of Mademoiselle de Montpensier, 3 vols, ed. A. Cheruel, Paris, 1891

Memoirs of the Embassy of the Marshal de Bassompierre to the Court of England in 1626, Trans., anon., John Murray, 1819

My Dearest Minette, Letters between Charles II and Henrietta, Duchesse d'Orléans, with a commentary by Ruth Norrington, Peter Owen, 1996

The Nicholas Papers, 3 vols, The Correspondence of Sir Edward Nicholas ed. G.F. Warner, Camden Soc., N.S. 40 and 50, 1886 and 1892

Notestein, W. and Relf, F.H., *Commons Debates for 1629*, Univ. of Minnesota, 1921

Oman, Carola, *Henrietta Maria*, Hodder & Stoughton, 1936

Panzani, Gregorio, *Memoirs with Introduction and Supplement*, Trans., Reverend Joseph Berington, Birmingham, 1793

Patmore, K.A., *The Court of Louis XIII*, Methuen, 1909

Pepys, Samuel, *Diary*, ed. Richard, Lord Braybrooke, 4 vols, 1858

Documents relating to the proceedings against William Prynne in 1634 and 1637, ed. S.R. Gardiner, Camden Soc., N.S. 18, 1877

Reresby, Sir John, *Memoirs*, ed. Andrew Browning, 2nd edition with new Preface and Note by M. Geiter and W.A. Speck, R.H.S., 1991

Richelieu, Cardinal de, *Mémoires*, ed. R. Lavollée, 10 vols, Société de l'Histoire de France, Paris, 1931

Rinuccini, Mons. G.B., *The Embassy in Ireland in the years 1645–1649*, Trans., Annie Hutton, Dublin, 1873

Rous, John, *Diary*, ed. M.A.E. Green, Camden Soc., No. 66, 1856

Rushworth, John, *Historical Collections of Private Passages of State*, 8 vols, 1659–1701

Salvetti Correspondence, Manuscripts of Henry Duncan Skrine, Hist. MSS Commission, 11th Report, Appendix I, HMSO, 1887

Sharpe, Kevin, *The Personal Rule of Charles I*, Yale U.P., New Haven, 1992

Smuts, R.M., *The Puritan Followers of Henrietta Maria in the 1630s*, English Hist. Review, Vol. 93, 1978

Narrative of the Spanish Marriage Treaty, Francisco de Jesús, ed. and trans. S.R. Gardiner, Camden Soc., No. 101, 1869

State Papers Collected by Edward Earl of Clarendon, ed. R. Scrope and T. Monkhouse, 3 vols, Oxford, 1767–86

Strickland, Agnes, *Lives of the Queens of England*, 8 vols, 1845

——, *Lives of the Last Four Princesses of Stuart*, 1872

Taylor, I.A., *The Life of Queen Henrietta Maria*, 2 vols, Hutchinson, 1905

Tillières, Comte Leveneur de, *Mémoires*, ed. M.C. Hippeau, Paris, 1863

Townshend, Aurelian, *Poems and Masks*, ed. E.K. Chambers, Oxford, 1912

Thurloe, John, *Collection of State Papers*, ed. Thomas Birch, 7 vols, 1742

Veevers, Erica, *Images of Love and Religion – Queen Henrietta Maria and Court Entertainments*, C.U.P., 1989

Warburton, Eliot, *Memoirs of Prince Rupert and the Cavaliers*, 3 vols, 1849

Wedgwood, C.V., *The King's Peace*, Collins, 1955

——, *The King's War*, Collins, 1958

——, *Richelieu and the French Monarchy*, Hodder & Stoughton for E.U.P., 1949

——, *Thomas Wentworth, 1st Earl of Strafford, A Revaluation*, Cape, 1961

Williams, Hugh, *A Gallant of Lorraine* (François, Seigneur de Bassompierre) 2 vols, 1921

Witt, Mme Guizot de, *The Lady of Lathom*, 1869

Wotton, Sir Henry, *Life and Death of George Villiers, Duke of Buckingham*, Harleian Miscellany, Vol. VIII, 1811

Index